Conquest and Community

A closeup of the Ghazi Miyan flag, Sohbatiya Bagh Fair, May 1994

Photograph by Sanjay Kak

'Bala Miyan; Bale Miyan (1) Standard of Ghazi Mian. (2) Ghazi Mian himself.'
—*Azamgarh Glossary of Eastern UP Rural Terms, 1881.*

Conquest and Community

The Afterlife of Warrior Saint *Ghazi Miyan*

Shahid Amin

THE UNIVERSITY OF CHICAGO PRESS
CHICAGO AND LONDON

The University of Chicago Press, Chicago 60637
The University of Chicago Press, Ltd., London

University of Chicago Press edition published 2016.
Printed in the United States of America

Conquest and Community: The Afterlife of Warrior Saint Ghazi Miyan by Shahid Amin was first published by Orient Blackswan Private Limited 2015, for the territory of South Asia (India, Pakistan, Bangladesh, Bhutan, Nepal, Sri Lanka, and the Maldives).

25 24 23 22 21 20 19 18 17 16   1 2 3 4 5

ISBN-13: 978-0-226-37257-0 (cloth)
ISBN-13: 978-0-226-37260-0 (paper)
ISBN-13: 978-0-226-37274-7 (e-book)
DOI: 10.7208/chicago/9780226372747.001.0001

LIBRARY OF CONGRESS CATALOGING-IN-PUBLICATION DATA
Names: Amin, Shahid, author.
Title: Conquest and community : the afterlife of warrior saint Ghazi Miyan / Shahid Amin.
Description: Chicago ; London : The University of Chicago Press, 2016. | Includes bibliographical references and index.
Identifiers: LCCN 2016016551 | ISBN 9780226372570 (cloth : alk. paper) | ISBN 9780226372600 (pbk. : alk. paper) | ISBN 9780226372747 (e-book)
Subjects: LCSH: Sayyid Sālār Mas'ūd G̱ẖāzī, 1014–1032—Cult. | Muslim saints—India—Uttar Pradesh—Biography. | Uttar Pradesh (India)—Folklore.
Classification: LCC BP80.S357 A43 2016 | DDC 297.092—dc23 LC record available at https://lccn.loc.gov/2016016551

∞ This paper meets the requirements of ANSI/NISO Z39.48-1992 (Permanence of Paper).

For

Simon Digby

Connoisseur, Linguist, Scholar, and Friend

Born Jabalpur 1932; died Basti Nizamuddin, Delhi, 2010

Diya khāmosh hai lekin kisi ka dil to jalta hai
Chale āo jahān tak raushini mālum hoti hai

—Nushoor Wahidi

Saiyed ki sarguzasht ko Hāli se pūchiye,
Ghazi Miyan ka hāl Dafāli se pūchiye.

—Akbar Ilahabadi

'For Sir Syed, [the great educationist's] tale, ask Hali, his biographer,
For Ghazi Miyan's story, ask Dafali, his balladeer.'

Contents

Maps and Figures

Maps

Figures

Abbreviations

BL	British Library, London
EI	*Encyclopaedia of Islam*
INQ	*Indian Notes and Queries*
JASB	*Journal of Royal Asiatic Society*
NINQ	*North Indian Notes and Queries*
PRFL	W. Crooke, *An Introduction to the Popular Religion and Folklore of Northern India*. Allahabad: North-Western Provinces and Oudh Government Press, 1893.
UPSA	Uttar Pradesh State Archives, Lucknow

Abbreviations for Versions of the *Mirat-i-Masudi*

MM F	Abdur Rahman Chishti, *Mirat-i-Masudi*. Persian Manuscript no. MS. Or. 1837. BL.
MM C	R. W. Chapman, English translation of *Mirat-i-Masudi*. Addl. MS 30776. BL.
MM E	English translation in H. M. Elliot and John Dowson (eds), *The History of India as Told by Its Own Historians*, vol. 2., New Delhi: Low Price Publications, 2001, reprint. First published 1869. London: Trübner & Company.
MM IH	Inayat Husain, *Tarikh Salar Masud Ghazi Masud Ghazi, Be-ihtemam... Mohammad Abdullah Siddiqui, Lakhnavi, Tajir Kutub-wa Chikan, Chowk*. Third edition, Lucknow: Matba-i-Mujtabai, 1916.
MM JS	Jagdeo Singh, *Mirat-i-Masudi: Izzat Mab Abdur Rahman Chishti ki Maruf Tasneef*. Urdu *tarjuma*, Lucknow: Books India International, 1997.
MM Q	in H. A. Qureshi, *Sufis: Classics II: Mirat-i-Masudi of Abdur Rahman Danethwi* (translation). Lucknow: New Royal Book Depot, 2009.

Storyline

It is the year 1014, the fifth century of the Islamic calendar. A son is born to Sultan Mahmud of Ghazni's sister at Ajmer in present-day Rajasthan, western India. It is foretold that he will die on the day of his marriage.

The young warrior travels to the middle Gangetic plains and wages war against local Hindu rulers. He gets addressed as a Ghazi and attracts recruits and adherents as an exceptional, pious Indo-Muslim warrior. This Ghazi Miyan gathers four close associates around him, forming the quintet 'Panchon Pir'—the Five Holies venerated across religious divides in the Gangetic corridor.

Ghazi Miyan combines hunting game with principled jihad and a calibrated sense of iconoclasm. Equally, the Miyan is the harbinger of succour: he blesses infertile women with male children; a putative brother, he brings news of the natal village to housewives in distant households.

Hunting through the jungles of Bahraich, the Ghazi develops a special affinity with this northeastern corner of Hindustan, bordering present-day Nepal. He grows attached to a local *mahua*, a tree with pungent flowers whose fruit is the source of subaltern sustenance and nourishing country liquor.

The day of Ghazi Miyan's marriage, the first Sunday of the lunar month of Jeth in the summer of 1034 CE, ends up being the defining moment in his life as in the memory of the Turkic conquest of north India. Conquering invader or protector of the locality? The popular celebrations of Ghazi Miyan's life give the lie to clear-cut verities as the only way of doing and understanding history.

Prominent Figures in the Cult of Ghazi Miyan

Abdur Rahman Chishti (d. 1683): A leading Awadh-based Sufi; translated and commented upon portions of the Bhagavad Gita and other ancient Hindu texts; also the author of the hagiographies of Salar Masud (*Mirat-i-Masudi*) and Shah Madar (*Mirat-i-Madari*), two important saints of north India with a considerable following.

Amina Sati: The virtuous Hindu wife of Raja Lorchand/Nurchand, banished by her husband for feasting 'brother' Ghazi Miyan who had come visiting from her natal home.

Baba Birahna or **Sikandar Diwana:** Accompanied Masud in all his adventures and battles; grave adjacent to his master's at the Bahraich shrine.

Dafalis: The caste of Muslim balladeers who sing the deeds of Ghazi Miyan and act as officiants in the ritual worship of the saint.

Ganga: The holy river, here, the sister of Amina Sati who stands by her for having feasted Ghazi Miyan in her Hindu marital home.

Ghazi Miyan: The common name by which Syed Salar Masud is known in north India; Miyan connotes a Musalman more generally (see also **Salar Masud**).

Jaswa or **Jashoda:** Yashoda is the name of Krishna's foster mother. In Ghazi Miyan folklore, the barren wife of the cowherd chief Nand; granted the boon of a son by the Ghazi.

Lilli Ghori: The prize mare that Ghazi Miyan wrests from uncle, Sultan Mahmud of Ghazni, and on which he rides to his eventual martyrdom; buried inside the Bahraich shrine.

Mahmud of Ghazni: Sultan of Ghazni (r. 998–1030 CE). Brother of Sitr-i-Mualla and uncle of Salar Masud on whom he dotes in the seventeenth-century Persian text *Mirat-i-Masudi*. In folklore, a villainous brother and uncle. Notorious for his repeated invasions of Hindustan.

Mamla, Mamul or **Mamula:** The sister of Sultan Mahmud and mother of Salar Masud; in folklore, derided as a barren woman who conceives Masud after supplications at an important Sufi shrine (see also **Sitr-i-Mualla**).

Masud: Short for Salar Masud, or Syed Salar Masud, popularly known as **Ghazi Miyan.**

Pabuji: The legendary 'Bhomia' or cow saviour of Rajasthan who is killed saving cows on the day of his marriage.

Salar Masud, aka **Ghazi Miyan**, **Bale Miyan**, **Bala Dulha**, **Pir Bahlim:** The hero of the story. Born in 1014 in Ajmer, died 1034 at Bahraich. Warrior saint hero of the *Mirat-i-Masudi* and of folklore; key figure in the cult of the Panchon Pir in the Gangetic valley.

Salar Sahu: General despatched by Sultan Mahmud of Ghazni to Ajmer, Rajasthan to fight infidels. Husband of the Sultan's sister, Sitr-i-Mualla, father of Salar Masud.

Sitr-i-Mualla (the 'veiled one'): Sister to Sultan Mahmud of Ghazni and mother of Syed Salar Masud.

Sohal Deo: Chief antagonist of Salar Masud in the Bahraich region.

Zohra Bibi: The blind girl of Rudauli who, on being cured by Ghazi Miyan, devotes her life as a servitor at his shrine, and with her death gets symbolically (and later ritually) betrothed to Ghazi Miyan.

Note on diacritical marks

Diacritics are used sparingly. Elongated vowel sounds for 'a' and 'u' are written with a macron as ā, ū. The elongated sound for 'e' is represented, as in the sources, alternatively by an 'i' (*Pir*= saint), or 'ee' (*Shaheed*= martyr). Diacritics are used *only for phrases* from Persian, Urdu and Hindi, Bhojpuri and Awadhi. Elongated vowel sounds ā and ū are also indicated for some crucial words from these dialects, for example *bānjh* (a barren woman).

Preface

Histories of conquest are written primarily as sagas of victory, even when tempered with doubt about their ability to persuade. Decimation or siring of *métissage* populations; supplanting of or accommodation with pre-existent beliefs; devaluation of native knowledge, forms and aesthetics; acculturation or racialisation; state formation and novel norms of rule and control—shorn of particularities, these are the tropes that order the history of events, post-conquest, when, after the fact, the chief antagonist has surrendered and the last rebel has been accounted for.

The conqueror as hero and the opponent who dies, or fights shy of battle, as in the case of Alexander the Greek and Darius the Persian, are chosen subjects of (victorious) chroniclers and subaltern myth-making. Far removed in time and space, Americo-Indian views of the historic clash with the conquistadors, for their part, are not purely adversarial; memories of past events are inflected with dramatic reversals and counterfactual folklore.[1] That spectral world where promiscuous accounts of the past are variedly embraced by victors and conquered alike is not amenable to unalloyed certitude; it is best explored by sidestepping the hubris of History.

With the martyred Turkic-Indian warrior hero Ghazi Miyan, who fell in battle against local chiefs 350 miles northeast of Delhi in 1034 CE, some two centuries before the establishment of a Sultanate at that imperial city, there are additional imponderables. Hagiographical literature maintains that he was the sister's son of Sultan Mahmud of Ghazni, but that sultan who invaded India seventeen times during the early eleventh century had no such nephew: contemporary chronicles are clear on this score. Yet the combined weight of folklore and a seventeenth-century text has had the effect of displacing the ruthless conqueror from Ghazni, Afghanistan by the virtuous nephew—the saintly warrior Salar Masud or Ghazi Miyan, as he is referred to in the Gangetic plains. What does this radical displacement mean for the multi-religious devotees of this youthful Turkic commander fighting 'infidel' Indian rajas and for a history of conquest? How are memory and history, the transmitted and the inscribed, juggled in the career of this ambiguous Ghazi over the *longue durée*, from the early thirteenth century to the present?

This book eschews definitive explanations—the big why questions—that in a commonsensical view are requisites for all historical accounts. It is not a perverse desire to undercut the ground from under Clio's feet, but the recognition, after Carlo Ginzburg, 'that a new field of investigation alters not only the method but also the criteria of evidence of a given discipline' that has motivated the manner of writing of the story of Ghazi Miyan.[2] And so, instead of documenting precisely *why* a particular Sufi scholar wrote a hagiographical account of the Warrior Saint at the time that he did, or offering a compelling reason for *why* Hindu castes have felt no compunction in installing a Muslim warrior on their domestic altar, I attempt to narrate both the manner in which the hagiography of Salar Masud has been written and the ways in which popular assent is generated across religious divides. This has required a close reading of textual, folkloric and archival material in the several languages and dialects of Hindustan. I have also sought to capture the sense of, say, a ballad about the warrior hero recorded over a century ago in a contemporary performance and its resonance in the world of kin and quotidian relations, and to map the contours of historically grounded beliefs by engaging with present-day devotees at the Fair of the Ghazi.

The book seeks to offer not so much an ethnography of devotion as a history of veneration and popular affirmation of both community and a conflictual past. I make no apologies for peopling the Ghazi story with things Indian and *mentalité* Gangetic, which alone make this tale intelligible. I hope that the story of 'our Ghazi groom', as he is affectionately referred to in folklore, is read as more than an evocation of a world fiercely local. Comparative analysis requires not so much the laying out of newer histories within pre-existing fields, as efforts, howsoever tenuous, to make the historically unfamiliar intelligible outside its particular location of space and time. The pitfalls of such an intellectual conceit are many, not least of which is a sort of special pleading. But to accede readily to the requirements of trans-regional comparison as a prerequisite for intelligibility is, to use that hackneyed phrase, to throw out the baby with the bath water.

Part I of the book begins with a consideration of the idealised portrayal of Syed Salar Masud and his eleventh-century jihad as described in a seventeenth-century Farsi hagiography. Turning to folklore, Part II (based on fieldwork) focuses on the image of this Indo-Turkic warrior in the mirror of the everyday, and the manner in which that representation has inspired devotion among both his Muslim and Hindu followers. The discussion in Part III turns to the routinised aspects of faith: domestic worship among the various peasant and artisanal groups, the role of a special set of Dafali balladeers, past and present, in the propagation of the cult, and the economy and geography of veneration. Part IV recounts the episodes of opposition to the person and the cult of the warrior saint, from both orthodox Muslims and Hindu publicists, especially in the early twentieth century when the solidification of communitarian identities saw a concerted attack on the popular veneration of the Islamic warrior by a largely Hindu populace. The concluding section, Part V, engages with the persistent figure of Ghazi Miyan in adages, proverbs and everyday memory, such that the fraught coupling of conquest and community is not so much elided as made to appear naturally so.

It is within the referents of religio-cultural affinities, peasant dialects and linguistic particularities, culinary etiquette and transgressive commensality that the image of the Turkic warrior Salar Masud gets redrawn into that of a youthful warrior—a Ghazi who has little compunction forsaking marriage for martyrdom. Here social responsibility is all encompassing, as a reckless bridegroom interrupts midway both familial expectations and the unfolding marital rites to ride to his death. What one could call the main currents of History function only as a backdrop; these do not quite exercise the determining influence that is a characteristic of the passage of chronological time. In the unfolding saga of the saintly warrior-groom, the eventful is on sufferance of the archetypal. This then is a story of the quotidian reshaping the historic. To broach such issues is to enter simultaneously the world of popular belief as it is to revisit the historiography of the Turkic conquest of India.

1

Introduction

Sufi and the Ghazi

The politics of the imagination of a 'Hindu India' has depended crucially on a particular reading of the oppression of the disunited denizens of the subcontinent by Muslim conquerors and rulers from the eleventh century till the establishment of British rule in the mid-eighteenth century.

> Believing in four Vedas, six Shastras, eighteen Purans and 33 crore devtas Hindus, to begin with, were differentiated according to language, beliefs and customs, and then the [war of the] Mahabharata caused further havoc. The one or two germs of valour that remained were finished off by the Ahimsa of Lord Buddha ... Our ferociousness simply disappeared; our sense of pride deserted us, and as for anger, all sorts of sins were laid at its door. The result: we became devtas, mahatmas, or for that matter nice fellows [*bhalmanus*], but our spunk, we lost that. No fire, no spark, simply cold ash, that's what we became ...
>
> And on the other side in the desert of Arabia a soul appeared who was brave as his word, and in whose religion killing, slaughtering, fighting and marauding were the principal elements...[1]

Thus wrote Manan Dwivedi, Bhojpuri poet, Hindi novelist and writer of nationalist prose in the prologue to an impressive two-part 'History of Muslim Rule in India', commissioned by the Hindi-nationalist Kashi Nagari Pracharini Sabha in the year 1920.[2]

There are obvious continuities here with what Partha Chatterjee has called the 'new nationalist history of India' written in Bengali some fifty years earlier in the late nineteenth century.[3] These vernacular histories transmitted the 'stereotypical figure of "the Muslim", endowed with a "national character", fanatical, bigoted, warlike, dissolute, cruel.' This distinct history, says Chatterjee,

> [o]riginates in, and acquires its identity from the life of Muhammad. In other words, the dynasty that will be founded in Delhi at the beginning of the thirteenth century and the many changes that will take place in the subsequent five centuries are not to be described merely as the period of Turko-Afghan or Mughal India: they are integral parts of the political history of Islam.
>
> The actors in this history are also given certain behavioural characteristics. They are warlike and believe it is their religious duty to kill infidels. Driven by the lust for plunder and the visions of cohabiting with the nymphs of paradise, they are even prepared to die in battle. They are not merely conquerors but 'delirious at the prospect of conquest' (*digvijayonmatta*), and consequently are by their very nature covetous of the riches of India.[4]

Jin jāvanān tuv dharam nari dhan tinhon līnhon: 'You Muslim foreigners! You have robbed us [Hindus] of [our] dharma, women and wealth—all three', wrote the Hindi poet Bharatendu Harishchandra in 1888, echoing pithily the stereotypical recollection of Muslim conquest and its effects on a Hindu India.[5]

Ruled by Muslim kings of different dynasties, the Sultanate of Delhi, c. 1200 CE, expanded over the next three centuries to encompass large portions of northern and peninsular India. And when it was snuffed out in the 1520s by Zahir-ud-din Babur, an adventurer from the petty principality of Farghana in present-day Uzbekistan, the Delhi Kingdom was replaced by the more glamorous Mughal Empire, which lasted as an expanding imperial venture till the early eighteenth century, and nominally till the suppression of the Rebellion of 1857. It was then that the last of the Mughals was exiled by the triumphant British to oblivion in distant Rangoon. In their exercise of imperial hegemony and subcontinental power, the Mughals totally transformed the predatory meaning of the term 'Mongol/Mughal', reconfiguring in the process (in active interaction with the indigenous/local/'Hindu') a wide swath of the social, cultural and intellectual world of India.

Medieval 'Muslim' warfare and rule, c. 1000 onwards, has understandably been the object of considerable narrative anxiety from the nineteenth century to the present. And for good reason, for at its heart is the issue of the pre-colonial conquest of the subcontinent—and of its consequences. How different was this medieval 'Muslim' India of Turkish sultans and Mughal padshahs from the conquest and colonisation of India by industrial Britain? Here most accounts have been unable to extricate themselves from the blame/praise format—and a good deal of this has to do with the tie-up between history-writing and nation-formation. For a large part, mainstream history-writing usually relates to one form of community—the national community. Modern history invokes the idea of a people as sovereign and historically constituted, and this has been productive of most national histories. The triumph of the idea of self-determination has meant that all conquest has come to be regarded as unjust. It is in this context, writes Camal Kafadar in his study of the formation of the Ottoman state, 'that the meaning of medieval Muslim invasions has been particularly problematic one to deal with among many Eurasian nations', for to take 'one's comingling with the "other" seriously in the historical reconstruction of heritages ... seems to demand too much of national historiographies'.[6] How can the historian's history then reengage in newer ways the issue of conquest—in this case, the Turkish conquest of north India, c. 1000–1200?

What was the nature of iconoclasm and pillage, especially of the notorious Sultan Mahmud of Ghazni, whose repeated raids into northern and western India, 1000–1026 CE, resulted in widespread despoliation and destruction? Writing in his wake, the eleventh-century savant Al Beruni seems to have predicted uncannily the path of the memories of Mahmud's invasions:

> Mahmud utterly ruined the prosperity of the country, and performed there wonderful exploits, by which the Hindus became like atoms of dust scattered in all directions, and like a tale of old in the mouth of the people. Their scattered remains cherish, of course, the most inveterate aversion towards all Muslims.[7]

Its metaphoric charge notwithstanding, this sentiment has been echoed in every textbook of Indian history, beginning with a

Bengali tract written in 1858: 'Of all the Muslims it was [Mahmud's] aggression which first brought devastation and disarray to India, and from that time the freedom of the Hindus has diminished and faded like the phases of the moon'.[8] Sultan Mahmud of Ghazni is then the familiar conqueror-marauder of history textbooks, as he is the idealised iconoclast of Indo-Persian chronicles, panegyrics and medieval treatises on governance.[9]

There have been a series of retorts to this 'communalisation of history', as it is called in South Asia, the term 'communal' implying an adherence to narrow religio-sectarian loyalties that colour and impede the development of a properly contextualised history and a composite cultural past and present, not exclusively Hindu or Muslim. The most powerful (and very nearly the first) such critique came from Professor Mohammad Habib, who in a series of essays, c. 1920–1950, sought to counter the communalisation of India's medieval history from a broadly Marxist perspective.[10] His ire was directed particularly against the partisan scholarship of British administrator-orientalists who had consistently projected the 'Muslim India' of c. 1000–1700 as a period of oppression and fanaticism from which colonial rule had finally liberated the grateful Hindus.

Habib countered by arguing that the 'real motives of the plundering expeditions' of the beginning of the eleventh century, associated with the name of Mahmud of Ghazni, were 'greed for treasure and gold. The iconoclastic pretensions were meant only for the applause of the gallery'.[11] The Muslims of India were not so much the progeny of Turkish conquerors, he wrote, as local converts from the artisanal classes, socially and spatially at the margins of both Hindu society and early medieval towns: 'an Indian Muslim had as little chance of becoming a warlord of the empire of Delhi as a [low caste] Hindu *Sudra* of ascending a Rajasthan throne' occupied by Hindu rajas and maharajas. For Habib, 'such limited success as Islam achieved in India' as a proselytising force 'was not due to its kings and politicians but to its saints'.[12]

In this view, 'the Indo-Muslim mystics, without perhaps consciously knowing it, followed the footsteps of their great Hindu predecessors … And Hinduism in its cosmopolitan outlook enrolled the Muslim mystics among its rishis, and neighbourly feelings soon developed a common calendar of saints. So it was in the thirteenth century and so it remains today'.[13] A part of the 'age-old moral and spiritual traditions of our people', syncretism for Habib and several others delineates an essential Indian characteristic, one marked by emotive floral, faunal and cultural signifiers. In such an understanding, syncretism is not a historical process, a product of coming to terms with events like political conquest and the otherworldly challenge posed to the indigenous *jogi*s (yogis) by what must have seemed like *arriviste* Sufis. It springs, fully formed, so to speak, from the same 'sacred land where the black gazelles graze, the *munja* grass grows and the *pān* [betel] leaf is eaten, and where the material and the spiritual are organically intermixed'. I take these evocative markers of India's sacred topology from Habib's powerful address to the Indian History Congress in the immediate aftermath of Independence and Partition in December 1947.[14]

But we know that the medieval Sufis, though gentle in their persona, especially in archetypal opposition to the 'holy warrior', had to forcefully carve out their spiritual domain against the locally ensconced authority of *jogi*s. Hagiographies constantly harp on contests between the Sufi and the *jogi* for spiritual supremacy, contests in which the *jogi* is invariably bested: he either converts along with his disciples, or retires, leaving the Sufi in triumphant possession of a prior holy and tranquil spot (often by a lake). One of India's most venerable Sufis, Muinuddin Chishti of Ajmer, is said to have established his hospice only after successfully overcoming ogres and warriors attached to a pre-existing site commanded by a *jogi* and his entourage.[15] Sometimes, all that remains of the preceding *jogi* is a wisp of a name, carrying the toponymic stigmata of a 'historic' defeat for all to utter. Many place names in the Gangetic heartland enshrine the memory of such holy victories and defeats (though I am far from arguing that every time a local mentions, say, the name Mau-nāth-bhanjan, she necessarily recollects the destruction [*bhanjan*] of the lord and master [*nāth*] of Mau, a thriving manufacturing town near Banaras since the seventeenth century). In other cases, the defeated spiritual master is transformed into an ogre by the sheer act of transcription from one language to another. While the Sanskrit *dev* stands for a god, or the title of a revered person, when written in Persian without this gloss the word *deo* stands for a ghost, demon or monster. Spiritually and linguistically mastered, the holy-harmful figure often submits before the majestic Sufi, who grants the vanquished and now subservient *deo* his last wish that his memory be recorded for posterity in terms of some trace. This frequently gets enshrined in the nomenclature of a place—for example, Maunath Bhanjan, or Deoband, the place of the incarcerated *deo*-demon, incidentally the locale of an Islamic seminary since the 1860s. The trace could be retained as a visible sign of an equally monstrous sort. At the Bahraich shrine of Salar Masud Ghazi in northeastern Uttar Pradesh (UP), for example the earrings of the subdued *deo* Nirmal are the size of grindstones.

These are some of the ways in which eventful encounters between the holy men of Islam and of the Hindus get enshrined in the life histories of popular Sufi sites. And of course these shrines attract both Hindus and Muslims as devotees. Muzaffar Alam has shown with great acuity how many descriptions of such Sufi saints are *subsequent* representations, probably guided by the political necessity, either to overcompensate for a founding head's politically incorrect dealings with an earlier Sultan, or to elevate him (as with Muinuddin Chishti of Ajmer) into a full-fledged Indian prophet (*Nabi-yi-Hind*). As the dominant Chishtiya *silsilah* faced threats in the seventeenth century from 'new Central Asian sheikhs' from the erstwhile homelands of the Mughals and their Indian disciples, such efforts to save the phenomena of dominance and fame of the Chishti Sufis became more pronounced.[16]

Let me clarify. My point is not to deny the composite following of India's justly famous Sufi saints. All I wish to do is to create a space for encounter, clash and conquest as necessary elements of the conflictual prehistory of such cultic sites as that of Muinuddin Chishti of Ajmer, and Nizamuddin Auliya, medieval and modern Delhi's greatest Sufi saint. Wrathful, hypostatical, miraculous events and encounters, I am suggesting, not a simple, longstanding Indian spirit of accommodation, go into the making of India's vaunted syncretism. Or, to put it sharply: accommodation is predicated, necessarily in such stories, on a prior clash of two opposing wills. The hermetically cloistered figures of rosary-fondling Sufis (saints) and saber-rattling *ghazis* (warriors), even when yoked to the cause of good pluralistic politics, produce bad history. Not History with a capital 'H', but the representation and recollection of their exploits outside proper, verifiable, contemporary medieval archives are some of the elements of a new history that we should strive towards. I say this for two reasons: one, because irrespective of their specificities of time and place, such accounts feed into the life stories of prominent Sufis, forming the template for recollecting the exploits of subsequent, lesser, (but no less important) local figures. And also because standard tropes such as the dumb idol breaking its silence under the power of a Sufi shaikh to recite the *shahada* (the Islamic credo), as found in medieval Persian texts, contribute to the valorisation of that credo—There is no God but Allah and Muhammad is His Messenger. Even everyday Indian-Muslim signs (like the index finger which is raised during prayers in testimony of the singularity of Allah, or the ablutionary water-pot *badhna*) become imbued with a certain power in a whole range of popular accounts of warriors and Sufis in the east-UP countryside.[17]

The notion of syncretism has come in for criticism recently from several scholars working with a variety of historical and ethnographic materials. Tony Stewart in his analysis of the Janus-faced popular Bengali deity Satya Pir, criticises the votaries of syncretism for taking recourse to metaphor to underscore their point, comparing the category 'to some other entity that is impermanent, the most popular being organic (such as hybrid or half-breed), alchemical (such as mixture or solution), or construction (bricoleur)'. This metaphorical charge, in Stewart's view, 'implies that no syncretic entity is viable in its own right', for it is after all a mixture of two very separate elements—Hindus and Muslims—and hence, in a sense, inherently unstable. Aditya Behl characterises the Awadh-based Hindvi Sufi poets of the fourteenth to sixteenth centuries as 'fully part of the Indian cultural landscape, indigenized yet *competing* with other groups to articulate their distinct theology'.[18] Muzaffar Alam has analysed the north Indian Sufis' output and attitudes in the context of their complex relationship to state and society between the thirteenth and eighteenth centuries, which was as political, theological and cultural as it was competitive, adversarial and contributory. Such a multi-layered relationship, with its own chronology and politics, was moulded firmly by the development of Indo-Islamic concepts such as *wahdat-al wujud* (unity of being), tending towards 'the process of religious synthesis and cultural amalgam'. The same seventeenth-century Sufi writer, writes Alam, while appreciating certain portions of the Gita that he found 'close to some Quranic verses and hadises as read by proponents of *wahdat-al-wujud*', could write another text which 'reads like a polemic against Hindu beliefs and traditions'.[19] Faced as we are today with a Manichean clash between Islam and Hinduism in India's medieval past, and a conflictual present in many parts of the world, historians need to fashion newer histories of this encounter.

The shared worship of worthies—heroes, warriors, saints—by a multi-religious populace is rightly portrayed in most writings as evidence of the remarkable composite religiosity of the Indian people. Muinuddin Chishti of Ajmer; Nizamuddin Auliya of Delhi, Khwaja Khizr, the patron saint of boatmen—all have received their fair share in most scholarly accounts of Indian Islam.[20] These personages continue to have their importance in the uncertain India of today. But the focus on syncretism sans conflict amounts to taking only half a step. And this is so because our concentration on inter-communal goodwill and harmony, though necessary, leaves the field of sectarian strife as the special preserve of sectarian and 'communal' historians. Mine is a plea for essaying non-sectarian histories of conquest and conflict in India specially, and elsewhere more generally.

This book argues a fairly simple proposition: If the sites of the martyrdom of Islam's holy warriors in India are equally the sites of long-lasting multi-religious cults, then clearly this is attributable neither to popular amnesia nor to the triumph of thaumaturgy over 'facts of history'. The tales of Muslim warrior saints retailed by balladeers, which bear a complicated relationship to the standard hagiographies, are evidence of the refashioning of sagas of 'religious' conflict in order to create communities in the past and in the present. To focus exclusively on the syncretism of such cults, without taking on board the narrative refashionings of conquest that these cults invariably entail, is to miss out on the creation of India's composite culture as a process. It is also to hitch popular remembrance to the temporal career of superstition, while remaining impervious to the literary, cultural and mnemonic devices through which popular assent is generated across religious divides.

There are many Muslim warrior saints and saintly shrines scattered throughout India. Numerous place names with the prefix 'Ghazi', humble shrines of 'manly martyrs' (*shahīd mard*) and their graveyards, genealogies of camp followers, and of course folklore testify to the widespread memorialisation of Ghazis and *shahīds*—warriors and martyrs—over large parts of India.[21] In his exemplary study of the Sufis of Bijapur, Richard Eaton has related the historical presence of warrior Sufis in peninsular India to the military campaigns into the Deccan launched from the late thirteenth century by armies of the Sultanate of Delhi. Unable to exist 'entirely independent[ly] of some kind of Muslim presence', these Sufis seem to have lost their raison d'être 'after Islam had achieved full political presence' by the establishment of the Bahmani kingdom (1347–1489) 'in a region that had theretofore had been a Muslim frontier', suggests Eaton.[22] We are concerned here with arguably the most intriguing of warrior saints from the subcontinent: Syed Salar Masud. According to a seventeenth-century Persian hagiography, assiduously translated and commented upon in the nineteenth and twentieth centuries, and in ballads sung over large parts of north India, this dashing warrior was martyred at the young age of nineteen in 1034 CE at Bahraich in northeastern Uttar Pradesh bordering Nepal.

I do not set out to establish a credible chronology for Syed Salar Masud, also known as Ghazi Miyan, Bale Miyan, Bala Pir, Pir Bahlim or Gajan Dulha; it is rather the widespread recognition of this 'eleventh-century Jihadi' as India's premier warrior saint that requires the historian's consideration. Not that the Ghazi went completely unnoticed in medieval chronicles, travellers' accounts and reminiscences of both kings and humbler soldiers. The hallowed warrior could well invade the dreams of one who, wish fulfilled, had reneged on paying obeisance to this saint of Bahraich; equally, exuberant devotee-pilgrims en route to his tomb in northeastern UP could, during their nocturnal sojourn outside the imperial capital at Agra, unsettle the equanimity of the Mughal Emperor Akbar. The historian Ziauddin Barani described this Salar (commander) as 'one of the heroes of Sultan Mahmud['s]' campaigns in India in his *Tarikh-i-Ferozshahi* (1357CE); and according to the *Akbar Nama*, the late-sixteenth century account of the reign of that Mughal king, 'Salar Masud … was connected by blood with Mahmud Ghazni … sold his life bravely in battle and left an imperishable name'.[23] However, the hiatus between Masud's total absence from the contemporary chronicles of the eleventh-century Ghaznavid dynasty and the recognition he elicited in varied accounts from the late-thirteenth century, still remains.

As with his connection to Sultan Mahmud of Ghazni, the pull and power of Masud's grave had begun to be noticed by writers affiliated to the relatively new political entity of the Delhi Sultanate from the late thirteenth century. In a letter c. 1290, Amir Khusro, the Delhi-based poet who had spent some time in Awadh, alluded elliptically to the 'fragrant tomb of Sipahsalar *Shahīd* [the martyred commander]' at Bahraich spreading the 'perfume of odorous wood' throughout Hindustan—the regional appellation referring to present-day eastern Uttar Pradesh (Figure 1.1).[24] The accolade was not undeserved, for in the next fifty years the 'fragrance' of this backwoods shrine had reached the Court at Delhi itself. In 1341, the famous Moroccan traveller Ibn Battuta accompanied the Delhi Sultan Mohammad bin Tughlaq to the Bahraich *dargah*—a sure sign of its prior popularity. Ferozshah, the next ruler of the Delhi Sultanate, had a special attachment for the *mazar*, once getting his head shaved at the shrine in the manner of a recluse, after the deceased warrior had paid him a visit in a dream.[25] Interestingly, an armed foray by the ruler of Lakhnauti (Bengal) to the Bahraich shrine in 1353, purportedly seeking a remedy for his *bars* (vitiligo), led to a quick retribution by the Sultan of Delhi. Taking umbrage at a regional ruler's military incursion into an outlying part of his kingdom, Ferozshah Tughlaq in turn invaded the principality of Bengal.[26] Two centuries later, one Dattu Sarvani, an Indo-Afghan soldier, recalled the saint's wrathful appearance in a sequence of his dreams. The 'vividness and immediate ring of truth', writes the pioneering medievalist Simon Digby, is suggestive of the fact that Dattu 'could have hardly recorded them had he not dreamt of them'.[27] As with other such saints, the *jalāli* or ominous aspect of the beneficient Salar Masud is best brought out by recalling *in extenso* the vivid nocturnal record of the encounters of soldier Dattu with the spirit of Masud:

> Once I was very ill and in pain. And some people said, 'You should vow to go to the tomb of Salar Masud Ghazi. Say that when you are well you will go to the tomb.' I stayed silent, and the people said again very earnestly. 'You should make a vow to go to the tomb of Salar Masud Ghazi. For he is a powerful saint, and whoever makes a vow to him attains his desire'.
>
> I was obliged to make a vow to him, but the whole of my vow was that first I would go to the tomb of Hazrat Qutb-i-Alam [Shaikh

Fig. 1.1 A page from Amir Khusro's Ijaz-i-Khusrawi with the couplet about the dargah at Bahraich

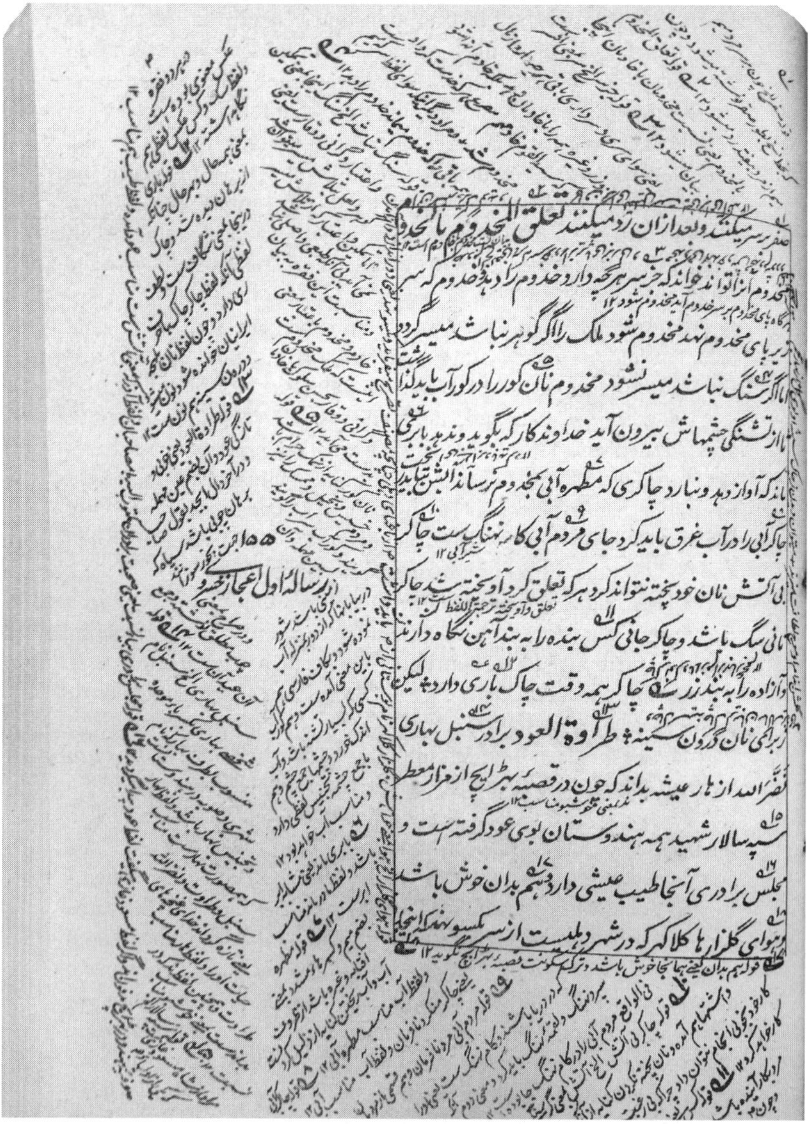

Source: Amir Khusrau, *Ijaz-i-Khusravi*, Risala I (Lucknow: Neval Kishore Press, 1867), p. 155

Abdul Quddus Chishti Sabri Gangohi, d. 1531], my Pir and helper. Later when God granted me a measure of health, Hazrat Salar Masud Ghazi appeared in a dream and said, 'Come visit me.' When I woke up I did not tell of this appearance to anyone. After some days he said to me again in a dream. 'My tomb is near. Why do you not come and visit it? Lo! Behold my tomb'. The domed tomb came before my eyes. I woke up and told what I had seen to several people. 'Hazrat Salar Masud is clearly summoning you', they said. 'Go immediately to his tomb,' ... However much people urged me I could not agree, because the vow fixed in my mind was that first I would visit the tomb of my Pir and helper, [Hazrat Qutub-i-Alam Gangohi] and kiss the feet of the Pirzada: and then I would go to the tomb of Hazrat Salar.

One day a Madari Darvesh came into the house and said, 'Hazrat Salar has told me to tell Dattu to visit him first, and not to delay'. I told the Madari, 'I have a vow that when I have the strength and ability to do so I will go, if God wills: and I do not deny that I will benefit from it.' 'I have warned you', he said, 'Salar is a powerful saint. Take care lest harm occur to you.' In short I began to feel afraid, but the resolve remained in my mind, that first I would visit my Pir and helper and kiss the feet of his sons and then the other. One night Hazrat Qutub-i-Alam appeared and said, 'Dattu, it is better for you first to visit my grave.'

I woke up and grew stronger; and then one night I saw in a dream that Salar Masud had come into my room. He seized me by the hair and dragged me out in anger. When we had gone some steps, a man came and said, 'Who are you that has seized Dattu by the hair and are taking him away.'

He [Salar Masud] seized him also by the hair, and all three of us went on, and we could not get free. Suddenly I saw that like a hawk Hazrat Qutub-i-Alam was coming to our aid, and Hazrat Salar, when he saw Hazrat Qutub-i-Alam let go of our hair and remained standing there. I wondered why he had let go of me. Then when I looked behind I saw Hazrat Qutbi was standing there ... The same moment another man appeared and said, 'What fault has Dattu committed that you are carrying him off by the hair?' 'He vowed', Hazrat Salar said 'that when he was well again, he would visit my tomb. He is evading his vow.' 'This fellow does not have the strength at present', the other man said. 'When he is strong to come to your place he will come.' Salar smiled and said, 'Very well.' In short when I saw the signs from Salar Masud and also the signs from Hazrat Qutb-i-Alam, my thoughts were confused and I was overawed.'[28]

That a vow (unfulfilled, hence the nightmares) to visit the Bahraich shrine for regaining health could commend itself to an Afghan soldier embroiled in the mid-sixteenth century struggle over the fledgling Mughal empire, speaks for the entrenched position of Masud in the mental universe of rulers and subalterns alike.

Mainstream sixteenth-century sources had begun to reflect this wide devotional arc of the Bahraich shrine, as also the exuberant involvement of *menu peuple* in commemorating the martyrdom of warrior hero Masud. The Delhi Sultan Sikandar Lodi (1481–1517), had tried banning, it seems unsuccessfully, 'the festival of the spears [pennons] of Masud in his kingdom', which included the better portion of northern India between the Punjab and Bihar. Half a century later, the Mughal emperor Akbar was sufficiently shaken by his close encounter with the Bahraich-bound pilgrims on the outskirts of Agra, to relate it to the ideologue and court historian soon after. 'It is the custom of India', noted Abul Fazl's official account of the reign of Akbar, 'for people to make flags of various colours in different places and convey them with numerous presents' to Bahraich. One such large pilgrim party—'a great concourse' comprising 'both the good and the bad'—had camped at the capital city of Agra one summer night in the lunar month of Jeth (May–June) 1560–1561 CE. They would have started at day break on their 250-mile joyous trudge which would take them across the rivers Jamuna, Ganga and Ghaghra to the shrine a couple of days later. Sufficiently intrigued, the Emperor decided to observe the assemblage incognito. Recognised by 'some ruffian', Akbar in his own words, 'without the least delay or hesitation rolled my eyes and squinted so as to make a wonderful change in my appearance'. The rustic devotees of Masud Ghazi did not press further. 'I quietly moved away from the scene and went to my place', recounted the Emperor to his minister Abul Fazl, who duly recorded it in the *Akbar Nama*.[29]

It was Emperor Akbar who made a land grant for the upkeep of the Bahraich shrine in 1571 CE, an arrangement that was reinforced by a royal decree by Nawab Shuja-ud-daula of Awadh in the last year of his life in 1765. Asaf-ud-daula, the next Nawab is known to have made annual visits to the shrine.[30] Two accounts of popular religion and the fetes of Hindustan published in the first decade of the nineteenth century provide more detailed descriptions of the festivities at the concourse of pilgrims at Bahraich—the sort that Emperor Akbar had encountered outside the capital city in 1561 CE. Mirza Muhammad Qateel's 'Haft Tamasha' (written in 1811–12 at the behest of the Nawab of Awadh) and Cazim Ali Javan's poetic narrative of the fair and festivals of Hindustan, published by the Hindustani Press, Calcutta again in 1812, each refer to the folklore and ceremonies around the wedding of young Salar Masud, performed at his annual festival at the dargah in Bahraich and elsewhere. These may safely be taken to describe the happenings at the Ghazi Miyan Fair for the latter half of the eighteenth century. Qateel's *Haft Tamasha* mentions synoptically the ceremonial viewing of a replica of Masud's nuptial bed which was brought out every year in *qasba* Rudauli, commemorating the tragic death of the warrior, martyred on the night of his wedding in 'a fight against [unnamed] kafirs'. Cazim Ali Javan's longer poetical account provides a fuller description of the summer fair at Bahraich, the site of Masud's martyrdom and of his shrine—to which we shall turn later on in the book (see also, Appendix 3). Neither of these texts on popular culture of Hindustan, however, provides a connected narrative of the life of Salar Masud.[31]

For the present, one fact stands out from the mid-sixteenth century. Compared to the palpable presence of Ghazi Miyan's devotees outside Akbar's imperial capital at Agra, a gazetteer of the reign of that emperor made only the briefest of mentions about the life of the warrior saint to whose shrine at Bahraich his exuberant followers were headed: 'Salar Masud … [who] was connected by blood with Mahmud Ghazni … sold his life bravely in battle and left an imperishable name' is all there is to Salar Masud in the *Ain-i-Akbari*.[32]

This was scanty detail about a saint so famous for his military exploits, who was attracting thousands of milling pilgrims to his shrine every year. Aimed at filling this narrative gap, there appeared in the early seventeenth century a most remarkable life of Masud, which reads virtually like a screenplay of the short but brilliant career of the youthful commander ('connected by blood with Mahmud Ghazni'), who died aged nineteen fighting infidels at Bahraich in 1034 CE. It is to this hagiography that we now turn, with the caveat that rather than its facticity, it is the picture of a virtual Salar Masud which it portrays that is more interesting. Suggestive of the almost real time narrative that this Life sought to convey to its medieval readers, I too narrate its events in the present tense.

Map 1.1 *Main sites connected with Salar Masud's life and campaigns in northern India and neighbouring regions*

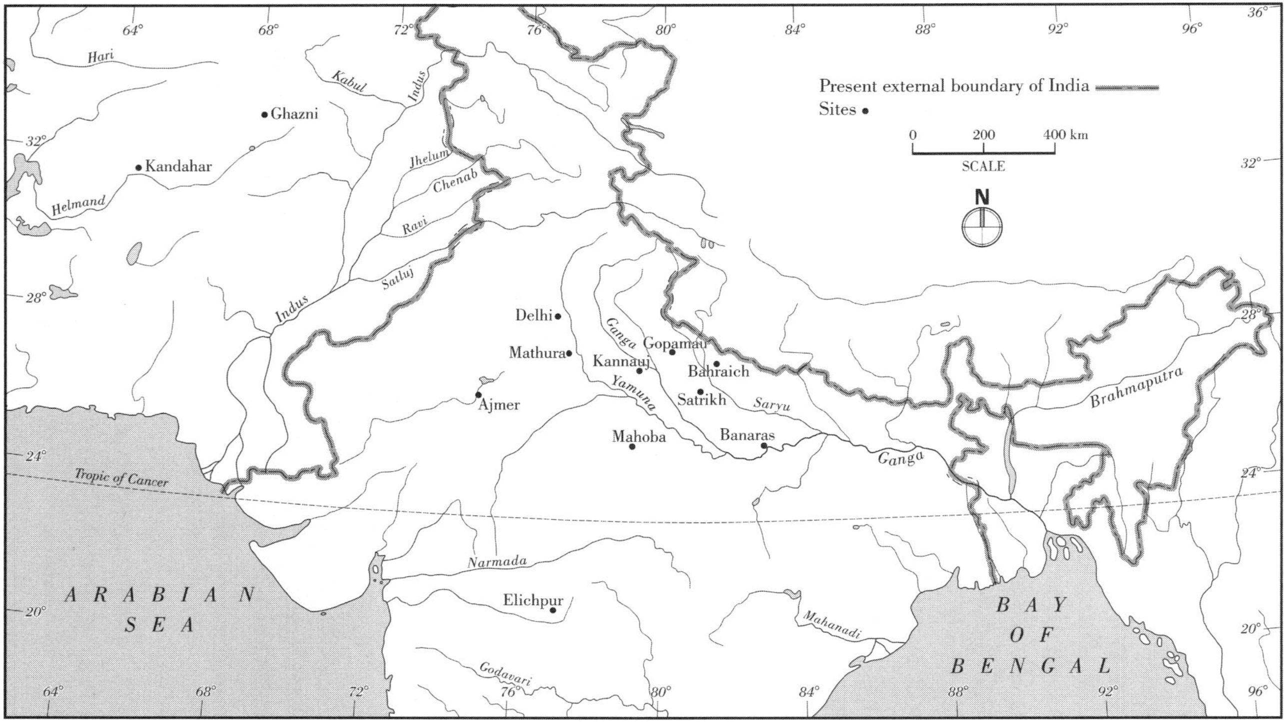

PART ONE A LIFE

2

The Hagiography

In the 1620s, Abdur Rahman Chishti, a prominent Sufi shaikh of north India whose prodigious outpourings spanned the regimes of three Mughal emperors, Jahangir, Shah Jahan and Aurangzeb, set about writing the Life of Salar Masud—*Sultan-us-Shuhda*, or the Prince of Martyrs as he dubbed him, and Ghazi Miyan, Bale Miyan, Bale Pir, Gajna Dulha as he was and is variously known even today. This was not the only mirror the prolific Sufi from Rudauli in central Uttar Pradesh held up to the north Indian past. Abdur Rahman's considerable corpus included a 'verse treatise on Hindu cosmogony', an 'abridged translation and Islamising explanation of the Bhagvad Gita', a biographical compendium of a long list of Islamic saints, the life of Shah Madar of Makanpur and *Mirat-i-Masudi*, the text that concerns us here.[1] The medievalist Muzaffar Alam locates the several works of Abdur Rahman within the context of his desire to elevate the Chishtiya branch of Sufis and Khwaja Muinuddin Chishti, its founder in India, in order to counter the seventeenth-century influence of the Naqsbandia Sufi school at the Mughal court. Alam suggests that Abdur Rahman wrote the biographies of the two popular north Indian saints, Shah Madar of Makanpur and Salar Masud of Bahraich, 'in order to integrate and associate legends that had developed around these figures with the life and work of Khwaja Muinuddin'.[2]

Abdur Rahman most likely composed *Mirat-i-Masudi*, the hagiography of Salar Masud (born 14 February 1014, died 10 June 1034), as a labour of love at the Chishti Sufi hospice of Rudauli, thirty miles from Ayodhya in central Awadh. By the late fourteenth century, Rudauli had emerged as a major Sufi centre, with the Chishtiya *khanqah* of Shaikh Abdul Haq (died 1434 CE) functioning as a 'clearing house… [which] … encouraged religious and cultural accommodation to local social beliefs and customs'.[3] A lineal descendant of the founder of that hospice, Abdur Rahman had assumed its headship through a chain of family succession in 1622 CE. A long-time devotee of the Bahraich Ghazi, Abdur Rahman 'the insignificant', as he proformally debased himself, was beset by a medley of oral accounts of Salar Masud's birth, of his coming to Hindustan, of his martyrdom, but of their absence from any historical work of repute.[4] In a word, there *was* evidence about the cult and the person Masud, but no connected narrative of his life. The seventeenth-century Sufi had profound belief in Salar Masud.[5] His own spiritual awakening—the crucial release from the worldly turmoil of profane love to the elevated state of the 'unveiling of the spirits' where one has 'unimpeded access to all'—was induced by the inner grace of the Prince of Martyrs, as Abdur Rahman chose to dub Masud Ghazi.* And this happened during the forty days' fasting practised by Sufis in India to 'induce [a] state outside normal experience.'[6]

Returning to this inner transformation in a later work, Abdur Rahman exulted:

> Twenty seven years have elapsed since this humble servant observed the spiritual presence of the Sultan-us-Shuhda, and during that whole period not one event, either esoteric or exoteric, has taken place which has more enlightened me than the occurrence of the [appearance] of his spirituality, neither has any physical or metaphysical assistance [greater than this] shown itself.[7]

Abdur Rahman, who had 'long endeavoured to ascertain the real facts' was in search of a contemporary chronicle about Salar Masud. He finally dug out an 'Old History' written by one Mulla Mahmud Ghaznavi. An eyewitness account, it gave him a narrative opening, for the story of *shahadat* (martyrdom) in Islam, as in Judaism, derives its tellability from the presence of a witness—a *shahid*.[8] Mulla

* Abdur Rahman was here claiming a special boon from God. He did not just get a visit from the Salar but also an entry into a realm where all spirits reside, many of whom spoke to him. A martyr retains both his body and spirit till Judgement Day, and so Abdur Rahman had separate visits from the martyr as well.

Muhammad Ghaznavi's history met that important requirement without lessening the role of Abdur Rahman as author, for the Chishti shaikh of Rudauli was no ordinary chronicler of Sufis and saints: his persona was honed by the propensity for the visionary he shared with other mystics.[9]

Understandably, the call to narrate came from beyond the world of the living. 'Several of the beloved friends and attendants of the Martyr … in the abodes of the blessed', he writes, had pressed him to write the Life of Salar Masud. The 'pure spirit' of the Bahraich martyr appeared in a dream and accorded permission to narrate, assuring help with his life story as it was being transcribed. Abdur Rahman had no hesitation in vouching for the veracity of what he had written. Indeed, the helping hand of the hero was proof that he had not dreamt it all up.

> Sundry incidents, and miraculous statements, which have been found in trustworthy books, have been selected, and after being verified by oral communications with the author's spiritual visitors, have been inserted in the present work.[10]

Whenever doubts assailed the author about the Ghazi's lineage or his rank in the 'court of God', the martyr's spirit would quite literally take him by the hand—often all the way to Kaba—for confirmation. Once, Abdur Rahman had a vision of Masud emerging from the grave of the Prophet, only to return on horseback to Bahraich, the site of his martyrdom. In a reverse journey to the hallowed courtyard at Mecca, Abdur Rahman saw Masud as a lineal descendant of Hazrat Ali, the Prophet's son-in-law.[11]

Quite clearly, *Mirat-i-Masudi* or the 'Mirror of Masud' was the artefact of a Sufi savant's febrile intellect. Suffused with Sufi notions and states, it sought to convey more than an esoteric message, for it had a clear story line: the righteous exertions of the Prince of Martyrs in Hindustan. Imprecations against *kafirs* notwithstanding, it could not do without their side of the story. In a fortuitous encounter on one of his visits 'into the north country at the foot of the mountains … by the order of the Emperor Nuru-d-din Muhammad Jahangir', Abdur Rahman claimed he came across a Brahman 'perfectly versed in the works of Hindu historians'. And as they 'chanced to speak of the Prince of Martyrs' and his expeditions in Hindustan, there emerged almost a perfect congruence between the Brahman's account and that contained in the 'Old History' of Mulla Ghaznavi discovered by Abdur Rahman himself![12] It was for all these reasons that Abdur Rahman 'believed his work to be an authentic history of Salar Masud'.[13] The *Mirat* was addressed simultaneously to the 'ordinary readers' as a Sufi account of Islam's glorious militant past, while being open to a more elevated 'read[ing] with a spiritual object'.[14]

An audacious text, the *Mirat* was unlike other accounts of the 'Sword of Islam in India' in several respects—its professed reliance on 'Hindi histories'; its imbrication in Gangetic popular culture, its narration of the life of a historically recalcitrant personage. Mahmud, the Sultan of Ghazni, did not have a nephew called Masud, the *Mirat-i-Masudi* is the only extant work on his life, and Mulla Muhammad's *Twarikh*, on which it is purportedly based, is lost to history—if its very existence is not to be attributed to Abdur Rahman's own, self-serving 'historicist' exertions alone! For all these reasons, the *Mirat* has been a difficult text to engage within works of history. Its mid-nineteenth-century English editor called it 'a historical romance … in [which] fact and fiction are freely mingled, and the great actions and exploits of other men are appropriated, without scruple to the hero of the tale'.[15] Twentieth-century medievalists have not found much use for it either—a lacuna that has now been filled in a recent work by Sunil Kumar.[16] Yet, to limit oneself to slapping ripostes for the *Mirat*'s cavalier citations from standard chronicles is to let go of the hagiography altogether; to try and untangle its truths and their affiliation to popular culture and lore, is, paradoxically, to reclaim it for history—the history of one of the most intriguing warrior saints from the Indo-Muslim encounter of the last millennium.[17]

The *Mirat* begins with the Sultan of Ghazni, 'subduer of the kingdom of Rum, and the whole of the countries of Turan and Iran [modern day Central Asia and Anatolia], spreading everywhere the religion of Muhammad', seated on his throne 'awaiting an occasion' to further execute 'the purposes of Allah'.[18] It is the beginning of the fifth-century Hijri, the year 1011 of the Christian era. Sultan Mahmud has already made several incursions across the river Indus into the Punjab. Now a group of beleaguered Muslims from the western Indian town of Ajmer appeal to him for help: 'The infidels surround us on all sides … Rai Bhairun and Rai Somgiriya are tightening the noose', plead the camel-riding emissaries. Moved by the plight of 'these poor followers of Islam', Sultan Mahmud promises succour and exacts a political promise. Should the Ajmer-Muslims triumph with his help, they will incorporate the Sultan's name in the *khutba* read at the Friday public prayers.* In a word, Mahmud would be invested with the attributes of a sovereign in the lands beyond the river Indus.[19]

A fabulous contingent of 700,000 cavalry, led by General Salar Sahu leaves for Ajmer from Kandahar, where the court had shifted temporarily. The Sultan honours the officers with gifts of ceremonial dresses; on the General, his brother-in law, he bestows his own scimitar, girdle and dagger and a pedigreed Arab charger. The officers are told to obey General Sahu as implicitly as if they were obeying the Sultan. Three days' march from Ajmer, spirits reveal to the General that he will be victorious, and that a male child will be born to him.

General Sahu routs the 'unbelievers', builds a mosque at the gate of the fort and gets the *khutba* read in the name of the Sultan.[20] Muzaffar Khan's administrative control over Ajmer and the surrounding countryside is re-established. The Sultan is overjoyed, and confers 'the government of the country' on 'his faithful brother [in-law]', asking him to force Rai Ajaipal, the Prince of Kannauj—an important political centre on the banks of the Ganges—into submission, else face the Ghaznavid scourge. The General's wife, carrying the royal order, now rejoins her husband. Masud is conceived the night of their first reunion and born in the garrison town of Ajmer.[21]

The Sultan is delighted at the birth of his sister's son, and now re-confers 'the government of the Kingdom of Hindustan' on General Sahu and the infant Masud. Salar Sahu tries to persuade Rai Ajaipal 'to cast his lot in the scale of justice', but that prince instead encourages the rebels who had taken refuge at Kannauj after fleeing the Ajmer rout. Sultan Mahmud takes the 'road to Hindustan' and reaches Ajmer. Here he feasts his eyes on his sister's son, not 'letting him go out of his sight' for days.[22] In the *Mirat* the uncle Sultan halts at Ajmer simply for the adoration of the infant Masud.**

---

* The *khutba* is a sermon at the end of congregational prayers, in which the name of the ruler was traditionally included.

** The 'chief relative who is bound to bring … presents to a new-born child is the maternal uncle [mamu] of the baby', states Ram Gharib Chaube, the famous native ethnographer, in his 'Ethnographic Note on Eastern U.P.', c. 1900. Grierson Papers, MS Eur. E-223, BL.

Masud grows up in Ajmer, precociously devout, and with an equal mastery in all the arts of war. 'By the time he was nine, he had acquired most sciences, practical and abstract, and at ten years of age he was so given … to devotion that he passed the whole night in deep study, and never left his chamber' till past sunrise.[23] A youthful holy figure with a Jesus-like countenance, destined to 'take possession of a country which has not fallen into the hands of any Musalman', Masud had a preference for chewing betel leaf, a practice particular to India.

> He was constantly performing ablutions, though if he had prayed without bathing, so pure was he in body and mind, it would not have been wrong. He had clean carpets spread where he was wont to sit, he wore pure garments and delighted in fragrant essences and eating betel leaf.[24]

Abdur Rahman continues the paean in fulsome fashion. Masud's piousness was the envy of ascetics and dervishes whom he engaged in learned converse: 'so elegantly did he turn every phrase in conversation that bystanders were astonished'; his magnanimity, like that of the legendary Hatim, famous in Arab, Persian and Indian lore and films for his generosity, was boundless; his command over civil and military affairs breathtaking.[25] 'Whoever saw his Joseph-like beauty fell in love with his affability and polished manner for the rest of his life'. His life-long followers—those who accompanied him from Ghazni on the road to Hindustan—were equally resplendent.[26] And so, Abdur Rahman leaves his seventeenth-century readers in no doubt about the high station of Masud within Islam: the 'whole of the perfection of Mohammad' shone on his forehead 'as to draw comparison' with the original 'pure Imams' or Caliphs 'in the worship of one God'.[27]

In the ten years that it takes Masud to ascend to the high state of the first five Caliphs (here, Hasan is counted along with Abu Bakr, Umar, Usman and Ali), his father 'subdues many of the countries of India', ensuring the regular inflow of revenue.[28] Commander Sahu sends a military dispatch of his successes to the Sultan, who confers 'the province of Kalihar' as a personal fiefdom.[29] The General now asks his son and wife to join him—the campaigns described in the *Mirat* have a lot of male bonding, specially between Masud and his followers, but till the hero takes the road to martyrdom, familial matters will continue to occupy him a good deal.

Accompanied by several thousand horsemen, Masud proceeds with his mother to Kalihar. The journey is uneventful, till 'engaging in the chase ... he reached the town of Rawal'. The local *zamindar* was an affine of the Sultan's wazir, Khwaja Hasan Maimandi: his sister had been given in marriage to the Khwaja.[30] The *Mirat* underlines that Wazir Maimandi 'had an hereditary feud' with Salar Sahu and was 'jealous of the honours and favours bestowed on him by the Sultan'.[31]

Satgun, the inferior-ranked sister-giver of Indian kinship, comes forward to proffer the customary obsequies, 'insisting that Masud should do him the favour' of staying at his house, 'so that he might get honour'. But 'as the star of Hasan Maimandi's bad faith shone' on his forehead, Salar Masud would 'by no means consent to alight at the abode of such a treacherous unbeliever'. The family feud with Maimandi, overlaid by the expected dislike of Indian chiefs here yields the figure of the treacherous kafir: Satgun—literally 'truth-value'—functions as the long arm of the devious wazir. And so this Hindu raja of Rawal, a relative of Maimandi, tries to poison the young warrior. Masud spurns the offer of the raja to eat the food he has prepared for his party with the retort—'Following the religion of the Prophet and his close kin, I don't eat food prepared in the house of a Hindu'.[32] The raja then entreats him to 'take sugar, rice and all things necessary, and have his food prepared by his own cooks', thereby maintaining both his own Islamic as well as Hindu notions of purity. Even this offer is spurned. Satgun then brings large quantities of sweets—commonly accepted across religious and caste divides— but Masud 'with divine perception suspects the truth'. He returns Satgun's courtesy with an appropriate gift of a robe of honour.

At the next stage on the route, the sweets are given to the dogs of chase accompanying the contingent; they die immediately. Turning to his attendants, the effulgent Masud utters what would normally be a boyish boast: 'The little unbelievers thought me, too, one of the undiscerning'. His attendants are astonished at this early proof of Masud's superior foreknowledge and bowing to the ground, begin to extol him. His mother gives away alms in thanksgiving; she is equally certain that 'the unbelievers had attempted to commit this treachery at the instigation of the deceitful Hasan Maimandi'.[33]

Not wishing to alarm his mother, Masud takes her leave on the pretext of *shikar* (hunting). Spies bring news that the treacherous

Satgun is busy 'worshipping his idols.' Masud attacks immediately. 'The unbelievers' are routed; the place torched, and Satgun, his wife and children bound and brought to the camp.[34] Salar Masud now sits down to write an account of the affair to Sultan Mahmud. Meanwhile, Satgun's brother has teamed up with Wazir Maimandi at the Ghazni court to convey a contrary picture of how the intemperate Masud had gratuitously plundered the town and taken the raja and his family hostage. A prior affinal communication between Indian chiefs and their relative, Wazir Maimandi in Ghazni, poisons the Sultan's ear before Masud's true version of Satgun's perfidy reaches the court. Now aware of the truth, the Sultan orders his nephew to keep Satgun prisoner till 'enquiries are made to punish him.'* 'The Prince of Martyrs was filled with joy on the receipt of this *farman*; but mourning fell on the house of Maimandi and his hidden treachery was made manifest.'[35]

Several elements which would propel the story of young Masud into the big bad world of Hindustan are already in place here: the play on the idea of the hunt/war; the perfidious local chiefs, here abetted by an internal enemy at the Ghazni court; young Masud's inner foreknowledge of events; the grafting of his adventure on to the established facts of Ghaznavid history. Masud now proceeds to meet with his father. The General, 'smitten with the longing desire to behold his son, who was like a second Joseph … started off … like Jacob, regardless of ceremony, to meet him.'[36] As the doting father and the dashing son enter the palace, whoever beheld Masud

> was astonished crying out 'whether Jesus has descended from the fourth heaven and does the light of Mohammad shine forth, or what is it on the face of the boy that makes the whole world burn around him like a moth in a flame.' They did not understand that the hidden treasure described by a [wise] man had come to light.

---

* The English agnatic term 'nephew' used here does not completely convey the nuances of the fact that Masud is the Sultan's sister's son, for which there is a separate north Indian term: *bhanja/bhaneja/bhaina*. This has implications for the story, as a 'sister's son' has a rather special place in both Islamic and north Indian kinship.

> 'Though that Great Monarch had firmly
> closed the door,
> Attired in the habit of darweshes,
> one person appeared
> through the door
> and "came suddenly forth".'

Abdur Rahman adds, after quoting this Persian couplet, 'How are people of the Lower World to recognise him. Those of the Upper World alone can delight and rejoice in the adorement of the divine among men'.[37] The passage and the verse are illustrative of the theological and literary conventions of the world of Abdur Rahman, which he thought his readers to be conversant with. Parallels with Jesus are invoked alongside the majestic awe of Prophet Mohammad adorning the hero's brow. Radiant and beautiful, Masud is endowed with signs of divinity and piety which only the highly literate can truly recognise. The 'divine grace' imagery is invoked here, as elsewhere, through literary allusions. By age twelve, the young boy has already developed an elevated spiritual disposition. As Masud grows up, he will go into deep meditation after the evening prayers, 'remaining alone with the Lord of the Universe the whole night'.[38]

Father and son are only briefly together, when summons arrive from the Sultan to proceed to the court in Ghazni. Salar Sahu hurries back. The Sultan 'showed such great kindness to Masud that his Wazir became jealous'. So central is the enmity of the Wazir towards young Masud that the two cannot be in Ghazni together without the bile between them staining the narrative. And, as with such visceral enmities, it has consequences for the unfolding of the story. The Sultan seeks Salar Sahu's opinion on the desirability of an expedition to 'destroy the temple at Somnath, a place of great sanctity to all Hindus' on the western coast of India. The General recommends immediate attack. The Wazir, with his family connections with Indian chiefs, prevaricates but is overruled. The Sultan elects to take Masud with his 'victorious army' to attack Somnath, an expedition upon which his fantastic reputation as an iconoclast would rest in contemporary Persian chronicle and histories. Abdur Rahman writes that Masud 'with several thousand youths in the flower of their age … performed many illustrious deeds' under the Sultan's command, and the Sultan in turn showed both Masud and his followers 'increasing favour and kindness'.[39]

There is very little in the *Mirat* beyond this fluffy passage about the actual exertions of Masud during the famous Somnath expedition—still a byword for Turkish despoliation of India and things Indic.[40] The inconsequential description of Masud's role in the sack of the Somnath temple appears almost as a storyteller's ploy. To describe in imaginary detail the nephew's activities alongside the uncle would have forced the author to square up to the young man's complete absence in the consistently bloated historical accounts of that expedition.[41] By contrast, building on an 'Old Book', Abdur Rahman would expatiate on Masud's forays into Awadh, as Sultan Mahmud did not raid this far into the Gangetic heartland. The absence of Masud from the standard Ghaznavid histories was not a problem here, for there was no possibility of the events described in the *Mirat* clashing with the court chronicles of those times.

Apart from an account of the attack on the temple of Somnath, the 'Old History' of Mulla Ghaznawi relied upon by Abdur Rahman resurfaces in the discussion about the fate of the dislodged and dismembered idol from that temple town. And with that Masud returns once again to centre stage. Sultan Mahmud, so goes the story, placed one portion of the dismembered stone idol at the entrance of the main mosque in Ghazni—to be trod upon by believers going in and out of that Jama Masjid. The 'unbelievers' approach Wazir Maimandi for help in striking a deal to ransom the remaining portion of the mutilated idol. A bargain for twice its weight in gold is struck. Masud persuades the iconoclast Sultan from becoming, in effect, an 'idol seller'. Sultan Mahmud draws back from the deal, and redirects the unbelievers to his nephew. In a sadistic move, Masud offers the idol, ground with quicklime paste and wrapped as betel (*pān*) to those who have come to purchase the remnants of their god!

'A fabrication of inferior quality' elaborated memorably in a fourteenth-century political epic about the wondrous Mahmud Ghazni, Abdur Rahman reworks the fable to reduce the iconoclast-Sultan to a narrative peg.[42] In the *Mirat*, it is not so much the legendary Sultan, but Salar Masud and Wazir Maimandi who by their clash push the story forward. The chronicled facts: that Hasan al-Maimandi was a 'man of great scholarship and vast experience in administration', that he was a 'foster brother of Sultan Mahmud and had been brought up with him'[43] are omitted in the *Mirat*. Instead, it is Maimandi's affinal links with the Indian rajas, and his hereditary feud with Salar Masud that pockmark the Wazir's every appearance in Abdur Rahman's text. The fact of foster kinship between Wazir Maimandi and the Ghazni Sultan is pushed aside by a purported kin relationship between Masud and his royal uncle. 'And Khwaja Hasan from that day, resigned the office of Wazir, [and] became disaffected', we read in the *Mirat*.[44] An opening of narrative significance now comes about; the Wazir's disaffection leads the Sultan to try and conciliate him by asking Masud to leave Ghazni temporarily for Hindustan.

Put in the context of 'broader historical facts' (as we say in our trade) the *Mirat-i-Masudi* effects a significant shift in the story of the Somnath idol that has so dominated the discussion about Muslim iconoclasm in India.[45] For Abdur Rahman Chishti, writing in the reign of Mughal Emperor Jahangir, it is not so much the historical Sultan of Ghazni (the hero of Persian chronicles and Islamic treatises on governance) but nephew Masud and Wazir Maimandi who push the story forward. In the *Mirat*, the fate of the Somnath idol brings family feuds out into the open, catapulting the young hero, much against the wishes of his loving uncle, into Hindustan, never to return to the land of his parents and extended kin. The historical Wazir al-Maimandi, a stickler for 'official procedure', 'exacting in his dealings with the dignitaries of the empire', such that 'many intrigued to bring his downfall',[46] here plots rebellion in Hindustan with his Hindu friends come to retrieve the dismembered Somnath idol.

Forced for reasons of state to prod Masud into a short exile, the Sultan is loath to let the nephew depart. He bestows 'a dress of special honour, five Arabian horses, and two elephants' upon his dear *bhanja* (nephew) and writes to his father 'to conciliate' the young man 'in every way and keep him' at Kalihar, 'as he would be recalled' to Ghazni shortly.[47] Zealous Masud is unbridled in his ambition.

> With your permission, [he tells the Sultan] I will make an expedition into Hindustan, and wresting the kingdoms now in the hands of pagans, out of their hands, will spread the true faith, and cause the *khutba* to be read in your majesty's name.[48]

And so, much like his father who had earlier led a crack contingent to relieve the siege of Ajmer, young Masud leaves 'the Court like a fierce lion', and pitches his tent outside the capital city, Ghazni. The 'religious zeal of those times', Abdur Rahman writes from Awadh six hundred years later (in early seventeenth century), 'is well known'. Hundreds from the city and its neighbourhood joined Masud 'and all the Amirs, Princes and Tartars who were of his kindred also came out of the city to accompany him'. Buttressing his narrative with literary allusions, Abdur Rahman writes:

> The world-adoring beauty of Masud was their life. Love cannot brook delay and scorns everything but possession of the beloved. So they all, with one accord, joined the service of the loved one of the Lord of the Universe.[49]

Masud gathers several thousand followers, each struck by his beauty and awed by his valour. Turning their back on 'home and family', they exemplify to a man what the great poet Hafiz had to say on the surrender of the self to the will of another.

> When summoned by my friend my courage rose;
> at the first step, I left all thought of life,
> He loved not learning, I became a fool;
> He sought not wisdom—I too became mad.[50]

The young Ghazi marches towards Hindustan by rapid stages. He discovers a hidden treasure that helps pay his volunteer army and enlist fresh recruits. After a successful engagement, Delhi falls into his lap, but he refuses the throne, 'affirming that he was only fighting for the glory of God'.[51] The chastened Raja Ajaipal of Kannauj now welcomes the young warrior on the banks of the Ganges. Masud crosses the river in pursuit of shikar. Marching in the direction of Satrikh, he arrives at the holy city of the Seven Rishis on the outskirts of the present-day town of Bara Banki, twenty-three miles from Lucknow. This is virgin territory in the heart of the Awadh countryside. The Sultan is far away, never to be heard of again; there will be no more military dispatches to Uncle Mahmud, no fresh accretion of strength from Ghazni. The young hero is now in the thick of the local ecology of war and intrigue; he will soon begin losing important commanders to action; his parents will die of grief and old age.

Abdur Rahman opens his account of Awadh with a hyperbolic digression on Satrikh: 'the most flourishing of all the cities of India', abounding equally 'in good hunting ground', 'it was a sacred shrine of the Hindus. Masud fixed his head quarters there and sent out armies on every side to conquer the surrounding country.'[52] Half a day's ride from Abdur Rahman's hospice, it was familiar country for the author of this hagiography. And so, while recounting the exploits of Masud's commanders, Abdur Rahman would adduce the continued popularity of their graves as signposts of a *longue durée* memory. With Satrikh, we also get the first mention of Bahraich, across the river Ghaghra, which is also known as the Saru or Saryu. Forested and unsettled, Bahraich was the northern frontier of Awadh in Abdur Rahman's time and down to the mid-nineteenth century, and so it is characterised in his reconstruction of the eleventh century.[53] The advance party sent there is in danger of starving until supplies are arranged from the grain surplus tract of Siddhaura and Amethi, in the more settled part of Awadh, between the rivers Ghaghra and Gomti.[54]

From his headquarters in Satrikh, Masud dispatched his commanders to 'every side to conquer the surrounding countryside', that is, present-day central and eastern UP: Amir Hasan to Mahoba, Azizuddin to Gopamau in Partabgarh District, Malik Fazal to the holy city of Banaras.[55] Following his master's brief, Mir Bakhtiyar, they say, subdued '*mulk-i-firo-dast*', tasting the cup of martyrdom at Kanur.[56] Mir Bakhtiyar, a general who in the *Mirat* leaves his Ghazni home to join Masud in Delhi, and the conquest of the *firo-dast* tract are telltale instances of Abdur Rahman's proclivity to populate his description of the eleventh century with events and personalities from a later date. Bakhtiyar (Khalji), the Mir Bakhtiyar of the *Mirat* (died 1206 CE), was a Turkic general who 'supplanted the petty Gahadavala chiefs' of the Banaras-Mirzapur tract, made incursions into Bihar and led a daring cavalry charge down the Gangetic corridor to bring the eastern kingdom of Bengal under the Delhi Sultanate.[57] Similarly, the term *mulk-i-firo-dast*—literally, 'beyond the borders of the cultivated plains'—though apposite for parts of Awadh in the thirteenth century, had, by Abdur Rahman's, time come to convey the sense of the country of eastern Bihar and Bengal.[58] It appears that the author of *Mirat* could not always keep clear of the changing connotations of geographical terms; Abdur Rahman's careful construction of an eleventh century, 600 years distant from his own age, still carried the possibility of such slippages and anachronisms.

While his commanders march through the Awadh countryside, laying down their lives and the foundations of medieval memory, Masud continues 'to reside with great magnificence at Satrakh, enjoying the pleasures of the chase'.[59] This is not the first time that shikar would overlap with war. In this life story, the harsh choice for kafir chiefs between death and conversion becomes braided with much else. The daring Ghazi is unconcerned with political power. The Masud of the *Mirat* is both zealous and saintly; a warrior, a hunter, a leader of men, but also a diviner of signs. A devout, emotional youth, he would retire after a military skirmish to savour the delights of a garden; a heroic warrior, he would march off into the jungle if the chase was inviting. It is for these reasons that the *Mirat-i-Masudi* as a 'Warrior's-Life' is unlike the better known medieval chronicles of conquest, where the narrative becomes exhausted by an excess of blood and gore.

As Masud hunts around Satrikh, surviving the attempts of the rajas of Awadh country (Kara Manikpur and Gopamau) to bewitch and poison him, an urgent message for help arrives from the frontier post of Bahraich. Masud now crosses the Ghaghra river and enters the inhospitable Bahraich country. Off the beaten track, connected obliquely from the early twentieth century by a looping branch line to the trunk rail route and abutting Nepal, Bahraich, even today, is something of a frontier district. In the eleventh century, as etched by Abdur Rahman, it appears to have produced insufficient food grains to support a small advance party dispatched by Masud from his Satrikh redoubt. Populated largely by cattle and herdsmen—both would insert themselves into the hero's life in his penultimate days—Bahraich, the *Mirat* implies, had not yet ceded ground to agriculturalists. In the early seventeenth century, the time of Abdur Rahman's writing, Bahraich is said to have produced 'quality rice'.[60] Sunil Kumar has recently drawn attention to two interrelated developments in the Bahraich region vis-à-vis the Sultanate of Delhi: 'On the one hand the growing regional popularity of a Sufi shrine' of Salar Masud 'in the forested sub-Himalayan foothills, and on the other the presence of military elites who relied upon the local terrain and alliances … sometimes … reaching accommodative relationships with neighbouring pastoral groups ... to create a regional stronghold that aspired to challenge the might of the [Delhi] Sultanate'.[61]

Masud's forays into 'the country around Bahraich' are therefore primarily hunting expeditions, and on one of these, he encounters a Suraj Kund—a water body devoted to the worship of the sun god. The *Mirat* presents the Suraj Kund with typical hyperbole as 'a sacred site for all the unbelievers of India'. The sun tank and the stone-engraved image of the sun (*Bāla rikh*)—a hallowed spot for the Hindus—are in a jungle, and it is 'this idol that had lent its name to the habitation Bahraich' and the administrative headquarter of that name going back to the early thirteenth century.[62] The name *Bāla rich/rikh*[63] appears to be a compound of *Bāla* = sun, and *rich* = *rish*, from 'rishi', as in, the place-name 'Satrikh' (*sapt-rikh* = 'abode of seven rishis'). The sun or *Bāla* cult is a non-Brahmanical, non-Vedic cult in the sub-Himalayan belt: witness, for example, *Bāl nāth ka tilla* (the mound of the lord Bāl or sun) in the Salt Range, twenty-five miles northwest of Jhelum, subsequently called Gorakh Tilla in the eighteenth century, as mentioned in the *Ain-i-Akbari*.[64]

The weekly display of idolatry on Sundays distresses Masud, who looks forward to reappropriating the site for a proper mosque. But the gratuitous pulveriser of the dismembered idol of Somnath does not destroy this religious site at first encounter. Rather, for author Abdur Rahman, Ghazi Masud's repeated sighting of the Suraj Kund has a tragic premonition built into it. The warrior wishes to mark that 'piece of ground'—already his hunting ground—for a 'dwelling place', that is, a place to be reclaimed from the wilderness for rest and repose as a martyr.[65] In the month of Muharram, Masud has a dream. 'He thought he saw [his father] ... encamped with a large army on the banks of the Ganges whither he had just joined him'. Inside the private pavilion Salar Sahu presided 'over a festive assembly'. With a garland of roses in her hand Masud's mother now beckoned: '"Hasten hither my child Masud, we have prepared this feast for thee." Salar Masud approached and she crowned him with a garland of roses.' The Dervishes 'with one accord declared that he who had seen such a vision would certainly be a martyr for the faith'.[66] An inkling of impending martyrdom is implied here.

The chiefs of the country around Bahraich now serve an ultimatum: vacate this our domain, or else face our swords! 'Puffed with pride', the confederacy of the rajas had instructed their ambassador to convey this message to Masud:

> You come from the Upper Country (*mulk-i-bāla dast*), and know nothing of these parts. This is the land of nobles: never shall inhabitants of the Upper Country remain here. Think more wisely on this matter.[67]

Now, in the period in which Masud's story is set down to the thirteenth century, the phrase *mulk-i-bāla dast* referred to the highland beyond the passes, that is, the Ghaznavid domains. By Abdur Rahman's time in the seventeenth century, it had come to be applied to the Himachal and Kumaun hills as well, but the author quite consciously uses it in its archaic sense, contrasting it with the 'low country' or *mulk-i-firo-dast*, that is, the area of northern Awadh beyond the Sary or Saryu river. Masud's reply to the rajas' ultimatum is diplomatic, emphasising his desire for the hunt in this unsettled and wild country: 'This land is jungle and *kharāba uftāda*: we should agree to share it'. 'Peace is possible only after the defeat of one of us'; 'this is the land of our fathers and grandfathers, and this child wishes to take possession of it', the local chiefs retort.[68]

The 'unbelievers' advance and encamp in the jungle on the banks of river Kasahla or Kathela.[69] Masud draws out his army, and moves through the night. The next day, as he was preparing for the attack, 'news arrived that the enemy were driving off the cattle' attached to the army: '*hamān waqt khabar rasīdand ke kafirān maweshi-i-lashkar burdand*'.[70] Almost in the manner of Indian folk heroes who die battling cattle rustlers, this cuts the Ghazi to the quick.[71] Masud attacks forthwith at dawn. A pitched battle ensues: 'several thousand unbelievers were killed, and the soldiers of Islam too tasted the wine of martyrdom'. The Ghazi remains on the battlefield for a week, 'burying the soldiers who had attained martyrdom, and reading the *fatiha* for their pure souls'. On the eighth day, returning to Bahraich, as the weather was warm, he rests awhile under a large *mahua* tree by the Suraj Kund.

Here begins Masud's fascination for the mahua (*Bassia latifolia)*, which, though not a sacred tree, is much valued in those parts for its fruit, used as food and also fermented into liquor.[72] The choice of a mahua tree from the Bahraich forest is intriguing. Its associations—insects, bees, flies (drawn to its sweet and pungent fruit) and the fermentation of its flower into liquor are not genteel and hold no particular affection for a *sharif* Musalman. No Muslim landholder, natives opine, would plant a mahua tree in his orchard in this region. It is not even a shady tree. Yet it has many things in its favour, and because of these, its corolla, kernel and leaves figure in the origin myths of the castes of distillers, oil pressers and grain parchers of north India. Babur, the first Mughal, in his sixteenth-century account of India, had noted that 'the houses of the people of Hindustan are mostly made of Mahua wood'. Pradip Krishen, a modern historian of Indian trees, stresses that in the 'tribal belt in Central India it is valued above all trees for its many economic products and is never felled'.[73] In the Awadh region, of which Bahraich was a frontier outpost, the mahua, noted the 1877 *Gazetteer*, was 'by far the most important' of the floral products of the countryside. Growing in 'great quantities in the jungles all over the province', its full value surfaced specially for the rural poor, 'only once the jungles are cleared'. Its flowers, 'which formerly dropped into a tangled brake of grass and underwood', could now be picked clean from the bare ground. An ingredient of country liquor, dried mahua corolla, mixed with water, would be rolled into a poor man's *roti* during the lean agricultural months preceding the autumn harvest. 'So serviceable is the tree', added the official notice, that in areas of poor soil, peasants let it stand rather than 'break the land under *its barren shade*'.[74] It is apropos such a tree, alien to both Turkic and the refined Mughal sensibilities of the Awadhi author of the *Mirat* but of considerable local importance, that Masud says:

> The shade of this tree is very refreshing; and the spot is pleasing to me. It would be well to plant a garden here like those found in our own country. Here will I often come, till the crowd of unbelievers and the darkness of unbelief, be removed from hence.[75]

Salar Masud now orders the ground levelled, and all trees, save that solitary mahua, uprooted.[76] In a few days, the trusted Miyan Rajab clears some of the jungle around the Suraj Kund. Masud now takes 'the pioneers who had accompanied his troops from his own country, and ordered them to lay out the grounds in parterres and walks *after the manner of their native land*'.[77] He gets a *chabutra* (platform) built under the mahua tree 'to serve him as a seat, as he said he had taken a great fancy to that place'. After engaging in battle, Masud would retire to his garden to 'sit under the mahua tree where they had built a fine large platform. The tree was close to the Suraj Kund, with the idol Bāla [rikh] on its banks, and in its water the unbelievers were wont to bathe before offering it their worship. Masud grew angry whenever his eyes fell upon that tank and idol'.[78] Miyan Rajab, a family slave, suggests that if ordered he will demolish both the idol and the temple, considering that 'your lordship has completed this garden, and made it your constant place of worship and resort, the spot has become sacred to the faith of Islam', to which Masud replies:

> You do not consider that God is without equal as shall appear. In a short time the angels shall, by order of the Preserver of the Universe, remove the darkness of the unbelievers, and sprinkle upon them the true light of Islam, which is like the waters of life.[79]

In the final engagement, on Sunday, the 14th of the month of Rajab in the year 424 Hijri (14 June 1034 CE), the local commander at Bahraich and many others are martyred. Rather than wait for divine agency or angelic endeavour, Masud now acts on the Suraj Kund. He has the bodies of his slain soldiers cast into the tank, 'in the hope that through the odour of their martyrdom the darkness of unbelief might be dispelled from the spot'.[80] This desperate act of Masud—filling the sacred sun tank pell-mell with the bodies of Muslim soldiers in the face of impending defeat—*is* an act of major desecration of a site 'sacred … for all the unbelievers of India', as the *Mirat* puts it hyperbolically; it will be castigated vigorously in twentieth-century pamphlets opposing the Ghazi cult. Sahar/Sohal Deo and Har Deo, along with other chiefs, 'seeing that the army of Islam was reduced to nothing', now launch a final assault. The Prince of Martyrs readies himself. Cleansed in body and spirit and offering the appropriate prayer, he marches out on his favourite 'grey mare' (*asp māda-i-khing*)[81] to court martyrdom:

> As the time of evening prayers came on … a chance arrow pierced the main artery in the arm of Prince of the Faithful. His sun-like countenance became pale as the new moon. Repeating the text in

> praise of martyrdom, he dismounted. Sikandar Diwana, and the other servants of the loved-one of God, carried him to the shade of the mahua tree, and laid him down upon a couch. Sikandar Diwana taking his honoured head upon his lap, sat looking towards Mecca, weeping bitterly. The prince of Martyrs opened his eyes but once, then drew a sigh, and committed his soul to God …
>
> A sound of woe and lamentation broke from the people; they wept aloud, and brandishing their swords, rushed upon the enemy of the unbelievers, and gave up their lives … By the time of the evening prayers not one was left. All the servants of Masud lay scattered like stars.[82]

And so the young warrior of the *Mirat* and folklore dies: wilts like a flower in a fragrant garden, as the balladeers sing today.

The story as told by Abdur Rahman is then a particular elaboration on the 'Sword of Islam' motif *in India*. The Sufi savant overreaches himself in establishing a most noble spiritual and genealogical pedigree for the Prince of Martyrs. The family tree is traced all the way back to the Prophet's son-in-law Ali Murtaza on the one hand, and to the family of Syed Ahmed Yasavi (here a first cousin of Masud) on the other. Abdur Rahman implies that Salar Masud is the South Asian counterpart to Ahmad Yasavi (d. 1167 CE), who played a stellar role in the conversion of Central Asia to Islam in the twelfth century.[83]

Doubtful Islamic parallels notwithstanding, a clutch of things Indian adhere to the personable Ghazi: restrictions on the acceptance of cooked food, the constant chewing of betel leaf with areca nut (*supāri*) and quicklime; Masud's stress on personal hygiene and his penchant for 'pure garments and fragrant essences', though part of a Sufi comportment, seem almost brahmanically Indian. His peculiar attachment to a local mahua tree, a favourite of the low castes, and the rush to save cows from the cattle rustlers of the hills, place him firmly within the world of Gangetic popular culture and the deeds of the heroic dead.

Replanting that particular patch of the Bahraich forest harbouring the temple and the sun tank and shaping it into a garden à la Ghazni, while according great importance to the mahua tree, indicates Masud's double-edged relationship to Hindustan: destruction/appropriation as well attachment/reconfiguration of the local ecology of Awadh. As with any commander fighting his way through unfamiliar territory, Masud too is a harried man, yet, in a way, he finds the countryside to his liking.

> Since we have come into India, not a day has passed at ease, or without trouble, especially in the waste wilderness. I never enjoy peace for an hour. Notwithstanding which I like the country and this place is agreeable and pleasant to me.[84]

His Garden and the *chabutara* (platform)[85]—mark the local Hindawi word—under the mahua is a place of solace from the din and gore of battle. Taking his mind off the battles, Masud would come here in the evenings to recuperate and ruminate. The garden motif seems to humanise warrior Masud in an attractive yet alien land.

Salar Masud's kinship with the Sultan of Ghazni is balanced in the *Mirat* by the fact of his being an Indo-Turkic warrior. Born in the Indian desert city of Ajmer, the pān-chewing Masud comes of age in Hindustan. He returns briefly to Ghazni only be to be cast back into the lands beyond the Indus—Rawal, Delhi, Kannauj, Satrikh and Bahraich. This blurring—being from Hindustan and bursting into it from across the Indus—is as novel as it is ingenious. Masud is unlike the archetypal despoiler who swoops down from the northern passes, returning each time, like uncle Mahmud, after disgorging the booty from Indian temples into the royal treasury in present-day Afghanistan. As portrayed in the *Mirat*, Ghazi Salar Masud straddles the two worlds of Ghazni and the central and northeastern parts of the present-day province of Uttar Pradesh.

To return to the final day of the battle of Bahraich, 14 June 1034: As the evening shades fall, and Masud 'commit[s] his soul to God', his followers 'rushed upon the enemy… and gave up their lives… *By the time of evening prayers not one was left*'. Once Masud is martyred, no one from his contingent can possibly remain alive, for that would devalue the heroic death of the Prince of Martyrs as Salar Masud is called in the *Mirat-i-Masudi*. Yet the need to build a connected account of his shrine required that some from the original contingent remain alive to tend the martyr's grave. In the account of the final engagement, we read at several places that all died, yet a few somehow survived in order to perform specific tasks. And so, while all perish subsequent to Masud's martyrdom, 'some … who were only wounded' manage to escape and reach the camp at Bahraich. These survivors inform the base-camp commander Syed Ibrahim of the chief's martyrdom. Ibrahim inters Masud under the mahua tree, burying Syed Birahna and the warrior's favourite grey mare besides him. As instructed by Masud in a dream, Syed Ibrahim kills enemy Sohal Deo, and is in turn martyred in a final combat. Now, most definitely, 'both sides lay dead on the field, *not one remained alive, except a few followers of the Prince of the Martyrs*, who were only wounded and determined, on their recovery, to spend their lives in attendance upon the blessed shrine'.[86]

But these survivors do not mark the continuity between the crucial battles of the eleventh century and the Bahraich dargah, certainly in existence from the late thirteenth century, and whose seventeenth-century servitors were commended by Abdur Rahman Chishti as the proper claimants to the offerings made at the shrine. In the *Mirat*, the martyrdom of Masud marks a return to the ascendancy of 'unbelievers'. Implied here is also the suggestion that for at least 300 years there might have been only an ill-kempt grave of Masud, an idea present in folklore as well. And so the glorious death of the Prince of Martyrs at Bahraich in 1034 fails to register as a consequential event in the history of Islam in Hindustan. Salar Masud does defeat various 'unbeliever' rajas in the Gangetic plains. However, save minor instances, there is little in the hagiography about the acceptance of the Islamic creed by the local ruler, his courtiers and the general population.[87] In eleventh-century north India, as described in the *Mirat*, the martyrdom of Masud in the wilds of Bahraich is followed immediately by the death of Muzaffar Khan, the military commander of Ajmer, whose travails in the western desert were the goad that had brought Masud's father into the land of unbelief. With these two deaths at the two corners of Upper India, one in the desert of Rajasthan, the other in the *tarai* wet-country beyond the river Saryu, 'idolatry again reigned over the land of India … for 200 years', till the Prophet himself appeared in a vision to India's premier Sufi saint at the Kaba and directed him thus:

> Muin-al Din, you are the essence of my faith, yet you must go to Hindustan. There is a place called Ajmer where one of my sons (descendants) went for holy war. Now he has become a martyr and the place has passed once again into the hands of the infidels. By the grace of your footsteps Islam shall once more be manifest there, and the infidels punished by God's wrath.[88]

Muinuddin Chishti proceeds to Ajmer and appropriates it as a sacred site for Islam by a magical contest with the existing temporal and spiritual protectors of that place.[89] After the establishment of his Sufi hospice at Ajmer, maintains the *Mirat*, Khwaja Muinuddin 'through the powerful assistance of his prayers, brought the whole country of India into the hands of Kutub-ud-din Aibak'. Aibak, and after him Syed Husain Khingsawar ('grey horse-rider'), with the grace of sage Muinuddin Chishti, helped stabilise the setting up of a Turkic state in northern India in the early thirteenth century, '[s]uch that since that time no kafir has been Badshah of Hind', as Abdur Rahman concluded at the end of the 1620s in the narrative portion of the *Mirat-i-Masudi*.[90]

The martyrdom of Masud then does not quite inaugurate the history of Islam in north India. Though focused on the career of Salar Masud, the *Mirat* ascribes the long-lasting political ascendancy of Islam in India to the spiritual might of Khwaja Muinuddin Chishti (died 1236 CE). Preceding the prophetic move of the Khwaja from the Kaba to the holy city of Ajmer in Rajasthan by some 200 years, Masud's death marks a hiatus between the pre-history and history of Islam in north India. The memorability of his death lies in its poignancy, not in its 'historic' consequences. And yet Masud's martyrdom has been one of the most eventful deaths of the last millennium, such that in a wide swath of north India, it has continued to elicit affirmation and devotion across denominational divides, since at least the thirteenth or fourteenth centuries.

3

An Urdu Mirror of Masud

Akin to its protagonist, the *Mirat-i-Masudi* had a long afterlife, but again, only after a hiatus. Masud's grave had to await the patronage, c. 1370, of the Delhi Sultan Ferozshah Tughlaq. Similarly, Abdur Rahman Chishti's seventeenth-century hagiography appears to have lain dormant for the next 200 years. The original manuscript, c. 1620, has not survived; the earliest extant Persian copy is dated 1709, followed by another from 1748; the rest were all transcribed in the early nineteenth century, one as late as the 1860s. These manuscripts were preserved at the Bahraich dargah and at subsidiary shrines in the vicinity of that town (for example, the shrine of Hathile), or copied and catalogued for the edification of prominent landholders in Awadh, the region of Ghazi Miyan's legendary exploits. And yet, there is scant evidence to suggest that the *Mirat* elicited any significant discussion among the north Indian literati during the eighteenth century.[1] The *Khulasatu-t-Tawarikh* (1695–96), while noticing the festivities at the Bahraich shrine, shows scant awareness of Abdur Rahman Chishti's by now seventy-year-old Farsi *Mirat-i-Masudi*. 'All manner of people carrying golden banners (*alam*: pennons/lances) come from distant lands to Bahraich'—a mart for trade with the produce of the hills—'for pilgrimage, whereupon they hold lavish festivities and leave copious offerings in tribute', we read in Sujan Rai Bhandari's dynastic and geographical compendium of north India, written in the fortieth year of Emperor Aurangzeb's reign.[2]

Outside the libraries of a select few, Abdur Rahman's *Mirat-i-Masudi* appears to have remained somewhat of a lost text. This seems to have changed in the 1860s when an abridged English version was published as 'a historical romance … unknown to the European reader … [which] will probably satisfy, rather than excite further curiosity'.[3] For the denizens of Awadh though, the *Mirat* was to become a source of continuous 'excitement' and contestation from the last quarter of the nineteenth century. The *Mirat-i-Masudi* now came to be worked upon in Urdu, the Persian-aligned high-vernacular of Hindustan, deprecated by Hindi pamphleteers as epitomising the egregious ways of the Muslims in India. An Urdu version was published in 1879. Simultaneously, the English shorter *Mirat*, published in a compendium (1861) of source material by H. M. Elliot, became a key reference for colonial administrators busy ferreting out local histories of 'Masud's Crescentade' in Awadh, which had come under their complete sway post-1857. It was in the context of colonial modernity, marked in northern India by a decline of the Muslim aristocracy of land and the pen, and the concomitant rise of a new Hindu literati and mercantile groups who began welding Hindi (language) with Hindu communitarian initiatives, that the vernacularisation of the *Mirat* flared into almost Rabelaisian polemics.[4]

The incitement to translate *Mirat-i-Masudi* into Urdu came from a Lucknow-based publisher aware of the declining fortunes of Persian in late-nineteenth-century Hindustan. Inayat Husain Bilgrami's 1879 Urdu text was the first real induction of the seventeenth-century hagiography into the print culture of Upper India.[5] Driven by a profitable print run—its publisher (*tajir kutb* in Urdu; lit., 'trader in books') doubled as a *chikan* cloth merchant—it became the definitive 'History of Masud', to be trumpeted or trashed during the increasing politicisation of medieval memory that marked the birth of modern Hindu/Muslim communities in north India.

In his Urdu translation, Inayat Husain deployed a rhymed prose style to impart narrative drive to the text while making it enjoyable to a presumed Muslim-only readership. This high Urdu version was peppered with offensively rhymed words. This, in turn, resulted in an unsettling excess of meaning, the spitfire phrases yielding a picture of innate Muslim valour and timeless Hindu cowardice. Bilious and offensive, Inayat Husain's 'Tarikh Salar Masud' was peopled by stereotypical Hindus and Musalmans, unchanged from the time of the battles of the early eleventh century down to the author's nineteenth-century present! In short, Husain's Urdu *Mirat* was a gratuitously ungenerous account of 'Hindu defeat' at the hands of the forces of Islam in India.

As examples, we may take Inayat Husain's rendition of the two battles fought at the beginning and end of the *Mirat-i-Masudi*. The first, where General Salar Sahu, Masud's father, engages Hindu forces near Ajmer, occupies very little space in the seventeenth-century text: the kafirs run away from commander Salar Sahu; they are pursued for several miles; Muslim martyrs are buried; the booty shared out, a mosque built at the gate of the fort of Ajmer, the khutba read in Sultan Mahmud Ghazni's name and the administration around that city set on an even keel.[6]

We get the following description of the battle of Ajmer-Pushkar in the Farsi *Mirat*:

> When the news of the arrival of the General [Salar Sahu] reached Muzaffar Khan [the besieged commander of Ajmer] he was overjoyed, and caused music to be played. The unbelievers who had assembled to besiege Ajmir were struck with a panic ... So they raised the siege of Ajmir, and retiring to a distance of seven kos, encamped near Koh-pukhar ...
>
> [Salar Sahu] pitched his tent on the banks of tank Pukhar [Hindi. *Pokhar*, Sanskrit. Pushkar: Elliot], sacred among the unbelievers; and, having taken a few days rest, again put himself in motion ... The enemy also drew up their forces in line, *and the flower of both armies joined in battle*. The field raged with the conflict for three days; but on the third day the breeze of victory began to blow on the side of the General [Salar Sahu], and the unbelievers yielded and fled. The Faithful pursued them to a distance of several parasangs, slew a great number of their officers', took a few prisoners, and then returned. The General took possession of the enemy's camp that day, and, having interred such of the Faithful as had been blessed with the honour of martyrdom, and distributed the whole spoils of the unbelievers among the soldiers of his army, he returned the next day towards Ajmir.[7]

This appears to be a measured description of a battle among what appear to be two armies of equals: true, 'Faithful' and 'Unbelievers' are value-loaded terms; however, it is not inherently unequal antagonists but 'the flower of both armies' that engage in three days of pitched combat before the kafirs retreat. No offence, so to speak, is meant in this description of the first battle between the soldiers of Islam and of Unbelief.

In his late nineteenth-century Urdu version, Husain elaborates on this battle scene thus: the opposition is in disarray, while Salar Sahu's troops are in battle-ready formation. And when the Ajmer rajas take on the Muslim General freshly arrived from Ghazni, a presumed partisan reader is regaled with an account of a representative slice of Hindu society articulating battle fright in queer dispositions and involuntary bodily functions!

> *Hārne ke shagun par har-har karte āye, lashkar-i-Islam ko dekh-kar kaleja tharrāye. Kisi ke dil mein khauf sama gaya, kisi ko ghush aa gaya ... Koi chillāya hamen be-khāye rāt bhar dast āye, dhoti kharāb hai, jāri peshāb hai, yahān hum kya banāte hain, jhāre-jangal hokar bistar par jāte hain.*[8]

Here, Inayat Husain, the *mualif* (compiler) of the Urdu *Mirat* is functioning literally as a traducer—a defamer, slanderer, calumniator, vilifier, denigrator, deprecator, abuser, smearer, detractor, as the Oxford English Dictionary defines that word. What we have here is a scatology of Hindu cowardice, something entirely missing from the seventeenth-century originary text of Abdur Rahman Chishti. The mocking phrase *Hārne ke shagun par har-har karte āye* is a clever allusion to the practice of divining an auspicious occasion (*shagun*) for almost everything, from undertaking a journey to fixing the exact time for assuming a high office, a practice that endures to the present. The *Har-har* battle cry in this overture here turns into the perfect dénouement for its phonetically similar but semantically opposite *hār*—defeat! One look at the 'contingent of Islam' is enough to put the dread of defeat into the hearts of Hindu adversaries.

The excess of words that Husain as Urdu translator (or rather compiler or *mualif* as the title of the text has it) puts in the mouths of the 'kafirs' conveys an imaginary glee at the discomfiture of the Salar's Hindu antagonists, portrayed here with a flurry of offensive jests. The recurring imagery is the dread felt by a cross-section of frightened Hindu opponents, some of them not warriors at all. In Inayat Husain's Urdu *Mirat*, the drug-addled warriors curse their stars, for away from the din and gore their days are consumed by puffing harmlessly at *ganja* pipes! The salaciously 'tender and juicy' Brahman boys are similarly dying to run away without giving battle. Accustomed to passing their days making harmless astrological predictions, these 'pigtailed Brahmans' cry out: 'We are prepared to live off peasant charity. No more rich fare from high tables for us; we will be content roasting our own potato-wheat *bhaunri-litties* over improvised stoves … O Almighty! Save us from a dog's death in this encounter.'[9]

As battles rage in Hindustan, Husain sprays his Urdu account with the spittle of additional distaste. Towards the end of the story, Masud is dressed up to become a *shahīd*. Adorning his favourite grey mare in the manner of a bride, the young Ghazi gallops fearlessly towards his martyrdom.[10] The Hindus of the text are again at the receiving end of the Urdu translator's spleen: 'The conch-shell blowers had the shells of their ears flapping desperately to catch the sound of the gong of retreat ... The worshippers of *Lāt* and *Manāt** had their bodies pulverised under the hoofs (*tāp*) of horses and by the kicks (*lāt*) of rampaging infantry'!

> *Lāt-wa-Manāt par* [*jo*] *jān-o-dil se fida thei,*
> *jism unke ghoron ki tāpon-se,*
> *pyādon ki lāton-se halwa thei.*[11]

To translate this passage fully is to catch ineptly the play between the violence of language and the language of violence, as the idols (*Lāt* and *Manāt*) are made to rhyme with *tāp* and *lāt*—kicks administered to a supine enemy by horses and soldiers alike! It was this kind of pornography of valour and cowardice, far in excess of the descriptions in the seventeenth-century original *Mirat*, that fed into the production of equally vituperative Hindu counter-histories about the despicable Ghazi Miyan. Initially priced cheaply at four annas, the going daily wage rate for a field labourer, Inayat Husain's Urdu text saw four imprints between 1879 and 1926.[12] In these fifty years, a spate of anti-Ghazi Miyan tracts rolled off the Hindi presses of small-town Uttar Pradesh as well. It is to these demotic fist fights about a hero missing from authoritative chronicles, but extolled and quartered in demotic pamphlets, that we shall turn in the latter part of the story of Masud.

---

* These were two idols, thrown, so it was said, by the Prophet into the Arabian Sea, and washed ashore on the coast of India.

4

The Author as Hero

At roughly the same time when the seventeenth-century 'Life' of Masud was being expounded and castigated in its vernacular versions, a legendary account of one Shah Abdur Rahman was collated and published in the *Journal of the Asiatic Society of Bengal*. No Sufi savant, this Abdur Rahman was a warrior saint in his own right, rising from his nuptials in Ghazni to further the cause of Islam at Elichpur—the capital of the Imadshahi dynasty in the Deccan from 1490 to 1572 CE. Much like Syed Salar Masud Ghazi, the Elichpur martyr, it turns out, was also a nephew of Mahmud of Ghazni! Indeed, in this late nineteenth-century account, Abdur Rahman Chishti, the author of the *Mirat*, seems to have himself donned the mantle of his warrior-hero, 600 miles southwest of the site of the latter's 'historic' martyrdom in 1034 CE. The Elichpur 'legend' has come down to us through a summary translation published in 1900 of a text and local tradition garnered in the northern Deccan by the administrator-historian Wolseley Haig.[1] Much flatter than the folk accounts of the Bahraich Ghazi, it has, nevertheless, some intriguing parallels and divergences with both the *Mirat-i-Masudi* and what the balladeers of north India continue to sing about Salar Masud, or Ghazi Miyan as he is popularly known.

The story begins with a wandering *faqir* arriving at the court of the 'fierce and bigoted idolator' Raja Eil, 'preaching Islam and holding religious disputations'. This greatly incensed the Raja: 'a tyrant like Pharaoh and Namrud, eaten with vainglory and pride' was he. The Raja cut off the faqir's hands (shades of Nimrod?) and drove him out of the kingdom. The dervish went all the way to

Ghazni to lay his plaint before Amir Subuktagin, 'then famous for his incursions into India and for the wars he had waged with idolatrous Hindus'.[2] The Amir had died recently and his kingdom plunged into chaos because of a battle for succession to the throne. The faqir was advised by knowledgeable local people to seek Shah Abdur Rahman, the son of Subuktagin's daughter, instead. Now, Abdur Rahman, whose 'nuptials were being celebrated' at that very moment, was a callow youth consumed by 'zeal against the idolatrous'. The faqir interrupted Abdur Rahman's marriage with an account of his punishment for preaching Islam in the kingdom of Eil and 'the young bridegroom, in his religious zeal, stopped the wedding festivities at once, and announced his intention of setting out on a jihad'.[3]

Abdur Rahman immediately set out from Ghazni at the head of a contingent to avenge the humiliation of the Muslim faqir. He was joined by his mother. At Kherla, near Elichpur, he engaged in battle with the Raja and his five associates for a full twenty-seven days. Abdur Rahman was forced to retreat, and in common with many historical and fabulist accounts, offered a special prayer to Allah for victory. The trope of divine inspiration, or the aid of a distinguished holy man, which wins the day for a beleaguered Muslim warrior, is a fairly common one. In the *Mirat*, the saint of Chisht, near Herat in present-day Afghanistan, arranges assistance for Sultan Mahmud's assault on the Somnath temple: a miller-devotee pulverises a mountain with his pestle, thereby affording long-distance help to Mahmud on the distant Gujarat coast.[4]

By contrast, the divine or saintly response to the Elichpur Ghazi's prayer for victory is drastic: 'Cut off your head', thunders a heavenly voice, 'and so, slaying thyself, thou shall embrace the bride, victory'. The son seeks his mother's advice, who has no hesitation in commending this extreme action.[5] The hero performs a quick self-decapitation; now a 'headless horseman', the Elichpur warrior engages the infidels once again. This time he is victorious.

> The Hindus were signally defeated, and were pursued as far as Elichpur itself with great slaughter. Wherever the pursuers halted they took the opportunity to bury their dead; and their tombs are still resorted to by the pious Muslims, whose prayers are said to be answered by means of the intercession of the martyrs.[6]

This spread of warriors' graves in and around Kherla and Elichpur parallels the *ganj-i-shahīdān,* war cemeteries of Salar Masud's army, though the latter cover a wide area in northern India. In the final battle, Abdur Rahman's sister's son and mother's brother assist the young hero by dispatching key enemy figures to hell. The Raja flees the battlefield, and takes refuge in his citadel.

In keeping with the strict Islamic tenor of this story, things Indian hold no attraction for the Elichpur warrior. There is no attachment to a favourite local tree, no ambiguity here about the supplanting of a previous holy site by a graveyard for Muslim martyrs. By contrast, the Elichpur Ghazi aims at a wanton destruction of the image of the locally powerful goddess Bhavani. There is also a similar need for a ritual disposal of martyred soldiers for which warrior Abdur Rahman selects a cave next to the temple of Bhavani. Uprooting the image, he throws it 'face downwards into the cave', piling up Muslim bodies on the back of this ferocious goddess, now made supine. Not just iconoclasm but a symbolic negation is involved here, for with eight arms, each bearing a weapon, Bhavani is depicted iconically holding the head of a slain demon.

The warrior accomplishes these deeds as a 'headless horseman'. Five brothers, now called, in the vulgar idiom, 'Panchpir' ('Five Pirs'), the author of this local history avers, capture the Raja and bring him to the Muslim warrior. A headless Abdur Rahman invites the captive king to accept Islam; the Raja in turn spits in his face—both literal impossibilities! Rather than order an immediate execution, he asks Raja Eil to name his own punishment. 'I would have flayed you, stuffed your skin with straw, and burnt it, and I would have buried your carcass' is the defiant reply. The Islamic warrior puts the Hindu Raja's words into immediate effect, dispatching 'him to be one of the chiefs of hell'.[7] Abdur Rahman now lets his truncated body rest at Elichpur. His tutor buries him, and stays back to tend the martyr's grave. The present servitors are descendants from his family. Thus ends the story of this Abdur Rahman Ghazi of Elichpur.

As with the *Mirat-i-Masudi*, the author of the Elichpur text, a late nineteenth-century special magistrate and *khatīb* (one who gives the *khutba*, the sermon in a mosque after prayers), also accords this legend a high gloss. The major difference is that while Salar Masud is martyred on the battlefield, the Elichpur hero decapitates himself before engaging the infidels; with victory achieved, he, so to speak, dies of his own accord. And as with Masud, the genealogical tree of the warrior-martyr Shah Abdur Rahman is traced, in almost identical stages, all the way to the Prophet's grandson.[8] Similarly, the Elichpur *Tarikh* cites the *Jihad-ur Rahman*, typically an earlier text, to establish that the mother of the hero is a sibling of Bibi Mamal, Ghazi Miyan's mother in folklore. Both the heroes (Ghazi Miyan and Abdur Rahman) are then Sultan Mahmud's sisters' sons. The wronged faqir comes to Ghazni, looking not for Sultan Mahmud but his father who had died recently. Instead of going to his son, the faqir is directed to young Abdur Rahman, his young nephew. Indeed, Sultan Mahmud as *mamu* (mother's brother) to the young lad has no role to play in the Elichpur story.[9]

We don't have the text or the translation of the *Tarikh-i-Amjadi*. The only source, an English summary, suggests that it is a much later (late nineteenth-century) reworking of the three centuries older *Mirat-i-Masudi*, with variations. The Old Book (*Tarikh-i-kuhna*) that helped the seventeenth-century Sufi of Awadh write his *Mirat*, is replaced in the Elichpur legend, by a text 'named, carelessly enough "*Jihad-ur Rahman*" or the Jihad of [Abdur] Rahman'![10] Sitr-i-Mualla (the 'veiled one'), mother of Salar Masud, with a possible rustic echo of the 'Mamula' of the ballads, is here graced with the grandiose name, 'Empress of the World'. She is a sibling of Adral and Majhul, the latter two featuring as sisters eager to beget sons in the story of the birth of another popular saint, Zahir or Gugga Pir, as he is variously called from Lucknow to Banaras.[11]

In folklore, Masud (better known as Ghazi Miyan), is a bridegroom hero, that is, one who interrupts his marital rites never to return to his bride; Abdur Rahman of the Elichpur legend is also called *Dulha* (bridegroom) *Rahman*. However, the latter does not lay down his life on the battlefield; rather he decides to decapitate himself in response to a divine commandment. Headlessness, so important with the Elichpur legend, is not central to Salar Masud of Bahraich, either in the *Mirat* or in folklore. No doubt the Ghazi's insignia at the annual pilgrimage is a tuft of hair atop a colourful flagpole, but balladeers don't dwell on Ghazi Miyan as a hero who loses his head on divine instruction! Nor, as with some other accounts of martyrs, is there any allusion to parts of the hero's body being scattered at different places, thereby marking the sites of his cenotaphs and the spatial arc of devotion. And if, as in an intriguing account of the battle of Banaras, Ghazi Miyan literally pockets his head, it is to avert his eyes from falling on the naked virgins that the raja of that holy Hindu city had shamelessly paraded to upset the hero's pure resolve![12] There may be the odd 'headless horseman' among Masud's commanders, such as the one who rides back from battle to Bijlaur near Lucknow, to be buried alongside his horse. Or Chandan Shahīd of Banaras, who galloped some distance headless, only to be told by a woman betel leaf seller, as folklore has it, that in the present state he would be unable to enjoy her delicious *pān*![13] However, unlike the Elichpur warrior, the appellation *Ghorwa-Shahīd* ('the headless equestrian martyr') is never applied to Ghazi Miyan.

So what relation does the Elichpur legend bear to the *Mirat-i-Masudi* and the lore about martyr Salar Masud? A knowledgeable colonial officer rightly discounted the possibility of an eleventh-century Muslim attack on Elichpur—adding sardonically that 'battles are not commonly won by the general losing his head at a critical moment'.[14] Instead, the British officer A.C. Lyall wagered the guess that the legend is perhaps 'founded historically on the assassination (about 1400 CE) of a Bahmani commander at Kherla just as he had taken the fort'. The monument at Kherla still stood in the 1870s for the 'bridegroom Rahman's head', that is, the author of the *Mirat-i-Masudi* transmogrified into a variant of the martyred bridegroom Ghazi Miyan of north Indian folklore.[15] Wolseley Haig, to whom we owe an account of the Elichpur text, was less sanguine about finding an historical basis for the cult even in the fourteenth century. The 'cult and the legend', in his view, '*were originated by a wandering faqir from Hindustan* who was well versed in the legends of Ghazi Miyan, and was himself, probably, a member of the *pacpiriya* cult'—the quintet formed by the warrior and his four assorted associates and commonly worshipped in eastern UP and Awadh.[16]

This is an interesting possibility, but not without its problems. There is the parallel with Panchon Pir (*pacpiriya* cult), the popular quintet of the Punjab and northern India more generally. However, the Five Worthies of Elichpur are not an amalgam of the Ghazi's close associates, tossed together with assorted village godlings; rather lamely, they are five brothers who chase and capture the fleeing Raja Eil. Nor is there any evidence that the worship of these central Indian worthies extended beyond the local Muslims to include a wider mixed population of both Musalmans and Hindus. And so, rather than ascribe the Elichpur story to a *single* faqir-minstrel, it might make better sense to regard it as another case of the braiding of popular lore and the high textual.

The Elichpur *Tarikh-i-Amjadi*, presented by Wolseley Haig, shows clear traces of borrowings from the seventeenth-century *Mirat-i-Masudi*: Ghazni as the land of succour for Muslims harried in Hindustan, the hero as Sultan Mahmud's sister's son, the Syed pedigree of the warrior all the way to Ali in the Prophet's family and the trope of a lost book containing recorded details about the warrior absent from standard chronicles. Clearly, the Ghazi of Elichpur is the work of more than one wandering faqir enamoured of the Pachpiriya cult, fashioning single handed a 'Ghazi Miyan' appropriate to that locality. Ballads and popular traditions do indeed travel, but unlike written texts, they are seldom the creation of a single febrile mind. The tale of the Elichpur Ghazi suggests, instead, a roughly hewn interface between Abdur Rahman's Farsi *Mirat* and travelling tales about the Bahraich Ghazi, as overlaid by local military events. The power of the Ghazi bridegroom in its myriad ecologies is well-attested in colonial ethnographies all the way down the Gangetic corridor into the Sunderban Delta where the Ganga-Hooghly meanders through tiger-infested mangroves into the Bay of Bengal.[17]

Contrived and wooden as the Elichpur Ghazi story may be, its significance lies equally in the outreach of the cult of Salar Masud, and as yet another instance of the long impress of the seventeenth-century 'Life' of Masud. For the Elichpur faqir to be redirected on reaching Ghazni to Sultan Mahmud's nephew—the young zealot here called Abdur Rahman—is a remarkable apotheosis of the author of the *Mirat-i-Masudi* as its hero! And for warrior Abdur Rahman to forsake marriage for martyrdom, a trope present allegorically in the *Mirat* in the shape of a *tabīr* or interpretation of a dream (by dervishes) but central to the folkloric imaginary of the cult, testifies to the pull of popular culture in shaping the legends of both the Ellichpur and the Bahraich Ghazi.[18] It is to these legends, tales and folklore about Salar Masud, popularly known as Ghazi Miyan, that we now turn.

PART TWO LORE

5

Tales and the Text

When did the ballads and the folklore about Ghazi Miyan first come into being? What exactly is the connection between these two? This cannot be established with any degree of certainty. After a visit to the shrine in 1341 CE, Ibn Battuta had remarked on the 'many marvellous stories [that] are told about him [Salar Masud].[1] Three centuries later, it was the express desire of Abdur Rahman to reign in the multiplicity of popular accounts, couched, perhaps, as ballads—for demotic tales are invariably cast as verse narratives—within an historicist hagiography.'* The references in the *Mirat* to multiple views regarding 'the facts of ... [Masud's] birth ... and... martyrdom', the regional spread of his appellations, the exuberant processions sought to be banned by the Sultan of Delhi in the early sixteenth century are all indicative of the varied popular retellings of the life story of Masud[2]. The central figures—*Dafali*s or Muslim balladeers leading small parties to the annual fair—are attested to from the late eighteenth century, and it is doubtful whether 'the numerous presents' made to the tomb of the warrior saint by the pilgrims from the fourteenth century onwards would have gone unaccompanied by songs, dance and stories—*sarodgoyān wa raqskuna*, as the Farsi text of the *Mirat* puts it.

For his part, Abdur Rahman Chishti closed his hagiography of the warrior saint with a section devoted to the *karamāt* and *khwariq*

* Compare: 'The history of the ... [Prince] of Martyrs, the facts of his birth, of his coming to Hindustan, and of his martyrdom are told by different men in different ways, which have not found a place in any historical work of repute'. *MM* E, p. 103.

(miracles) of Masud Ghazi after his martyrdom as well as an account of the building of the saint's shrine. Apart from recounting the personal encounters that the author had had with the spirit of the deceased hero, which he claimed enabled him to write the story of his lodestar, he included in the fifth and final section of the *Mirat* a medley of stories concerning the grace of the martyred saint. It recounted the spiritual blessings that the Delhi sultans, specially the Tughlaq kings, derived from the Bahraich shrine and the boons bestowed by Salar Masud on select elite Muslim families of Awadh, as recounted in the *malfuzāt* (anecdotes) of prominent Sufi saints. Significantly, this last chapter of the *Mirat* also contained the first two *khwariqs* (supernatural happenings), which, by the early seventeenth century, or indeed earlier, had passed into folklore—and which are still sung today by Dafali balladeers in and around Bahraich. The first of these concerned a son being born to an infertile milkmaid by the grace of the grave at Bahraich, the initial raising of the grave by the cowherd couple and the attraction that the consecrated site subsequently held subsequently for the 'cowherd tribe' and the needy and afflicted of the area. As Abdur Rahman Chishti, c. 1620, put it in the *Mirat-i-Masudi*:

> This miracle became divulged all-around. Whosoever had a wish regarding any affair [or] obstacle, Most Glorious God granted it (within) no time. And the coming[s] and the going[s] of the people [increased] more and more … [with each passing] … day. Since it was the manifestation (*urooj-i-zahoor*), [the] *karamāt* of that loved one of the Lord of the Universe Salar Masud Ghazi fell like the rains upon the people at large during those days. Therefore, the blind, palsied and (lepers), etc., who reached the *Dargah* of the loved one of the God got cured. Therefore his *karamāt* got currency from village to village, city to city … country to country. Therefore his *Astāna* is the centre of the hope of the world.[3]

The second miracle expatiated in the *Mirat* concerned the ethereal love of a blind girl of Rudauli for the Bahraich saint, and her construction of a regular *mazār* (mausoleum) and her raising of a cupola over the dome of the warrior saint. The text does not provide any clues for dating these two 'events' in the development of the Ghazi lore, though clearly these would post-date his martyrdom by some time—perhaps two or three centuries. The patronage of the Bahraich shrine by the Tughlaq sultans of Delhi, beginning with the visit of Mohammad bin

Tughlaq accompanied by Ibn Battuta in 1341, testifies to the existence of prior popular veneration in which the granting of the boon of a son to a low-caste woman and the selfless devotion of a daughter of an elite Rudauli-based Muslim family in the heart of the Awadh country, seem to have played an important role. Beyond a point, it serves no real purpose to speculate whether or not the folklore and the half dozen ballads about the Bahraich Ghazi recorded in the late nineteenth century and gathered during fieldwork a century later, pre- or post-date the writing of Abdur Rahman Chishti's early-seventeenth-century hagiography; in such matters, an improbable certitude has a tendency to yield very little. In any event, the author of the Mirat had himself moved in the last section from the elevated plane of an event-packed Sufi hagiography to the porous world of hearsay, sentiments, auguries and lore.

The saga of the Bahraich Ghazi is then better told by braiding the *Mirat* and the ballads sung to this day in the Awadhi and Bhojpuri dialects of north India. As Abdur Rahman's hagiography did not forswear the prevalent lore about Masud, the tales told (then and now) move in and out of his text, as they hone in on the quotidian and the familial. Cutting a life tragically short at nineteen, Masud's martyrdom has become lodged at the cusp of common anxieties and historic events. Not that Abdur Rahman had refrained from flirting with the verities of History in his seventeenth-century *Mirat-i-Masudi*: Sultan Mahmud Ghazni no doubt had sisters, but none were called Sitr-i-Mualla, the name of Masud's mother. His father Salar Sahu was *not* the commander of the Ghaznavid forces in Hindustan; it was another Turk named Eryaruq whose wife was indeed called 'Sitr-i-Mualla', the name of the hero's mother in the *Mirat*; Wazir Maimandi, the evil schemer of the text, was in fact the foster brother and a favourite of the Sultan of Ghazni and a companion of much wit and wisdom as well.[4] Eliding this *rida* (milk-sharing) bond, Abdur Rahman seems to have substituted a fictive uncle–nephew relationship between Sultan Mahmud and Salar Masud.

The overlap and divergences between the ballads and the *Mirat* are equally remarkable. Dafali balladeers also refer to Masud as the sister's son of the Sultan of Ghazni, rendering that town 'Garh Gajan', literally, 'stronghold of the Ghazis.' The mahua tree is central to both the *Mirat* and the ballads extant today. On the other hand, Masud's mother, named 'Sitr-i-Mualla' (the veiled one), in the *Mirat*, is in the ballads a homely Bibi Mamula; Sikandar Diwana, the trusted lieutenant who perishes while cradling the martyr's body under that mahua tree is rendered in folklore as Baba Birahna, an eleventh-century naked faqir who follows the Prince with a hammer and chain, and can sire, when required, a large number of warriors by simply loosening his *langot*—the equivalent of a celibate's jockstrap—and unfurling it in the air!* Most remarkably, while Sultan Mahmud of the *Mirat* dotes on nephew Masud, the ballads cast him, in contrast, as a mean spirited uncle. In terms of similarities, the first miracle that spreads the fame of Masud (*urooj-i-zahoor*) in the text is the birth of son to a barren milkmaid after she has made her supplication at the Bahraich shrine; balladeers even today sing the 'Lay of Jaswa', featuring the trials and tribulations that marriage brings for a woman in north India. In another ballad, the birth of Ghazi Miyan to a 'barren Mamula' is made conditional on her undergoing austerities at Ajmer and Makanpur, two of the major Sufi shrines of north India. It is these ballads about the Ghazi's grace to childless women that we shall now explore.

* Compare '*diya langot jhariyāe*': ballad sung by a Dafali of Basaurhi, recorded in village Karaundi, Bara Banki, June 1994. Sikandar Diwana's sectarian habit as a follower of Ibrahim Adhan, of uncovered head and unshod feet (*MM* C, p. 30), yields the term 'Barahna', lit. naked. His stout stick (*sonta*) is replicated at the shrine as a string of handy bats used for driving evil spirits from those possessed by djinns.

6

Reproductive Anxiety

To marry in northern India is not just to raise a family; it is to beget a male child quickly. 'Only the Almighty granting the boon of a son can make the married woman truly so'. Thus spoke the saint of Makanpur to Ghazi Miyan's mother who had come seeking the boon of a male child.[1] In such a world the girl child did not count. Songs celebrating birth in north India are invariably about the male child; if it is a girl, 'there are no birth songs, bands or beating of trays', noted the anthropologist Bernard Cohn about a village in eastern UP in the early 1950s. In one such *sohar* birth song, a fecund woman castigates her silly 'girl-producing womb', which attains to its fullness only with the birth of a son.[2] It is the male child that makes for a woman's deliverance in a household where, even while gravid, she has little claim to her husband's attention. For example, in a folksong, when heavy with child, the wife asks her man to stay back from a distant job and help her catch some sleep by gathering the cool air with a hand-held fan, all she gets is a rebuke at the desired inversion of caring roles. But as a new dawn breaks with the birth cry of a boy child, accompanied by celebratory kettledrums, the husband rushes back, fan in one hand and a neatly folded pān in another. Delivered of a male child, the proud mother can afford to be dismissive: 'go fan your mother and your aunt, I now have my darling son, my body has become cool of itself…'[3]

In perhaps the most poignant of such folksongs, a woman turned out for her inadequacy in producing sons can find no shelter, no deliverance. Infertility in a woman, the story implies, is clearly at odds with a world calibrated for reproduction. In the song, it is the mother- and sisters-in-law who turn out the woman who had come into their household as a barely pubescent bride (*Sāsu mori kaheli banjhaniya nanad brijbāsini ho*; *Rama jinki main bāri re biyāhi uee ghar-se nikrareni ho*; in plain English, 'My mother-in-law calls me a barren—*bānjh*; my sister-in-law a wanton woman. O Rama! The house I entered as a young bride, I am now being thrown out of').[4] The cast away *bānjh* (infertile woman) now stands alone in the wilderness. She encounters wild animals that turn down her request to devour her, for any contact with such a woman might affect, in turn, their own fertility! Her own mother, too, has daughters-in-law to think of; to keep such a daughter at home would affect their fecundity adversely. In a telling dénouement, the woman seeks the deathly embrace of mother earth. And again, she gets turned down, for the earth is concerned about going barren after opening up to the *bānjh*![5]

Balladeers recount the story where the plight of such a castaway *bānjhin* is made to follow the contours of the Ghazi Miyan cult. Taking her name from Jashoda, Lord Krishna's foster mother, the Jaswa of the ballads is the wife of the chief of the cowherds.

The scene of the ballad is Gaura Got—a large pasture, adjacent to a major watering place, which also doubles as a cattle fair.[6] 'Hear ye the story of Salar and Gaura Got where grazed 125,000 cows and lived 1,400 cowherds', begins Bashir Dafali, straining his neck to emit the high-pitched opening note (most older balladeers develop a pronounced swelling of the larynx from the overuse of their vocal chords.) In the ballad, an indigent bard makes his way on a festive occasion to the gathering at Gaura Got. He recites an epigramatic composition, and is rewarded with copper coins by the herdsmen and gold sovereigns by Nanda, their chief. Returning home he tells his wife about the rich donor. Shaking her head the wife retorts: return he must the gold coins of Nanda, for *Nanda ki Rani re Jasau rang-rāti; janam-janam ki wo tau bānjh kahlāti*. Nanda's queen Jasau is a *bānjh*, says the bard's wife: 'she has been born *bānjh* in each of her several births': no deity, no demigod will accept alms given by her husband as offerings from us. The gold coins are returned respectfully, but the insult has been administered. Head bent in shame, Nanda the proud chief of 1,400 cowherds, stands alone. The bard tells him off:

no *deuta*, no deity would accept these gifts from us, he spells out his wife's warning.[7] There ends the shorter version of the ballad of Jaswa sung by Bashir Dafali.

In the fuller two-hour saga recited by Shubrati Dafali, one of the most accomplished balladeers of Bahraich, the Jaswa story takes a crucial turn with the returning of alms to the cowherd chief in full public view. His clansmen immediately suggest a line of action: 'You have been maligned; no fault of yours though! The blame attaches to her infertile womb.'[8] 'Cast away your woman; it is only then that you can retain the headship of the brotherhood.'[9] 'Forsake the food and the money I have given you', orders her cruel master. A tearful Jaswa hands over her jewellery to her mother-in-law: with tearful eyes she returns to natal home. But her mother who had nursed her at her ample breasts—*battis-dhār ka dūdh pilāya*—is now unwilling to give her shelter! 'Beti!' she prefaces her denial with a word of endearment, 'Beti, I have your brother's wives living in this house ... There's no room here even for a moment for an infertile woman.'[10] 'My husband's home is wealthy, and my natal home even more "Duplicut"'—Shubrati Dafali's Jaswa uses the English word to signify equivalence in wealth. But her 'duplicate' mother turns her back on her *bānjh* daughter.

Now beyond the pale of society, only wilderness awaits Jaswa. Deep inside the jungle, she starts wailing. And with good effect, for now the jungle itself began to wilt. All the beasts then go up to the Goddess of the Forest. 'We are being forced to leave the jungle of our birth', they plead, 'for everything here is wilting, lake Anarkali is drying up—some calamity, perhaps the end of your jungle is at hand.' Cubs and kids in tow, the beasts depart. Soon the forest emptied out. In a sympathetic reversal, as the tears of the *bānjh* dry up, so does the jungle, which now catches fire. Coming out of her preferred perch, Bansapti Mai, the goddess of vegetation, shows Jaswa the way: 'Six wildernesses you have traversed on your own; yet there is a seventh, that is Hazrat Syed Salar. A person of great *barkat* (powers), his fame is yet to reverberate through Hindustan':

> He lies interred in an earthen grave under [the mahua] tree, unattended and overgrown with weeds. Go ye thither! Serve him well; supplicate; put in your *arzi*, your application. It is indeed time for him to come out and reveal himself.[11]

The reference to the Ghazi's 'gong of fame awaiting the reverberation of the first devotional success' (*Abhi unka danka nahin baja hai*),[12] is of interest, for it covers nicely the gap of three hundred years between the martyrdom of the Ghazi in 1034 CE and the earliest evidence of pilgrimage, c. 1340. Both in the *Mirat* and in Shubrati's ballad, barren Jaswa's story is the first eventful occurrence in the birth of the saint's cult.

Jaswa locates the unmarked grave under a mound of dried leaves. Lifting the dust with her eyelashes, she sweeps it clean with her long tresses (*Palkon se buhārna/jārobkashi*). As night falls, fear overwhelms her: she tries drowning herself in the Anarkali lake. The lake recedes, as the saint rising from his grave makes a circular movement over it with his index finger (*kalmi ungli*), which Muslims raise ever so slightly during prayers to invoke the singularity of Allah. Ghazi Miyan now advises Jaswa to rush home, for 'your husband is about to take a second wife'. Jaswa gets transported to her husband's marriage pavilion. Husband Nanda is furious. He asks his clansmen to beat up Jaswa in full public view. The succour of Ghazi Miyan is at hand; it is the cowherds themselves who are miraculously beaten up. Roles reversed, the mother-in-law now begs Jaswa to spare her son's life. 'When you were at our home, no Pir no Deuta no demi god you had for saviour, and in seven days you have acquired such a powerful being—Hindu/Musalman I know not which—by your side'. 'Forgive my crazed son, do something so that all these whose life is ebbing away are brought back to life'. And, oh yes, 'get me a grandson; even a granddaughter will do', says the old woman in a conciliatory voice. Jaswa in turn requires all the 700 cowherds to become devotees of Syed Salar.

Humbled, yet unrepentant, Nand follows alongside his clansmen to the Bahraich shrine. Ever so insolent, he tries testing the powers of Ghazi Miyan. Sticking his dry-as-a-bone stave into the ground, he demands that the Ghazi transform it into a mahua tree. Ghazi Miyan's special relationship with the Bahraich jungle symbolised by the mahua tree is clearly at stake here. As both Nand and Jaswa pour water from the Anarkali lake on to the wooden *lathi*, the stave sprouts leaf-buds, and soon, pungent-smelling mahua fruits begin dropping from its branches! The first fruits are offered to Ghazi Miyan, the second lot eaten by Nand himself, and (understandably) the leftovers ingested by the wife. With Ghazi's intercession, Allah ensures that Jaswa's womb is fructified. And in the ninth month, sings Shubrati, baby Kanhaya or Krishna is born to Jaswa.[13]

This, of course, is contrary to both the epics and to medieval Krishnite devotional poetry: Yashoda (Jaswa of the ballads) is childless; she is not Krishna's biological mother, though, as that demigod's foster parents, both she and Nand have come to enjoy iconic status—Krishna, after all, is 'Nand lala' or Nand's lad and Jashoda the archetypal doting mother. The overstretching by Shubrati Dafali is significant, as making Krishna's birth consequent on the Bahraich saint's benediction strengthens the cowherds' connection with Ghazi Miyan.

The Jaswa trope works for another reason as well. The first miracle, which, according to the *Mirat*, spread the fame of the Pir far and wide, was of a *bānjh* milkmaid being blessed with a son. The seventeenth-century text is sparse, but it has the structure of feeling that constitutes *bānjh*-ness in north Indian villages. The *aqeema* of the Persian *Mirat* is the straightforward *bānjh* of north India; the husband is characterised as a 'Gobal'/Gopal in the Persian text, and its more common equivalents 'Ahir' and 'Gaddi' in nineteenth- and twentieth-century Urdu-Hindi tracts.[14] This unfortunate woman from village Nagraur, not far from the shrine, has been thrown out by her mother-in-law, with a view to getting a second wife for her cowherd son. Out in the cold, the wife locates the few servitors tending the rude Bahraich grave and is advised to pray to Allah, seeking the intercession of the warrior saint. Her husband, somewhat more caring than the Nand of the ballads, comes looking for her: he also prays at the grave, promising to offer *shirni* (sweets). Husband and wife go back home together. Conception is almost immediate, and a male child is born after nine months. This, according to the *Mirat*, marked the beginning of the fame (*tāza urūj zuhūr*) of the shrine.'[15] In sum, it is a milkmaid's yearning for motherhood that makes Ghazi Miyan *qua* saint come into his own!

7

Zohra Bibi

As the news of the miracle of Ghazi Miyan—the infertile milkmaid conceiving—spread through the villages and towns of Awadh, two Syed brothers newly arrived from Central Asia settled down in *qasba* Rudauli* near Faizabad. Rudauli was a few hours' ride from Satrikh, the place where Salar Masud had dropped anchor in the spring of 1034. By the late fourteenth century, it was a major Sufi centre, with the hospice of Shaikh Abdul Haq (d. 1434) functioning as a 'clearing house … [which] … encouraged religious and cultural accommodation to local social beliefs and customs'.[1] Abdur Rahman (died c. 1683), the author of *Mirat* and successor to the Sufi hospice of Rudauli, tells the story of Zohra Bibi as an example of how an elite family, newly arrived from Central Asia, began to partake of the popular culture of Awadh.[2]

Pubescent at twelve, Zohra was blind from birth. Her father, new to the ways of Hindustan, came to know of people from neighbouring towns and villages making a beeline for the Bahraich shrine.[3] There were stories about the milkmaid being blessed with a son, and of the blind gaining sight by applying (metaphorically) 'the dust of that pure shrine to their darkened eyes'.[4] With pure heart, the father prayed for a cure for his daughter's affliction, vowing to get a *pukka* masonary tomb for the Ghazi built at Bahraich. It is his daughter Zohra who raised a roof over the saint's grave, which, according to a Delhi poet,

---

* *Qasba*: a small central place with a fair sprinkling of Muslim literati, landholders and a multi-religious artisanate, such as specialist weavers; the bigger qasbas boast a major Sufi hospice or shrine, as in the case of Rudauli.

had begun exuding the fragrance of his benediction throughout Hindustan from the late thirteenth century.[5]

On hearing about the legendary Salar Masud, Zohra was consumed by a pining for the warrior saint. Blind and impetuous, the twelve-year-old vowed that if cured (by the intercession of the Ghazi), she would devote her life to serving his shrine. One night, exhausted, she sensed the Ghazi approaching. 'If I be possessed of true love', prayed Zohra in her dream, 'may I regain my vision, so that I may be able to set my eyes on Masud'. Riding his favourite grey mare, the Prince of Martyrs appeared in her vision; the girl chased her dream: when she awoke she had gained sight, but Masud was lost from view.[6]

A veritable madness now descended upon Zohra; once again, Masud appeared in her sleep, this time directing her to come to Bahraich. Her grateful father immediately set her up for the journey, which would have meant crossing the wide Saryu river at Belkhara, as people from villages around Rudauli still do today. Accompanied by her uncle and a cousin, she left for Bahraich with a tidy sum of money. Zohra's father, though a wealthy patron, was *dervesh*-like in his disposition: he had his own promise to keep to the saint, which his daughter was now going to fulfil.

At Bahraich, Zohra busied herself cleaning up the Ghazi's unkempt grave. Money in hand, her close relatives (implies the *Mirat*) negotiated with the servitors of the makeshift shrine. A dome embellished with a gold cupola now rose over the sepulchre. Regular, pukka graves for Masud's close associates—Birahna, the constant companion and Syed Ibrahim, who had avenged Masud's death by killing Sohal Deo—were also laid out. Zohra also constructed a martyrs' graveyard (*ganj-i-shahīdān*) over the sun tank, which Masud had hurriedly filled with his slain soldiers.[7] And in a final gesture, reminiscent more of Mughal royalty than of a forlorn devotee, Zohra got her own tomb constructed adjacent to the saint's. Her two close relatives who had served the Ghazi well were also buried inside the Bahraich shrine.

Bibi Zohra served the shrine for six years and died at the same age as Masud Ghazi, and on the same day and month, that is, the fourteenth day of the Islamic month of Rajab—*dar-qāyda Hind awwal roz māh Jeth,* as Abdur Rahman reworked it in terms of the local agricultural and ritual calendar.[8] This first day of the Indian solar month of Jeth translates for purposes of the Bahraich Fair roughly as the first Sunday of May, provided a Thursday in the same month precedes it.[9] And it is on the day that the marriage of Ghazi Miyan has been celebrated by thousands of pilgrim-devotees for centuries. Inayat Husain wrote in his nineteenth-century Urdu edition of the *Mirat,* 'Praise be to Allah, for the date and age of the martyrdom of Masud and of the death of Zohra [while serving the shrine] is exactly the same', even though a considerable time had elapsed between the two events![10] The term *urs* (Arabic for 'wedding'), used in South Asia in the dual sense of the death and the union of a Sufi saint with God, acquired, in this case, an additional coat of meaning. For Abdur Rahman, this *urs-i-ursiana* (marriage of all marriages) also came to stand for the marriage-in-death of Zohra with the warrior saint of Bahraich, who had also embraced his death/bride on the day of his martyrdom.

Zohra's mother began to visit Bahraich with her family every year on the day of the saint's *urs* (and also of Zohra's death), as if she was coming to get her daughter married to her saint.[11] Subsequently pilgrims began bringing the *daija* or mini trousseaux to the shrine during the Jeth Fair. It was such a wedding party of 'singing and dancing' rustic enthusiasts en route to Bahraich that aroused the curiosity of Emperor Akbar outside the capital city Agra in 1560–61 CE.[12]

'A monument to pure love, the *rauza* (shrine) built by Zohra for Salar Masud has stood the vagaries of time', wrote Abdur Rahman in his hagiography of the saint, c. 1620. When some people, claiming that it did not quite come up to the mark, attempted to rebuild the original structure, Masud persuaded them in their dreams against upsetting the purity of that design.[13] And for good reason: for the shrine conjoined the martyrdom of a warrior with the death of a nubile servitor who had snuffed out her life, so to speak, as a moth doting over an eternal flame.

Abdur Rahman, the author of *Mirat*, caps the story of Zohra by allowing himself a literary conceit: 'It is the belief of this nobody', writes Abdur Rahman deprecatingly, that the rite of getting the saint married is the fulfillment of the dream Salar Masud once had of his deceased parents arranging for his *shādi* with the houries—which the learned had interpreted during his lifetime as a foreshadowing of martyrdom.[14] And, 'since the inner part, the heart of the martyr is ever happiness and passion (*shādi wa zauq*), the reflection of this happiness is noticed in this world as well. This is what we see on the occasion of the urs'. Abdur Rahman concluded this esoteric reflection with a forceful defence of the pilgrimage and popular veneration of the Ghazi, and an attack on the orthodox *Ulema*, the opponents of the cult:

> To regard such things [as the pilgrimage to Bahraich] *bi'dat* (innovation within Islam) is sheer ignorance and stupidity. Those who call themselves '*Alim*' and object to such happenings around saints do not know what they are talking about. They can never fathom the depths of [real] knowledge.[15]

In an early twentieth-century *masnavi* verse narrative, what had been the measured anger of the author of *Mirat* at the shallow learned opponents of the Ghazi now cascaded into an shower of abuse against such veritable anti-Christs—the one-eyed *dajjāl* mentioned in the Book. *Murtid*s or bad characters that had turned their face away from Islam, such evil persons were fit only to be punched and kicked:

> *Jo bid'at kahe usko mār aur lāt, ki jāhil kahe mardūd aur kambhakt zāt; Nahin Maulvi balki dajjāl hai; badāfāl, murtib, badāmāl hai.*[16]

There is a local tradition that makes Zohra and Salar Masud contemporaries. Ghazi Miyan was thirsty; he found Zohra sitting by a well and asked her for water. 'Are you blind as me that you can't see? she shot back.'[17] So begins the story of the blind girl cured by the Ghazi. The usual storyline of such well-side encounters features Krishna, or even a gallant low-caste wayfarer's dalliance with a nubile upper-caste damsel as he offers in amorous distance to help lift the heavy pitcher on to the girl's head.[18] In the case of Zohra, the roles are reversed. Tired from his travels, Masud (in an hour-long ballad recited in May 1994 by a Dafali near Rudauli; see Appendix 1) asks the blind Zohra for some drinking water. She is unable to oblige, and in turn gets annoyed. Possessed already of sufficient powers, the young wayfarer now prays on Zohra's behalf: 'Please Allah, please restore her eyesight fast'. She of course needs it most, but so does Masud, for faced with a blind girl's inability to draw water, he is dying of thirst: *ehka to parwar digār ānkhi jaldi dī hau / hamre-tau māre piyās-ke jān hamra jāi.*

Zohra gains eyesight, and then follows a peculiar dalliance, with the girl playing the propositioner to a bemused Masud. An excited Zohra runs home to inform her parents, and also fetch a *lota* to draw water from the well.[19] She is unwilling to let go; she thinks of sundry excuses to detain Masud: it is so hot, she says, why not rest awhile before taking the high road? It was he, words keep pouring out, it was this gentleman, who politely asked me for some water, and then prayed to Allah 'to send me a pair of eyes fast', she confides in her mother.

Zohra procures a copy of the Quran, and opening it at random pushes the Book in Masud's face: tell me the month of your birth, and I shall mine, she gushes.* 'The month of Jeth in the summer season', replies Masud; 'so is mine', the girl chimes in excitedly. For Zohra it is all neatly sewed up. Our marriage is fated in the month of our birth; it is fixed for now; as good as done, Zohra keeps rattling about the month of Jeth. Curiously, with the balladeer, the coincidence of the date and month of Masud's and Zohra's deaths (as mentioned in the *Mirat*) has here changed into the sharing of a zodiac sign.

A dampener is in the offing. Heavens forbid; prophets and wise men all negate Masud's wedding: 'His marriage has been blotted out of his fate', they say in unison. 'There will be *pachka*', a conjunction of five unlucky stars when it is bad karma, so to speak, to commence any work, much less a wedding—for even persons dying during this period are not accorded full cremation rites.[20] The requisite rituals shall proceed without a hitch: sitting on a small stool, the groom will be anointed with unguents preparatory to going out to the bride's place. But then the planets will stymie the proceedings: *Tel hoyi, mel hoyi, biyāh mein pachka pari*... The marriage will not take place, only the preparatory rituals, sang the Dafali of Basaurhi on the night of 16 May 1994.[21]

Masud's mother now reaches the scene. An elite Syedani, here she calls for a Brahman (and not an Islamic officiant, a *qazi*) to fix an auspicious date for the marriage of 'my (little) saint', as she puts it lovingly. The pandit can only reconfirm what the prophets had decreed—it will go as far as the anointing of the groom, but the marriage shall not take place. So ends the Basaurhi Dafali's tale of Zohra Bibi and Ghazi Miyan. Interestingly, the balladeer insists that Zohra, 'born of [elite] Syed parents, was raised by a Rudauli Teli'—a low caste whose occupation is the pressing of oil from oilseeds. In folklore, this curious divergence between birth and upbringing is stated

* *Istikhāra*: Finding meaning or significance by opening randomly a verse of the Quran and interpreting it in terms of the current issue or problem.

as a popularly held fact, requiring no further gloss or explanation. This merits a pause, for in the seventeenth-century *Mirat*, Zohra is a regular Syedani—that is, a female with a purported genealogy stretching all the way to the Prophet's family, with no possible connection with the Rudauli 'low-breds'. The trope of attributing a low-caste upbringing to the young girl is most probably a successful local grafting, post *Mirat-i-Masudi*, c. 1620. Or perhaps the author of the seventeenth-century *Mirat* had purged the story of Zohra of its local low-caste associations? Chronological sequence apart, this local Lay of Zohra, suggests that the town of Rudauli, home to Sufis and Muslim gentry dating back to the fourteenth century, is not allowed to lay exclusive claim to the most important female character in the Ghazi Miyan legend.[22]

The two stories about a previously infertile milkmaid blessed with a son and the divine love of a fourteenth-century elite Rudauli girl for the long-dead Masud are significant events in the afterlife of the Bahraich hero. They mark successively the outreach, so to speak, of belief in the *barkat* (blessings) of the shrine. Together, they recount the story of the emergence of the cult through acts of intense devotion by the low and the middle castes of Awadh: Zohra, a girl born in an elite Muslim family, is raised in a local low-caste household. And it is such a girl who gets the tomb of the Ghazi constructed.

The story of Zohra Bibi is the longest of the lores about Salar Masud recorded in the *Mirat*. In engaging with the blind girl's resolve to devote her life to the service of the makeshift Bahraich shrine, the *Mirat* opens itself fully to local tradition. Receptive to folk beliefs and practices, Abdur Rahman, the learned Sufi of Rudauli, here becomes acerbic in his defence of the popular practice of seeking to enact the Ghazi's marriage to Zohra. To regard such things as the pilgrimage to Bahraich as *bid'at*, that is, unacceptable innovation within Islam, is nothing short of 'ignorance and stupidity', the learned head of the Chishti Sufi school at Rudauli (the birthplace of Zohra), railed against the doubting Ulema.

Pilgrimage is of course central to the longevity of a cult. And it usually involves leaving behind a trace for wish-fulfilment—a piece of thread, a supplicatory chit tied to the lattice of a shrine. With Ghazi Miyan, there is equally a collective desire to get the Ghazi bridegroom married. The annual pilgrimage replicates the journeys that Zohra's mother had made to Bahraich after the death of her nubile daughter at the shrine. What is important for the Ghazi's devotees is that this ritualised effort after marriage has retained a connection with the 'historic' Life and Times of Masud. For, just as recorded in the seventeenth-century *Mirat-i-Masudi*, the intrepid Ghazi had rushed at his antagonist Sohal after hearing of 'the enemy rustling the cattle of the army'; the balladeers still continue to recount the martyrdom of Masud while fighting for *his* cows and cowherds. And as there are (and have been) a large number of women who make the pilgrimage in the hope of being blessed with a son, the ballads have combined the travails of such infertile *bānjhin* women with the tragedy of one such—the Ghazi's mother—losing her only son, born with the blessings of a saint, on the day of his marriage!

8

Birth-Marriage-Martyrdom

The memorable thing about the marriage of Masud is that it never quite takes place. 'Bale Miyan's *biyāh*' is the annual pilgrimage to get the saint married … without success. It indicates, proverbially, the absurdity of the recurring male failure to tie the nuptial knot, and by extension, any inordinate deferral.

The story of Masud's marriage is about a mother trying to buy back fate, and getting short changed in the process. And as the groom in question is a warrior Ghazi, it is equally about supplanting *kufr* (unbelief) with Islam.[1] In a ballad recorded in the late nineteenth century, gravid after tireless supplications, Mamula gives birth to a son who decimates *kufr* with the sword of Islam, making ogres and demons scamper into the woods. A hundred years later, in May 1994, a Dafali of village Basaurhi was singing the same tune, this time making the frightful idols themselves affirm the Islamic faith: *Khule bhāg Bahraich ke, jab base Gaji Pīr; bhāge yahān se deo-dānu, kānpe sakal jamīn / ki mūrat kalma sab parhin.*[2] The demons of Bahraich run away, the earth trembles and as the Ghazi 'settles down' in these parts, the idols themselves recite in unison recite the Islamic credo. Allusion to the profession of faith aside, these ballads are no starched, sectarian sagas, recording aggressively the march of Islam in India. The warrior-hero straddles a malleable historical past, for 'Gajan', the moniker for Masud of the ballads, is a conjoint of Ghazi and Ghazna, conflating, in one dialectal move, the mission of the young lad, his parental home and the iconoclasm of his uncle, Sultan Mahmud of Ghazni. And while the ballads focus on an Islamic warrior sacrificing his life for cows and cowherds, the Ghazi's birth echoes feminine anxieties about conception and barrenness.

Taunted as a 'barren' woman even by low caste women—*jāt ki bhujāin o dhobāin mohe tāna māren: sun Mamal, tuhe Rabb ne bānjh banāi*—Mamula keeps running from one shrine to another.[3] Her first hospice of call is the famous dargah at Ajmer, but unlike in the *Mirat*, where Masud is conceived in that holy city on the first night of parental union, Mamula of the ballads is turned away by the Ajmer saint. Shattered, she is redirected to the shrine of Shah Madar at Makanpur, where she undergoes the standard obsequies: kissing the threshold of the shrine and sweeping the floor with her unbraided tresses—a gesture of humility and submission that a woman employs while seeking the intercession of saints.[4]

Mamula finally gets the blessings of Saint Madar, who asks her to take a dip in the tank of the shrine and come up with whatever she craves: diamonds, pearls, or rubies—the latter also a term of endearment for a son. She conceives soon after. As Mamula oversleeps that crucial night of conception, Ahir cowherds crowd her dreams, foretelling martyrdom for her embryonic son on the day of marriage. Startled, as she sleeps lazily with the child welling inside her—*nindiya alsāni, so gaun bete sang*—Mamula rushes for the daybreak pilgrimage stipulated by the saint. But it is already too late. The *Pir* who had earlier given his blessings now curses Mamula cruelly, and in terms identical to her nightmare: 'may your son die the day he is decked as groom'!

In another version, the saint desires that should Mamula have a son, she must present the child at the shrine before severing the umbilical cord—*Jo bānjhin hoe tera bans, mujhe deo dekhāi-leo nār bewāra.*[5] This seems like an impossible stipulation as it is obligatory as a marker of rootedness to bury the navel string in the place of the child's birth.[6] A male child is born to a delighted Mamula, but the midwife—Nona Chamain, a notorious low-caste witch of north Indian lore—reasons with the mother against offering the 'unclean navel string' to the saint. Severing it with a small sickle she buries it in the courtyard.[7] Mamula makes a thanksgiving journey to Makanpur, sans the shrivelled birth-cord. The *Pir* gets angry at the doting mother for disobeying his command. Sounding the death knell so soon after the blessing, he curses that the boy shall die on the day of his marriage (*mare tor beta jih din jāe sanwra*).[8] Mamula is shaken, not deterred. Casting caution to the winds, she prepares herself for the worst that Fate may have in store for her son: all she wishes is to see him dressed in full attire as a fetching groom. (*Ab honi ho so hove; dekh leun jalwa Pir Bahlim ka. Ab rākhe khuda ya khove.*) She summons a Brahman (and, note, not a Muslim qazi) who suggests an auspicious date for Masud's marriage, marred unfortunately by the strong possibility of war and likely death disrupting violently the joyous occasion. Prepared to brazen it out, Mamula both laughs and cries, for she knows that her son's future is uncertain the moment he rides at the head of the marriage procession.

The marriage/martyrdom reversal is not fully narrated at the Bahraich Fair at least nowadays. 'Dressed as groom, kerchief in hand, cummerbund around his waist, antimony in his eyes, pān in mouth is Mamal's lad', sings Bashir Dafali from Faizabad. The journey of any other bridegroom would be fairly predictable, interrupted only by ritual obstacles, banter and stylised fights at the girl's house. In this rendition of the Dafali from Faizabad, there is no narrative unfolding of the story after this picture of 'our bridegroom', as most balladeers invariably address Ghazi Miyan lovingly. The sequence: marriage/martyrdom does not quite unfold through a playing out of a tragic story. Rather, it unravels linguistically by an inversion of the elements that go into the makeup of the groom himself—a case of a *rite de passage* forcing the pace of events. And so, the chaplet of flowers turns into a crown of martyrdom; the cummerbund so lovingly tied by a doting mother shrivels into a noose of separation: *shādi*—marriage, literally, the time of rejoicing—is overwhelmed by separation, warfare and mourning.

The pilgrim-audiences of these ballads would not have been entirely unfamiliar with this reversal of the groom's good fortune, for in both lore and rites, marriage as the enactment of the manly act of wife capture had its own dangers. In two prominent folk epics of the region, *Lorikayan* and *Alha*, the invitation to suitors carried with it the hazard of death in the marriage pavilion! A formal invitation soliciting a match for his daughter in the north Indian epic 'Alha-Rudal', carried a chilling rider from the prospective father-in-law: 'There shall be fighting at the doorway and valiant sword play around the wedding post, and when the groom comes in for the post-marriage feast, his head will I cut off'![9] In another version, as Rudal's marriage party—literally his *paltan* or platoon—enters the marriage *mandwa*, the girl's grandfather challenges the groom to a combat: a serious fight ensues; the groom finally cuts off the head of his grandfather-in-law, and is escorted with pomp and ceremony into the marriage pavilion![10] This scenario of marriage/death or marriage/war does not appear to have been a figment of bardic imagination. When a mid-fourteenth-century Delhi sultan offered the hand of his sister to an Arab, following the local custom the groom's party rode on their horses, each with 'a stick previously prepared' for the occasion. At the gate, they overwhelmed the bride's party, forcing them off their horses. This defeat of the bride's, that is, the Sultan's parents, seems to have pleased the sister-giver Sultan Mohammad bin Tughlaq appositely. And this, according to the fourteenth-century Moroccan traveller Ibn Battuta who was a witness to this quaint scene.[11] So much for marriage carrying the possibility of death for the groom.

Collected over a wide arc from Amballa in Punjab to Banaras and Bahraich in eastern UP, the marriage-ballads of the Ghazi vary in their emphasis. The Amballa version recorded in the Punjab is rich in the description of rites whereas the one collected close to Bahraich in the early 1890s focuses on cowherds and their place in the Ghazi-groom story.[12] Irrespective of regional inflections, all share a set of common motifs: the brahman and not the qazi fixing the date for marriage/war, the anointing and massage of the groom with oil and the calamitous appearance of milkmaid Jaswa whose 'Save the Cows' cry makes the Ghazi-groom forsake his nuptials for battle against the enemies of Islam and of local cowherds.

As they describe a mother's nervous preparations for her son's marriage, the ballads go over the rituals customary among the main followers of Ghazi Miyan—the lower- and middle-caste Hindus and Muslims of the Gangetic valley. There is the invitation to the members of the extended family, the calling upon the barber, the gardener and others who play specialised roles in the marriage; the offering of gifts to such service providers. And then come the erection of the marriage shed (*māndo*, *mandwa*) made of freshly-cut bamboo, adorned with banana and mango leaves;[13] the wake, when women sitting all night long by a sacral water-pot sang invocations to the heavens to bless the bride and the groom; and the night of 'the forty', mimicked by forty beggars performing *dhammāl*—a fire-jumping dance—to the accompaniment of drums and stringed instruments.[14]

Understandably, the ballads omit the one ceremony following in the story of the Ghazi groom, reported widely from lower caste Muslim households in the late nineteenth-century. This was the 'rite of Ghazi or Bale Miyan' himself. Women of the neighbourhood gathered under the marriage pavilion, erected a green standard of the Ghazi in the shape of a branch of a mango tree decorated with a red kerchief dyed in safflower, and sang the lay of the Warrior Saint's Spear.[15] The most important rite preparatory to marriage was the going into confinement for the regular anointing with oil and herbs, applied both to the bride and the groom. In common parlance, the phrase *mānjhe/māyūn baithna* connotes sitting idly, cutting oneself off from normal exertions: '...Mahomadan...persons about to be married are made to oil themselves, wearing dirty clothes, and sit still for a number of days before [being] married', is how a Rural Dictionary glossed *mānjha* in the late nineteenth century.[16] Travelling leisurely through north India, with stops in Patna, Faizabad and Lucknow in the early nineteenth century, an Iranian had also commented on the centrality of the *mānjha* ceremony:

> On the eve of a marriage, just a few days before the *Henna-band*[h]*an* or myrtle paint ceremony [the ubiquitous '*mehndi*' function of nearly all north Indian marriages of today], the bride and the bridegroom have a massage of turmeric or saffron and clad in yellow-coloured dress retire to a private apartment [in their respective homes]. During those days, they rarely come out of their apartments ... that period is called [*mānjha* or *māyun*].[17]

Ghazi Miyan, the ballads stress, is in such a state of enforced idleness, while female relatives massage him. Mother Mamula adorns his wrist with the safflower-dyed cotton threads marking the days left to marriage.[18] A chaplet of sweet-smelling *bela* and *mogra* buds hangs from Masud's forehead, as women sing lusty songs aimed at stirring the groom's desire at the demure bride making fulsome demands on the wedding night: *sughar mere banre banno mānge-gi rang raliyan*; *chatur mere banre banno mānge-gi rang raliyan*.[19] It is 'our Ghazi Groom' (as the Dafalis are wont to say) who is accosted in such an advanced stage of marital preparedness by Jaswa *gwalin*'s cry of 'Save your cows!' 'Pray! Listen to me before you tie the nuptial knot: The arrogant Sohal has rustled your cows! Pir, your herdsmen are dead!' wails Jaswa, the chief of the milkmaids as she rushes to the marriage pavilion. Hearing this, the young groom rises up in anger and begins lacing himself with scimitar and sword. Mother Mamula is distraught: the dreaded future is now coming to pass. 'Don't go to war, my little one; I have got you by reversing the wheel of fortune', she entreats him: *tum mat jao ran ko lālre, tumhen bare bhāg se pāi.*[20] 'Sit still, let me feast my eyes on you.' The Ghazi groom begins to show signs of annoyance: 'Mother! Don't you see? Sohaldal has challenged me to a fight. Try and see beyond the rites, give me something to do for *deen* and Islam.' 'Don't stop me today': *Māmal māi*, the intimate Bhojpuri phrase for mother here rhymes with *rār machāi*—the enemy's deceitful affray. Not easily denied, Mamula counters with a mother's special pleading: 'A maid with locks as dark as night I bring thee for thy bride';[21] 'eat the choicest viands, claim your wife on the wedding night. As for the cattle-rustling, well that's not all, is it—you have so many more! Sit under the canopied pavilion; this is no time to fret about some stolen cows and calves.'[22]

The son rebuts the mother on each count: 'How can I not respond to the Save the Cows Cry; look, there is milkmaid Jaswa appealing for help; and mother, life is ephemeral, "*fāni*", we all have to go some day'. Cursing her ill fortune, Mamula tears her hair in despair.[23] 'Pir Bahlim', her son—here called a 'Pir' (saint) by the mother—stands firm and duty-bound. In other versions of this ballad, the Ghazi foresees his death saving cows in a reverie. Masud wishes the mother to rejoice at the impending martyrdom of her fully groomed son. 'Only after cutting Sohal's head shall I return, else let this chaplet adorn my very grave.'[24] In the English translation of the version recorded near Bahraich in the 1880s, Masud says:

> Nay, mother, nay, he said, there waits / A martyr's death for me: A mausoleum and mosque / my monument shall be / I shall be laid in Hind to rest / But still my fame will grow, And all the four worlds hither come / Their tribute to bestow.[25]

Ghazi Miyan gets up, washes the henna off his hands, and knotting his hair in a bun, jumps astride his favourite Lilli mare. Taking leave, he asks two favours of his distraught mother: 'Free me of the debt of life that I owe to your milk'—for in sallying forth to his death, Masud is about to waste the mother's milk that has nurtured him.[26] 'And please untie the ceremonial threads'—the *kalewa* (with which the loving mother marks the countdown to the son's wedding).[27]

Such, then, is the trajectory of events of Ghazi Miyan's marriage ballads as transcribed from popular renditions in the late nineteenth century. A hundred years later, at the 1996 Bahraich Fair, I heard a Dafali reworking this well-known story.

> The first Sunday of Jeth it was,
> when bedecked the groom
> Made town Rudauli a stop
> To confront Raja Sohal. ...
> 'Enrapted in rites I was,
> My cowherds you ambushed'?
> 'Hold your tongue you Turkic brat,
> lest push you I to Ghazni hills ...
> For it was a Sunday,
> the first in May
> The *shādi*-day, as willed.[28]

The battle is fought. Sohal's army is decimated; his five brothers run home for reinforcements; the women shamed them for showing their backs to the *Turukas*. And this is the beginning of the end of Raja Sohal Deo. There, on the battlefield itself, Masud Ghazi prays to God: 'Let every other lineage save Sohal's remain in this world: may his progeny be decimated so that none remain to ease his death rattle with a last drink of water.' And so everything—his army, his fort, his palace bites dust, sinking and '*dhus*-ing' into the ground: what they call Sahet-Mahet (the historic city of Sravasti, the site of Buddha's four month monsoon sojourn) ... 'that *jhaua-jhār* of ruins and wilderness, that's what became of the fort of Sohal after the Ghazi took the measure of this wicked king', declaimed a Dafali in May 1996 at the Bahraich Fair.[29]

Hum to lubhāvan byāh mein, apne lagāya ghāt! 'Here I was engrossed in my nuptial rites and you ambushed my cows and cowherds!' It is this obscene opportunism, not political opposition or the tussle over enlarging the realm of Islam, that seals the fate of Raja Sohal. 'By God's decree the Gajan killed / Those kings who wisdom lacked / He took possession of their fort / Their palace razed and sacked'.[30] This translation of a ballad recorded by an English civil servant in the 1880s echoes a similar sentiment.

In most ballads the sword of Islam motif, though prominent, gets overlaid by the tragic fate of a groom losing his life on the eve of marriage. Not that the sword stays sheathed; violence is not belittled, it is made anodyne. The term 'Kafir' here denotes not so much an adversarial category as the deceitful 'kafirish behaviour' of Raja Sohal rustling the cows belonging to the Ghazi at the time he chooses for the deed. In the ballad collected at Amballa in the 1880s, as the troops are arrayed in battle formation, Masud challenges Raja Sohal:

> Listen you, you slayed my cowherds, rustled my cows;
> You, you are kafir
> for the *dagha* [deceit] that you have wrought.[31]

No doubt in other ballads there is a clear mention of Masud spreading Islam by putting adversary Sohal to the sword.[32] But if the young Ghazi claims to further the 'religion of the Prophet', the prognosis at birth of his militant service to Islam is couched explicitly as the destruction of demons and ogres.[33]

Ghazi Miyan ends up freeing the cows that Sohal had carried away. Returning to the camp, he seeks the shade of a sandalwood tree*—for it is the dead of summer—where he reads the Quran. And it is there that archangel Gabriel brings a message from Allah: 'Ask if you so wish for long life', the Gibreel (Gabriel) says. Ghazi Miyan nods his head in the negative. The archangel returns. Now the Ghazi finally asks for a favour: 'Go, please tell the Almighty I wish my name to be known'. There and then Gabriel conveys the decree of Allah: 'Raja and beggar, rich and poor—all thirty six castes and sub-castes, each one of them shall remember you and take your name'.[34] And there ends one of the ballads of marriage and death as retold by a Dafali at the Ghazi Miyan Fair in May 1996. In other versions, the victorious Ghazi after recovering 'his cows', seeks protection from the midday sun under a tree. As fated, an unseen arrow pierces the aorta of the Pir; the bridegroom dies, wilts like a flower as the Dafalis put it.[35]

---

* The sandalwood tree in this particular ballad usurps the importance of the mahua tree of the *Mirat*.

9

Ghazi Miyan and Cowherds

So much for the tragedy that cuts short the life of Gajan Pir, beloved of the thirty-six (*chattīs*) castes and sub-castes (standing for all of society) but specially of the Ahir-cowherds. It is in a ballad gathered c. 1890 close to Bahraich that cowherds really come into their own. The ballad of Set Mahet (Shravasti) opens with the Ahirs or Gwal cowherds, 'wild with mirth', dancing in the forest to mark the Ghazi's marriage. Raja Sohal sends a formal request to Nand for 'curds and milk'. Nand, the cowherd chief, flatly refuses this gratuitous levy, while arranging for the time-honoured tribute to the Ghazi, this special time for his nuptials. Rebuffing the local Raja Sohal, he exhorts his cowherds to be steadfast in their fealty to their protector.

> 'Hear me my Gwals', said he, 'be brave'
> 'And to your salt be true.
> Be up and bear in mind today
> The Mian's claim on you.' [1]

The 'wanton Raja seize[s] the cattle of the Pir', but the brave Ahirs beat back this first assault: 'Then quailed the raja Suhil Dal / He left the cows and fled.' The carefree Ahirs literally get drunk on victory. Crafty stratagems follow. Suhil Dal sends a Brahman spy bearing gifts to the Gwala chief. Nand insults Suhil Dal by telling the messenger that these are not quite the presents that should accompany a proposal from the Raja for the marriage of his daughter to Kunwar Kandhaiya (the young Krishna), *his son*—an allusion to Nand being the foster father of Krishna in another set of poetry and lore![2]

In the next decisive round, Sohil Dal masters his forces well: he aligns with other rajas and 'sweeps off the cows' by slaying the drunk Gwals in an unfair contest. As Nand lies dying, Masud's mother asks Jaso—Nand's wife—to bring the propitious curds for her son's marriage ceremony.[3] Jaso or Jaswa proceeds to the Gaura Got pasture with 700 milkmaids, and braves the scene of rout and massacre. She manages to locate her dying husband. Nand expires in her lap, as she gets him a last drink of water blessed by the Pir.[4] She returns to Ghazi Miyan's marriage-shed with 700 milk pails brimming with the blood of the Pir's cowherds. And so, in this Ahir-centric ballad, it is not just Jaso reporting the massacre, but the dramatic entry of 700 blood-smeared milkmaids that turns the tide at the Ghazi's marriage.[5] In this version, Salar Masud is not martyred; rather his victory at Gaura Got is followed by a more general attack on all 'those kings who wisdom lacked / He took possession of their fort / Their palace razed and sacked'. With God's grace, the Ghazi brings Nand and the other 700 Gwalas back to life.[6]

Ghazi Miyan is then the protector of 'cows and cowherds'; Raja Sohal a despicable cattle thief. By extension, the Ghazi is the Pir par excellence of the cowherds (he dies for them, and they for him); the Ahir-killer, cow-rustler Sohal is the archetypal Kafir—a saintless, faithless *be-Pir*. So strong is the popular association of Gwal uprightness with Ghazi Pir that in an early twentieth-century Bhojpuri love ditty, the heartless lover is cursed by the heroine as a *Be-Pir Ahir*, that is, a cowherd unable, literally, to keep faith.[7]

The idea of a Ghazi-warrior with firm ties to local pastoralists may appear odd, for in textbook memory, the Muslims of India are portrayed as adamant beef eaters, who, unmindful of Hindu sensibilities, slaughtered cows for the table. It is precisely in these terms that publicists since the early twentieth century have sought to undermine the appeal of the Ghazi Miyan cult. Balladeers and lay devotees of the Ghazi, however, have continued to recount the protection that the young warrior afforded the cowherds in rural Awadh.

> [Ghazi Miyan] had 1600 Ahir-cowherds and 125,000 cows.
>
> He had given his cowherds the freedom to do as they pleased; what he expected of them was the auspicious present of milk every eighth day. Raja Sohal Deo got annoyed at this. He said: 'A Turuk like him takes the *shagun* [present] of milk, and I, a Kshatriya, am

> ignored!' The gwalins disregard him, and took the *shagun* to the Ghazi's wedding in front of Sohal Deo.[8]

So recounted Zainulla balladeer at the summer fair of Ghazi Miyan in May 1996. Sixty miles southeast in village Guleria near Rudauli, the town of Zohra Bibi, Raja Sohal Deo is still condemned by the local Muslim gentry for his oppression of the Ahirs and for taxing dairy products heavily.[9] Much further east, in deltaic Bengal, the veneration of the Ghazi by cattle-rearers had found elaborate iconic and ritual expressions by the late nineteenth century. A shrine to the 'Ghazi saheb' was a common feature of most villages. Faqirs who sang about the Ghazi were rewarded with money and grain; the first milk given by a cow was offered at the Ghazi's mound outside the village, and bovine sickness occasioned a fresh round of offerings.[10] Unlike eastern Bengal, Ghazi Miyan is not credited with curative powers over cattle in rural Awadh. Further west in the Punjab though, there existed a quaint association between Muslim saints and dairy products. 'Neither Hindus nor Muslims will churn milk on Thursday ... as that day is held in honour of the Muhamadan saints', reported a native informant in early 1887. Consequently only a 'part of the milk got that day was used, and the rest given over to beggars and religionists (sic!)'.[11]

In a large swath of Muslim-dominated villages in Awadh (from Ram Sanehi Ghat and Rudauli and beyond Bhelsar to Ichauli), the oppression of cowherds under the local rajas figures to this day as the backdrop to the wondrous exploits of Ghazi Miyan. 'There were two principal crimes perpetrated by the rulers on hapless peasants: one, the sacrifice of the eldest son to powerful local idols, and second, the practice of the newly-wedded bride spending the first night at the raja's bedchamber'. So recounted a recluse Sufi of Kinaura, near Rudauli, in the winter of 1995. This imagery of sexual oppression seems to echo the Ahir epic *Loriki*, where through the artifice of a game of dice the local raja establishes claims on the proud cowherd chief's property, and crucially over the womb of his wife. All Ahir daughters would henceforth do time as the King's concubines; the sons as grooms in the royal stables.[12] In another version, the king ties a blue tag around the neck of newborn daughters, marking his right to abduct and impregnate the grown-up virgin bride immediately after her marriage to a cowherd. The epic Ahir hero Lorik shows his valour by winning over, after stupendous acts of bravery, one such girl, Manjiri, his first love, from the clutches of the raja.[13]

A chilling example of feudal barbarity striking at the moral economy of reproduction, it is perhaps this trope that has fed into the stylised remembrance of the oppressive conditions in Awadh at the time of Ghazi Miyan's campaigns. According to the recluse of Kinaura, the locals of this area appealed to Masud Ghazi, encamped some twenty miles away at Satrikh, to come to these parts and rid them of such oppressive practices. Salar Masud put an end to human sacrifice and the landlord's right to impregnate virgin brides. And that is why all the castes of this area have forever been grateful to Salar Masud.[14]

This remembrance of virgin brides routinely enlisted into royal harems is at variance with the other lore about the north Indian milkmaids. Here, it is the *Ahirin* milkmaids, hips swaying under their head-loads of milk and yogurt pots, that are a familiar object of male desire. Medieval poetry in the Braj dialect of Hindi brims with sexual banter between Krishna and the milkmaid who knows well that it is not so much milk as something else that the cowherd-lover is really after (see Figure 9.1).

> You grab my scarf and demand milk.
> Well, here is milk. How much do you want?
> You say you want to taste my butter.
> Well, here is my butter—have your fill.
> (Raskhan says) Don't try tricks on me
> For I know what you're really after Krishna.
> A cow can't give you what you want.
> And as for me—you haven't a chance.[15]

The Gwalin or Ahirin milkmaid of folklore is coquettish and vain. An itinerant seller of milk and yogurt, she is that familiar outsider who walks some distance from her village into the homes of clients; she is physically strong, and capable of whiplash retorts to the innuendos and double entendres that invariably assail her in unfamiliar surroundings where she ventures for the day's sales.[16] Money received from the day's rounds must be accounted for. The silly girl always dreams of spending her day's coins on herself, a desire seldom fulfilled, for accounts must be rendered to the male householder, or worse, to the mother-in-law.[17]

Fig. 9.1 *A Braj Bhasha verse of Raskhan about Krishna and the milkmaid*

Source: Courtesy of Richard Harris from Simon Digby Collection, Jersey, Channel Islands

Any earnings beyond the ordinary would be an aspersion on her character, for which she will have to come out of the fire of censure unscathed. The suspicion that debases virtue and the coin brought home from such hawking errands figure as a crucial turning point in *Lorikayan*, the major epic of the cowherds of northern India. In the penultimate episode, Lorik, the Ahir hero, has just returned after numerous sexual and military escapades to his natal habitat. During his long absence the cows of his village have been rustled by strangers; his duly wedded wife Manjiri (left behind) reduced to dire straits. Playing the Ahir king, Lorik commands the local Gwalins to come with buttermilk and curd to his royal seat. And when he rewards his destitute wife by putting gold and silver coins surreptitiously in her basket, Manjiri is suspected by her mother-in-law of having acquired this small fortune by offering illicit favours. She herself suggests an ordeal by fire. Her earnings—gold and silver coins—are thrown into a pot of boiling oil. The virtuous Ahirin prays and takes out the *mohur*s and sovereigns, with her hand and virtue unscathed.[18]

The daring of the Gwalin is proverbial, and it is this toughness that forms the recurring motif in folkloric encounters between the Muslim/'Mughal' and the intrepid milkmaid. This genre of ballads from central and western India pits the Mughal in Delhi or in his peripatetic imperial camp and the decked-up but by no means demure Ahir woman who, unmindful of sage counsel, insists on taking the high road to sell her curd to the Mirza or the Mughal. The result is predictable: the lascivious 'Mughal' is keener on taking the fetching Ahirin into his harem than striking an honest bargain for her products. The milkmaid rebuffs his advances, insulting him as she goes about contrasting the constrictive grandeur of the Mughal harem with the wonderful life she enjoys as a milkmaid. As she turns the attempted dalliance into a volley of earthy insults, royal anger flares up. The king takes the Gwalin forcibly into his harem; the newly wedded girl manages to convey her plight to her husband, who leads a charge of enraged Ahirs and rescues his strong-headed wife.[19] This archetypal encounter between an Ahirin and a Mughal ruler seems to be a retro-projection of solidified religious identities of a later period—the nineteenth century. It is perhaps for this reason that the milkmaid's response to the sexual advances expands from four-lettered ripostes—'your wife and mother copulate out of wedlock'— into a frontal attack on the religion of Islam:

> I will put fire on Allah's head: I do the work of an Ahir.
> My Ahir stave is of ebony ... and whosever that
> Stick chastises
> Will soon desert the name of Allah.[20]

By contrast, in Ghazi Miyan country (rural Awadh), we get several stories where a Muslim recluse or wise man's fatherly dealings with milkmaids is misconstrued through the prism of sexual desire—often with historic consequences. One such story positioned by an informant to have occurred in the eleventh century goes as follows:

> There lived a *buzurg*, a wise man, in these parts. The curds that [the Ahir maidens] took through the village was, uncut [literally, untouched] curd. One day this holy man dipped his finger in a big flat earthen curd-dish and licked it [thereby 'polluting' the rest of the curd, a move pregnant with sexual overtones]. A complaint was preferred to the Raja. In response this worthy severed his finger there and then. Anointing his forehead with blood, he took to moving about the area, tracing with his bleeding finger 'the line of Islam', as he put it. And sure enough, the advent of Syed Salar Masud Ghazi took place in this area a few years later.[21]

In this account from the winter of 1995, it is a local Faqir's self-mortification at a suspected pollution (and, by extension, an unfair reading of symbolic sexual advance towards a milkmaid in an innocent gesture by a fatherly recluse) that makes him mark the end of the line of the Hindu rajas of central Awadh.

At a more general level, thirteenth-century sources offer insights for placing the Ahir-Ghazi-Sufi connection in terms of forest clearance, with the possibility of cowherds (operating from inside the forests and its margins) being the first productive group to enter into a relationship with the Turks, both of the sword-wielding and the Sufi variety. As the area to the east and the south of the city of Delhi was heavily wooded in the thirteenth century, most of the energies of migrant communities coming into the Gangetic valley from the northwest were directed at forest clearance and 'extension of settlement and cultivation rather than the subjugation of a pre-existing urban population or of a settled peasantry', writes the great medievalist Simon Digby. And 'this course of extending cultivation was often marked by and centred upon the establishment of a tomb-cult with the appurtenances of Sufi shrine and servitors'.[22] Digby cites the story of a Sufi shaikh, sitting c. 1200 CE, at the entrance of his lodging at the edge of the town of Badaun, encountering a curd seller emerging with a pot of yogurt on his head from the forest refuge of Katehar. The encounter led to the conversion of the *zughrāt-farosh*, who also offered a large sum of money (100,000 bullion coins) to the shaikh, which could only have been amassed by the brigandage facilitated by the widespread forest cover.[23]

It could well be that the cattle-related cult of Ghazi Miyan arose during the phase when forests and pastures had begun to yield ground to agriculture in the plains of Central Awadh—a political instantiation, concurrently, of 'the struggles of remote and garrison-like Muslim communities in a hostile and imperfectly subordinated Hindu enviornment', as Digby puts it.[24] Pastoralism is common on the fringes of forests, and this goes back to the Mahabharata. That Salar Masud is pushed back into the eleventh century and is associated closely with Sultan Mahmud of Ghazni remains somewhat of a puzzle. Could it be due to the persistence of long memory of the first incursions of Turkic warriors in the Gangetic plains? What we know for certain is that Ghazi Miyan was a cult figure in the politics of the Gangetic plain in the fourteenth century, as suggested by the close patronage the Bahraich shrine enjoyed from the Tughlaq Delhi sultans. What seems irreducible about the Ghazi is that the narrative of his life and deeds, learned and plebeian, borrowed creatively both from the historical time of the eleventh-century Sultan of Ghazni and the folk literature about cowherd heroes of north India more generally. For that matter, the canonical stories of the Pahlavi literature of Iran, 'whether based ultimately on historical events or even on sheer fiction … were taken from the ancient horsemen culture of the cow-rearing Iranians—the chief hero Rustam, was a cowboy, and the lasso was not the least of his weapons.'[25]

Some of the central motifs of the Ghazi Miyan ballads: his birth to Mamula after a good deal of supplicatory effort, the fight against cattle rustlers, death on the day of marriage—all have parallels in the folk epics of north India with a cow-protector as hero. The mother of Lorik, a major cowherd-hero, is also derided as a barren hag and gets blessed with a son after much pleading at the court of Brahma, the cosmic creator.[26] The midwife who facilitates this birth is the same Nona Chamain who tricks Masud's mother into parting with the umbilical cord, meant to be shown to the Pir who had blessed her with a son.[27] Moving to the animal associates of the folk heroes, both Lorik and Ghazi Miyan are sent away (by a raja and uncle Sultan Mahmud respectively) to recover long outstanding revenue dues, in the hope that they will perish in the effort. They agree to the wager, as both are in search of that super steed they alone are destined to ride. Both tame this dangerous charger kept locked in the royal dungeon, known to kill any rider approaching it. As cowherd hero Lorik rides to the kingdom of Neuri for tax collection, a battle royal takes place, whose chief interest for us lies in the 'immortal bitch Sakuli', which the defalcating raja lets loose at Lorik's horse. Now Sankul, Sakul, or Sakuli (*sag-i-sakul* of the Persian *Mirat*) is the faithful dog that kept awake that dreadful night of 13 June 1034 and for three more days, howling and keeping watch over the body of Masud,[28] preventing its removal and desecration by Raja Sohal Deo. This watchdog role of Sakul in ensuring that Masud got a burial befitting a martyr was of course crucial, for it is this interment in the blood-soaked clothes of a *shahīd* that marks the beginning of the *barkat* of the Bahraich saint's grave—as indeed, it is one of the key markers of any Islamic martyr's burial. And it is in recognition of Sakul's importance that the canine's grave still exists inside the Bahraich dargah—a notable exception for Muslim shrines.[29]

A premier cowherd-brigand folk deity from Rajasthan also gets up, like Ghazi Miyan, from his wedding, and is killed while rescuing cows.[30] This hero Pabuji must have his special war horse. So he approaches a woman named Deval, 'known for her skill in the rearing and trading of horses, cows, and bullocks'. She asks Pabuji to pick any horse, but as with Ghazi Miyan, Pabuji will have none other than that one special horse which the horse trader is loath to part for fear of attracting the enmity of a local strongman.[31] 'Give me the mare on any condition', Pabuji insists. 'You will have to protect my herd of cows even at the cost of your life' demands Deval.[32] Pabuji puts the seal of honour on this tragic pact. Like Ghazi Miyan, he too will die saving cows. The most elevated of cattle savers, Pabuji dies tragically as he interrupts his marriage rites to respond to the 'Save the Cows' cry whispered in his ear by the cattle breeder, transmogrified as a golden bird. 'O Pabuji', the bird chirps, 'the cows whose sweet boiled milk I drink, Khichi has driven them off and is striking them with his whip! O Pabuji, my cowhouse lies empty; the cow's little calves are lowing in their enclosure.'[33] The bridegroom-hero rushes off to rescue the cows successfully, but like Ghazi Miyan, is killed in the bargain.

The remarkable association of a Turkic warrior with herdsmen does not mean that Muslims figure uniformly in all cowherd epics as cow-protectors. Indeed, in a subsidiary episode, Pabuji himself leads a campaign against the Muslim King of Patan, because 'in Patan daily calves and white cows are slain / In Patan are slain the frogs and the peacocks of the garden'.[34] In *Chandayan*, an earlier fourteenth-century version of the *Lorikayan* epic by the great Sufi Mulla Daud, the hero Lorik returns home after numerous exploits, to reclaim his prize cows which have been stolen in his absence by Kol tribals with the help of the 'Turks of Garh Gajan'—the ancestral home of Ghazi Miyan in popular lore![35] The *Lorikayan* is regarded as the 'oldest expression of Ahir self-image',[36] but the complicity of the Garh Gajan Turks in the theft of Lorik's cattle does not seem to have upset the Ahirs' devotion to their Ghazi, who—as local folklore has it—dies fighting for Ahirs and cows.

The heroic cattle deity par excellence is Kuar Bir of south Bihar, and even here in the historical evolution of the cult, a Muslim connection seems to have been grafted onto the story. This particular hero is a repository of bovine fertility, whose propitiation enables she-buffaloes to come into heat. He is a model protector of cows against tigers, and loses his life in one such encounter with wild beasts—an Ahir so completely (almost sexually) obsessed with his she-buffaloes as to be remiss in his conjugal obligation to his wife.[37]

The Kuar Bir myth operates within the natural economy of pastoralism, outside any 'historical' claims made by overlords on dairy products. In several allied myths though, Kuar Bir appears to lose his life defending cows against human depredators, and if worshipped, continues to protect the cattle of the villagers. In these variants, an unmarked cattle thief is replaced with a 'Mohammadan ruler', but more often by a nameless Muslim servant of the landlord. The servant arrives demanding the milk that has been ritually set aside for the worship of Kuar Bir. The Ahirs dare him to take the dedicated milk away; the interloper either dies in the ensuing fight, or is mauled by wild animals on his way back with the milk sequestered from the Kuar Bir worship. Curiously, such a death in the fight over sacred milk binds the assembled cowherds to worship this Musalman as well![38]

Ghazi Miyan ballads, of course, paint a Turkic warrior as a martyr to the cause of '*his* cowherds'—a hero who forsakes marriage, family and life for the sake of cows! Could it be that latter-day balladeers have inverted a prior, necessarily antagonistic relationship between Turkish warriors and herdsmen, and made it palatable for 'Hindu' devotees by adding a tragic and heroic denouement (death of a bridegroom) to it? This seems doubtful as there is no evidence that such a conscious inversion and superimposition of the Ghazi Miyan cult took place.

What about the intercalations with characters and events from the great Sanskrit epics, the Ramayana and Mahabharata? In his cow-protecting role, Ghazi Miyan is almost Krishnaite, but then in the Jaswa ballad, the birth of Krishna itself takes place due to the benediction of the Ghazi. Such connections or 'borrowings' are not uncommon. In the Pabuji ballad from Rajasthan, the hero is referred to as 'mounted Lakshman [Rama's brother], the ascetic deity of the sand desert'. His antagonist is painted in the scrolls that accompany the narration as Ravana, the villain of the Ramayana.[39] The folklorist Komal Kothari is categorical that resemblances notwithstanding, there neither is 'any direct transference of identities between the characters in the Ramayana and the Pabuji story', nor a 'thematic correspondence between the two texts. What is common is a 'general belief among communities like the Nayaks, the Bhils, and the Jogis, that the Pabuji story has mythic links with the epic of Rama'.[40]

One way out is not to let these great pan-Indian epics colonise all discussions of folk narratives with a final proof of resemblance, borrowing or concordance. A preoccupation with resonances with the Mahabharata, for instance, would denude all specific sagas, such as that of Ghazi Miyan or Pabuji, of their rich particularities, which accord them a texture of their own. Here Komal Kothari makes a helpful distinction between the 'historical warrior and kings' and the 'epic heroes' of Rajasthan. The great Rajasthani braves and royalty are 'commemorated in classical stories, myths, genealogies and hagiographies'. But hardly any are 'remembered through an oral epic, as Pabuji is today'. Kothari suggests that it makes better sense to see the historical figures as 'absentee heroes', as they 'are literally absent from folk memory and ritual'. The *real* hero, in his view, is 'present' in a dual sense: he lives in popular commemoration, and he is enshrined in the daily lives of ordinary people—ever-present 'to intervene in life's manifold problems through possible solutions and blessings'. It is 'not so much Pabuji's achievements in the epic that make him so memorable to this day, but this capacity to intervene in everyday life', concludes Kothari.[41]

An important insight, yet it leaves little room for studying the life of such 'present' heroes as specific reconfigurations of the popular mind. The difficult question of 'the fit' between narrative and cult, even when rephrased as a relationship between remembrance/commemoration and devotion/propitiation, would still resist an easy resolution. For, apart from the boon-granting, distress-obviating rites of Ghazi Miyan and their imbrication with familial concerns, the persistence of his ballads surely involves the giving of assent, at some level, to the intricately woven tales belonging to times past. This is not an idealised past, but a contentious, ambiguous and variedly crafted historical past: the time of Sultan Mahmud and the 'Turks of Garh Gajan.' There is a seventeenth-century hagiography which fills in this past with the exploits of Ghazi Masud and his chief adversary Raja Sohal Deo. Superheroes on the popular stage, both these personages are absent from the chronicles of those times. And then of course there is a clutch of ballads that spin an enticing web of stories about the warrior saint—Ghazi Miyan, Bale Miyan, Ghazi Dulha, or Pir Bahlim of popular lore. The persistence of the cult of Ghazi Miyan inheres in the ballads about his heroic quest for a war horse, the story of a putative brother bringing news of the natal home to housewives married into distant households, or his peculiar iconoclasm in the temple city of Banaras, which are still sung in his honour. It is to a few more of these tall tales and their continuing tellability that we now turn.

10

Grey Mare, Lilli

As with many other equestrian heroes Ghazi Miyan must wrest his horse from royalty, in this case, from his uncle Mahmud, the Sultan of Ghazni. Interred alongside the warrior saint at the Bahraich shrine, Ghazi Miyan's 'Lilli Mare' has come to share some of the attributes of the deified dead whose spirits were invoked by shamans for wish fulfilment. A convoluted mantra (recorded in 1930), prefatory to a woman asking for the boon of a son, refers midway to the Leela horse, astride which sits the Musalman warrior.[1]

In the valley of the Ganga and its tributary, the Ghaghra—the locale of Salar Masud's exploits—folklore has fashioned 'Lilli mare' in strikingly varied ways. Here, Lilli is the mare of every brother come home to help with a sister's wedding; and it is this mount that he saddles to fetch the sister back from her in-laws.[2] *Neela* (blue) or *Leela ghora* is also the horse astride which the groom arrives to take away the daughter, causing financial ruin to her natal household: while marrying her off, the mother ritually curses the daughter for having denuded the family so.[3] In Etawah, abutting the town of Kanpur, the restless warrior 'Kale Khan' lived in rustic imagination till a century ago, wandering on a bedecked 'Lila horse', for somewhere on the banks of the Ganga, Turkish scimitars and Indian swords had clashed in the medieval past.[4] The prize mare for which the young Ghazi Miyan would unsettle his uncle's ribcage in a cunning embrace, besting Sultan Mahmud at his own game of duplicity, was in local memory a gold-saddled stallion—Lila Ghora, *zeen sonehra*.

In the *Mirat*, Masud's unnamed favourite grey horse—an Iraqi mare—is a present from his uncle Sultan Mahmud. And it is this mare which the hero decks with a golden saddle, riding sans 'defensive armour' to his tragic martyrdom in June 1034.[5] The phrase *asp māda-i-khing*, the 'grey mare', used for Masud's horse in the *Mirat-i-Masudi*, is not unrelated to Nili (blue) or Lilli in its Bhojpuri inflection; *khing*, grey, or 'dark as night', is the common colour of the hero's horse in some of the major Turkish and Persian epics. The mounts of the heroes Koroghlu and Bamsi Beyrek are called 'Kyrat' and 'Bozat', Turkish equivalents of the *asp-i-khing* ('grey horse'). Other famous horses from the classic, *Shahnameh*, are Bizhan's horse 'Shabrang' (night-hued), and Khusraw Parwiz's 'Shabdiz' (midnight).[6] Nearer home, a twentieth-century verse romance suffused with folklore terms Masud's mare 'Neeli' (blue).[7]

Unlike the text of the *Mirat* where Sultan Mahmud bestows the choicest horses on his nephew, in popular lore the uncle is loath to let go of Lilli. And if boy Masud or his mother, the Sultan's sister, would as much as ask for the gift of that one mare, the King would not part with even a blue rag or a blue string! *Lilli ke nām leel dhāga nahin hai*, sang balladeer Zainuddin in May 1996, echoing the dialectal shift of *la* and *na* :Lilli > Leel > Neel = blue.[8]

A closer look at the ballads of Lilli mare sung around Banaras in the 1880s and extant today allows us to peel the layers of meaning that have come to adhere to the hero's war horse in popular lore. In a late-nineteenth-century version, Ghazi Miyan when twelve 'became … on a sudden enrapt in anxious musing', to quote a late nineteenth-century ethnographic notice. Mamula, with a mother's instinct, attributes this 'to passion for some woman or the malign influence of some demon': *Ki beta lāge deo- danu … ki tirya … ki sūrat dekh lobhāni*, worried, she inquires in the printed version of the ballad (1880s). The reason for the son going into a sulk is his obsession with Lilli. He will surely ride her:

> Amma! There is this beautiful mare Lilli in *mamu*'s place;
> Amma! I must, I surely must ride Lilli, whatever it takes;
> I shall be worthy of *mamu*'s name; Amma I tell you;
> Else Amma, I shall run away;
> Join I will a band of jogis and faqirs,
> I surely would Amma! I tell you.[9]

So sang Zainullah Dafail near Bahraich in 1996. In the versions recorded in the 1880s, mother Mamula is forced by her petulant son to undertake a journey to her brother in Ghazni. 'Ask me for land, I will give thee a province.' 'Ask me for a charger, I will give thee a whole stall ... Hollow-backed steeds of Cutch, steed dark as musk, fleet Arab, Turkish chargers', but not Lilli, or even a blue (*neela*, *neeli*) rag approximating that name, replies Sultan Mahmud harshly.[10] Sister Mamula withdraws in a huff, showering curses on her brother for not entertaining the one demand of the Bala child.

Sultan Mahmud's refusal seems a bit strange, as it is expected of uncles in north India to meet every wish of even fictive *bhānjas*.* In one such song, a clever calf wards off a ravenous lion by addressing him as 'uncle': '*Mama* you better devour me first and mother Surain [Sura] cow afterwards'. Now tied in the web of fictive kinship, the lion can only respond by offering an avuncular largesse to the clever 'nephew' out to save his mother: He grants his *bhanja* the run of the Kajli forest as pasture and access to Ganges water to quench his thirst. *Jāo bhanaija, ban tumheen ko deenho, bhor hot char jāwo; Charne ko kajli ban dai deenho; peene ko Ganga-jal pāni ri.*[11]

A real sister, Mamula's anger at her brother for denying Lilli to her son is understandable: she wishes the lion-hearted brother dead, his wife widowed. And this for not honouring a sister come a-begging on behalf of her son to his resourceful uncle.[12]

Mother Mamula returns home empty handed. A disconsolate Masud will not take no for an answer. Blind with childish rage, he dashes off into the jungle, a toy drum still dangling from his neck. Lost in the woods, he instinctively 'offers a prayer to heaven': a hidden treasure stands revealed. 'A few strokes on the drum soon collected all the urchins of the neighbourhood'. The young 'leader of men' gives each a gold *mohur* and asks them to obtain their parent's permission for a few days' absence.

A prayer is offered by the boy Masud, and the neighbourhood boys get transformed into regular riders. Further, each juvenile horseman is a spitting image of Ghazi Miyan: a disconcerting horde of identical nephews cantering towards *Sultan* Mahmud to wrest that special mare Lilli. This curious cavalry stops for the night at a tank where 'Mahmud's vaunted chargers were being watered'; the young

---

* *Mama/mamu*: mother's brother; *bhanja/bhaneja/bhanaija*: sister's son.

fellow heralds his arrival 'by stretching them lifeless'.[13] Ghazi Miyan, 'who had been absorbed in the Quran' the entire night, welcomes his uncle warmly at dawn '... crushing in 2 ½ of his ribs in the embrace'. Mahmud is furious at the temerity of the young nephew. 'Gently', replies Ghazi Miyan:

> Well I know that starting from your place, you blustered before your underlings saying 'this fellow is but a youngster. If I kiss his lips, I shall set the mother's milk suckling, and if I embrace his body I shall crush in two ribs or more.' Now that you know me better, peradventure you will yield me the mare Lilli.[14]

A firm 'Never' is the uncle's answer. Ghazi Miyan tries to reason; the Sultan is uninterested, and instead throws a challenge: 'If you have enough wit to find the mare Lilli, she is yours.' The nephew is more than a match. 'In an instant it is revealed to Ghazi Miyan' that due to her 'ungovernable viciousness', the mare was confined in 'an underground chamber barricaded by four gateways where water was poured down a tube and food lowered down a bamboo'.[15]

Invoking the name of Allah, Ghazi Miyan flings the four barricades open, and Lilli comes out whining demurely, her bridle firmly in the determined lad's hand. The miracle of the taming of vicious Lilli, hitherto kept chained, is applauded by all present. Masud grants her the power of speech; she implores the young hero to release her momentarily. With a scream of delight she gallops eight miles to the east and eight miles to the west, 'careering wildly through the gateway of Mahmud, who with his retainers, stampeded at her approach'. Satisfied by this outburst that her former owner has abandoned her, and she now stands absolved of allegiance to the Sultan, 'Lilli returned gentle and submissive to her new master'.[16] It is so that Ghazi Miyan acquires his prize mare, but without a saddle, the quest for which would take him (in another version) to the city of Banaras and to another round of adventure.

In ballads circulated today in the Bahraich region, Lilli continues to be of central importance, its story revolving round the claim of the married woman on her kin, of the *bhanja* on his *mamu*—uncle. In Zainullah Dafali's ballad, recited on the banks of the Chittaura lake near the Bahraich shrine in May 1996, the story of 'Lilli' begins on a somewhat contrived note, with sister Mamula's alienation from her brothers at her marriage. It then takes a detour, with a novel gloss on the modality of the young Ghazi's hunt/war in the Bahraich jungle. In this version, Mamula's father loved his daughter almost to distraction; unable to bear her loss in marriage to Salar Sahu, he died of a broken heart. Sultan Mahmud blamed sister Mamula for his father's death, and relations had been strained ever since. This would account partially for Sultan Mahmud's refusal to meet his young nephew's request for the mare Lilli. Having contrived to prepare the ground for the long-drawn alienation of Mamula from her natal home, Zainullah Dafali suddenly turns the narrative in the direction of the young Ghazi, hunting in the jungle of Bahraich.

Fig. 10.1 A toy replica of the grey mare, Lilli Ghori, in a clearing near Lake Anarkali, May 1996

Source: All figures are courtesy of the author unless mentioned otherwise

'Our Ghazi *dulha* was very fond of shikar, and would go hunting with his four associates', so declaims Zainulah Dafali. Mamula warned him not to stray northwards, for that way lay enemy jungle—Raja Sohal Deo's forest. But it was teeming with game. 'Let's ignore what mother says—let's go hunting there', the Miyan said to his associates. As Zainullah's narrative unfolds, it turns out that the Ghazi's hunting was not so, properly speaking. 'No taking of life by the Ghazi', declaimed the balladeer. 'He wouldn't kill the animals; just a quick clipping of nose and ears, and he would set them free'. Parallelisms abound, both with the Ghazi's doings in the idol-packed city of Banaras and with temple desecrations elsewhere. This minimal violence motif was not confined to a single Dafali's story about the Masud's hunting style. In a late nineteenth-century ballad, the warrior saint marks his iconoclastic presence in Banaras by similarly humiliating and subjugating the powerful idols of that holy city. As he approaches Banaras, idols scamper from their pedestals. Durga, the ferocious goddess, proffers gifts of fowl and sweets, craving all the while for the lowly position of a groom in Masud's stables! The tender-hearted Ghazi spares Durga her life, but clips the idol's nose to mark her subjection.[17]

The chiselling of the noses of human figures by the Turks in the early thirteenth century in temple-turned-mosque Quwat-ul Islam in Delhi seems to be yet another act of culturally specific iconoclasm that makes these 'deities' literally lose face in the local milieu.[18] It is equally common for a father humiliated (and unable to face society) because of the wayward actions of a son or a daughter to say, 'You have had my nose cut'! Among all the body parts, it is the nose that is the bodily projection of status. To actually clip someone's nose is therefore a sure sign of having extracted revenge—as when the Bhil tribals led an assault on the olfactory organs of mean-spirited moneylenders in colonial western India, or the cutting of noses of village revenue officials in Bara Banki district, Uttar Pradesh in the early 1950s for making fraudulent changes in land registers after the enactment of a major land reform legislation.[19]

In Zainul Dafali's ballad, the young Ghazi treads nimbly in the Bahraich jungle, hunting game by the cultural rules that gird the sense of human worth and loss of face: 'He wouldn't kill [animals], just a sharp and quick clipping of nose and ears and then he would set them free'. 'And there was my Ghazi Groom', says another Dafali, establishing a personal connection with the medieval hero. 'My Ghazi Groom was very fond of shikar ... By the Anarkali lake he was, sitting atop his platform, which doubled as his fishing perch'. Adept angler that he was, the Ghazi would put the fish he caught back into the lake.[20] Was this an outlandish practice, thought up by a present-day apologist to lessen metaphorically the violence of the Ghazi's shikar/war in his own times? It does not appear to be so, for in an ethnographic account of a village in the same ecological zone, fishing in living memory was prohibited in certain ponds, and so following the religious injunction, anglers would set the fish caught free after attaching a nose-ring (of brass, even gold) as a mark of their bloodless sport![21] Zainullah Dafali then goes over some of the elements of the ballads recorded over a hundred years ago—the refusal of the uncle to part with Lilli—but introduces crucially a novel gloss on Ghazi Miyan's iconoclasm—the clipping of the nose of the ferocious goddess Durga in the idol-packed city of Banaras—making it both anodyne and semiotically significant.

The Lilli mare stories recorded by late nineteenth-century folklorists and collected during fieldwork a hundred years later, afford an entry point for grasping some of the elements that have gone into the crafting of the Ghazi Miyan cult. The name 'Lilli ghori' that permeates popular culture is a dialectal inflection of 'Neeli' or blue (mare). And this blue, or 'dark as night' mount was written up as *asp māda-i-khing*, the grey mare, by Abdur Rahman Chishti in his seventeenth-century Life of Masud. The wide currency that 'Lilli' still enjoys in songs and ballads, could lead one to suggest that our medieval author may have copied this name, affixed already to the horse of the Ghazi hero. Conversely, given the wide prevalence of the motif of 'the dark horse' in Turkish and Persian epics, it could equally be that the Sufi savant had borrowed from the Persian classic *Shahnameh* while thinking up a name for Salar Masud's mare, and that 'Lilli' is a Bhojpuri inflection of 'grey' or dark blue, 'neeli'. But would that not imply that Neeli/Lilli had no provenance in Gangetic popular culture independent of the writing of the Persian *Mirat-i-Masudi*? If so, that would accord this arcane seventeenth-century text the power of impacting popular culture in myriad ways. But it would be hasty to be so conclusive. And for the good reason that the *Mirat* was itself marked by an engagement with folk accounts of Salar Masud.[22] It is difficult—and perhaps fruitless—to adjudicate between these two possibilities.

11

Cooking for a Turkic Brother

Could it be that Masud's need to wrest his prize mount from the king has led to the Sultan's inexplicable meanness towards his sister and her son in popular lore? In the normal case, the relationship between siblings *should* have been of one of longing and affection, for post-marriage, such bonds tend to get stronger, as the sister, now living in another's home, eagerly awaits the occasional visit from her brother.

In eastern UP, notes a folklorist, 'nobody is required to visit a girl in her husband's house to the extent that a brother is'. And so 'the arrival of a brother is always the most exciting event in … [her] life', such that folksongs picture the eager sibling seeking her mother-in-law's permission 'to run and meet him on the boundary of the village'. Often referred in songs as *Bir* or a hero, a brother 'is a beloved visitor who brings presents and news of their parents'.[1] Such visits are all the more precious for being few and far between.[2]

Framed as an invitation to such a brother, a women's work song, sung late at night by poor women operating the heavy corn grinders in the backyard of landed homes, speaks for the hard work that is the common lot of all married women. The song begins with the forlorn sister beseeching her brother to come and see just once how she is getting along. The sibling proffers formulaic excuses: the way to your home, sister, he says, is prowling with wild animals; surely you can come with a sword and shield is the uppity reply.[3] And when the married woman sees two men coming towards her house, she immediately recognises the brother as 'my mother's fair-skinned son', and her husband as the dark-skinned brother of her husband's sister! Lonely in her (husband's) home, she has eyes only for the agnatic kin.[4]

'How may I feast my brother?', she asks her mother-in-law dutifully. 'Cook some rotten millet rotis, and for vegetables the shrivelled potherbs by the kerb'. 'In a broken earthen pot give him drinking water from the nearby puddle.' As for pān, the customary welcoming betel leaf, 'a peepal leaf laced with bird droppings should do', is the cruel reply. The woman boldly curses her mother-in-law, for come what may, she is going to prepare a royal feast for her brother And as she bends to pour ghee on to the 'golden plate' of fine rice, *pooris* and choicest potherbs, she sees tears rolling down the brother's cheeks, for he has noticed how pale her visage has become. Ignoring her husband who eats alongside, the sister now complains to the brother about the hard work she endures in this house. 'And don't pass on my woes to our parents, our sisters, even your wife', she pleads. 'Get hold of the Brahmin who solemnised the marriage, and the match-maker, and ask them … Better still, don't say anything to any one; just bundle all my woes into a *gathri* and open it whenever you feel like lamenting my fate'![5]

Of course, Ghazi Miyan is not a real brother to Amina Sati, who is married to a Hindu raja: he is a 'Turuk' warrior-hunter come into the jungle for shikar. At the Ghazi Miyan Fair in May 1996, a Dafali from Banaras began his 'Lay of Amina' with the fast-paced opening lines about a thirsty Salar Masud hunting in the famous kadli forest.[6] The hunt motif, which is central to the Ghazi's campaign in the *Mirat*, is here merely a catalyst pushing the story of Hindu sister and Muslim brother further. It is not shikar, but the Ghazi 'athirst while hunting' that brings Masud to Amina's door, for no one will so much as offer water to the 'impure' Muslim. In the 1996 Banaras version, both common wayfarers and the drawers of water cry out at this exemplary meanness.[7]

In a longer late nineteenth-century version, Ghazi Miyan goes to Banaspati Mai, the Goddess of the Forest, for a drink of water. Banaspati Ma declines: there is no *lota-pota* and no rope with me 'my dear Miyan', she tells him, the familiar address mitigating somewhat the act of crass refusal to draw water for a thirsty Musalman hunter. The jungle goddess is not entirely unhelpful though; she redirects Masud to Amina's: 'a lofty palace with a lowly wicket; there sits Amina before her door.' Ma Banaspati's directions are vague, so Palihar, the demon captured from Lanka by the Ghazi, raises himself to his full height and locates beyond the horizon a morose Amina sitting at her door—scouring the high road for signs of the familiar brotherly figure.

> Stuffy her town,
> lonely her *des*,
> No messenger, no missive
> to relieve the tedium
> At the in-law's place.[8]

Even though a Musalman, Ghazi Miyan (plural, Panchon Pir, in those variants where the Ghazi shows up with his companions) is from Amina's natal home, and addresses her instinctively as 'sister'. This is one word Amina has been thirsting for: she rushes out, for though 'Turuks', she recognises them as 'brothers' from her village—her momentary hesitation overtaken by joy at seeing a 'brother' come to see her. 'Tell me how goes it in my place.' 'All are fine back home ... we are day and night at your house', reply the Panchon Pirs,* strengthening the bonds of putative kinship.[9] And they joke: 'We can't be sitting here forever waiting for a drink of water, you know; come early morning and we are off for shikar!'

Amina, the married sister, has decided already to transgress the boundaries of 'us' and 'them.' She won't just offer her 'Turuka' (Muslim) brothers water; she is going to cook them a regular feast, and with the etiquette requisite for laying the table well. She brings out a special cot for them to sit under the sandalwood tree, she rushes to take the regulation bath preparatory to entering the kitchen ... But there still remains one boundary between Hindu 'us' and Muslim 'them', which has been breached only very recently, and only in the towns. Amina is aware of the requirement to serve the 'Turukas' not in plates from her husband's scullery, but in disposable leaf plates, freshly ordered from the platter-maker, the town *bāri.*** Commensality across religious boundaries is taboo in this kingdom as well. In the Remembered Account, c. 1940s of his east-UP village, a Hindi scholar recalls that when his grandfather invited his Muslim friends home on festive

---

* Here Ghazi Miyan is called Panchon Pir, the five saints of north India which usually include the Ghazi and four other associates. A follower of the Ghazi is called *Pachpiriya* or a believer in the Saintly Five.

** A bāri makes *pattals*, dishes made of leaves, for Hindu households on occasions of feasting.

occasions, all the eating utensils had to be borrowed from Muslim neighbours. In this representative village, Muslims reciprocated within the boundedness of Hindu commensality, feasting them by sending flour, sweets and uncooked portions of the sacrificial lamb on the occasion of the festivals of Eid-ul-Fitr and Eid-ul-Zuha.[10]

And so Amina goes to the bazaar, and asks for disposable leaf platters. The town bāri makes an excuse, suggesting mischievously that she serve her guests in golden dishes, presumably from the raja's pantry. Gilded plates descend from the heavens; Amina will get blamed, though, for feasting Turkas in 'the raja's dishes'.[11] Amina cooks for the Panchon Pir who had come merely asking for water. 'Wash your face and feet and sit down to lunch', she tells them: *utho bhaiyya charan pakhāro, rasoi leu tum khāi*. Ghazi Miyan warns her: 'Don't feast us, for ill fortune will befall you because of this meal'—served to us Turkas, he leaves unsaid. Amina is philosophical about the outcome.[12] After the feast, Ghazi Miyan wishes to grant her a boon. Retorts Amina, 'My dearest desire was fulfilled when my two children Amat and Nimat were granted me. However, I ask you come to my rescue in the hour of my need'.[13] A little banter follows, with the Ghazi quipping that such an open ended promise binds him 'for all time and all places. Nevertheless for my oath's sake, I must consent'.[14]

Meanwhile, a neighbour—a fork-tongued widow—has been straining her eyes and ears to figure out what exactly Amina is doing with these 'Turkas'. She now accosts Amina, threatening to spill the beans. Amina's mother-in-law returns from her bath: in one version she is such a devout Hindu that 'she bathed hundred times daily in the Ganges.' 'What is it with you people that the plate that the raja eats in gets polluted by Turkas in your absence', the neighbour taunts the old lady.[15]

Raja Lorchand comes home and asks for his supper. His mother refuses 'to assist in preparing the repast of which Amina had defiled the dishes by banqueting outcast Musalmans'. The son tries to reason: 'What if they are defiled? I'll order another set from the potters'—a reference to earthen pots used specially in the cooking of *dāl* (lentils) that will figure at an important juncture of the story. The mother rebukes her son for being henpecked, and demands that Amina be thrown out; otherwise she will starve to death and come back to haunt her married son all his life. The Raja now entreats his wife, 'Let the old woman have her way. Anything for peace and quiet. Leave the house for a day or two. Stay with a friend and then return'.

Amina is furious: 'I'll go, never to return'. She snatches her two sons, and flinging out the garments and jewellery given to her by her in-laws, she storms out; the raja's mother laughs in triumph at her head-strong daughter-in-law turned out of the house with only a single sari in her possession.[16] In the longer ballad, the king turns Amina out, without bothering to hear her side of the story. Her sons in tow, and parched mustard seeds in the fold of her sari, Amina walks out proud and angry. With every step that she takes, greater and still greater misfortune befalls the raja. Amina goes out into wilderness; her children get hungry; she sprinkles the parched mustard seeds, invoking the name of Ghazi Miyan, and a fresh plant comes into existence—a miracle, for parched seeds cannot sprout, and mustard potherbs are not nourishment enough in themselves. Her two boys eat their fill. She prays for water; a stream jets out from Garh Gajan—Ghazni or the abode of Ghazis.

While the two sons are sitting content by her Sita-like mother, whom Raja Rama of the Ramayana had similarly turned out of the house by giving ear to gossip about her impugned chastity,[17] Lorchand, the king in this story, returns home where his triumphant mother now reigns supreme. When the mother tries to cook for the son, a reverse of the miraculous happenings of the wilderness takes place. Having discarded Amina as an unclean *pātr* (a word which can mean both 'utensil' and 'character')—the mother-in-law is unable to cook for the son: whichever pot she holds becomes empty; whichever way she looks in the kitchen, the foodstuff burns to ashes: *Jaune bartan mein hāth dālen sab bartan chūnch ho jāe ... jaune or tāken bhasm-sur dekhāe*'.[18]

Stripped of all majesty, the raja manages somehow to procure a lame mare, and ride in search of Amina. Traversing one jungle after another, he finds his wife and two sons in the third jungle. Lorchand asks Amina to come back; Amina refuses, suggesting instead that he go meet Ganga, her sister. Raja Lorchand (Nurchand in other versions) goes to the sacred river, and requests her to flow westwards just once: 'for on your bank sits Amina; were you to change course she will come home to me'. The holy Ganges puts it starkly: 'Look, Raja!' she tells him, 'There is an earthen pot lying on the dung heap; go and cook your meals in that soiled pot, and I'll oblige you by changing direction' (*Dekho Raja Nurchand ghūre par handiya pari bāe; wuhi handiya mein jewan karo to hum pacchum bah jāe*).[19] 'Despite your sense of right and wrong, she is a clean *pātra* [utensil/character]. Accept your wife Amina for what she is [has become: a sister/devotee of Ghazi Miyan!] irrespective of your notions of purity/pollution'—this is what Ganga seems to be telling the Raja. In the prose version, the river says it in as many words: 'Go … Amina is that [earthen] vessel. Heedlessly didst thou cast her from thee. Yet by that act was she dishonoured, and may never return.'[20]

Taking back Amina who has gone into the fold of the Muslim Ghazi Miyan is like picking up a soiled pot and cooking in it! Concerned with conversion-as-pollution, the story is couched in terms of eating and cooking vessels. The ballad takes care to specify that the plates had not been soiled by the Turkas eating from them. Aware of the requisite norms, Amina had first gone looking for leaf platters (400 of them!), and when the lowly bari had refused to supply them, golden dishes (with Ghazi Miyan's blessings) had descended from heaven itself. The Panchon Pir had not quite eaten in the Raja's vessels after all. But that mattered little: the act of cooking for Turkas had made that one dish, the earthen dish, which unlike metal pots can not be scoured clean, impure. For, as late as the early 1950s, traditional cooking in eastern UP was done in an earthen vessel (*patuki*) in which lentils, specially the regional favourite *arhar dāl*, was cooked.

Meanwhile at the river front, the Raja understandably declines to eat out of the dung-heap dish—'Mother Ganga this I can't do, for I would lose my *nem-dharam*, my religion, my entire being', he replies.[21] The die has been cast; a major threshold crossed for good. Ganga tells the Raja to forget Amina, and return home sans wife. Lorchand flares up in anger. He tries to take Amina home forcefully; she in turn appeals to Mother Earth to open up, so that she may be saved from the clutches of her husband! Amina sinks peacefully into the earth; her two sons Amat and Nimat turn into mango and neem trees—their nonsensical sounding names now amenable to easy diminution into *am* (mango) and *neem* (*Azadirachta indica*), a medicinal tree of the mahogany family. Unsuccessful in taking his wife back home on his own terms, the king fades from the narrative.

Amina now cries out to the Ghazi in the familiar register of a woman devotee addressing a male lord: *Jahān piya ho tuhār, wahān mangta hamār*. 'Wheresoever thou art worshipped, there let me be honoured', translates an English collector valiantly, unable to quite capture the attachment of a woman for a male overlord—called *piya* or darling, even as with Amina, this attraction is empty of sexual desire. For, not only is Ghazi Miyan her fictive brother from her natal home, Amina, the mother of two, is empty of all sexual desire. She is Amina Sati, Amina, the virtuous!

Lacking the sibling focus, the shorter version brings Amina and the Ghazi into a similar relationship towards the very end of the story. Here, the Miyan, on hearing of Amina's distress— the raja pulling her out of the earth by her tresses—hurries to her rescue. The Ghazi tries to persuade Amina to return to her lord and master 'so earnestly that he addressed her by the title sister'. 'Am I your sister?' cries Amina, 'then though thou art Turk and I a Brahman, verily *for my children's sake*, will I claim the privilege of dwelling with [my] brother.' The story ends thus: thenceforth they resided at Garh Ganjan 'as brother and sister in the spirit (*dīni bhāi bahin*) until the "great martyrdom".'[22]

In a third version, hearing of her plight, the Panchon Pir ride hard on their horses, and carry Amina on a litter (taking care to quite literally pluck out her two sons Amat and Nimat, fast turning into trees). They take Amina to Bahraich, and there raise a shrine to her—which is located in the inner courtyard of the dargah. 'And to this day', ends this late nineteenth-century 'Lay of Amina', the Miyan is offered goats and roosters at the shrine of Ghazi Miyan and to Amina's grave the devotees present a shred of cloth—in commemoration, one suspects, of the one piece of unstitched cloth with which she was banished from her marital home for feasting brother Ghazi Miyan. When propitiated at home, Amina Sati is offered a *patua*: the sari that poor women put on when the other remaining dhoti has gone to the dhobi for washing![23]

At the Ghazi Miyan Fair in May 1996, I heard three more versions of the Amina story. One balladeer opened with the common trope of Ghazi Miyan getting thirsty in the forest, and trailed off with Amina turning her back on her in-laws with the refrain *ab na jaibe oie ghare, na jaibe oie ghare, na jaibe sasure*—'I shan't return to my husband's place, my in-laws' house, no I shan't, no I shan't'.[24] The version by another Dafali is as interesting as it has contemporary resonance: Ghazi Miyan had chased the enemy till Dikauli—twelve miles northeast of Bahraich—where the purported graves of Amina and her two sons are still pointed out.[25] Amina was a Brahman's wife.

She was with Ghazi Miyan; people levelled an *abjes*, 'objection' in the Awadhi dialect (!), at which the Ghazi inducted her as 'his sister-in-faith'. She was *Sati-satvanti*, pure and virtuous.

In the version sung by Bashir Dafali of Faizabad—one of my chief informants—the storyline is as simple as the welcoming gestures are elaborate. A Brahman's daughter, Sati Amina is married to Lorchand. She lives in the house of her in-laws. Here, a sandalwood tree, the evergreen *Santalum Album*, has dried up. Amina asks her family priest whether the tree will be green again. She is told that its regeneration awaits the Ghazi's arrival. Both Sati Amina and, so to speak, tree bide their time. Her mother-in-law is away bathing in the Ganga when Masud Ghazi suddenly appears. The dried up sandalwood sprouts leaves. *Sati Amina ka Imān durust ho jāta hai*, interjects Bashir, referring obliquely to the 'rightening' of her faith—suggestive of her becoming a devotee of the Ghazi, if not a convert to Islam. Amina welcomes the Panchon Pir by washing their feet and sprinkling the water purified by the touch of the Ghazi's feet onto the inner courtyard—the prescribed gesture meant to welcome Brahman or other superior beings, both familial and social, visiting one's house after a long trudge on dusty roads; in its more 'developed' form, such a ritual act involves ingesting, even if symbolically, the water so sanctified (*charnāmrit*: the nectar or *amrit* of the feet). The entire courtyard and not just that one sandalwood tree becomes verdant.[26] Amina then serves the Panchon Pir a sumptuous meal. The Ghazi warns her that she will be turned out for feasting him so. But she is not to worry, for come misfortune and he shall come to her aid.[27] And when banished by her husband, Amina wanders around and meets the Ghazi in the forest, famous for Krishna's exploits—he tries to console her: 'Why didn't you listen, when I told you so': *Ghazi Miyan samjhāven, Amina manyu kāhe na!* Though focused on the sandalwood tree, this ballad has the cooking metaphor as its capstone. For, when Ghazi Miyan gives his word to Amina about her impending canonisation—worshippers will first approach her before repairing to him for boons—the creator of this ballad throws in a line about Amina receiving cooking vessels from Ghazi Miyan. So ends Bashir's ballad, with the devotee/convert Amina doing her cooking in vessels provided by the Ghazi himself!

The Amina Sati story in its different versions is about the transgression of religious boundaries by a married woman overdoing the reception for a 'brother' come from home. Even as a putative sibling from one's natal village, a Turuk/Turka (a Muslim) remains necessarily an outsider in a Hindu household. The fiction—or the fact—of a shared village, where strict boundaries of commensality would be enforced, cannot override the religious demarcation of Hindu and Muslim, especially as these pertain to intermarriage and inter-dining. Come what may, a Muslim *can never* be a brother to a Hindu woman. This is the normal ethical position against which the story plays out. And the narrative drive for this is the act of cooking for a Turkic brother—a transgressive term in itself.

But the initial act of naming the heroine Amina Sati forcibly jostles Hindu and Muslim identities into familial relations, such that the banishment of the 'sister' (of a Muslim) as a Hindu wife is foredoomed, even before the ploy of cooking across religious thresholds comes into play. 'Amina' is a name with a connotation that can be grasped only from a specific Muslim religious threshold, for Amina is the Prophet's mother. And 'Sati', the woman of utmost purity, expresses a sublime connotation that can similarly be appreciated only from the standpoint of Hindu religiosity. Feeding the hungry, clothing the naked, putting the wayfarer on the high road—it is such deeds that characterise Amina's 'sati-ness' in the ballad.[28] And yet, someone's 'becoming' Amina Sati amounts virtually to traversing that forbidden space between two religious spheres.

The Amina Sati story, as a part of the Ghazi Miyan cycle, consists of the ethical adaptation of 'cooking for a Turkic brother' as an earnest call for the blurring of inter-community boundaries, both in the everyday and in times past.[29] Or could it be that my own sensibilities are here running ahead of the storyline—that something has been lost in an historian's attempt to engage with a softly historicised past, wherein the standard 'facts of history' get juxtaposed in unsettling ways? Could it be that in her natal home only Amina's brother had affirmed the Islamic credo—a tantalising possibility about individual members of a family crossing over, without the head of the house or the clan leaving the parental fold? The English officer to whom we owe the late nineteenth-century version was quite sure about this 'pathetic story [sic!] as an 'illustra[tion] … of the division of families in consequence of conversion'. [30]

Let us dilate a bit on the 'cooking for an outsider' trope in Amina's banishment. Clearly, with Amina there is no desire. Hers is not the case of divine love, or the yearning for a male child. Amina has two sons, Amat and Nimat. Her life is complete. She simply responds in an appropriate way by recognising Ghazi Miyan for who he is: a 'brother' from home. And she does this knowing that he is Turuka. When the Ghazi tries to persuade her to return to her husband 'so earnestly that he addressed her by the title sister', she cries out, 'Am I your sister? Then though thou art Turk and I a Brahman, verily *for my children's sake*, will I claim the privilege of dwelling with her brother.' With that one act Amina defiles not just the cooking space, she also unsettles, so to speak, the idols from their pedestals in the Raja's *puja* room—the equivalent of a family chapel.

12

Idols

The theme of destruction of temples and idols by Muslim kings and warriors, so central to medieval chronicles, is touched upon but obliquely in both text and Ghazi lore. Curiously, for a hagiography of a Turkic Ghazi, the *Mirat-i-Masudi* has very little on assaults on temples and much more on its hero's engagements with disingenuous Hindu rajas of Hindustan. Even when the *Mirat* celebrates uncle Mahmud's attack on the temple of Somnath, Masud plays practically no part in the actual destruction of that famous idol.[1] The ballads of Banaras dealing with that idol-city are couched in terms of a surreal poetics of violence. The intended effect is to cast the young Ghazi Miyan as a somewhat brazen figure, as he works his ire on the idols and godlings of one of the holiest temple towns of India. Seemingly unconnected with doctrinaire animus, desecration, iconoclasm and conversion all operate here in the realm of the wondrous. In such portrayal, there is no effort at exculpation or the lessening of the sense of hurt for the Hindu followers of the Ghazi. For the balladeers, desecration appears to be playful as it is monstrous, natural as it is gratuitous. In any event, the Ghazi's eventful brush with the 'bloody idols' of that city hangs as a pendant to the familiar story of his quest for the grey mare Lilli.

We are at that point in the Lilli Mare story where Ghazi Miyan has just won and mastered, sans saddle, the vicious mare from uncle Sultan's subterranean stables. To quote from the late-Victorian prose version of R. Greeven:

> Then Sultan Mahmud bethought him, how he could banish his nephew for ever by a device. "Who shall saddle the untamed Lilli", he

> uttered, "save only Karwan, the leather-seller?" "Where dwells he?" demanded Ghazi Miyan, little dreaming that Karwan was a cobbler of Ghazni. "Hast thou the heart", inquired the Sultan doubtfully, well knowing that his question goaded the hearer like a whip-cut. "Hast thou the heart to seek him"? "If earth holds him, I'll find him, Name his home." "Then seek him in Benares", chuckled the Sultan, gleefully conjuring up a vision of his nephew weltering in his heart-blood, under the knives of the Brahman priesthood, on the altar of the monstrous image of Sobhnath.[2]

In the contemporary version of Zainullah Dafali, the condition put forward by the Sultan uncle for parting with the mare is for the young Masud to recover outstanding dues from the recalcitrant (Hindu) ruler of Banaras. On the outskirts of that city, Masud meets an old Muslim woman who had lost six of her sons at the sacrificial altar of the idol Shobnath of that city. She forewarns Masud. Regardless, the young Ghazi makes straight for the temple: he finds a kettledrum, kept for heralding the time of puja. With one massive strike he cleaves the instrument that percussioned the daily human sacrifice at the temple of Shobhnath. An axe was kept beside it for splitting the logs into wooden platters. With that very axe, the young Ghazi strikes the idols dead; Hathile the Adamant follows wielding his heavy trident.

In the Banaras ballads collected in the late nineteenth-century, it is the prospect of being dismembered that makes the chief idol plead for some human kindness: 'Please don't beat me; forsaking my idolatrous self, I shall become a follower of Islam'.

> *Jin tu mārab* [*māra*], *Miyan lāt.*
> *Ham āpan puja chorab pāt*[*h*];
> *Ab ham chalte tuhre sāth,*
> *kahte kalima, lete nām Khuda*![3]

With folded hands the chief idol Shobhnath renounces his own worship to join the Ghazi as a Musalman! 'It is the King who implicates me unjustly, blood-letting all this while in my name', adds the idol metamorphosed. And so, the idol Shobhnath is converted dramatically in full court. A *badhna*, the ablutionary earthen vessel with a spout—quotidian marker of Muslimness in India—is ordered. (In fourteenth-century Bengal, peasants used to hang a *badhna* from their roof tops as a marker of having converted to Islam.) Ghazi

Miyan makes the ogre-idol a believer by making him affirm the Islamic credo, not once but five times. The imbibing of milk (here Islam) continues, a regulated jet streaming down the curved spout of the *badhna*, mimicking the way most Indian Muslims ritually ablute themselves preparatory to prayers. The idol adds the reflexive 'Praise be to Allah'—to mark the sanctity of the occasion.[4] In passages marked by violence and stereotypical reversals, the high priests run for dear life and godlings tear themselves from their rude platforms and makeshift straw huts. The triumph of iconoclasm and the verbal assault on Hindu sensibilities continues, with Saiyid Birahna, Masud's lieutenant, smashing their dwellings with his hammer and chain. And so, Mahabir leapt across the Ganga, while the other idols drowned in that river or scrambled into the woods. Bisheshar, the patron deity of Banaras nose-dived into a well, Bhagwan ran for dear life, leaving his trusted loin cloth behind, and in a demeaning reversal, Mahadeo, or Shiva, invoking his own war cry of 'Har-Har Mahadeo', ran for cover! The ferocious Durga turned herself into a devotee of the Ghazi, lining up with the requisite offering of cockerel and *sinni*—sweets: 'spare me my Gaji, from now on I'll live by stall-feeding your horses', she pleads. As a demeaning act, 'the manly Ghazi' lets her off after slashing the idol's nose.[5]

In a prose version collected near Banaras, the heavens thunder, the earth shakes as the Ghazi riding bareback reins in Lilli Mare inside the temple precinct. Shobhnath, the head idol, receives two whip cuts and begins complaining about the king who sacrifices Musalmans in his name. Now a slave of Ghazi Miyan, he awaits the new master's command.[6] Aware that his patron idols had failed him, Raja Banar, the ruler of Banaras, now leans on his astrologers. As they gaze expertly at the heavens, it is not so much to divine the military outcome as to reduce this towering Ghazi 'protected by Khuda' to the base essentials of the lascivious Turk. The astrologers suggest that if offered sufficient temptation, Masud, sheathing his scimitar, would be likely to turn, mid-battle, in hot pursuit of comely virgins. In the Banaras ballad, this pornographic display—'the virgins of the city, flinging off their apparel, wander[ing] in a dreamy and sensuous procession over the ramparts of the fortress'—appears as a shameless raja's last stand to stave off defeat by offering his harem to the powerful conqueror. This base ruse elicits a most dramatic response from the virtuous Ghazi Miyan/the Panchon Pir.[7] To quote from the Ballad of Banaras:

Kāfir beghairat sabhon ne aurat apni pahunchāya;
Behaya khare kihin aurat ke, nange mādarzād tahlāya!
Pānchon Pir pahile to uth kar namāj parhāya,
Jab aurat par pari najar, sir kātke āpan jeb mein dhaya.[8]

In plain prose: The Ghazi's response to this shameless offering of nubile women is to first make himself ritually pure by offering supererogatory prayers. Raising his eyes from the prayer mat, he severs his head, pocketing it till this particular battle is over and the Banaras kingdom done with. Headless, the Ghazi and companions now engage the Raja's forces. Invoking the trusted *Sura-i-Fatiha* from the Quran, Ghazi Miyan kills the seven kings (the Raja and six princes), upturning the Banaras Rajghat fort with one finger. And only then does he affix his head to his shoulders![9] The very first Turkish horseman to ride into Banaras, Ghazi Miyan is here viewed from the historic-literary lens of a later period that yielded the image of the rapacious Muslim foreigners who appropriated '[Hindu] *dharma*, women and wealth, all three'.[10] Chronologically ahead of his times, the eleventh-century Ghazi Miyan is unlike all Miyans (Musalmans) that are yet to invest and inhabit Hindustan!

The Banaras episode, linked variously to the quest for Lilli Mare by the Dafalis, is crucially about smashing the idols of that most holy of Hindu cities. In Banaras, opined an English officer-folklorist, Ghazi Miyan 'has become associated with a local tradition ... [which] is a conscious reproduction of the iconoclasm of the seventeenth-century Mughal emperor Aurangzeb, over the living effects of which every Magistrate of Benares has expended a stock of impatient language.' Ethnographer Greeven selected the statement: 'Bisheshar leapt into a well' from the ballad as an 'obvious allusion to the submerged figure of Vishwanath, popularly supposed to have flung himself into a tank, no doubt with the assistance of its priests, in order to escape desecration at the hands of the approaching Aurangzeb', who sought out the temples of Banaras.[11] People in the Muslim quarters of Banaras may have refrained from reciting or paraphrasing these ballads to visiting scholars in the mid-1990s,[12] and others have surely found it demeaning, but Bashir Dafali was quite forthright about the appreciation his 'Banaras ballad' receives at the annual Bahraich concourse: 'When I sing it with my full party ... at the mela, then currency notes start raining', he boasted at the Fair in May 1996.[13]

What the Banaras stories, collected from the mouths of 'Pachpiriya Ballad-mongers' in the 1880s and 1890s, and sung to this day by Zainullah and Bashir Dafali, underscore is the power that seems to inhere in the common markers of Muslimness in India.[14] It is not that the balladeers elide the Ghazi's force of arms, for it is 'the sight of the unsheathed sword', as Bashir Dafali puts it, that makes 'the goat-devouring Goddess Durga run for dear life.'[15] But equally, it is the humble *badhna*, the spouted earthen pot used by Muslims for daily ablutions, that plays a stellar role in the spectacular conversion of the bloodthirsty idol Shobhnath. Blood and gore and the transference of Aurangzeb's iconoclasm to Ghazi Miyan aside, in the sacred geography of Salar Masud, Banaras yields to Bahraich where Ghazi Miyan achieved his martyrdom.

In the early 1890s 'an annual pilgrimage … depart[ed] from Adampura [a quarter of Banaras] in time to visit Bahraich on [the date of] Jeth Sudi 6th, in order to commemorate the hero's marriage with offerings of miniature bedsteads … and [*peerha*—stools]… supposed to represent the wedding presents'.[16] In fact, a hundred years later, an advance party would leave the city a week before, repairing to the local 'grave of Ghazi Miyan' in time to kickstart the week-long festivities marking the 'marriage of the Ghazi' in the holy Hindu city of Banaras itself. Roosters and cockerels would be offered to the warrior saint, the cenotaph in Bari Bazar given a ritual ablution, and the sanctified water ingested or applied to the eyes by devotees who, forsaking a regular midday meal, would make do with an uncooked fare of gur and *sattu* (dough of ground parched gram). The novelist Abdul Bismillah, to whose evocative Life, c. 1980, of the *menu peuple* (especially weavers) of Banaras we owe this portrayal, adds a sardonic caveat: *aur unka pratap dekhiye, yahan ek mohalle ka nām hi par gaya hai—Ghazi Miyan*! When translated, this approximates to 'And behold his grace and glory, for there is even a quarter in the city simply called Ghazi Miyan!'[17] Indicative of the integration of the cult of Ghazi Miyan in the lives of the Banarasi lower orders, much like the itinerant bazaars of the Indian countryside, the fair of Ghazi Miyan moved from one mohalla (quarter) of the town to another for the full duration of a week—Kazi Sadullapura on Saturday till Monday morning, Nakkighat (Monday evening), then on to Kacchi

Bagh on Tuesday, Chittanpura the next day, Beniabagh on Thursday and ending with mohalla Purana Pul on Friday.[18]

For its part, at the main fair at Bahraich in the summer of 1996, the 'Banaras marriage party' led by Ganesh and Tulsi Sardar, consisting for a large part of Hindu devotees, was one of the most boisterous of the two dozen that converged at the tomb of the Ghazi that night (Sunday, 19 May) to get 'their Gaji groom' married.[19] Ghazi Miyan's excesses, as retold in ballads, did not seem to have lessened the enthusiasm of at least this party of present-day Banaras devotees.

PART THREE SHRINE

13

Altars

There were two facets to the devotees' exertions on behalf of Ghazi Miyan: pilgrimage to Bahraich or to a surrogate fair nearer home, and the worship of the Ghazi at domestic altars. The common appellation of Salar Masud's devotees was *Panchpiriya*, that is, the followers of the quintet consisting of Ghazi Miyan and his four associates. 'Panchpiriya' was the country demotic for Panj Pir, the 'five saints' of Islam, especially Shia Islam: the Prophet; Fatima, his daughter; Ali, her husband; and their sons, Hasan and Husain, whose tragic death at the battle of Karbala is mourned widely across the Hindu-Muslim divide.

Late nineteenth-century accounts of north Indian religious life present a bewildering variety of 'Panch Pirs' or five personages worthy of devotion and propitiation. In western Punjab, the quintet frequently consisted of the pedigreed Indian saints of Multan, Ucch, Pakpattan, Ajmer and Delhi. In eastern Punjab and the Gangetic corridor, the Panchpiriya was a demotic concatenation, led invariably by Ghazi Miyan, yet malleable enough to accommodate more generally the myriad 'deified worthies propitiated by the lowest classes'.[1] The 1.7 million individuals who were recorded at the 1891 Census as belonging to the Panchpiriya sect—almost entirely in the Gorakhpur and Banaras divisions of eastern UP—did not have a uniform set of Five Worthies. That year's census reported Ghazi Miyan, Buhana Pir, Palihar, Amina Sati and Hathile in that order of popularity.[2] These were some of the principal characters from the Ghazi Miyan lore: Hathile the Adamant who helps attack idols in Banaras; the virtuous Amina Sati, banished for feeding a

Turkic brother; and Buhana, or Birahana the naked, a marijuanated bodyguard of Masud, in whose lap the warrior saint breathed his last on that first Sunday of June in 1034 .

In the villages of eastern UP, the term 'Panchpiriya' encompassed equally godlings, worthies and local Muslim saints. Ghazi Miyan and the upright Amina Sati figured in most such groupings, but with curious anomalies.[3] Among the caste of Kahar-palanquin bearers, the ferocious Amina Bhavani was 'the most venerated' of their Panchon Pirs—a bloody mother goddess who, uncharacteristically for a Panchpiriya godling, received 'libations of wine and a young pig' as offerings. The potters of Basti who worshipped Panchon Pir alongside a clutch of local godlings and forest deities were careful not to offer pigs to these Muslim godlings—'Musalmani *deotār*' as the Panchpiriyas were called generically.[4] Muslim devotees of the Ghazi also shared their Five Pirs with sundry local deified beings, mother goddesses, guardian deities, and disease-causing and repelling worthies. Musalman bangle sellers and armourers propitiated the Hindu goddesses of destruction. Similarly, darzi-tailors and Ghosi herdsmen, ardent worshippers of Ghazi Miyan, retained 'like many other lower Muhammadan tribes, some Hindu belief and practices'.[5]

The archetypal Panchpiriya follower was a low-caste Hindu, usually from the eastern Banaras-Gorakhpur region. 'A panchpiriya is a Hindu who worships Musalman saints'—Ghazi Miyan, Hathila, Parihar, Sahja Mai, and Ajab Salar—noted an authoritative compendium on *Bihar Peasant Life*.[6] The 1911 Census of UP put the 'total population of the Hindu castes who worship[ped] these five saints' at 13.5 million, laying stress on the fact that 'of the 53 castes devoted to the Panchpiriyas in the province, 44 were 'wholly or partly Hindus'.[7] That was for the province as a whole. Forty years earlier in 1873 at the Bahraich Fair, 'the proportion of Mahomedans ... was ... [found to be] less than the Hindoos'. The Muslim devotees were largely weavers, cotton carders, butchers and Jats—low-bred *razla* as these were characterised in a major historical work of early nineteenth century.[8] As for the Hindus, Koris, Kurmi and Ahir peasants and cowherds were the largest groups among the 105,306 pilgrims who entered the shrine on Sunday, 18 May 1873. We know the exact number as entry to the fair that year to was regulated by district officials by the sale of 1 paisa tickets.[9]

Local officials were emphatic that it were the Hindu *menu peuple* (*nānh jāt* in the local dialect) who were the pukka or 'real' devotees of the Miyan. These non-Muslim lower castes appeared 'to have more belief in Syud Salar than the rest'; they came into the shrine 'leaping and jumping with the flag bearer[s]' and made the most offerings of flags, *chadar*s and cash at the Bahraich shrine. Akbar Ali, a junior functionary stationed at the fair in 1873, identified them as 'the people of the East'—the *purabiya*s from Gorakhpur-Banaras—'who came only wearing a "Dhoti"'.[10] The translation from the Urdu is jarring, but the awkward sartorial image of the true devotee is intriguing and requires some unpacking. Clearly, these pilgrims—members of the Ghazi's 'marriage parties' as they perceived themselves—did not march bare-chested in the scorching heat of May all the way from their villages 'only wearing a long *dhoti*' tied at the waist. Something has been lost in the translation, for it was customary both for the groom and for male members of a marriage party to wear yellow *dhoti*s, dyed traditionally with turmeric or safflower. The curious allusion to the Hindu devotees' attire, it seems, is a pointer rather to their coloured *dhoti*s, for the same officer set them apart from the 'white clothes wearing … people of Bahraich who had gone' to the shrine 'for the purpose of witnessing the fair', and who 'seldom went inside to offer anything'.[11]

Now the dyeing of dhotis was not the norm in eastern UP and Bihar. *Mārkīn*, that is, mill-made cloth with the distinguishing 'mark' of English or Indian mills, was the cloth most used for dhotis, and it was usually white. Where white was customary, the dyeing of cloth had a special significance attached to it. Dhotis are still dyed primarily for marriages and other special occasions, ritual and social—even political. When in 1922, peasants in the Gorakhpur district of eastern UP consciously donned the mantle of Congress volunteers as part of Gandhi's 'army' of non-cooperators, they marched wearing yellow-dyed dhotis.[12] *Piyari*, or the coloured dhotis worn by males of a groom's party, were clearly in evidence at Bahraich that summer of 1873—an extension to the fair of a ritual practice followed more routinely at home. Indeed, the Panchon Pir or 'Heroes Five', when propitiated at domestic altars, received the special presents due to a groom: the characteristic *maur* head dress, the full-length *dhoti*, or the smaller 'langot' which grooms put on for a full body massage.[13] The offering of the yellow dhoti or the smaller *langot* was also the norm with two other groom-godlings: Hardiha Lala and the eponymous Dulha Deo.

Hardiha Lala or Hardaul was the 'great cholera godling' of north India, propitiated during an epidemic with the sacrifice of 'goats, fowls and suckers.'[14] However, among the potters, Hardaul had become 'a household godling', worshipped with the cooked food and condiments associated with marriage rituals. And this groom-godling was offered 'a pair of loin-cloths (*dhoti*) dyed with turmeric'.[15] In central India, Hardaul, if propitiated, ensured that weddings took place as scheduled, unmarred by rain or storm. At the slightest sign of a brewing storm, a prayer was offered in praise of the hero.[16] The trope of a storm disrupting marriage is also central to the Ghazi Miyan pilgrimage: an early nineteenth-century poetic description of the festivals of north India alluded to the popular belief that the storm is caused every year by an ogre trying to sweep the fairground clean. For the pilgrims constituting the Ghazi's marriage party, it is a dust storm that disrupts his marriage at Bahraich on a yearly basis.[17]

The preeminent groom-godling of the tribal communities of the plateau of the Son in Mirzapur and central India was Dulha Deo. In several variants, the groom is killed by lightening or turned to stone on his way to the bride.[18] During the marriage season he was worshipped in the family's kitchen, and 'at weddings oil and turmeric [were] offered to him'[19]—as these are routinely rubbed on the groom's body in all marriages, including the fateful one of Ghazi Miyan in the month of Jeth in 1034 CE.

It is these intriguing parallels that appear to make Dulha Deo and Ghazi Miyan so alike—both 'of the class of divine youths, snatched away from life at the height of their strength and beauty', as a nineteenth-century ethnographer put it.[20] Killed by a tiger before the consummation of his marriage in one variant, for some scholars Dulha Deo was perhaps 'absorbed into the Ghazi Miyan corpus ... to facilitate ... the adoption of the [warrior saint] cult by the non-Muslims' of north India.[21] Whether parallels suggest that key structural elements of one, presumably prior cult are consciously grafted on to a subsequent cult remains an open question. In any event, merely seeking structural parallels subtracts from the particular inversion of marriage/death embedded in the Ghazi Miyan story.

The poignancy of the Ghazi-Groom story lies crucially in the unraveling of the lines of fate: a mother forewarned of the death of her (long-desired) son at his marriage, yet persisting with the celebrations. It is this tragic figure of mother Mamula straining at the wheel of fortune and failing to turn it around that makes the Ghazi saga more than a death of a bridegroom story. That destiny intervenes, not as the bland binary of victory and death in battle, but as a righteous call to 'save the cows', imbues a social dimension to the relatively straightforward tragedy of a groom's death, foreclosing the possibility of consummation and procreation. And crucially for history, it is not the transposition of a prior groom-godling on to the figure of Ghazi Miyan, but the obeisance paid to a Turkic warrior saint by a representative swath of Hindu society over several centuries, that propels continually the afterlife of Salar Masud as a hero located in an identifiable conflictual past of the early eleventh century—the time of seventeen incursions into northern India by purported uncle Sultan Mahmud of Ghazni.

That the tensility of the Ghazi Miyan cult may have inhered in a layered memorialisation of medieval Turkish conquerors bewildered the late nineteenth-century British officer-ethnographers. The writer of the 1891 Census Report, which recorded over 1.5 million 'special worshippers of Panchon Pir' in UP, faced some difficulty explaining the origin and development of the cult. It was the sheer incredibility, matched by numbers 'of the adoption into the Hindu system as ... beneficient ... divinities ... those men who were most instrumental in the subjection of Hindus to an alien rule' that puzzled the Census Commissioner. For the data were unequivocal that 'even the Brahman makes his daily offerings of food and water to the spirits of the great [Ghazi] Pir and his associates, and for the low caste man the household worship of the five Pirs is in many districts his sole religious trust'.[22]

Officer D. C. Bailee ventured that the cult 'probably spread through its early adoption by low caste converts [to Islam] who ... found their gods ... [whom] they had abandoned ... in the dead heroes, whom genuine Muhammadans reverenced [sic] as martyrs who had fallen on behalf of their faith'. Unable to quite explain the wide appeal of the cult, Bailee asked his readers to imagine a sequence by which 'the worship of the low caste Muhammadans at shrines dotted all over the country and known by all extended to the low caste and then to all Hindus'. One additional feature added to the puzzlement of the English officer: 'the Muhammdan origin of the worship even when adopted into the households of Hindus is never forgotten'. It is Muslim Dafalis and servitors of the shrine who benefit from this conundrum of Hindu religiosity, concluded this official notice on the Ghazi Miyan phenomenon—a theme picked up in subsequent decades by publicists out to wean 'innocent Hindu peasants' from the clutches of charlatan Dafalis.[23]

Late nineteenth-century notices marvelled at the amazing cross-religious hold of the Ghazi cult even among the most unlikely of communities. It was reported that while thieving in the great fairs of north India, the nefarious Bawarias scrupulously abstained from plundering the tomb and the fair of Ghazi Miyan. Instead, they went annually as pilgrims, and offered their own *lahbar* (flag) to the Bahraich shrine. There seems to be no reason to believe that this was a new development. Another such 'criminal caste', the Barwars, laid aside 1 per cent of their pickings from other fairs while propitiating the Panchpiriya, their 'tutelary god', in an elaborate domestic ritual:

> Each Barwar family keeps a small altar in honour of this tutelary god in his house, in the shape of a tomb, at which in the month of Bhadon (August) of every year, on the third or the fifth day of the first half of the month, he sacrifices a domestic fowl and bakes thin loaves of bread called "lugra", and then gives both the bread and the meat of the sacrificed fowl, together with cooked *dāl* of gram [*chane ki dāl*], to a Musalman beggar [Dafali?], who goes about from house to house beating on a kettle-drum.[24]

That was in the 1880s. In the Mewat region of villages near Delhi, Dafalis on the day of his martyrdom carried a procession of the Ghazi's flag, singing in his honour and begging through the main village site and its satellite settlements.[25] At the other end of the sprawling province of UP, an ethnographic study of an eastern UP village suggests that well into the 1940s, each household of the caste of Teli oil pressers similarly had a clay altar in its house dedicated to Ghazi Miyan. Every year on return from the Bahraich pilgrimage, householders would offer a big feast (*kandūri*): goats were sacrificed to the saint and money gifted to the Dafali. At the key domestic puja, the Dafalis were treated like Brahmans: the Teli householders washing their feet, and sprinkling this water inside their houses. The Dafalis would then sing and drum, in an effort to induce Ghazi Miyan to possess one member of the family.[26] In Senapur (the village studied by Cornell University anthropologists in early 1950s), all Teli oil pressers, Kalwar distillers and 'a majority of clean shudra and untouchable population as well, worshipped Ghazi Miyan as a family god'.[27]

By 1953, the 'ethnographic present' of the anthropologist Jack Planalp, the cult of Ghazi Miyan had suffered a decline in Senapur. Only two Nonia makers of saltpeter, earth-diggers, households and a few untouchable Chamar leather tanners and more generally agricultural labourers' families worshipped the Ghazi in the early 1950s, and that too as an individual deity rather than as a 'family god'. The dominant Thakur landlords of the village had succeeded in enforcing a ban on the public display of the Ghazi's flag. Dafalis were now restricted to taking out their procession in the segregated untouchable Chamar quarters, away from the main village site. Even then, women of all castes continued to ascribe misfortunes in the family to the dereliction of the Ghazi's worship.[28] Oil presser Telis seem to have retained their close association with Ghazi Miyan. To this day, a miniature nuptial cot is taken out annually to Bahraich from the house of a Rudauli Teli in celebration of that marriage that death had stymied in the summer of 1034 CE! Nor has the Bahraich Fair been reduced to a solely Muslim affair.

14

Dafalis and Servitors

At the 1996 Bahraich Fair, I came across Bashir Dafali and his Teli patron from Tharia Kalan village of Faizabad district in eastern UP. Both stressed the Ghazi's wide following cutting across social groups. 'There are thirty-six *qaums* [here, castes] in Hindustan; all worship Syed Salar Masud Ghazi', stressed balladeer Bashir. His patron added: 'each and every *jati* in the country, all thirty-six of them'—a stock number—'come to this fair'.[1] Echoing the 1873 report of the functionary charged by the government to tax each and every person entering the shrine, Bashir Dafali maintained that 'seven-eighths of the devotees of the Ghazi are Hindus, and better ones at that ... their desires [are] also fulfilled by the *barkat* (blessings) of the Ghazi's tomb'.[2] 'Of course they retain their own religious ways', but in sickness and in happiness, after a marriage or at a birth, 'even if not commanded by the Bahraich saint', they will call upon their local Dafali. Not so the Musalman cotton carders, tailors and weavers, insisted Bashir: 'they, they will turn to Ghazi Miyan only when in a real fix, cutting corners, combining a marriage feast with the Ghazi's *kandūri*'; not so the Hindus: 'they would always call the Dafali specially for a proper *kandūri* offering...'[3]

When I met Bashir again on the last day of the fair in mid-May 1996, the Dafali from Faizabad was all set for a *fatiha* and *kandūri* (prayers for the deceased over an offering of sanctified food) for the Teli family from his village.[4] The conversation turned to the Hindu devotees' religiosity and the reasons for their continuing pilgrimage to Bahraich. '*Ahl-i-Hunūd* come here', announced Bashir, using the high Persian for the more common 'Hindu', as their 'faith is genuine'.

'They don't visit Bahraich thinking that they are coming to Bala Deo (a local demon subdued by the Ghazi, in Bashir's version—resonances of *bala-rikh* of the Farsi *Mirat*); they are pretty sure that they are coming to Syed Salar Masud Ghazi'. 'He is a Hindu Teli—one of my patrons and a pilgrim', Bashir, now in full flow, brought the Teli into the conversation. 'He will tell you the name of Masud Ghazi's parents!'

Fig. 14.1 *Bashir Dafali supervising the preparation of the kanduri offering to Ghazi Miyan at the Bahraich Fair, May 1996*

'We have come here to the shrine of Syed Salar Masud Ghazi', began the Teli oil presser from Tharia Kalan. Warming up, he recounted how starting from Arab[ia], Masud reached Hindustan to 'display his *karamat*'; '*Hazrat* is regarded as a *Mahapurush*', he expounded, combining the Islamic honorific with the Sanskrit term for a 'great personage'. 'His is the top rank among the martyrs of Hindustan.' The Teli now moved on to recollect Salar Masud's life: how as he was an *auliya-faqir*, he refused the throne of Delhi; how he destroyed the fort and the temple of Somnath of Banaras (Sobhnath of the ballads); how it was at the Suraj Kund at Anarkali lake—'a site originally of the Hindus—that the mare Lilli and the bitch Sankuli took the plunge'! The sequence, which lumps the lore and the *Mirat* together, is confusing. Here we have an idiosyncratic allusion to the desecration of the sun temple tank at Bahraich, but outside the frame of Islamic iconoclasm. The Teli devotee of Ghazi Miyan then went on to establish correspondences: Ghazi Miyan is an incarnation of Rama,

Hathile of Hanuman, Nirmal-Palihar is the night-stalker (*nishachar*) of Lanka.[5]

This modern-day *panchpiriya* continued: 'We have our gods and godlings for sure—*deh*, the village site and Kali [the goddess of destruction] whom we offer cooked food—the unattainable we ask of the Ghazi'. 'Our ancestors were short of a family', that is, a male child. 'They asked of the Ghazi, and received the boon; they were devotees', and so are we, he implied. He then turned to the perceived difference between Hindus and Muslims: *agar hum nāpāki mein hum charhāein* ('if we make our offerings in a state of impurity'—he used an Islamic term for ritual impurity), 'Salar Masud would have to accept it, as we are Hindus, and so not fully aware of the finer points of Islamic ritual.' It is the Dafalis' business to help such devotees beseech the Almighty properly, intervened Bashir: The Hindus ask for a boon directly from Salar Masud; that of course is impermissible, for an *auliya*, literally, one near to God, can only intercede on behalf of Allah, he cannot grant the boon himself. Asking for a boon involves crucially the Dafali saying the *fātiha* and the offering of sanctified food (*kandūri*). The food consists of a sacrificial animal, a goat, more often a fowl, and a pot pourri of lentils and rice, *maleeda*, even sherbet, as ethnographic accounts from the 1890s testify. The preferred lentil is chickpea or gram, never *arhar*, the staple *dal* of eastern UP.[6]

Fig. 14.2 A Dafali and his son singing during a kanduri session, May 1996

Fig. 14.3 *Bashir Dafali poses with his Daf after the conclusion of the Bahraich Fair, May 1994*

At the 1996 fair, Bashir Dafali set the stage by planting a small trident (*sāng*) in the ground. Earthen lamps and joss sticks stuck into a small mound completed the wish fulfilment paraphernalia.[7] The Dafali begins by singing the praises of Ghazi Miyan on his *rabāna*, a Daf-like tambourine with cymbals, seen often in Mughal paintings of devotees of Sufi acolytes working themselves into trance-like reverie.[8] As Bashir Dafali begins singing praises of the saint, one member of the Teli family gets possessed by the Ghazi's spirit and starts shaking his head and body. The devotee would recite the Muslim credo ('There is no God but Allah and Mohammad is His Prophet') but as this is done in a paranormal state, the Dafali, who is dependent on his Hindu clientele, does not insist that the person has converted to Islam. Bashir Dafali begins, 'your devotees and worshippers are here; they are here with their offerings, do you accept them?' Uttering a medley of invocations in Arabic and Urdu, the Dafali ritually slaughters the fowl. Wish fulfilment should follow.

Confident about what he did and said, Bashir Dafali cut an impressive figure at the 1996 Bahraich Fair. Knowledgeable about both Islamic and Hindu rites and lore, transiting with ease from one to the other, Bashir was in full flow at that year's *mela* (fair). Clearly, the mammoth May fair, where hundreds of Dafalis converged along with thousands of pilgrims, taking them through the rituals was where the Dafalis would be at their powerful best. This self-assured image is at odds with the picture of the lowly drummer recorded in nineteenth century colonial ethnographies, and subsequent descriptions. An early-nineteenth-century account described the 'daphalis [as] mendicant musicians' who 'not only play on the Damph [Daf] but hawk trinkets and spices'.[9] That the Dafalis were not very well regarded in village society is borne out by the numerous proverbs that targeted them. According to a late nineteenth-century compendium of peasant proverbs, *Dafali kai Rāg* meant 'inconsequent talk, prating'.[10] Yet, excellent communicators, they held their own in the village: 'Work your land with a Dafali, singing and narrating, he will take all', recorded another compendium of village witticisms, c. 1920s.[11] Late nineteenth-century ethnographies alluded to the multifaceted occupations of the rural Dafalis: 'The *Dafali* is a beggar, and goes about with a wallet in which he collects what he can get. But he also acts as a sort of hedge priest to the lower class Musalmans, and officiates at marriages, funerals and the like for people who cannot afford to pay for the services of a regular Qazi.'[12] They solemnised the marriages, for instance, of Kingarias, an allied group of balladeer-alms seeker and trinket-sellers.[13] An early twentieth-century report labelled the Dafali 'a beggar, drummer and hedge priest', placing him derisively on the same footing as dancing girls, buffoons, pimps and prostitutes.[14]

The Dafalis had, as they do today, several strings to their bow. Tailoring, and quilt-sewing, repairing utensils, small-time Maulvi, maker of drums—these were some of the vocations recorded for Dafalis by an anthropologist in the middle of the last century.[15] The Dafalis of Rudauli plied horse carriages and also made jewellery and drawstrings for quilted purses.[16] Bashir Dafali of neighbouring Faizabad district did not live by Ghazi Miyan alone: he set up shop in nearby itinerant markets; his younger son traded in goats; the eldest trained as a Dafali, and as also played musical instruments in dance performances in the countryside.[17]

'One of their chief duties', wrote the late nineteenth-century ethnographer William Crooke, 'is the exorcising of evil spirits by beating the drum, driving the effect of the Evil Eye from children'.[18] In Bihar, the worship of Panchon Pir, with Dafalis officiating, was a part of a village's attempts during epidemics to transfer diseases such as cholera across its boundary to an adjacent habitation. Even today Bashir Dafali is called upon by his patrons at child birth and for driving out the illness-causing evil spirits.[19]

Fig. 14.4 The rush of decorated palang-peerhis (nuptial bedsteads and trousseaux), as the gates of the shrine are opened on the first Sunday of Jeth (mid-May) 1994 for the 'marriage parties'

Source: Photograph by Sanjay Kak

The main role of these rural Dafalis was to lead their pilgrim-clients to Bahraich and in association with the servitors (*mujawirs* and *khadims*) of the shrine, to gain them access to the saint's munificence. One rendition of Ibn Battuta's account mentions that there already were a large number of persons dependent on the shrine for their livelihood.

Historian Barani, in his mid-fourteenth-century *Tarikh-i-Ferozshahi* records that the Sultan returned to Delhi after showering royal largesse on the *mujawirs* of the rauza (*ziyārat kard wa mujāwirān-i rauza-i u ra sadaqāt bisyār dād*).[20] It was the Mughal emperor Akbar who gifted in 1571 the revenue-paying village of Singha Parasi in which the dargah was located. As with other such 'maintenance grants', the Bahraich servitors became in effect the landed proprietors of this large village with scant obligation to the state; in addition to collecting tax-free rent from the village, they were also entitled to other allied receipts, in this case, offerings made at the shrine by royalty and commoners alike.[21]

Fig. 14.5 A veteran Dafali reciting a short ballad at the Bahraich shrine

The khadims appear to have appropriated for the next 300 years the proceeds from the village (and a couple of neighboring hamlets), and the offerings and levies from the shops that sprang up during the fair. An order of the Nawab of Awadh (in 1180 A.H.: 1766 CE) enjoined officials, present and future, to facilitate this arrangement. Proceeds from the revenue of a half a dozen villages in the vicinity of the shrine were now earmarked for meeting the daily expenses and for the burning of incense, lamps, etc. at the shrine; a considerable sum of Rs 3000 was set aside for the maintenance of the khadims. The dues from the shops were meant to offset the 'expenses of the fort', that is inside of the dargah proper, and this included the *fātiha* for the saint together with alms and funerary expenses for the indigent. The land, market and grazing dues of village Singha Parasi, in which the shrine fell, and of Jaldapur village had been alienated revenue-free to one Ghulam Ali's family from 'earlier times'. The 1766 official order from the Nawab of Awadh reiterated this time-honoured arrangement, reaffirming for 'all times and [to] all concerned' that the entire offerings made by devotees were to devolve to Ghulam Ali acting as the superintendent of the shrine and for him to allocate the shares of all the other khadims subordinated to him in this and other matters.[22] The validity of the revenue-free grant, and of the above order by Nawab Shujauddaulah (1753–95) was recognised by the East India Company at the annexation of Awadh in 1856, confiscated along with other private properties in the aftermath of the Great Rebellion and restored, in view of absence of a clear proof of resistance to the Raj, on the same terms and conditions at the post-Mutiny land settlement of 1870. That both the shrine and the fair were indeed historic helped, but so did the fact that the servitors had kept their noses clean during the Great Rebellion of 1857. At a time when a single day's prayer for the end of Firangi Raj could result in the billeting of 'European soldiery' in nondescript mosques,[23] to have kept the dargah free from any suspicion of disloyalty during those rebellious summer months (also the time of the fair) was achievement indeed. And so it came to pass that when a resurgent colonial state moved to divest the khadims of their income from the shrine, it did so for mendacious 'peculation' and not for any perceived disloyalty during the upheaval of 1857.

Fig. 14.6 *Ghazi Miyan flags fluttering in the wind at the Fair Ground, May 1996. Notice the bushy tops, symbolising the martyr's head*

Fig. 14.7 The eighteenth-century Farman from Nawab of Awadh about the role of servitors at the Bahraich shrine

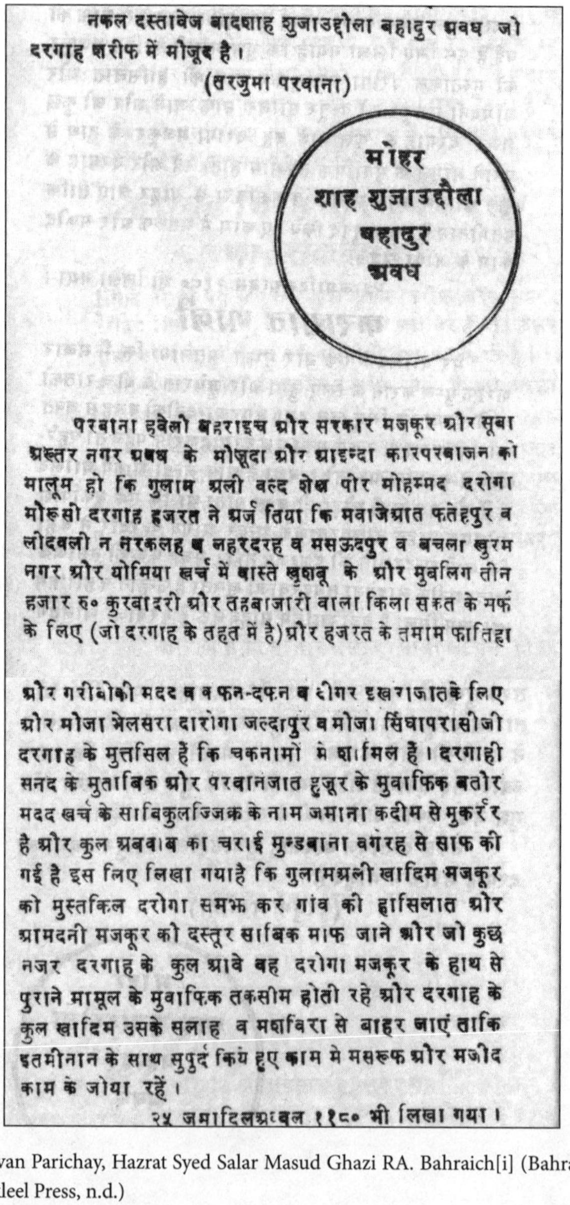

नकल दस्तावेज बादशाह शुजाउद्दौला बहादुर अवध जो दरगाह शरीफ में मौजूद है।

(तरजुमा परवाना)

मोहर
शाह शुजाउद्दौला
बहादुर
अवध

परवाना हवेली बहराइच और सरकार मजकूर और सूबा अख्तर नगर अवध के मौजूदा और आइन्दा कारपरदाजन को मालूम हो कि गुलाम अली वल्द शेख पीर मोहम्मद दरोगा मौरूसी दरगाह हजरत ने अर्ज तिया कि मवाजेआत फतेहपुर व लीदवली न नरकलह व नहरदरह व मसऊदपुर व बचला खुरम नगर और योमिया खर्च में वास्ते खुशबू के और मुबलिग तीन हजार रु० कुरबादरी और तहबाजारी वाला किला सकत के मर्फ के लिए (जो दरगाह के तहत में है) और हजरत के तमाम फातिहा

और गरीबोंकी मदद व व फन-दफन व दीगर इखराजातके लिए और मौजा भेलसरा दारोगा जल्दापुर व मौजा सिंघापरासीजी दरगाह के मुत्तसिल हैं कि चकनामों मे शामिल हैं। दरगाही सनद के मुताबिक और परवानजात हुजूर के मुवाफिक बतौर मदद खर्च के साबिकुलज्जिक्र के नाम जमाना कदीम से मुकर्रर है और कुल अबवाब का चराई मुन्डवाना वगैरह से साफ की गई है इस लिए लिखा गया है कि गुलामअली खादिम मजकूर को मुस्तकिल दरोगा समझ कर गांव की हासिलात और आमदनी मजकूर को दस्तूर साबिक माफ जाने और जो कुछ नजर दरगाह के कुल आवे वह दरोगा मजकूर के हाथ से पुराने मामूल के मुवाफिक तकसीम होती रहे और दरगाह के कुल खादिम उसके सलाह व मशविरा से बाहर जाएं ताकि इतमीनान के साथ सुपुर्द किये हुए काम मे मसरूफ और मजीद काम के जोया रहें।

२५ जमादिलअव्वल ११८० भी लिखा गया।

Source: Jeevan Parichay, Hazrat Syed Salar Masud Ghazi RA. Bahraich[i] (Bahraich, Uttar Pradesh: Ikleel Press, n.d.)

15

The Bahraich Shrine

A listing of the claims against the khadims for monies borrowed against the customary collections at the shrine presents a clearer picture of the ritual economy of the Bahraich shrine in the nineteenth century. But as the coins showered at the dargah issued forth from devotional piety, popular belief bubbles under the surface of what (for local English officials) was simply another case of pelf practised at yet another Indian shrine. The primary attraction for the Bahraich pilgrims at the shrine was the tomb of Ghazi Miyan. But the graves of Zohra Bibi, the Rudauli girl who got the tomb built, of the wondrous mare Lilli, and even dog Sakul who had saved the Ghazi's body from desecration on the night of his martyrdom (in the *Mirat*) were also objects of veneration. The largest source of income for the shrine (and its servitors) was *kalandri*: 'contributions thrown up upon the canopy of the shrine', as a District Officer put it somewhat awkwardly.[1] Devotees habitually showered coins at the dome of the tomb, which the servitor khadims garnered by attaching a canopy of stout cloth at the base of the dome. Functioning as a safety net, it prevented the offerings of the pious from getting dissipated on the ground.

Kalandari accounted for full half of the proceeds from the shrine. It was much prized by its manager (*mutawalli*) and servitors (khadims). In 1878, for which we have detailed information, Rs 1,415 out of the total income of Rs 3,102 from the fair was accounted for by *kalandari* offerings. This apparently was a low intake from a total of 120,000 devotees who had converged on the shrine that year during the last ten days of the fair. An agricultural downturn and the drop in numbers of *purabiya* devotees from the eastern districts—'the class

Map 15.1 The Bahraich Dargah and camping sites earmarked for pilgrims

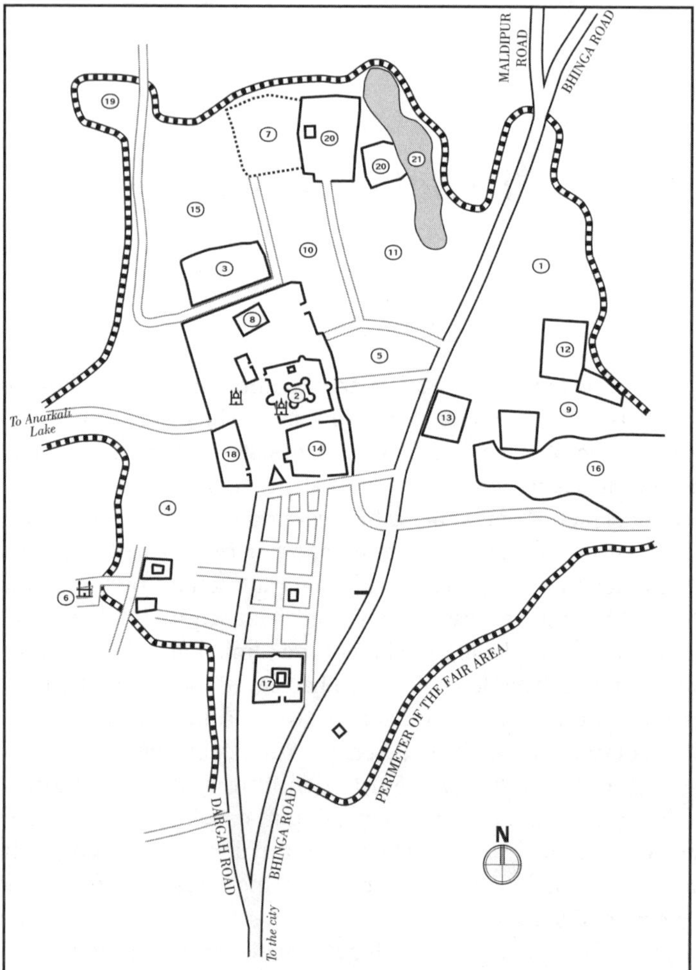

Index to the places shown with numbers in the fair area:

1. Abadi Ghosiana
2. Big Qila
3. Chamargarhi Bagh
4. Churni Bagh
5. Dargah Habitatious
6. Eidgah
7. Graveyard
8. Guest House
9. Ilas Gara
10. Jali Bagh
11. Khatīb Bagh
12. Lohar Bagh
13. Malin Bagh
14. Mehfil Khana
15. Naurang Bagh
16. Parli Bagh
17. Qadam Rasul
18. Salar Bagh
19. Sarain Bagh
20. Zohra Bagh
21. Zohra Talab (Pond)

The Bahraich Dargah, Fair Grounds and Camping Sites Earmarked for Pilgrim Parties

Bands of pilgrims, *Mednis* or Marriage Parties as they are called, stay at designated Baghs around the shrine, entering the main door of the *Qila*, following a set order of precedent (see Map 15.1). The following list gives a rough idea of location of various pilgrim groups during the Fair. If there is more than one 'medni' from a particular area/district, it is often designated by the name of a head Dafali (for example, Korabardar), or as in the case of Banaras party, interviewed during the May 1996 Fair, by name: Ramchandra's Banaras Party.

Qadam Rasul	Banaras Party
Parhli Bagh	Gorakhpur; Ayodhya; Partabgarh
Zohra Bagh	Basti
Naurang Bagh	Azamgarh; Sultanpur; Atraulia, Azamgarh
Malin Bagh	Ghazipur; Dostpur, District Sultanpur
Ghosiana	Faizabad
Tanda Bagh	Tanda
Khatīb Bagh	Basti; Gonda; Banaras; Korabardar's Barat, Siddharthnagar; Mustaqim Ansari's Barat, District Maharajganj
Salar Bagh	Banaras
Masudia Bagh	Balrampur; Ramchandra's Banaras Party
Sahu Bagh	Deoria, District Faizabad
Lohar Bagh	Jaunpur

Source: List of Medni/Barat/ Marriage/Pilgrims' Parties, Dargah office, May 1996

of pilgrims that present rich gifts'—were partly responsible for the diminution in the recorded income from that year's festive gathering.[2] But the 'chief reason', colonial officials felt, lay elsewhere. Aware that the local administration was now keeping an eagle eye on the proceeds from the mela, Dafalis and servitors had colluded to ensure that the really valuable offerings—the silver rupees, etc., 'tied to the flag very tightly'—were taken out and removed at the khadims' homes outside the dargah, or shared with the Dafalis at the camping places specified for the different groups of pilgrims. Only cowrie shells and bags of copper coins attached to the flags were cut and thrown into the *kalandari*. For the richer pilgrims to have abstained from depositing coin at the saint's dome was a telling instance of the servitors' hold over the ritual economy of the shrine: devotees and Dafalis had faithfully put the money into the care of the chief khadims who, unlike the colonial state had an organic connection with the dargah.

The dome of Ghazi Miyan's tomb (reputedly built by Zohra Bibi) was as much the focus of pilgrimage as his grave which lay underneath it. Pilgrims then, as now, tried to touch the dome with their colourful standards, or shower coins at the cupola. If the coins rebounded off the dome, this was seen to signify that the craving drawing the boon-seeker in the blistering heat of May to the shrine stood a chance of being fulfilled. And if by the next trip the desire had been fulfilled, the bamboo pennants with the attached bits of monies were left behind at the dargah—in effect for the khadims. On an average, fully 60 per cent of these insignias were left to the dargah every year—indicating a high perception of wish fulfilment indeed![3]

It was for this reason that over the centuries the Bahraich Fair had become synonymous with the Ghazi's standards—lances, *nishāns* or *lahbar*s as these were termed in the region (for a map of the Bahraich Fair grounds, see Map 15.1). This was no invention of a recent tradition: the 'Fair of the Ghazi's *neza*' (lance), the 'gathering' of his *charis*' (sticks/poles) were common names for the Bahraich Fair in the Gangetic plains from at least the fifteenth century. The official history of the reign of Akbar noted people customarily 'mak[ing] flags of various colours in different places and convey[ing] them along with numerous presents' to Bahraich. The *Mirat-i-Masudi*, c. 1620, refers to pilgrims walking to Bahraich displaying their lances and flags (*chatrahās*); it were these 'long bamboo poles with coloured pennons and horse-hair tied on the top' that were the focus of singing and dancing by both Hindus and Muslims pilgrims in the sixteenth century as well.[4] 'Thousands of Dafalis accompany low-caste persons carrying their red-pennoned neza lances from their townships en route to the Baharich May Fair', noted a late eighteenth-century account.[5] The words 'pennoned *neza*s' or lances and 'bamboo-poles', often used interchangeably, may well indicate a switch over time from the militant display of actual lances by Qalandar and Madari mendicant followers of Masud till the late eighteenth century to the ordinary bamboo poles easily available in the innumerable *banswari* clumps in the countryside.[6] It was customary to plant these flag poles by the nearby Chittaura lake, light earthen lamps and spend the night listening to the ballads and *sohla* songs of the Ghazi. The choice of this latter musical genre was specially apt, for *sohla*s celebrated (as they did in the time of the Mughal emperor Akbar) the twin occasions of birth and marriage—specially apposite to Ghazi Miyan whose marriage-martyrdom were prophesied at the time of his eventful birth.[7]

*Lahbar*s, as these pennons are termed in Bhojpuri, were king-size flags, up to 20 cubits long, embroidered with figures of elephants and horses, and capped by a tuft of hair that was widely held to symbolise the martyr's head.* The Sanskritist Monier Williams was sufficiently intrigued to publish in 1879 a communication regarding the Ghazi Miyan flag: 'The standard', he wrote from Oxford, 'is generally about 25 or 30 feet high, and is adorned with a fine large flag of brilliant colours ornamented with numerous representations in needle-work of men on horseback, etc.'[8] To this was tied a bag of coins. These massive flag poles, crafted from full-length bamboos and the flags, which required the village tailor the better part of a year to embroider, stood for Ghazi Miyan.[9] Such was the association of the warrior saint with his standard that in eastern UP, the word 'Bale Miyan', a popular sobriquet for the Ghazi, signified primarily Masud's flag, only secondarily the warrior saint.[10] In these parts, the Bhojpuri term *lahbar* connoted both the flagpole and the tuft of the martyr's hair which capped it. The extension of the word *lahbar*, 'the hair of the newborn', to Bale Miyan—(literally, 'the Muslim lad') made good

* In point of fact, only an enemy's head was carried afloat, and the Central Asian Turks were wont to tie yak's hair to their banners, as noticed by a missionary familiar with the Bahraich Fair.

linguistic sense, for though the hero fell in his adolescence, *bāla/bāle* in east-UP dialects meant both 'baby' as well as 'lad'.[11] After touching the dome of the saint's tomb, the pilgrim 'standard bearers' would leave the shrine with their pressing desires—a long-awaited male child, a cure for leprosy or leucoderma or the 'return of light' to their opaque eyes. Indeed Tulsidas, the great sixteenth-century poet, had commented on the entire world blindly making a beeline for Bahraich (*Lahi ānkh kab āndhre, bānjh pūt kab biyāe; kab korhi kāya lahi, jag Bahraich jāy*). Tulsi's sardonic couplet on pilgrimage to Bahraich can be read as literary evidence of faith in the powers of Ghazi Miyan—popular belief renewed by the annual 'cured-of-affliction' list that has been circulated at the fair at least since the late nineteenth century (see endpaper to this book).[12]

Martyrs in India as elsewhere are often represented as headless horsemen.[13] However, neither the *Mirat* nor the ballads mention the Ghazi literally losing his head. Yet, tufts of hair on flagpoles have come to stand both for the hero and his insignia in battle. '…A long pole is paraded about', at the annual fair, 'crowned at the top with bushy hair … said to represent the head of the martyr, which kept rolling on long after it was separated from the trunk', noted a rural glossary compiled in the early 1840s by the same colonial official who had commissioned the translation of the *Mirat-i-Masudi*.[14] 'Bale Miyan unfurls his tresses sans his head in the summer month of May'—this from a village boy in a novel set in early twentieth-century eastern UP.[15] Around the same time as when the novelist Manan Dwivedi wrote these lines in 1913, a missionary was marvelling at the large crowds carrying the 'fantastic banners of every size and construction, one forty feet long and fifteen wide on a great bamboo, erect, the whole thirty-eight miles', from Gonda to the Bahraich Fair and back again.[16] A quarter century earlier, a tub-thumping Methodist had let off evangelical steam at these Bahraich-bound *lahbars*. 'One striking peculiarity of this reeking *mela*', wrote Reverend Knowles in 1884, 'is the multitude of its flaunting glittering banners … each … surrounded by a black, shaggy yak's tail', conveying 'the idea of a cruel victorious army proudly displaying the scalps of their fallen heroes.'

> Every district and tribe represented come marching into the fair with a flourish of trumpets and drums, bearing their gaudy flags fiercely vibrating in the hot west wind. Every emblem that mythology can

> feign, every animal and memorial connected with the stories of poor dead Saiyid Salar's former life, serpents, wolves, lions, horses, gods, geniis, stars, moons and suns, with other cabalistic signs, in all the colours of the rainbow, were emblazoned upon these waving crowds of dashing pennants and proud ensigns.[17]

These mammoth standards exited the dargah after their bearers had touched the sacred dome with the top of the banner pole. Ruing over 'the deluded devotees' shying money at the 'golden pinnacle', a local missionary calculated £100 sterling a day as 'an ordinary collection' during the important days of the Bahraich Fair. This was a lot of copper pice and cowries, current as coin of the value of 1/140 of a cent each, or seventy to a farthing, as the missionary helpfully calculated for his British and American readers.[18]

The coins that peasants handled routinely in the region were copper pice, cowrie shells, and the regionally minted low-value Gorakhpuri *kaccha* paisa. For the rural poor, *Chehrashahi*, the silver rupee with the face (*chehra*) of the British sovereign, was for hoarding, not spending: 'I'd rather die than get you changed into smaller coins' (*Main mar jāun par tujhe na bhujāun*), went a local proverb. The rich no doubt left silver rupees, even an occasional gold coin at the dome.[19] But copper pice and cowrie shells made for the bulk of the current coin withdrawn from active circulation in the region and cast into the cotton fold that girded the dome of the Bahraich shrine. This affected the exchange ratio of copper and cowrie shells each year after the end of the Bahraich Fair, with the mollusc dimes emerging temporarily stronger vis-à-vis coppers till the shells made their way back into local circulation.[20] Or it could well be that poorer devotees who could ill afford to part with a lot of copper coins exchanged these for cowries from moneychangers in the village marts (or outside the shrine), where shroffs or money dealers would set up shop for this purpose (see Figure 15.1).[21] This was the practice in rural Bengal, from where these shells, imported from the Maldives were sent upcountry.[22] Ibn Battuta, the renowned fourteenth-century traveller who visited both Bengal and the Bahraich shrine, reported of the Maldives:

> All transactions take place in this country by means of the cowrie, which is an animal picked from the sea and deposited in pits on the shore ... They are used for buying and selling ... They are sold to the

> inhabitants of Bengal for rice, because the cowries are also current in Bengal, and also to the inhabitants of Yemen, who use these instead of sand for ballast in their ships. The cowrie is also the currency of the Sudanese …[23]

Fig. 15.1 A Delhi shroff or moneylender changing coins for cowrie shells, c. 1860

Source: Shepherd and Robinson in John Forbes Watson and John William Kaye (eds), *The People of India: A Series of Photographic Illustrations with Descriptive Letterpress of the Races and Tribes of Hindustan* (London [India Museum]: India Office [W. H. Allen and Co.], 1868)

In any case, both the cloth and the fiscal standing of the chief administrators were in tatters in the 1860s, as over 200 claims had been decreed against the *mutwalli* and his cousin in Court. In 1867, the principal that creditors agreed to 'putting up the kalandari' cloth, provided the offerings at the dome were 'given over to them at the earliest possible opportunity.' The thousands of cowries and coppers that had rained on the canopy during the four years of collection by peons appointed by Court seem to have frayed the cloth a good deal,[24] for in 1871, the senior khadim took on credit from one Nanku Teli Rs 10 'worth of cloth for the use of *kalandari*'.[25] And when a committee of local notables virtually took over the shrine under the stewardship of the District Magistrate, a 'raised shutter of iron netting above the dome' was installed, so as to do away with the khadim's recurrent borrowings for the renewal of kalandari cloth. 'Now a permanent *Qalandari Tatti*', or an iron shutter, was in place for 'safeguarding the income' of the 'noble shrine', wrote a sympathetic native official in 1891.[26]

Apart from *kalandari*, the two chief khadims had a share in a wide range of payments and offerings that the shrine attracted throughout the year and specially during the festive month. These were dues from shopkeepers during the fair, and monies offered at the several sites of veneration, both inside and outside the dargah. Such were the assets that the principal servitors could mortgage for raising loans in the local money market. Offerings were made inside the shrine at wide-mouthed funnels attached to leather bags or brass and iron receptacles to allow easy ingress of fistfuls of devotees' copper. The donation box with a narrow slit found in mosques and departure lounges is designed to allow the insertion of folded currency notes; the average Ghazi Miyan devotee was a copper-and cowrie-throwing subaltern. Two large lamps burnt continuously at the foot and by the side of saint's grave; these attracted a fair amount of baser metals and some silver coins as well.

In the early nineteenth century, the khadims seemed to have 'bathed the *lungi** and the wooden stool' of the saint, and distributed the blessed water which was received as 'the spring of life' by eager pilgrims in return for cash offerings.[27] We are back here to the

---

* *Lungi*: A north Indian sarong, somewhat looser than the Southeast Asian one. Worn only by men, it can be pulled up to expose the legs for massage.

symbolic importance of the peerha-stool and the deep cleansing of grooms with full body massages. If 'bathing the lungi' was indeed the practice in the 1800s, it was discontinued over the next seventy years. What was fought over now were the shares in the offerings connected with the daily ablutions given to the martyr's grave and the brocaded covers that adorned it. The water flowing out into a pit after this ritual bathing was considered to have therapeutic value, it was argued later, because of its sulphur content. This is where the lepers wallowed to receive aqua-treatment with the blessings of the saint. It was benedictory water, worthy equally of the attention of pilgrims in general. The offerings netted income to the khadims, which could be mortgaged to raise money for the upkeep of their families and for the shrine. In 1865, one Salamat Julaha appropriated in lieu of a cash advance the right to three-fourths of the collections made at the point where the water fell into the small 'lepers' pond'.[28] Offerings at the grave of Lilli Mare or the tomb of Zohra could be similarly capitalised by the khadims taking loans by pledging these as sureties.

It was official indignation at such 'peculation'—the mortgaging by khadims of offerings elicited, for instance by the 'the drain water' to 'private ends', that led to their being stripped in the late 1870s of their traditional claims to the shrine's proceeds. In 1876, a miffed District Commissioner found a radical solution to such private capitalisation of devotional piety. All the major offerings—*kalandari* predominantly, but equally petty cash thrown into receptacles, income from Singha Parasi village and from shops at the fair—were now decreed to be 'the property of the shrine', and 'no[t] personal rights.' Recovered fully from the Great Rebellion of 1857, the colonial state was willing, at most, to recognise a prescriptive right of the servitors to the smaller offerings made in and around the shrine—and even these had to be ceded in lieu of a fixed monthly stipend.[29] The longstanding rights of khadims to 'public charity' now stood abrogated.[30] Henceforth, the colonial state was to manage the Trust through a Committee of local notables.

A problem still remained: an extant statute exempted all religious endowments from the direct control of the state.[31] Hemmed in by its own laws, colonial officials now began redefining the very character of the shrine. And so it was decreed by executive fiat that the shrine of the Bahraich Ghazi, martyred in the cause of Islam, which attracted equally non-Muslim devotees, was not a

Muslim institution in the legal sense of the term but 'evidentally cosmopolitan.'[32] The ruse resorted to by the administration was to dub the Bahraich Trust, certainly in existence since 1564 in the service of an Indo-Muslim saint, as a non-denominational, indeed non-religious establishment! 'For the future—the origin of the shrine, and its attendance now does not invest it with the character of a special religious endowment of the Mohammedan or any other cult', noted the District Officer of Bahraich. Its management could then be taken over under the terms of another colonial statute.[33] The local government was set upon getting rid of the peculative khadims in the interest of the secular public good.

The ideological thrust of this colonial intervention was that of 'improvement': regular collection and audit of offerings, the opening of a hospital for pilgrims, school for the khadims' sons, and proper ventilation of the stuffy tomb, dangerously crammed with devotees during the hot mela month of May. The tomb of the saint—to quote a local officer, stood 'inside a dark and narrow cell which one enter[s] by a single door some five feet high.'[34] The congestion, humidity and perspiration of the milling devotees during the summer months were overpowering. A king-sized lamp burning constantly at the head of the grave added to the sweltering atmosphere, sufficient to 'melt the fat off human bodies', as Meer Ufsos noted in his nineteenth-century History of Hindustan. No wonder, then, that women entering the claustrophobic chamber emerged deliriously dehydrated. 'But such wretched females' seemed to welcome being 'sucked dry' by the distinguished occupant of the tomb: *Par woh murdār yeh samajhti hai ki sāheb-i-qabr ne mujhe chūs liya*. And this, ventured Ufsos, was the reason for the appellation *chinla* (libertine) that has come to be attached to the warrior saint.[35]

This seems intriguing, for folklore does not dwell upon the sexuality of the virgin-warrior. Was it then a case of a psychosomatic connect that lower and middle-caste women made after their heady brush with the Ghazi's grave? Could the portrayal of Ghazi Miyan as a bridegroom, who dies before consummation, eliciting miniature nuptial cots every year to his pilgrimage, could this story of a proximate honeymoon that is never to be, have elicited such a charged intimacy for and from women within grasping distance of his mortal remains?[36] There is no way to be sure. What is as palpable is the press of pilgrims and the stuffiness pervading the inside of the low-ceilinged dome. Even Ibn Battuta, while accompanying the Delhi Sultan did not quite succeed in entering the 'tomb … which lay under a dome … on account of the crowds'.[37]

The danger to pilgrims, male and female, was real indeed: twenty-odd had been 'crushed and suffocated to death' in the early 1870s. In 1878, the Deputy Commissioner succeeded, against opposition from the khadims, 'in getting a window opened in the wall of the holy of the holies', as he put it, 'the application to which of a thermantidote has considerably cooled and purified the air inside.'[38] A hand-propelled 'winnowing machine fitted to a window aperture', the thermantidote (like the solar topee) was a pukka colonial construct: 'A rotating fan fixed in a window opening and incased in wet tatties, used in India to drive in a current of cool air', is how the Oxford English Dictionary defines it.[39] The Deputy Commissioner reported that the mela pilgrims had begun to 'call the current of air from' the "English Fan" … the breath of the martyred saint', even placing 'offerings of pice, cowrie and flowers upon it'![40] The focus of attention of 'credulous pilgrims' of the nineteenth century, the thermantidote still lies unused in a corner of the shrine (Figure 15.2).

Fig. 15.2 The thermantidote installed in an opening in the wall of the Ghazi's tomb in 1878, now lying discarded in a corner of the shrine, May 1996

Cooling contraption notwithstanding, the chief servitors were greatly aggrieved at the official takeover of the management of the shrine. In 1887 managers Inayatullah and Daulat were finally permitted to petition the Lieutenant Governor against the arbitrary and illegal action of the local administration.[41] In response, local officers harked back to the quarter century of 'beneficent supervision of official authority' and the 'evidently cosmopolitan' character of the shrine. But after prolonged hearings, the Government ultimately lost the suit.[42] In 1902, the management of the shrine reverted to a Waqf Committee, that is, a trust organised in accordance with Islamic principles, but with the safeguards provided under the relevant colonial statute. However, this was not the end of legal wranglings. After a series of internecine disputes, the dargah was placed in 1964 under the management of the Sunni Waqf Board.[43] And that is where matters stand today.

16

Sites and Cenotaphs

The annual commemoration of the Ghazi was not limited to the principal shrine at Bahraich; the trope of a military campaign had resulted in the sacralisation of numerous sites where the commanders of Masud's army were said to have laid down their lives. In the *Mirat*, Abdur Rahman had provided a roll call of commanders whom Masud had despatched from his Satrikh redoubt: Amir Hasan to Mahoba (Banda District), Mir Bakhtiyar to the 'lower country' (eastern Bihar and Bengal), Azizudin to Gopamau in Partabgarh, Malik Afzal to the eastern city of Banaras, where he drank the 'cup of martyrdom', and the advance party of Miyan Rajab and Saifuddin to Bahraich, which place was to draw the hero himself into the fateful battle in 1034 CE. A Masud-centric work, the *Mirat* flags these commanders largely as colourless entities. In another encyclopaedic text,[1] Abdur Rahman Chishti laced his account of Masud's campaigns with pointed references to several martyrs' memorials, whose long-lasting *barkat* or beneficience had continued well into the author's own time in the seventeenth century.

> And so it is that wherever this writer has gone [in Awadh] during his travels, at each and every place there is to be found the presence of Masud's companions (*asrāt-ashāb-i-sultan-us-Shuhda*), who are the object of popular veneration.[2]

'The blessed *mazar* of Salar Saifuddin', sent with an advance party to Bahraich 'continues to attract large numbers of pilgrims for its miracles and boons', wrote Abdur Rahman in the 1640s; Miyan

Nasarullah's grave—locally called Bare Purukh—attracts boon-seekers, especially during the months of the monsoon: pilgrims today repair to Dikauli (ten miles southeast of Bahraich) after attending the Summer Fair.[3] Miyan Rajab's tomb is located two miles to the east of the Bahraich shrine, where large numbers throng, and since he is literally 'awesome'—*tasarrufāt mein mumtāz hain*, as the Urdu translation puts it—people approach his shrine with due trepidation.[4] Innumerable followers of Masud are to be found buried ten miles north of Bahraich on the banks of river Kathela: prominent among these is Miyan Mubazar [Mubasshir?]—'the wretched writer of these words has himself benefited by a visit to his grave'.[5] A firm believer in the saint, Abdur Rahman had no reason to query the ascription of warriors' tombs to Masud and his lieutenants. It was only with the grave of Miyan Rajab or Rajab Salar, buried in the town of Bahraich, that Abdur Rahman took care to debunk popular notions about his association with the Tughlaq dynasty of Delhi (1320–1413),* stressing that he was a 'personal servant' of the house of Salar Masud. As the *Mirat-i-Masudi* has it:

> [P]eople at large have coined a lot of erroneous things about Miyan Rajjab after his martyrdom. Some persons of deficient wisdom say that he was the sister's son [bhanja] of Salar Masud [the Ajab Salar of folklore]. We seek refuge in God from ... [such] lies. ... And some have changed his name saying that he was a tyrant and of harsh disposition [,]that Rajjab has remained to be [sic] the name of Firoz Shah [Tughlaq]... By all means it is also false. What relationship could that servant have with the king? Malik Rajjab was the meanest servant of Hazrat Sultan-ush-Shohda. It is also current among the people at large that he was a tyrant and of harsh disposition [,] but it [too] has no worth in the eyes of [the] ... pruden[t].[6]

However, an important Farsi text written some seventy years after Abdur Rahman continued to make the connection. 'Bahraich is a large city of the ancients on the banks of the River Sarju [i.e., Sarayu], the environs of which are most pleasant', we read in Sujan Singh Bhandari's

* This may have stemmed from the visit by Mohammad-bin-Tughlaq along with Ibn Battuta to the Bahraich shrine and two subsequent visits by Firozshah Tughlaq, and the material help by the latter in the construction of masonry fortification, the Bara Qila as it is called today.

historical and geographical account, c. 1695–96, written independent of court patronage in the fortieth year of the reign of the Mughal Emperor Aurangzeb. 'The tomb of Salar Masud, who was a close kinsman of Sultan Mahmud Ghaznawi is there, along with that of Rajab Salar, the brother of Sulṭān [Ghias-ud-Dīn] Tughlaq Shah and the father of Firoz Shah, the ruler of Hindustan.'[7]

Local notices in the Gazetteers compiled in the late nineteenth century, three centuries after the *Mirat*, again reveal a bewildering ascription of 'historic' graves and *ganj-i-shahīdān* (martyrs' graveyards) to the fallen commanders of Masud's army. In qasba Bijlor, eight miles east of Lucknow, locals claimed, was the tomb of Malik Ambar, who was killed at Bahraich, but wandered back to his eventual burial site as a headless horseman. The earth seems to have opened to receive this *ghorwa shahīd*, the immense size of his tomb suggesting to the English officer that 'probably [Malik Ambar's] horse was buried with him'![8] Here, as elsewhere in the Awadh region, the mnemonic pull of Masud had tended to overwhelm local battles fought two to three centuries *after* the legendary campaigns of Masud Ghazi. It appears that even in the more historical nineteenth-century notices, there was no discounting the power of local tradition. At several places in southern Awadh, noted the Gazetteer, 'the earliest historical *event known to local memory*', remained in the 1870s—as it does today—'the passage of Sayyad Salar's army' through a particular tract in early eleventh century![9]

Some forty sites of *ganj-i-shahīdān* and warriors' tombs (reported in the late nineteenth-century Gazetteer) laid claim to a connection with the campaigns of Salar Masud: Gopamau and Bilgram in Hardoi, Jalalpur Debi, Rudauli and Tikaitganj in Bara Banki, Amethi and Salon in Rae Bareli, Malihabad, Bijlaur and Nagram (Lucknow), Zafrabad and Bhadohi further east, Badaun and Deoband in the upper Gangetic valley. These were some of the places where extant graves from the thirteenth to the sixteenth centuries were attributed in both elite and popular imagination to the campaigns of Salar Masud.[10] Commemorative graveyards aside, Ghazi Miyan's marriage/martyrdom was celebrated at a number of places in the north Indian states of UP and Bihar where boon-seekers gathered annually in May–June immediately after the spring harvest (see Maps 1.1 and 16.1). In a very real sense, the ill-defined 'long time ago' of Awadh and eastern

UP had got affixed to the exploits of the eleventh century warrior saint as etched in local lore and in the early seventeenth-century *Mirat*. The venerable desire for claiming Masud's commanders, often as lineage heads, had become a marker of status: the highest ranking Muslim families in various parts of eastern Awadh (and Allahabad), noted an official report, 'are [all] said to have come to this country in the time of Salar Masud'. Several of the old Awadh families asserted that their 'ancestors actually accompanied Salar Masud'![11]

The need to have Masud or his commanders fight in all the decisive early medieval battles had its dénouement in a piquant story from the town of Jais, the birthplace of the famous Awadhi poet Malik Mohammad Jaisi. Here, according to local tradition, one Rizvi Syed of Sabzwar of Persia invested the region at the head of a cavalry contingent, c. 1200 CE, and settled at Adyanagar, which place he called Ja-i-aish or 'happy residence', subsequently corrupted to Jais. His opponents, according to one version, were not the local Bhar chiefs, but Salar Masud himself: 'an instance of the application of a well-known name when the real name had passed out of recollection', as a British officer put it.[12] 'The Musalmans of Oudh [Awadh] are apt to associate with Syed Salar every object or tradition of antiquity to which they can ascribe no certain origin', noted a general history of the region.[13] An account of Unao district near Kanpur squared the circle with the suggestion that local legends about the 'places Masood is said to have passed through … may be so far accepted as proof that he did pass through them'![14] In the sub-Himalayan district of Saharanpur, the Musalmans of Deoband claimed that one of the first fortresses taken by 'the celebrated hero Sipah Salar Masud Ghazi' was the 'sacred forest' Devi-ban, the name changed to Deoband, literally, the 'incarcerated demon'. This was following the standard practice by which the term 'Devi' or more particularly 'Dev', an honorific attached to proper names of chiefs, was rendered into 'Deo', Persian/Urdu for demon or ogre.[15]

The oldest tomb of Bilgram in district Hardoi (central Awadh), suggested a splice of local history in an official Gazetteer, was that of 'a half mythical personage', Khwaje Madad-ul-din, a holy man and disciple of Khwaje Abu Muhammad Chishti'.[16] Unbeknowst to the English civilian, the author of this notice, the name 'Madad-ud-din' appears to have been an intriguing interpellation by the highly accomplished sheykhs of Bilgram.[17] To capture this ingenious bit of local history, one needs to revisit briefly the seventeenth-century hagiography of Ghazi Miyan. In the *Mirat-i-Masudi*, an ageing Khwaja Abu Mohammad of Chisht (of Chisht-i-Sharif, some 170 miles east of Herat, Afghanistan) calls out to his disciple, one Mohammad Kaku/ Kalu in that town, to extend help to Sultan Mahmud Ghazni in his famous attack on the temple of Somnath. Indulging in an exhibition of tele-warfare, Kaku, a miller and a devotee of the Khwaja, helps Sultan Mahmud vanquish the 'unbelievers' at a great distance, while pounding furiously a wall in his home town with his grinding mill! To quote the *Mirat*,

> The Khwaja called out 'Kaku assist.' Kaku was then seen in such a state that he was restlessly waging war (with great fury). At the time that the unbelievers [at Somnath] were getting routed, at that very moment Mohammad Kaku was seen in Chisht in such a state that carrying the grinding-mill under his armpit, he was smashing it furiously at a wall, [or rather] smashing the wall with his milling-pestle.[18]

In the *Mirat*-inflected memory of Bilgram, this 'helper' of Sultan Mahmud became 'Khwaja Madad-ud-din', quite literally 'the Khwaja Helper of Islam', and the occupant of the oldest shaykh tomb in town, over 1,600 km away from the Afghani town of Chisht.

While medieval graveyards were ascribed to Masud's commanders, ancient monuments were claimed as the forts and temples of Sohal Deo, the Ghazi's chief antagonist. Not only the ruins of Set Mahet (the Sravasti of Buddha's monsoon sojourns), but also the remnants of an old fort in Nanpara, 'like all the other old remains' of the Bahraich district, noted the Gazetteer, was 'assigned to Raja Sohal Deo, the opponent of Saiyid Salar'.[19] The temple of Mahadeo at Asokpur in neighbouring Gonda district, built over—according to tradition—by the tomb of Hathila Pir, killed in an assault, was said to have been constructed by Raja 'Suhel Deo, the opponent of Saiyid Salar'.[20] A late nineteenth-century archaeological digest averred that this 'low-domed building only 20 feet square, still much frequented as the shrine of a ghazi or martyr for the faith', was of Salar Saifuddin, sent out by Masud from his camp in Satrikh to Bahraich at the head of an advance column.[21] Further proof of the connection of this site with

Salar Masud, archaeologists felt, was provided by the existence of an old mahua tree! Given the centrality of the solitary mahua that Masud had allowed (according to the *Mirat*) to let stand in the replanted forest at Bahraich, the Director General of Archaeology had wanted in 1862 to make a proper excavation near the base of that large tree. However, 'a small Musalman tomb prevented him from digging in the centre'.[22] Cunningham, the Director of the Archaeological Survey of India, cut down a gigantic banyan tree instead, whose roots, thirty years later, still held the bricks of the remnants of the temple 'together by their interlacings'. For his part, a successor official interlaced local lore with dendrochronology to speculate:

> As the cut stem showed 849 annual rings, the tree must have been planted in 1013 A.D. during the reign of Mahmud of Ghazni.[!] This indeed is about the date of the temple itself, which is said to have been built by Suharidhdhvaja, the Raja of Asokpur, and antagonist of Saiyid Salar. The mound with the *mahua* tree is called raja *Sohil Deo-ka-khalang*, or Sohal Deo's seat.[23]

So much for mnemonic, monumental and arborial traces of the warrior saint and his chief antagonist. For his part, Abdur Rahman Chishti, the seventeenth-century author, concluded his geography of veneration with Qazi Tahir, 'the last in the line of martyrs' from the warrior saint's campaign, whose graveyard in qasba Anbathi (Dhanithi) in Lucknow district 'is shared by the author's ancestors', and where Abdur Rahman was himself buried in 1683 CE, 600 years later.[24] We have here the outer limit of textual ascription: the author's family graveyard standing, so to speak, as living proof of the veracity of a hagiography of his own writing!

The figure of Salar Masud of the *Mirat* and the dotting of the Awadh landscape by cenotaphs of his commanders appear then as a case of how elements of a romance concocted by a skilful literary ideologue in near pre-modern times (the seventeenth century) can take hold of the consciousness of the past prevalent in almost every group of the mainly illiterate population of an entire region. Masud's is then a fit case for suggesting that popular memory, when reinforced by literary inscriptions, is likely to survive over several centuries—often as genealogies of elites and subaltern remembrance alike.

And so, even to this day, in the tract around Mowai and Basaurhi parganas in Bara Banki district (abutting the historical town of Rudauli), the remains of a vanquished Bhar raja's fort, a martyrs' graveyard in the jungle beside Kinhaura (near Patranga railway station in Bara Banki district), or the exact spot in Belkhara village where the palanquin-bearer Karia Bhol is said to have helped Masud cross the wide Ghaghra river en route to his final battleground, are pointed with dead certainty as sites marked irrevocably by the presence of the Bahraich Ghazi.[25] Clearly, Salar Masud has had a long chain of recollectors besides Sheikh Abdur Rahman: among them, the fourteenth-century traveller Ibn Battuta who visited the shrine and alluded to the stories about the saint, Emperor Akbar who was nearly mobbed by Bahraich-bound pilgrims outside his palace in Agra, and the present-day Pathan landholders of a swath of villages in the Bhatiana tract in the Awadh region—purveyors of Ghazi anecdotes and proud claimants to a genealogical tree going back to the warrior saint.

Map 16.1 Sites and cenotaphs associated with Salar Masud in Uttar Pradesh

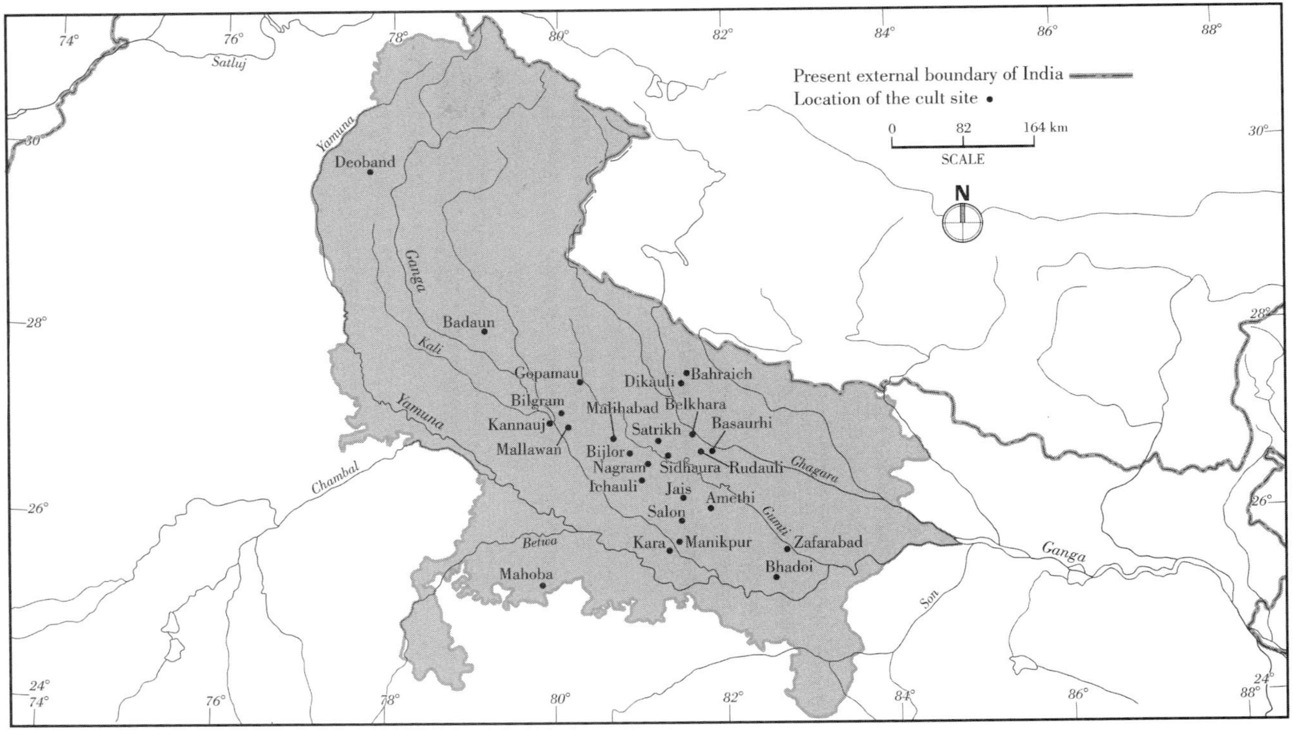

PART FOUR COUNTER-HISTORIES

17

Investing the Ghazi

Affective recollections aside, Ghazi Miyan has had an equally eventful presence from an imaginary eleventh century down to our own times. The attempt by Sikandar Lodi, a sixteenth-century Delhi Sultan, to ban 'the festival of the Spears of Salar Masud [for its unorthodox features] in his kingdom' had been unsuccessful.[1] The interdiction itself was evidence of the widespread veneration of the saint, with the Bahraich shrine attracting devotees from a wide arc between Agra and Banaras, looping upwards into the sub-montane tract bordering present-day Nepal. Did orthodox Muslims, specially the ulema, not frown upon the cult of Masud as an instance of neo-idolatry corrupting the ways of subaltern Musalmans? *Ashrāf* or Muslim elites clearly despised their low-caste brethren (ill-bred *razla*, as they called them), who together with Hindu *Panchpiriyas* made up the Ghazi-adoring public. In such a view, it was this uncouth populace that paraded boisterously through north Indian towns every May, colourful pennons aloft, declaiming the greatness of the Bahraich saint.

Abdur Rahman, the Sufi hagiographer of Masud, was clearly aware of the Islamicist disquiet at the 'worship' of his spiritual lodestar. He therefore took care to uphold the story about divine displeasure at a learned ulema's (to use a double attribute) belittling of the cult of the Bahraich Ghazi. The point in the *Mirat* where Abdur Rahman inserts this morality tale is significant. Masud has been dead for some time. The news of the milkmaid's conception after supplicating at his grave has brought the entire 'tribe of cowherds' into the saint's fold. The elites of Rudauli follow suit. The critical event here is the curing of blind girl Zohra and her symbolic marriage-in-death to the saint's grave. Together these have contributed to the 'rise in popular fervour for Masud'.

It is at this juncture in the text that Abdur Rahman inserts an incident symbolising the ineffective opposition to the cult from an Islamicist point of view. Singing and dancing, brandishing the lances and pennons of the Salar, a party of pilgrims from Banaras enters the town of Jaunpur in eastern UP, the seat of an independent Sharqi Sultanate (1394–1479 CE), which controlled large parts of eastern UP, Bihar and Awadh, including the frontier region of Bahraich. The exuberant crowd is joined by hundreds of local devotees. This adds to the din and clamour, the throng spilling over into the bylanes. Disturbed by the tumult, a local mulla seeks to 'exercise his religious authority' by attempting to put a stop to the un-Islamic ways of the Bahraich-bound pilgrims. Chastisement is almost immediate. A resounding slap is administered by an unseen hand; the maulvi falls senseless to the ground and dies. A curious crowd assembles. They observe that the mulla's cheek has turned black. 'Since that day most of the unwise and short-sighted persons [developed] a belief in the spiritual suzerainty of Masud and became his believers', records the *Mirat* with some satisfaction.[2]

The first Urdu translation of the *Mirat*, c. 1870, adds another episode at this point. Here the saint himself responds with unerring logic to a scholar questioning the un-Islamic practices at his shrine. The setting is quotidian. A scholar in a qasba in Awadh gets annoyed at the fidgety behaviour of his personal barber. A devotee of Ghazi Miyan, the barber is distraught at the prospect of missing the pilgrim-party setting out for Bahraich. On learning the reason for his distraction, the scholar hands him a letter addressed to (the long-martyred) Masud, expressing surprise at the saint condoning the un-Islamic practice of grave worship. The *nai* returns from the pilgrimage with a fitting response from Salar Masud himself! 'There is no stopping the honest devotion of the people, the Maker's own creation—their doings are the "works of God Almighty" (*kārkhāna-i-Khuda*). Who am I to forbid them? Besides, why query me about stopping the Bahraich concourse, when you yourself are unable to restrain the barber in Bahraich' an equestrian apparition had added at the back of the missive from Bahraich.[3]

The cult of Ghazi Miyan also attracted censure from sectarian preachers in their attempt to purify popular Islam. One such early nineteenth-century tract attacked the practice of pilgrimage and beseeching saints for 'every earthly desire—a (usually male) child, well-being or honour.' Such practices were excrescences that pockmarked the wayward faith of lower-class Muslims who needed redeeming. They were the result of 'social intercourse' with Hindus, resulting in a veritable *khichri* (potpourri) of Islamic and idolatrous practices. 'While Hindus have their Gaya, Mathura and Kashi (Banaras) as holy sites', rued Syed Ahmad Shahīd (1786–1831) in his *Sirat-i-Mustaqim* or 'The Straight Path', similarly 'Muslims go to Makanpur, then Bahraich and Ajmer'—all three places connected with Ghazi Miyan.[4] Occasional sectarian diatribes aside, however, neither Muslim nor Hindus elites considered it necessary till the 1870s to bleach this popular regard into the unsullied white of denominational rectitude.[5]

But what about the Ghazi's historic opponents, the Indian *kuffar* who were the objects of the Ghazi's militant exertions as depicted in the hagiography? The 1870s saw the beginning of a concerted attack from a narrowly sectarian view point on the life, shrine and cult of Masud. These were not occasioned by a systematic effort to mine the seams of a popular counter-memory. Popular lore, it appears, was unyielding for the purposes of an adversarial narrative, else the figure of 'our Ghazi groom' would not have persisted among the Hindu *menu peuple* well into the 1870s. It was this lacuna, this failure of 'Hindu memory', so to speak, that a new generation of modern Hindi writers set out to rectify from the last quarter of the nineteenth century. The backdrop to the print polemics against Ghazi Miyan was provided by developments in the fields of language, script and pedagogy in the second half of the nineteenth century. The espousal of Hindi and the distancing of the colonial state from Persian and Urdu were crucial to a new historicist forging of a reformed and unified Hindu community. The late nineteenth century also saw an acceleration in the colonial efforts by British officers in north India to encourage the publication of school primers in Hindi—a language that was becoming increasingly different from the standard Urdu of administration—and the large outpouring of literary productions occasioned by the development of printing presses. As a result, alongside the teaching of the 'Three Rs', a fair number of pedagogical tracts focused on rites and rituals far removed from the primary concerns of prepubescent children rolled off government presses as Hindi textbooks.[6] Spurred by subsidised print runs by the Department of Public Instruction, these early attacks on the deleterious effects of Parseek (sic: Persian) or 'Muslim rule' on Hindu society were written largely by a sprinkling of government school teachers of UP. And they were as novel as they were persistent in their inculcation of a generalised common sense about north India's oppressive medieval past.

These early attacks on Salar Masud were aimed at saving Hindu women from their blind adoration of the warrior saint. Often couched in the voice of the rational Hindu housewife, this rubbishing of Ghazi Miyan was of a piece with the construction of a common sense: the memory of 'Hindu Defeat' at the hands of Muslims in India's medieval past. Such a remembrance was linked equally to the logic of colonial modernity: for the siring of communities through print and the affixing of history to a persistent memory, here as elsewhere, went hand in hand. It is within this new 'Hindu History', increasingly abrasive, yet unable to fully dislodge Masud from familial altars, that the contest over the devotees of the Ghazi played itself out.

Classroom pedagogy and the recovery of a mutilated memory came together for the first time in such tracts as the 'Enlightenment of Women' (1871) and 'The Ocean of Rites' (1872). Written by Hindi school teachers, female attachment to Muslim shrines in these primers was likened to 'stubborn, noxious weeds from the parched fields' of Hindu India's subjugated past. Medieval Muslim dominance, these books argued, had left no aspect of Indian life unblemished, leading to an inability to distinguish between proper and improper mores. It was this historical numbing of the intellect that had led Hindu women to forsake their all-powerful God, *Ishwar*, while clinging to the shrines and cenotaphs of Ghazi Miyan. In partaking of holy unction, so to speak, at the altars of Muslim saints, Hindus were virtually ingesting the leftovers from their Muslim neigbours' kitchen. So argued one Ram Lal, First Master of a District School from south-central UP in 1871.[7] For this school teacher, the desperate desire of women to beget a male child was the reason for their attachment to Muslim saints. Yet, the patriarchal pressure to deliver a baby boy quickly—the goad behind the reproductive anxiety—was seldom addressed, even if the protagonist, as in this 1872 tract, was a woman.[8]

Maina, the heroine of *Ritiratnakar*, another such tract, is the upholder of feminine Hindu reason. Her interlocutors, all of them women, are of a status lower than this well-heeled, intelligent housewife from a middle-class Hindu home. The discussion on Ghazi Miyan, initiated by Maina, begins with a weak suggestion, left hanging in the air, that not all pregnant women yearn for a male child.[9] Neta, the lower-caste woman attached to Maina's household and the voice of the typical woman devotee, states matter-of-factly: 'Whoever goes to the Ghazi's Court comes back with her wishes fulfilled'. Faced with a catalogue of cured afflictions—epilepsy, blindness, possession, malignant fever—Maina, the literate housewife, gets frustrated. She will not believe any such stories unless furnished with an eyewitness account of the goings-on at the fair at Sikandara in Allahabad District.[10]

She pays a milkmaid to be a *bhedi*, her secret informant. The choice of an Ahirin, from the community with a great attachment to the saint, appears to be a narrative ploy. For it was Jaswa, an infertile woman of the same cowherd Ahir caste, tormented by her mother-in-law, who first supplicated at the Bahraich shrine and was blessed with a male child. This was the miracle recorded by the *Mirat* which appears to have led to the Ahir pastoral-peasant groups of the Gangetic plains becoming firm devotees of the warrior saint. By contrast, the late nineteenth-century milkmaid's commentary gets wedded to a condemnation of popular rites at the Ghazi Fair. Faced with a critical commentary on the Mela—a den of philanderers and crooks, teeming with rakes and rogues—the woman blurts out defensively: If Ghazi Miyan is not to be venerated, who else does one go to? Maina, the educated protagonist, tears her hair out at such superstition. Clearly, these women have to be disabused of their ill-placed faith in a Musalman saint by being taught what *these Musalmans have really been, and still are.* With History dislodging amnesia, self-knowledge will follow. Ghazi Miyan is no saint, no *devta*, lectures Maina to these 'forgetful' women:

> *Hai*! *Hai*! Have people here taken leave of their senses? *Aré Baurahi*!—Ghazi Miyan was a commander in the army of the Musalmans when coming from western countries [Turks from Turkey!] they attacked [us] here [in India]. There was a big fight between Hindus and Musalmans, at the end of which the Hindus slew Ghazi Miyan in Bahraich where

> his associates built a grave of [this Muslim commander]. Since then the bird-brained [among the Hindus] started worshipping him.[11]

The awkward question—why people should worship a slain foe 'senselessly'—is left hanging in the air. The reference to Ghazi Miyan as one of the principal actors in the Hindu–Muslim fight of yore is such as to evoke a contemporary resonance about present-day Musalmans. And so, Neta, the low-caste woman, makes sense of the slaying and entombment of the medieval Ghazi with reference to an event from the recent local past: the story of a Hindu–Muslim riot occasioned by a clash over a public festival, the death of a Muslim youth, and the affixing of the epithet 'martyr' to the dead boy. The analogy is forced, but the point is driven home by school teacher Ram Prasad Tiwari in this Hindi textbook subvented by the Director of Public Instruction, UP. The initial dialogue, the eyewitness report on the Fair, the quick uptake of history about the ways of *these contemporary Musalmans*, the critique of grave-worship—all these have the desired effect. Seeing reason (and the cunning of History), Neta, who was planning to take her daughter-in-law to the Ghazi Miyan shrine, recants. With the low-caste woman reposing her faith in the supreme Hindu God, the lesson on Ghazi Miyan can now end.[12]

18

Demotic Warfare

The first two decades of the twentieth century saw a spurt in the publication of such polemical Hindu histories of Masud. The goad was the availability of provocative Urdu renditions of the Mirat. First published in limited print runs in the 1870s, Inayat Husain's *History of Masud*—priced at a modest four annas (just short of a day's rural wages)—was by the 1910s in its third edition.[1] Over roughly the same period, a spate of Hindi tracts—subvented by the revivalist Arya Samaj—sought to project a singular Hindu national past: a 'history' alloyed with religious beliefs, stereotypical counterfactuals, and nuggets dug out from the seams of a newly excavated deep memory.[2] This included several 'modern Hindu histories', composed usually by publicists belonging to the district branches of the Arya Samaj in Awadh and eastern UP—the catchment area of the Ghazi Miyan cult.[3]

The starting point of these chapbooks was the requirement to study the 'Lives' of 'our ancient ancestors'. But there was also the need to recount the misdeeds of those Muslim conquerors who 'apart from playing football with our forefathers' heads [had] destroyed the history' of Hindu community as well.[4] Knowledge of one's history, in such a view, was a sure way to progress. 'Learned readers', began one such tract, 'the man who does not know his History, has no knowledge of his real situation', and till he knows his '"present" it is impossible for him to move along the path of progress.'[5] The professed aim of these pamphlets was to wean a large number of lower and middle caste persons away from venerating Ghazi Miyan. Their specific targets were those Hindu women who were thronging the Bahraich shrine, praying foolishly that the Ghazi, himself born to a long-time barren women, grant them their desire to be delivered of a son.

In a sixty-page pamphlet, *Ghazi Miyan or the Real Life Story of Masud Ghazi* (1916), a Brahman on way to his home town of Bahraich stops over at a large village in the province of Awadh. Both the topography and the vegetation suggest that the prosperous, decent Hindus living here have become indifferent in the practice of their true religion: in other words, they are being led astray by the likes of the warrior saint. The Brahman is met by a local trader from the caste of distillers, who invites him to stay back for the worship of the 'Big Deity Ghazi Miyan' of Bahraich. A native of that town, the Brahman is appalled at such ignorance. He calls for the culprit, the charlatan Muslim Dafali, deprecatingly dubbed Ghure, literally, 'dunghill'. A deconstruction of the web of dissimilitude with which Ghure had ensnared gullible rural Hindus takes place. The lowly Dafali is squarely worsted at his own game. The assembled villagers realise their mistake; the Brahman now proceeds to tell the 'real story of Ghazi Miyan' from authoritative 'Musalmani Histories'. In other words, a Hindu retelling of the expansive Urdu rendition of Abdur Rahman's seventeenth-century hagiography as History takes place.[6]

The Pandit starts with the question, 'Alright, Ghure! Tell me the name of Ghazi Miyan?' 'Salar Masud Ghazi' is the reply. 'Mother's and Father's name?'; 'they were from Ghazni, between Kabul and Kandahar'. 'Which castes live there?' 'Ghazi caste', replies the Dafali, and is made to add, 'in other words a Musalman caste'.[7] Nothing more would be required of the knowledgeable Pandit: incommensurable lines have been drawn in a village which had till then housed Ghazi Miyan's 'Hindu' devotees.

To assail the Dafali with the question: *Accha batāo Ghazi Miyan ka nām kya tha?* is to suggest that Ghazi Miyan, a linguistic marker of the domestication of the Islamic warrior is not a name, properly speaking.* It is a euphemism, a ruse to keep the Hindus ignorant about his real name—which is a Muslim name. Even the common

---

* Note that neither the warrior nor the Islamic/Muslim element is erased in the name 'Ghazi Miyan'. 'Ghazi' of course means 'holy warrior', while Miyan is a north Indian generic term for a Musalman. Miyan, as in the expression 'Bare Miyan', ('old chap'), has a certain honorific quality to it, but unlike the common Hindi honorific 'ji', it tends to reduce rather than create distance between the speaker and the addressee.

appellation 'Miyan' for male Muslims seems inadequate here. The term 'Musalman' functions as the marker of an explicit otherness: a recognisably Muslim proper name or the clear identification of a non-existent Muslim Ghazi caste is sorely needed. But it seems that villagers knew who a Ghazi was, or at least that a Miyan is a miyan, that is, a Musalman!

So the Arya Samaj tract goes over the idea of obfuscation to develop an argument about the ignorance of the Hindus: hence the need for pamphlets and the recounting of true demotic histories. Within such reasoning, not mentioning Musalman in the case of everything which is clearly so is an *obfuscation of the Musalmans*. We have arrived at the idea of two radically different cultures, societies, semiotic worlds. Muslims must identifiably be Muslim. Everything that is an interplay between the Islamic and the Indian (most notably Ghazi Miyan) is a Muslim ruse, because it does not mention that *we* Hindus are dealing with *them* Musalmans.

The stories told by the Dafalis are, therefore, figments of the imagination of these lowly rascals, out to make a quick buck by duping innocent Hindus with fabricated stories about the noble lineage and heroic deeds of Ghazi Miyan. One such tall tale is that Ghazi Miyan, or alternatively his nephew, is an incarnation of Rama's brother Lakshman. But the next positivist step, that Mahmud of Ghazni did not have a sister's son called Masud, and that the *Mirat* itself is a hagiography written in the early seventeenth century, uncorroborated by any known historical text, is not taken. Rather, embroidered nineteenth-century Urdu translations of the hagiography are considered definitive 'Muslim histories' dealing with the exploits of Masud, the fanatic.

For these publicists, endeavouring to purge common Hindus of all traces of an Indo-Muslim popular cult, the veneration of Ghazi Miyan needed to be tackled historically, even if it involved conferring a hagiography with the attributes of unalloyed certitude. Implied also is the suggestion that in a fundamental sense—the sense we Hindus have of our pasts and the ignoble deeds of the Musalmans—the *Mirat* is the definitive historical text and the tales told by Dafalis mere myth-making charades. Thus, the language of excess through which the deeds of Turkic, Afghan and Mughal conquerors in India are necessarily told in medieval chronicles fits snugly with the positivist 'Hindu' reading of such texts, yielding a supposedly true account of iconoclasm in eleventh-century north India. And this is the *real* history: 'apart from the life as recounted by me', says one pamphleteer, 'the rest that the *mujawir*-keepers of the shrine say is falsehood.' 'Readers should never trust anything that is not mentioned in my book', warns another.[8]

This 'real history' is elaborated through an essentialist reading of 'Hindu' and 'Muslim' pasts. Thus, Raja Sohal Deo and other members of the confederacy that challenged Masud in Bahraich are made into Kshatriya warriors by adding the suffix 'Singh' to the word 'Deo' (which is somewhat odd, for the normal practice is to write 'Singh Deo' rather than 'Deo Singh'). Sohal Deo is the ideal king: in one text, a Buddhist king of the famous city of Shravasti.[9] Further, he is a leading cow protector, maintaining water bodies and gifting cows to Brahmans.[10] We have here a neat inversion of the story of Raja Sohal rustling the Ghazi's cows, mentioned fleetingly in the *Mirat*, and dilated to great effect in the ballads.[11] Instead, the Raja gets portrayed as a mighty king, master of warfare and well served by his large army. It is his battle plan: first feign withdrawal, then decimate the charging cavalry of Masud with arrows as their horses trip over poisoned spikes—a standard trope in accounts of battles between Turks and Rajputs—that causes the rout of the Muslim cavalry.[12]

In the decisive battle of 14 Rajab 424 A.H.—there is no getting away from the Hijri era given in the Urdu version of the *Mirat*—the *yavana* (foreigner-Muslims), according to the Hindi pamphlet *Real Story of Masud Miyan*, were keen on attaining martyrdom; the kshatriyas committed to standing firm by their vow to protect their dharma. Carrying on in this vein, this History of Ghazi Miyan slips in the fact that the furious Hindu warriors were repeating during the battle the four-lettered verse, supposedly addressed by Ram's envoy Hanuman to Ravana, the demon king of Lanka, before that monkey god set the city ablaze![13]

The ambiguity about the desacralisation of the Suraj Kund (*pace Mirat*) is here seen as a straightforward case of iconoclasm, aimed at denying the Hindus the additional benefits of bathing in the sulphur enriched tank.[14] Imaginary dialogues are put into the mouth of Sohal Deo, here called, Suhridaya Dev, 'the good hearted'.

> In the end Raja Suhridaya Dev threw out the challenge: 'Oh you Ghazi! Let's see you show your Muhammadan ardour for which you

> have unnecessarily killed so many Hindus! Don't you forget, just as you pulverized the ears and nose of the Somnath idol into lime, so shall I crush today your bones to lime dust, and with that cement the nose and ears of that idol.[15]

The popular story about the Ghazi having come to do battle to save cows gets countered by the assertion that the cattle had been specially procured for his wedding banquet, and it was the kshatriya kings who were following their dharma by rescuing the cows before attacking the invaders—a case of using stereotypical counterfactuals to correct a literal fact present both in popular lore and the *Mirat*: 'As in Muslim religion it is proper to kill and eat cows rather than offer them protection, that's why the Ghazi had reared the cows for his and his army's consumption as food'.

> And so Ghazi Miyan cannot [by any stretch of the imagination] be a *Gau Guhari-Go-rakshak* (one who responds to the call: 'Protect the Cows'), for [in reality] he was a *Gaubhakshak* [that is, the devourer of cows].[16]

It was such a combination of facticity and stereotypical counterfactuality that enabled the Arya Samaj writers of the 1910s and 1920s to cut though the deceits of Dafalis and the conceits of the Urdu *Mirat*. And this so as to present their demotic accounts as the 'Real Life & Deeds of Masud Ghazi'. Abdur Rahman's text of the 1620s had come a long way. The hagiography of a warrior saint, written within the framework of the Chishti Sufi order, overlaid perhaps as a reaction to the non-sectarian state building of the previous Mughal Emperor, Akbar and propelled by the clutch of stories about the powers of a legendary warrior-saint, had been recast three centuries later by writers of Hindi chapbook histories.

Such 'Hindu Histories' can have no room for the saintly aspects of life of warrior Masud. And it is not just the hallowed Islamic persona of the hero of the *Mirat* that falls by the side. Minutiae of the hagiography such as manifestation of religious ecstasy, saintly premonition and humility as a curb on ambition also get excised as a matter of course. The Arya Samaj publicists would have none of this illicit coupling: Muslim/Hindu, Hindustani/Ghaznavid that enabled Abdur Rahman to write his hagiography as a saintly life of

Masud Ghazi. For the president of the local Arya Samaj of Bahraich, the *loot-maar* unleashed by this warrior is best told from 'Musalman histories', sans those portions which make the marauder appears less of a mindless iconoclast—in other words, braided with local, non-Muslim tropes, beliefs and practices from the Gangetic heartland. All references to Masud's attachment to things Indian which would seem to humanise the jihad of the Ghazi in Hindustan get expunged. There is no chewing of the Indian betel leaf and no affirmation of Masud's attachment to the Bahraich country or the mahua tree under which he wished to be buried.

The Hindi pamphlets end the story of the Masud–Sohal encounter with the Ghazi's death. There is practically nothing here on the fate of Sohal Deo after his victory on the battlefield. In the *Mirat*, Masud appears in the dream of his lieutenant left behind at the base camp, with the instruction to first bury him along with the *asp mada-i-khing* or the mare Lilli and Sikandar Diwana and then to slay Sohal Deo. The next day's events turn out as prophesised by the martyr: both Sohal Deo and Syed Ibrahim perish in mortal combat. The Hindi pamphlets skip this bit of the story, as if Sohal's life ends with the death of Masud and stopping the first of 'Islamic invasion of Awadh'.

If these tracts are ambiguous about the eventual fate of Sohal Deo, they are quite sanguine about what happened to Masud's body: With Masud dead, Sohal Deo now surveys the 'Islamic camp', and finds that not one among the 'foreigners' is alive; those soldiers who had miraculously survived appear almost dead—only a few servants remain. The raja does not think it fit to kill these non-combatants. The Hindus keep searching for Masud's body, but by now it is dark. They give up the search, saying that they could 'dispose of it properly' in the morning; the *Mirat* dilates instead on the watchdog role of the faithful dog Sakul, which kept the jackals away the entire night.[17] The Arya Samaj publicists strongly counter this: the battle had been fought on the outskirts of a jungle, teeming with wild animals who would have converged at the site of such a mass slaughter, making it impossible for a mere dog to guard Masud's corpse. The strong inference is that the Hindus must have taken Salar Masud's corpse away in the morning and 'despatched it in an appropriate manner'.[18] In other words, Salar Masud, a devout Muslim warrior, was denied a proper martyr's burial, which involved being interred in the blood-soaked clothes of a true *shahīd*. This is followed by extrapolating from the true dharma of kshatriya warriors. For the 'Kshatriyas of those days were known to sacrifice their life rather than renege on a promise': so if they had resolved that they would come looking for Salar Masud's body the next day, they must surely have found it. Besides, the Hindus would have prevented the few Musalmans that remained alive from burying Masud at that spot. And so it follows that the grave claimed to be Masud's does not contain that martyr's mortal remains. The *mujawir*s who have spread other tall tales about the Ghazi can be trusted to have spread this false story as well. It is thus that the 1916 pamphlet denies that it is the martyr's body that lies buried in what is purported to be his grave.[19]

Other publicists did not contest the fact of Masud's burial, but regretted that Raja Sohal lost the chance of restoring the sun tank to its original purity after the Ghazi had polluted it by dumping the bodies of his slain soldiers in it. This had long-term consequences. It was because Raja Sohal adhered to the idea of ritual purity of keeping distance from a site polluted by the dead *yavana*s that one or two servants of Masud were able to construct a rudimentary grave of the Ghazi.* It remained a nondescript earthen mound for 300 years, with people passing it by on their way to the desecrated ancient sun tank. Unfortunately, rued the Hindi pamphlet, this entire area fell into the hands of Muslim foreigners after two centuries. Sultan Ferozshah Tughlaq of Delhi came from Delhi to Bahraich 356 years after Masud's death in 776 Hijri, that is, 1374–75 CE. Wiping out all trace of the dilapidated sun tank, he rebuilt the shrine anew, enclosing it in the manner of medieval fort with a forbidding stone perimeter. 'A grave-protector called Mitrullah [a hybrid term, "friend", Sanskrit, *mitr* of Allah!] was assigned some revenue-free land for the maintenance of the shrine.' From this time on, concluded Braj Mohan Jha, an office bearer of the Bahraich branch of the Arya Samaj and the author of this particular pamphlet, the reputation of the Ghazi-shrine increased and the Suraj Kund Fair got converted into the mela of Syed Salar.

* *Yavanas*: a term used by the medieval period largely for foreigner Muslims. Relatively uncommon by the eighteenth century, it is used in this text to mark the extreme otherness of the Musalmans.

The angularity of the twentieth-century pamphlets derived then from a mode of demotic argumentation; their ire rose from a sense of frustration at the continued popularity of the Ghazi cult. Suffused with an earthy reasoning and inventive wordplay, these chapbooks sought to realign history, local geography and everyday practices to the crucial battle of Bahraich in 1034 CE. And so the Ghazi's invasion became the decisive 'Muslim event' of the last millennium. Hindu subjection, mutilated memory, even regional demographics, all had their origin in the *ghazza* of the Ghazi, such that the twentieth-century distribution of Muslims in Awadh bore the genetic footprint of the invading soldiery of the early eleventh century![20] The facts that the landed and military colonisation of Awadh (both by 'Hindu' and 'Muslim' gentry-military groups) took place nearly two to three centuries later, that the distribution of rural population by religion in the year 1926 (the date of one such pamphlet) could not have been determined by Masud's failed mission of nine hundred years ago, for then there would be no 'history' of conversion, all these were mere matters of detail.[21] When it came to Ghazi Miyan, what mattered was that *it happened the way it is remembered*. And this has been the case on both sides of the denominational divide: a good many landed Muslim families in Awadh have continued to trace their presence as the descendants of the commanders of Masud. Local memory, toponymy, medieval graveyards, all seem to unhinge calendric time, stapling it to the unchronicled certitude of Masud's campaigns in Bahraich and elsewhere.[22]

The concerns of Arya Samaj pamphlets were, therefore, many. A clutch of arguments, rational and materialist, religious and familial were deployed to wean 'ordinary and ignorant Hindu villagers' from the machinations of the Dafalis and the servitors of the shrine. The grave of Masud was itself a hoax; the talk of curing afflictions and inducing fertility by Sufi prayers was mere hogwash, else there would be no blind or childless Dafalis or Muslims for that matter; the large dispensary within the shrine was testimony to the lack of the Ghazi's healing powers; it was the religious duty of every Hindu wife to serve her husband and not rush yearning for sons to any 'male outsider', much less to the bundle of decalcified bones that lay interred in a suspect Ghazi's grave. It was maintained that Hindu wives who went to Bahraich were sure to be widowed; that an astronomical sum of

Rs 1 million was being gifted annually by Hindus to Muslims through their attachment to the Ghazi, and this was grist to the Muslim missionary mill.[23] All this, so as to persuade illiterate brethren not to believe a word of the lies the Dafalis were propagating about the virtuous Ghazi Miyan.[24]

But to rue the persistence of belief among misguided Hindus without pondering over how such an ingress could be sustained for so long, was to elevate peasant credulity to the status of surrogate reason; it was equally to deny these rustics any say in whom they chose to propitiate from a veritable pantheon of Deified Dead.[25] The publicists had a ready answer: if peasants carried the ideological stigmata of the Ghazi's invasion, calling a son Ghaziuddin or Dargahi (after the shrine which had blessed his conception), it could only be because a good many Hindus were still caught up in the web of an historic deception; or alternatively, because family heads were unable to show the light to a senile father, an errant brother or a wife in the grip of reproductive anxiety.[26] And though Musalman Dafalis were the chief culprits, the family priest and the village *purohit* were equally ill-informed accomplices, facilitating the access of Ghazi worship into the hearths of ordinary, simpleton Hindus.[27]

In the 1920s, both the pilgrimage and domestic worship of the Bahraich Ghazi came under concerted attack from the educated elites of middling and lower castes.[28] These tracts, aimed specifically at the Ghazi-adoring Ahir and Teli castes, were composed by a new generation of publicists who wished to paint a regular Hindu past for their communities. They were infused equally by a 'modernist spirit', where public reading rooms, women's education, the floating of joint stock companies were all part of an effort to pull these subordinate groups up by diligence, industry and, most crucially, complete control over the unbridled craving of their women for male offspring. According to such publicists, the neurotic desire for a son strained the bonds of conjugality, making these deluded women join hands (literally and metaphorically) with boon-dispensing Muslim and untouchable charlatans. Self-esteem and an overarching sense of Hinduness required that such wayward behaviour be stopped forthwith.[29]

Obsessed with getting pregnant, these women, argued such tracts, even managed to drag their husbands to disreputable shrines, attracting sundry loafers en route. A wife hurt to the quick by the harsh words of the mother-in-law, or desperate to 'untie her womb',* setting out with husband in tow was not in such views, the usual devotee, braving the long journey on foot. On the contrary, these women were the hip-swaying, attention-seeking eager conceivers, taking their husbands down the road to Bahraich. Unmindful of the contradiction, the pamphlets also laid down, so to speak, the fallow period allowed wives by Hindu law on pain of being cast aside by their husbands. The great Law Giver Manu was quoted to the effect that a husband saddled with an infertile *bānjh* wife should remarry in the eighth year; if her offspring had died in infancy, in the tenth year; if she delivered girls (repeatedly?), in the eleventh year, and immediately if she was loudmouthed![30]

'It is the lack of female education that makes such women seek out shady Chamar shamans, whose usual reward for a day's hard labour is two pounds of rotten grain and five shoe beatings', says the Ahir pamphlet *Four Sure Remedies for the Ills of Ahirs*, spitting out its visceral disdain for this caste of untouchables.[31] And it is this lack of knowledge—here, a sense of history—that leads women down the wanton slope of promiscuous boon-seeking. On reaching the shrine, such women seek out Muslim Dafalis, partake of the sanctified food, mixed, they say, with cow's blood, and so end up 'purifying their souls'! The irony and sexual imagery go into overdrive, with abuse sinking into the pleasures of pornographic contemplation. Becoming possessed, these women fall into ritualised trance, inviting the caresses of Muslim males. This is the opportune moment for unabashed licentiousness, as 'they get their entire body "purified" by the groping dafalis and *mujawirs* of the shrine'. And, if returning home, a child is born, then he is invariably called Makhdum or Dargahi in fond memory of the bodily pleasures (*indriya sukh*) experienced at Masud's dargah.[32]

While sticking to the reformist agenda of reining in women's sexuality, other publicists pressed for a boycott of Muslims *tout court*, and especially of the martyr Masud himself. Next in line was the Mulla of the mosque who would blow a benediction over the head of the child after reciting an appropriate verse from the Quran.[33] Such

---

* The common north Indian word *bānjh* (from the Sanskrit *vandhya*) literary means 'tied up'.

gatherings attracted Muslim rakes, ever ready to take advantage of lonely Hindu women gathering in unfamiliar quarters of the town. The bangle seller, another familiar Muslim, who would hawk door to door his glassware, was also to be shunned, for these male *churihārs* held Hindu women's hands to slip the bangles on to their wrists. But Hindu women out of shame hid such caressings from their families.[34]

In the mid-1920s, larger political and societal forces catapulted this ongoing campaign into a frontal attack on the cult of Ghazi Miyan. The fillip given to sectarian constituencies in the arena of electoral politics, the confrontational build up of proselytising groupings, a spate of Hindu–Muslim riots and the increased virulence of sectarian polemics all contributed to an effort to finally end the scandalous affair of 'our Hindu folks' seeking out the Jihadi of Bahraich.[35] Subvented by landed magnates whose properties fell within the devotional field of the Ghazi cult, this was a deployment of newer mobilisation techniques and marked by a renewed urgency. Meetings in several UP towns, often presided over by local notables, were held to prevent the low and middling castes from patronising the Bahraich Fair; articles rolled off the Hindi printing presses summarising the 'real history' of the Ghazi and inveigling against the domestic worship of the saint; money was collected, especially at Bahraich for the financing of anti-Ghazi propaganda.[36] Now in full cry, Arya Samaj activists sought to cordon off the halting places where faqirs, pilgrims and devotees rested en route to the fair and Brahmans brought religious pressure on 'poorbi pilgrims' (pilgrims from the eastern districts), with the result that only a small number of low-caste Hindus were reported to have attended the Bahraich Fair from the eastern UP district of Banaras, Mock Ghazi Miyan processions were staged;[37] chain letters were circulated threatening Hindu pilgrims with damnation. Greatly exercised, the Bahraich branch of the Arya Samaj tried to rush in firebrand anti-Ghazi Miyan preachers to the Fair, with a view to dissuading the pilgrims from actually entering the portals of the shrine.[38] Fearing a rise in sectarian tension, the local administration prohibited such mass meetings.

19

Downplaying the Iconoclast?

For its part, the dargah printed over 2,000 copies of a staid booklet, offering a reasoned account of the Life and Shrine of the Bahraich Ghazi. Cut to the quick by the local Arya Samaj's frontal assault, now wheeling in the heavy artillery of fiery preachers, the shrine put out for the first time a tract written in Hindi, aimed at its large number of Hindu devotees.[1] Downplaying the iconoclastic elements in Masud's career, this 'Brief Life' sought instead to highlight his large-hearted and pastoral dealings with the local population. This involved parsing the career of Masud (as laid out in the *Mirat*) in the low key voice of reason and rapprochement. The Ghazi's presence in the Bahraich jungle, the pamphlet argued, was not aimed at seeking out the sun tank and the *bāla-rikh* image but rather to spread, sans duress, the word of Allah and his Prophet, 'as Hindus, Sikhs and Christians seek to spread their respective truths in India even today'; Masud had paid ready cash for the provisioning of his advanced contingent, proof that even in dire need the Ghazi did not resort to looting; when he reached Bahraich he was unaware of the existence either of the image of *bāla-rikh/bālārk* or the sun tank—in other words, he was not seeking out idols to desecrate and destroy. In fact, when a trusted commander suggested a gratuitous iconoclastic assault, Masud expressly prohibited the destruction of that *suraj kund*. All this was aimed towards building a picture of Salar Masud as a Ghazi far ahead of his times, someone who 'did not believe in hurting the sentiments of others', as the dargah booklet put it, in quasi-modern terms.[2]

The historical portion of this tract put out by the officiants of the shrine cautioned contemporaries against imaging 'the deeds of nine hundred years ago' with presentist eyes, for 'in those days India was in turmoil, Rajas were at each other's throats, and Brahmans were bent upon uprooting Buddhism.' The pamphlet went on to seek support for its construction of 'those events of yore' by alluding to standard historical authorities. Keeping its distance from folklore, it asserted weakly, 'Ours are no made-up stories, and we have books to support us'. Books (the *Mirat* principally), 'about which the learned historian Sir Henry Elliot has said that one can't be sure whether it is true or false'![3] This was neither here nor there, but a historicist point was sought to be made.

Turning to the real object of the pamphlet war—the scandalous 'Hindu' pilgrimage to a 'Muslim' shrine—the rebuttal was again softly pedalled: No calculated demeaning of Hindu beliefs took place here; the income from offerings made to the shrine was used for non-sectarian ends (dispensary for the sick, scholarship for students, charity to the indigent). The devotees' continued devotion was the best proof of the cult's catholicity: the hundreds of insignias offered at the shrine's dome evidence of the boon-seekers' devotion. 'Come, see for yourself: the mela and the shrine are open to one and all'—such was this information sheet's subdued rhetoric.[4] Faced with a well-oiled campaign, the officiants of the shrine were hoping to ride out the storm by keeping a low profile.

This was not the case with a shrill Urdu pamphlet written in 1926 as a counter-blast to the *shuddhi* organisations out to reclaim neo-Muslim caste groupings back into a pure Hindu fold. Published in 1927 at the height of inter-religious tension in UP towns, it aimed to help Muslim proselytisers in their chosen activity.[5] Skirting all references to the Ghazi's reasonableness, it chose instead to highlight the warrior's iconoclasm. And it left its Arya Samaj opponents to stew in the juicy fat that the Ghazi's efforts at idol-smashing notwithstanding, a much larger number of Hindus continued to be his devotees to that very day.[6]

Dripping with loathing for the ignoramus *juhala* (a term originally used for the pre-Islamic Arabs), the 1927 tract nevertheless carried a revealing picture of the 'deviant' cult of Ghazi Miyan.[7] This impress of the popular in an overtly Islamic text is of considerable interest. Munshi Khalil, the author of this aggressive pamphlet, had picked up the gauntlet to counter the Arya Samaj, because as a widely travelled estate manager, he was familiar with the world of the low-caste Hindu devotees of the Ghazi in eastern UP and parts of Bihar and deltaic Bengal.[8] Interestingly, this Islamicist broadside against Hindu propagandists chose to append the demotic name 'Bale' on its cover, for in the dialects of the region the nineteen-year-old warrior of the *Mirat* was equally called Bala or Bale Miyan. The title *Tazkira Ghazi Bale Miyan* was yet another marker of the imbrication of the textual and the local-popular in almost everything that made up the Life, Death and Cult of Salar Masud.

Vigorous yet isolated counter-attacks notwithstanding, attendance at the Bahraich Fair may well have declined in the 1920s. The Arya Samajists claimed that their efforts had met with a large degree of success. Going by a local police report, the attendance at the fair dipped to 50,000 in the summer of 1926.[9] This was a considerable downturn compared to the more than 100,000 pilgrims who had thronged the fair fifty years before. Ethnographic enquiries from the early 1950s also suggest a downward curve in the role of Dafalis and the number of Hindu worshippers of Ghazi Miyan in a village of eastern UP.[10] Still, it would be far-fetched to see the 1920s as marking a definitive long-term decline in Hindu pilgrimage to Bahraich. If, influenced by the Arya Samaj, a large number of village households (as with the Telis of Senapur studied by the anthropologist Jack Planalp) had by the 1940s turned away from the Bahraich saint, this did not mark the end of lower and middle-caste attachment to Ghazi Miyan. Fieldwork at the dargah in the mid-1990s, and the continuing campaign against 'Hindu devotion to Ghazi Miyan' (ironically at stalls at the Fair rented by the Arya Samaj from the dargah) suggest that the hero of Bahraich is alive in a good many Ahir, Teli and Kalwar households of eastern UP.[11] The larger currents of modernisation and Hinduisation seem to have made a dent. Still, Ghazi Miyan retains his assured perch on that mahua tree under which he achieved martyrdom for Islam and for *his* cows and cowherds.

PART FIVE A LONG AFTERLIFE

20

Everyday Memories

Let me try and wrap up the story of Ghazi Miyan. It is a conflation of categories: the accretion of epithets around a Sultan's kinsman who is missing from the record; a martyr who is called a Ghazi (one who triumphs); a Muslim saint with his devoted dog (considered an impure animal in Islam); a celibate who is annually married, or nearly so; a Muslim man who does not choose his wife, but instead is chosen by her. Add to these, the success of a Mughal Sufi in bleaching stories (current at least since the fourteenth century) into an elevating narrative about Jihad-ul-Hind; the elevation of a Muslim martyr to Hindu altars; the domestication of the affairs of men by womanly concerns; the location of a cow-saving hero in the time of a notorious medieval despoiler of north India: such conundrums, I suggest, are not to be resolved; they are best narrated by thumbing through the weave of the text and traces of the culture of rural Hindustan. It is not a smooth commingling of things and pasts Hindu and Muslim—the common sense of mainstream Indian history and of a post-colonial secular consensus—that the Ghazi edifies. Rather, this is a cluttered yet meaningful story of conflict and community, warfare and domesticity, conquest and legendary empathy that has kept the pastoral presence of 'our Syed Salar' (a common moniker) alive for so many in the Gangetic valley. I have abjured a structural analysis of the *Mirat* text and the folklore, as deployed by Nathan Wachtel in making sense of the vision of the Indians who were vanquished by Spanish conquistadors in the early sixteenth century, though I have taken heart from Wachtel's masterful analysis of text and lore.[1] I have chosen to write about the

Bahraich Ghazi by holding on to a certain messiness, not trying to disentangle the threads that weave the story together.

What if a reader looking for an explanatory focus is not quite satisfied by the literally wonderful material about Ghazi Miyan? What *exactly* brings not only Muslims but crucially Hindu devotees to the shrine? How can an account of a historically recalcitrant figure be made 'adequate on the level of meaning', assigned in this case by devotees themselves, as also 'causally adequate', that is, in terms of Weber's 'correc[t] apprehen[sion]' of 'the relation[ship] between overt action and … motives'?[2]

It seemed appropriate then not to approach such issues solely as evidentiary problems, amenable to disciplinary resolutions of veracity and facticity. And so, rather than laying down a historically true account of the Ghazi, the book has aspired to sketching his cult's particular character. Indeed, to sound scientifically the depths of text and lore is to be sucked into that whirlpool where events and remembrances commingle, yet go their separate ways.

In a suggestive move, the French anthropologist Marc Gaborieu has situated the cult of Ghazi Masud in neighbouring Nepal in terms of its location during the agricultural calendar—in between the harvesting of the wheat and the anxiety about proper precipitation for the ploughing and transplantation of seedlings for the rice crop.[3] The placement of the social within the agricultural is clearly important, though curiously, it is the newly ripening mangoes rather than the freshly cut spring wheat that animates the symbolic agronomy of the cult. In any case, the pulls of a distant past and pressing everyday concerns appear equally to have propelled the Ghazi groom story in Hindustan over the past seven or eight centuries.

To view the career, death and afterlife of Panchon Pir-Ghazi Miyan as the unfolding of the temporal career of Indic superstition or as an illustration of 'the inveterate Hindu habit of venerating any manifestation of power', as a colonial historian put it, is to take recourse to home-truths about India and its time-honoured pasts.[4] My effort has been to nudge the reader towards assenting to a different manner of appreciating the duplex ways of the past and the popular. The ballads collected in the 1880s, and a century later during fieldwork, no doubt bear the impress of the seventeenth-century *Mirat*.[5] But they remain equally susceptible to tropes, figures and sequences from the saga of Imam Husain's martyrdom in Iraq, the travails of castaway Sita (the legendary Lord Rama's wife), and the cowherd epics of Lorik and Pabuji, without being reduced solely to retellings of any one of these masterly tales, so adored by the peasants of the Ganga valley.

The martyrdom of Husain, the Prophet's grandson, at Karbala (680 CE), has undoubtedly been an important element of Indian popular religiosity, mourned often in carnivalesque fashion in towns and larger villages—and even by emigrants in distant Fiji and Trinidad.[6] Situated on a battlefield in southern Iraq, the emotional pull of the 'Muharram' story lies in the theme of betrayal and suffering of the Prophet's kin and his family members. It poignancy is heightened by well-developed rituals of mourning and performance, yet it is not quite the same as a regional medieval past connecting a Muslim warrior to the toponymy and cultural immediacy of the Gangetic heartland. The archetypal Islamic martyr's tale and traces of Husain's *shahadat* (martyrdom) on the Ghazi Miyan story and cult have remained at best marginal. The yearly performance of Husain's classic martyrdom is predicated on the rotational rhythm of the Islamic lunar calendar, such that the ten-day rite of mourning has come to define the month of 'Muharram' in which it occurs annually. Muharram in India means the martyrdom of Husain (creolised to 'Hosay' in Trinidad). Ghazi Miyan's marriage-martyrdom happened on the first Sunday in the Indian solar month of Jyeshtha or Jeth: *dar-qāyda Hind awwal roz māh Jeth*, as Abdur Rahman put it in the *Mirat*. Its markers were not the waning and waxing of the moon, but the disposal of the spring harvest, more specifically the ripening of the cherished mango, a great delicacy with commoners and gentry alike.

Called *sīp*, *sīr* or *sīkar*, the loosing of these first fruits from *aam* trees was a sure sign, eagerly reported by watchmen, for landholders to begin plucking mangoes for subsequent maturing under heaps of straw. Such was the fit between *aam* and the Ghazi's wedding festivities that the symbolic nuptial cot (see Figure 20.1) kept under mango trees invariably saw a few ripening mangoes fall down on it on the assigned day! 'Irrespective of when exactly they ripen … some "*sīr* of *aam*", is sure to drop that day', says a character in a novel written as recently as the 1980s! A hundred years earlier, a native ethnographer had commented in 1894 on the 'popular belief … that the mango crop begins to ripen the day the mock marriage of Ghazi Miyan takes place … on Sunday in the month of Jeth'.[7]

Fig. 20.1 Decorated bedsteads with a set of pennons of Ghazi Miyan kept under a tree at Sohbatiya Bagh Fair, Rudauli, May 1994

The cult of Ghazi Miyan is then about things and events local: from a distant past, no doubt, but related to the seasonal and the quotidian. The valour of the virgin Miyan, a virtuous warrior from distant Garh-Gajan, was aimed at oppressive local chiefs, his marriage interrupted by the Ghazi groom dyeing his nuptial suit with the scarlet of a martyr killed protecting cows and Islam. Of alien seed, Salar Masud remains a local Muslim hero, venerated for centuries as much for his Muslimness as for his attachment to such things as quintessentially Indian as *pān*, that sturdy mahua tree and the cows that grazed under his protection in the Himalayan foothills.

However, it is not as a facsimile cowherd deity Krishna that Ghazi Miyan makes an unsettling claim upon history. The kin of Sultan Mahmud, the eleventh-century invader from beyond the river Indus, Salar Masud was an Indic Turuk *avant la lettre*. It was the legendary Hindawi-Farsi poet Amir Khusro (1253–1325 CE), the Delhi-based scion of a Turkish father and a Hindustani mother, who memorably styled himself an Indian Turk.[8] But Amir Khusro's Indic roots were nourished by over a hundred years of Turkish rule and a good deal of métissage. By contrast, Salar Masud's short life was lived in the frontier lands of Ajmer and Punjab. As for Awadh, the country between the rivers Ganga and Saryu and beyond to the foothills, a large part of it was quite literally *Ban Audha*—the Awadh wooded country—stranger to both Turkic horses and native ploughshares.[9] Yet, in his last days, Masud, according to the *Mirat*, grew increasingly attached to the Bahraich forest cover, his garden freshly laid out (in Mughal style) and that solitary mahua tree where he was to attain martyrdom for his cowherds and Islam. It was this marriage of contraries: local/foreign, Indic/Turkic, warrior/saint, virgin/virile, jihadi/protector of cows that has gone into the making of the warrior saint.

'Curious', 'incredible', 'typically Indian' are some of the epithets that have been used by modern observers while commenting on the career of Masud. This spell of disbelief, unless dispersed by a grounded explanation—History, in short—threatens to turn our telling into a trickster's tale, where the past stands exhausted in the very process of recounting it. What has been gained, the reader may well ask, by the hopscotch of elite and popular, public and familial when one is none the wiser whether or not Salar Masud existed at all? And if admittedly not in the eleventh century, then in which later century before the fourteenth *was* Ghazi Miyan? For clearly, a Delhi Sultan did visit the Bahraich shrine of the martyred warrior in 1341 CE—a sure sign of popular regard. There is of course no firm evidence of a commander called Masud in the Sultan of Ghazni's army, and certainly not of a nephew of that name: no identifiable Salar Masud sticks out from the pages of history. No eleventh-century logbook of that time lies sequestered in the cavernous hold of the British Library.

One way to establish warrior Masud in the eleventh century is to surmise that 'it is just possible that the legend of Ghazi Mian was the outcome of, or became mixed with the eastern raids of ... [another] Ghaznavid general, Ahmad Niyaltgin' who is known to have made a dashing cavalry charge into Banaras in 1033 CE, or to venture, rather expansively, that an equestrian raid into the Bahraich outback cannot be ruled out *a priori* for the eleventh century.[10] Another ingress would be to suggest that the thirteenth- to fourteenth-century incursions of soldiers and Sufis into the wooded expanse of Awadh yielded a pastiche of persons and events in the composite figure of the warrior saint Masud. But what then explains the ascription of a connection between martyr Masud and the eleventh-century Sultan of Ghazni in such texts as the historian Barani's fourteenth-century *Tarikh-i-Ferozshahi* and the mention of kin relationship in the classic Gazetteer of the Mughal Empire?[11] Who made Masud into a sister's son of Sultan Mahmud of Ghazni and a commander of Turkic forces in the inviting Gangetic plains northeast of Delhi? How was it that several 'marvellous stories' about the warrior hero were already in circulation in the mid-fourteenth century? Clearly, no one minstrel or Sufi savant could have consigned Masud single-handedly to a designated past. Abdur Rahman Chishti, learned Sufi and hagiographer, may have had his febrile converse with the spirit of his patron saint, but he did not invent an avuncular relationship between Sultan Mahmud of Ghazni and Salar Masud of Bahraich. The kinship between Commander Masud and the Sultan of Ghazni was already in the air and put into texts some three centuries or more ahead of the compilation of the *Mirat-i-Masudi*, c. 1620.

Try whichever way we may, there is no establishing the historicity of Masud Ghazi independent of lore and belief. If I have persisted with dating his death at Bahraich, it is because his martyrdom has been a social fact as much with poet Amir Khusro in thirteenth-century Delhi as with Mughal emperors, colonial ethnographers and twentieth-century pamphleteers. Paradoxical as it may sound, the historical proof of Masud lies in the entanglements of an arcane seventeenth-century Persian text with the lives and times of his really existent devotees—the 'Pachpiriyas', who have 'ma[d]e flags of various colours in different places [in Hindustan] and convey[ed] them along with numerous presents to' Bahraich for the last seven centuries.[12]

Scintillating works on the foundation and persistence of belief have been written by historians of pre-modern Europe. One such is the densely documented study of the birth, life and eventual demise of the idea, between the eleventh and eighteenth centuries, of the French and English monarchs' power to heal scrofula. Historian Marc Bloch prefaces his classic exploration of the perceived curative powers of *The Royal Touch* with a suggestive generalisation:

> For all religious phenomena, there are two traditional explanations. One ... prefers to see the fact under study as the conscious work of an individual thought very sure of what it is doing. The other ... looks rather for the expression of social forces of an obscure and profound nature ...[13]

Trawling through the royal archives on the curative powers of the sovereign, Bloch locates the origin of this belief in the rite of unction, its foundation 'in a certain concept of supreme political power', its longevity in what would come to be called the pre-modern *mentalité*. The great French historian then takes his readers on a tour of the times of believers, upholders, partial sceptics, and finally the active unbelievers—the modern European men and women of the nineteenth century. Bloch pays particular attention to the ambivalence of Renaissance thinkers in 'accept[ing] the fact as proven by common experience, even if it had to be explained by causes supplied by popular imagination', as well as the sceptic David Hume.[14] In a disarming move, Bloch allows himself the historian's ultimate conceit: to write as if from the inside of past events far away from one's own time. Relying on ample documentation about the perceived deeds of royalty, Marc

Bloch concludes his work with an imaginative sequence in the long life of a daring medieval idea.

> In the world of marvel inhabited by our ancestors, there was hardly any phenomenon they were not prepared to explain by cause outside the normal order of the universe. One day certain kings in Capetian France and Norman England—or perhaps certain counsellors on their behalf—conceived the idea of trying their hand as wonder workers, in order to strengthen their rather fragile prestige ...[15]

This current book has been able to trace the origin and career of the cult of the Ghazi only in a fitful manner. And that is not simply because of the paucity of evidence compared to the documents on the thaumaturgic powers of the Capetian and Norman Kings: all we have for our Ghazi is an early-modern hagiography about events c.1020–30, based purportedly on a contemporary account with no surety of its provenance. Even if we could establish the motivation for Abdur Rahman, the seventeenth-century Sufi, for writing his Life of Masud at the time when he did (and a scholar of medieval cultural history has tried to do so), an excess of meaning would still remain.[16] I have resisted in this book the idea that the story of Masud is solely the product of Abdur Rahman's disciplined reveries. And so the *Mirat-i-Masudi*—'the conscious work of an individual thought very sure of what it is doing' (Bloch)—does not quite mesh with the 'deeper currents of the collective consciousness' about the ways of Ghazi Miyan. Nor does it approximate the thesis about the circularity of ideas between elite and popular conceptions of culture,[17] for the more important issue is the assent of a diverse population to a common construction of a long and conflictual past.

Undoubtedly, Abdur Rahman was the crucial individual responsible for the bleaching of popular accounts extant when he crafted an edifying story of Warrior Masud. I have used the term 'bleached' in this book as a metaphor for the textual practice that marks the *Mirat* out as a singular work of hagiography. Stories already current had to be bleached of the hues of popular culture for the Rudauli Sufi to be able to impart the requisite Islamic colour to the career of Salar Masud. If the legendary Ghazi could not be imagined *ad novo* in the seventeenth century, his Life could not gain popular assent as a sectarian Islamic saga, for that would leave the large number of his low-caste non-Muslim devotees in the cold. Though his martyrdom failed to inaugurate the reign of Islam in India, Ghazi Miyan was a live presence in the seventeenth century, and so deserving of recognition by a Sufi ministering to the spiritual and cultural needs of a multi-religious population in Awadh.

One important question still needs to be addressed. How does one enter the life-world of belief and yet write a non-believer's account of it as a historian? It is salutary in this context to revisit the excitement felt by Marc Bloch in the 1920s, now that the royal touch miracle had exhausted itself in France and England more than a century previously. Bloch was clear that it was the death of belief at the hands of rationalism and democracy that had empowered him to essay its history—a 'rare privilege to be used to the full', as he exulted towards the end of his book.[18] Ghazi Miyan does not belong to the category of events and beliefs, which *pace* Collingwood, 'have finished happening',[19] and so afford the historian the safe conduct to ply her trade unmindful of notions of collective affront, hurt sentiments and the like. Writing from Delhi, I am doubly aware of the hitching of history and majoritarian belief in the service of undoing past wrongs, especially those perpetrated by Salar Masud's co-religionists. Indeed, it is for this reason alone that a history of Masud has to engage with the fairly strong modern move in India since the mid-nineteenth century to portray the Bahraich Ghazi as the first Muslim invader of India.

So it has certainly not been my endeavour to fashion a contrapuntal in Masud, the first though not the least of the jihadis to have swooped down the Khyber Pass into the inviting Punjab and Gangetic plains of modern-day Pakistan and India. But does the courting of an intractable warrior saint not burden historians with even greater responsibility? Such has been the argument recently of Eric Hobsbawm. Historians in such a view must concern themselves largely with stressing the centrality of the distinction between verifiable historical fact and fiction. Act as erudite whistleblowers; that is what Hobsbawm appears to charge historians with; uncover the ways in which the recourse to belief or 'appeal to history' often lie at the bottom of xenophobia, majoritarianism and nationalism. For 'History', says Hobsbawm, 'is the raw material for nationalist or ethnic or fundamentalist ideologies as poppies are the raw material for heroin addiction.' The historian has very little leeway in dealing with a cluttered past: 'Either Elvis Presley is dead or he isn't', writes

Hobsbawm in his book *On History*.[20] With us, the choice has not been whether Ghazi Miyan is dead, but how and in what ways he has been alive all these years.

Of course, the weight of a chronicled past cannot be brushed aside so easily. If one elects to write about a 'non-existent' historical personage, questions *will* be asked. Two further issues then need to be addressed. Why rake the past anew and that too in such uncertain terms? Why not keep the focus on the fount of it all—Sultan Mahmud of Ghazni (who invaded India seventeen times), opening the historical aperture to capture the actual pillage of the early eleventh century and the sentiments of those times? Why forsake the sturdy chronicles, howsoever flawed, for a slippery text written half a millennium after the event, and the even more malleable folklore? This takes us to the very beginning of our story. This book has tried to elicit the reader's assent for the argument that both in hagiography and in folklore, it is as Sultan Mahmud's sister's son that Masud (the familial 'Turuk') comes alive for his Hindu and Muslim devotees. As Sanjay Subrahmanyam puts it: 'the memory of … [such] social violence was not necessarily divisive, so long as it was not treated as a mode of "grievance"' by any identifiable group, caste of community'.[21]

Have the people who should have remembered indeed forgotten what happened to the likes of them during the Turkish invasion of India a millennium ago? Has the Ghazi saga been one big hoax perpetrated by crafty balladeers, recasting an avowedly 'jihadist' hagiography in anodyne and assuaging local terms? Isn't all belief blind? And haven't rustics been duped by charlatans through the ages? One could carry on in this vein, raising the stakes with ever harder questions about evidence and proof. To tell the story of Ghazi Miyan, improbably true as it is, is not to fudge the real issues about past violence and wrongs: conquest, pillage, desecration, destruction, conversions—the grating exercise of Islamic despotism in the land of the Buddha and Mahatma Gandhi. It is to essay a history of popular truths about each of these processes—but not by retreating into the interiority of an autochthonous 'popular'—the alley of acalendrical time, impervious to the real world of momentous events. Rather, it is to suggest with Partha Chatterjee 'a way out of the self-constructed cage of scientific history that has made the historian so fearful of the popular, virtually immobilizing him or her in its presence.'[22] And it is through an optic of the popular, with its danger of neologism and the ungrammatical turning of adjectives into nouns, that one can begin accounting for the displacement of pillaging 'uncle Mahmud' by the saintly Ghazi nephew. An extract from a contemporary chronicle about the Ghazni Sultan would indicate what a complete reversal the Ghazi ballads have wrought to the image of the ruthless times of that Turkic Sultan. The learned Abu Nasr Muhammad Ibn Abd al-Jabbar al-Utbi prefaces his celebrated work *Al Yāmini* crediting the Ghazni Sultan with

> … forcing the Hindoos to hide in the bosom of the earth at the mention of his name, and of making them shudder at the blasts coming from his country; for, from the time of his quitting the cradle and leaving the breast, from the moment that speech undid the knot of his tongue and that he could express his thoughts without the aid of signs, he occupied his tongue with prayer and with the Koran, enflamed his soul with the love of the sword and the spear … and fixed his wishes on the governing of the universe.[23]

Unlike his uncle, Ghazi Miyan was a warrior youth who hunted game in local forests and forded the wide turbulent Saryu where Ibn Battuta nearly drowned en route to his shrine in 1341 CE. A dutiful son who sacrificed maternal love at the altar of public duty (protecting cows and idolatrous cowherds), Masud of the ballads no doubt smashed 'blood-sucking' idols and deceitful Hindu chieftains, but also brought brotherly succour to the archetypal married woman pining for a message from her natal home. A Miyan, that is, a Musalman, he was unlike the fanatics of chronicles and textbook memory; the folklore that congealed around him concerned the travails and afflictions of the body and the mind, yet were not unrelated to the iconoclasm of those times (c. 1000 CE). His power as an *auliya pir*, that is, a friend of and intercessor with the Almighty, was based on a devout life lived as a warrior, and it arose poignantly from the aloe-like fragrance that spread from his Bahraich grave in the thirteenth century: 'In the qasba of Bahraich from the perfumed tomb of the martyred Sipah Salar the whole of Hindustan has taken the scent of *ud*', wrote the great Delhi poet Amir Khusro—the two letters making up the word *ud* also standing, as in the fourteenth-century Arabic manuscript of Ibn Battuta's travels, for the cursive way of writing 'Masud'.[24]

The longevity of this warrior hero of text, ritual and lore lies then in the tensility of his story and cult. And so this *Turuk* warrior of both Ghazni and Hindustan rides on, his recalcitrant presence averse to being clad either solely in mail and armour or the habit of a Sufi. With him, the homogenising trends of history have been unable to consign the Turkic conquest of India to an archaeology of bare fact—a 'Tale of Broken Limbs and Bleeding Wounds', to borrow an evocative phrase about Islamic iconoclasm in Medieval India.[25] The certitudes of a mutilated Hindu memory have fared no better. The clash of Turkish scimitars and 'Hindi swords' aside, popular lore has playfully domesticated that conquest by making this Ghazi a household figure of proverbs, adages and common anxieties.

And so, when a nursery rhyme about the unsaddling and death of Ghazi or Bale Miyan is echoed today by some of my graduate students from Awadh, the imagery of Masud rolling on the ground surfacing above the ticklish sensation of juvenile wordplay, it indicates not the erasure of 'history' but rather its permeation into everyday speech, including juvenile prattle.* So is the case with the riddle about needle-and-thread: 'This-short Ghazi Miyan, that-long the tale/tail', or its variant 'one finger-length Gaji Miyan, ten finger-length his tail; on moves Gaji Miyan, enmeshed gets the tail', as sung by a little girl in a game of riddles with her mother in the 1967 Hindi film *Majhli Didi*,[26] or the adage 'The Ghazi's war feats small, the drummers loudly call' cited in Fallon's classic Hindustani Dictionary.[27] In sum, the figure 'Ghazi Miyan', though located in the eleventh century, has become self-evident, as its referents are proverbial, that is, in no particular need of iterative recall of his Life and the facts of history.

Despite the evasion by much of history writing, this angular and powerful construction of eleventh-century Turkic raids into north India in terms of the person of Ghazi Miyan has had a long life. In a very real sense, Masud cannot be accommodated within the stern pages of History. Yet the state, both medieval and modern, has repeatedly afforded recognition to the dargah-shrine as a historical construct. The colonial state created a special station on the railway line which sprang annually into life during the summer Fair. Schools textbooks could ill afford to ignore the warrior saint. An 1872 geography primer 'based on the latest investigations and written in easy language for

---

* *Tāi-tāi pooriyān, ghee mein chaporiyān; Bale Miyan lot-gaye, dhar-kān mureriyān, jhāma-jhāma-jhāma*. 'Fried bread, splashed with ghee; Bale Miyan started rolling, (I) twist your ears … tickle, tickle, tickle, tickle'.

small school-goers of the Awadh Province', devoted a full paragraph to 'Syed Salar Masud Ghazi', his dargah, the massive Fair (complete with a reference to insignias and flagbearers) and the 'prior existence of a Hindu sun-tank' at that place.[28] One of the peasants who lodged a complaint against the European indigo planters with Gandhi—marking the beginning of the Mahatma's outreach in rural India—was called Salar Miyan (Muslim soldier/commander!)[29] And there are any number of 'Little Bahraichs', Ghazipurs and Salarpurs in north India. Indeed, the prefix 'Ghazi' is only slightly less common in place names than the ubiquitous 'Rama', standing for the legendary king of Ayodhya, a day's horse ride from Bahraich across the river Saryu.

21

Epilogue

Fifty years ago, well before the introduction of American-style zip codes, a poster commonly displayed at wayside railway stations in north India exhorted letter writers to mark carefully the particular locality their 'Rampur' was situated in, in order to enable the delivery of missives to their rightful recipients spread over hundreds of 'abodes of Rama'. Growing up in Ghazi Miyan country, I don't quite recall a similar advertisement asking people to be precise about which Ghazipur or Salarpur they meant. But there could well have been such a poster: on a rough count, there are four to six Ghazipurs in most districts of Awadh; eight Salarpurs in Bahraich alone, four each in Faizabad and Sultanpur, and two Ghazi-prefixed place names in and around Delhi.[1] So much for the toponymic traces of Ghazis in the Gangetic plains.

As I bring this book to a close, I wish to touch upon one last facet of the image of the Ghazi in the mirror of literature. In his novel *Adha Gaon* or 'Half a Village', c. 1954, one of the most innovative novelists of the Ganga valley seems, in the interest of syncretism, to elide over the historical past congealed in such warrior place names as Salartola and Ghaziabad—'abodes founded by Commanders and Ghazis'. Instead, in an authorial intervention, the novelist Rahi Masoom Raza suggests that the name of his own town, Ghazipur, is really a Persianisation of the local term 'Gadipur', after its conquest by a Turkic commander in the fourteenth century.[2] This was roughly the same time—1341—when the Moroccan traveller Ibn Battuta crossed the turbulent Saryu to visit the grave of the more famous Bahraich Ghazi. By underlining a mere linguistic switch—Gadipur/Ghazipur—Rahi Raza was being faithful, no doubt, to a composite view of India's medieval past, where even if Ghazis and Rajas cross swords, no real trace of that conflict—not even toponymic—survives on the ground. It is precisely this relationship of a 'history' to the local and the social, it is this momentous rupture amidst the quotidian, that Ghazi Miyan edifies.

In a novella, this time set in Bahraich proper, the imagery of Ghazi Miyan is overpowering, his nuptial rites laid out in detail by one who had grown up watching the Fair from up close. A work of early feminist fiction, Ismat Chughtai's *The Universe of the Heart* lacks a remembrance of the medieval conflict (from the 'time' of Ghazi Miyan). Rather, it is the empowerment in a male-dominated world of women devotees, enthralled in their devotion to a Krishnaite Ghazi Miyan, that impels the story forward. The bridegroom saviour of cows, the brotherly messenger from back home, the youthful figure who defeats local chiefs and unsettles the ribcage of his uncle Sultan to make him yield the prize mare Lilli—such a wondrous warrior finds no place in Chughtai's *Dil ki Duniya*. And so, where the novella dwells at some length on the story of Zohra Bibi, the blind girl of the *Mirat* cured by and enamoured of the martyred saint, it is not to make Zohra and Ghazi Miyan come fictionally alive. On the contrary, Ismat Chughtai, the ethnographer-novelist of north Indian womanhood, asserts, contra popular lore, that Bibi Zohra was simply a Muslim version of the legendary Radha Bai, the married milkmaid of Vaishnav devotional poetry and Krishnaite dalliance.[3] An equivalence between a major folk heroine and a latter-day Zohra of Rudauli thus stands established, but this comes about at the cost of stripping away the specifics of the story of the blind girl of Rudauli, whose devotion to Masud was instrumental in the birth of the Bahraich pilgrimage.

In the *Mirat*, the attraction of Ghazi Miyan towards the blind Rudauli girl, newly arrived with impeccable elite credentials from Central Asia, was the local popularity of the cult of the Bahraich saint. And it was the insistent belief that Zohra, born in a Syed family, was brought up in a low-caste Teli oil-presser family that has been one of the pillars of the Ghazi Miyan cult. The idea of pilgrims congregating annually in discrete marriage parties was not so much to celebrate a real-life romance, as to commemorate the fictive nuptials of nubile Zohra, maddened by divine love for a martyred Ghazi. Marriage and martyrdom, *shādi* and *shahādat* were conjoined every summer, beginning with the first ripe fruits falling on the nuptial cot kept under mango trees in Rudauli. The novella's attempt at locating Zohra and Ghazi Miyan in a generic Indic lore—Krishna and the besotted married milkmaid Radha—diminishes both the Rudauli girl and her warrior-saint, whom she rejoins in the next world with singular consequences for the shaping of the Bahraich cult. Its meaning is lodged beyond the overtly familial (the accursed birth of Masud), in eleventh-century Awadh 'history' and lore—'the enemy rustling the cattle attached to the army', milkmaid Jaswa interrupting the marriage rites, and the death of the Ghazi near the pasture of Gaura Got.

Perhaps Ghazi Dulha Syed Salar Masud, Bale Miyan, deserves one last story. And it is by the great Indian writer Premchand (d. 1936). We get a fleeting glimpse of Syed Salar in an early story by Premchand, first published in Urdu in 1916. *Panchayat* or 'The Assembly of Five' is a portrayal of the aesthetics of village justice, where a collegium of five adjudicators approved by both parties arrives, irrespective of past enmities, at a just resolution of a pressing dispute. The story is at that delicate juncture where an old aunt is making the round of the village, trying to gather five trusted worthies for convening a Panchayat. After knocking unsuccessfully at several doors, she finally comes breathless to Algu Chaudhuri, a childhood friend of her tormentor, the locally powerful Jumman Shaikh. Unwilling to weigh his friendship in the scales of village justice, Algu tries to wriggle out with an excuse. 'What use would I be to you? Others from the village will surely come to form your "Panchayat", won't they?' The old aunt replies haltingly, 'I have recounted my plaint to each and everyone. Now, who will come and who won't, only Allah knows.' And then, as this old woman knocks at the door of community justice, Premchand makes her utter this lore-laden sentence: 'Responding to the *guhār*-cry ['Save the cows'], our Syed Salar had got up from the *peerha*-stool [at his wedding]. Will no one heed my cry for help?'[4]

The poignant dénouement of this story holds no attraction for the present. What is significant is that Premchand finds it unnecessary to add any reference to a past event or local lore: no particulars besides the bare minimum about Salar Masud are proffered, but the point about the duty to shoulder responsibility for a just cause is made—readers *will* understand. That one phrase about Syed Salar responding to *Guhār* (a call for help, here, 'Save the cows!') encapsulates the pull of the Ghazi Miyan saga. It is another matter that no one reading this textbook story on village justice in Hindi or in translated anthologies will come across this passage now. Transcribing the short story into Hindi at a later date, the author or the publisher chose to replace that pregnant phrase with a nondescript 'Let's see who responds to my plight.' And with that, 'our Syed Salar' went for a toss. Is there a move here analogous to the syncretistic sentiment of the Urdu novella, where Zohra Bibi, the key female character in Ghazi Miyan lore gets quickly assimilated with Krishna's favourite milkmaid *gopi*, the lovestruck Radha? Perhaps it mattered to Premchand or the editor of the journal that the targeted audience of his Hindi version consisted largely of literate Hindus. But then it was the Hindu lower castes who were the 'real devotees' of Ghazi Miyan: 'A panchpiriya is a Hindu who worships Musalman saints' (Ghazi Miyan et al.), noted Grierson's authoritative nineteenth-century compendium, *Bihar Peasant Life*, a fact readily noticeable at the Ghazi Miyan Fair, imprecations by Hindu fundamentalists notwithstanding.[5]

As I end this book, that one cryptic sentence about 'Our Syed Salar forsaking his nuptials for the call of duty' keeps returning to me. The trope of Ghazi Miyan's righteous response to a call for succour in a story ostensibly about village justice, illustrates once again the presence of Salar Masud in the *mentalité* of north India. Its outward manifestations, apart from the numerous cenotaphs to the medieval hero, were the fair grounds, earmarked in some cases expressly for the annual festivities in honour of the saint. When Gandhi stopped in the town of Gorakhpur, in eastern UP, to address a mammoth nationalist gathering on 8 February 1921, the sprawling Bale or Ghazi Miyan grounds was the only open space big enough to accommodate the over 100,000 people who had come together to hear the message of satyagraha that day.

The issue with the Ghazi Miyan saga has not been how to put the historian's history back into it, but rather, how to get history out of it. To put it so is to suggest a dense imbrication of lore and history in the continued longevity of the cult of the Warrior Saint. Studies of tales of conquest and memories of defeat, in India and elsewhere, will be instructive in this regard. It is a curious verisimilitude—familial and momentous—that has enabled Salar Masud to remain true both to an Islamic warrior's life and the quotidian culture of north India. The popular celebration of Ghazi Miyan's life seems to give the lie to clear cut verities as the only way of doing and understanding History.

To return one last time to the warrior saint ... the person Ghazi Miyan and his martyrdom at Bahraich in 1034 are unchronicled. Yet his exploits, as recounted in ballads and in a seventeenth-century Persian hagiography relate to a history—that of the Turkish conquest of north India. Historically dubious as they are, these retellings nonetheless articulate aspects of a verifiable past conflict, creating, in the process, communities in the present—communities that are based in part on a memorialised recognition of difference and conquest. And this articulation has a definite narrative form which subverts the dominant account of difference and conquest. To retell the story of Ghazi Miyan involves grappling with more than a narrative understanding of the warrior saint as a 'just conqueror'. It also involves facing unexpected 'fabrications' of this virgin warrior in unexpected quarters. This then opens up the possibilities of creating a new and unfamiliar—and defamiliarising—historical narrative of the 'Sword of Islam' in India.

To overlook the story of Ghazi Miyan as recounted in hagiography and ballads, and to concentrate instead on the well-established aspects of the syncretic and thaumaturgic aspects of the cult, is, in other words, to forgo the opportunity of penning an alternative history of the Turkish conquest of northern India: one that is neither Turkiana (the Sword of Islam) nor Sufiana (the gentle ways of the Islamic mystics)—to borrow the polarity of Suniti Kumar Chatterjee[6]—but which rather focuses attention upon this recalcitrant and popular figure of north India's premier warrior saint. It is also to impoverish storytelling. The alternative history that I am advocating is not the writing of privileged textbook events which might involve a reworking and contextualising of the facticities of Mahmud of Ghazni's raids in this instance.[7] Rather, I am putting forward the case for alternative histories of submerged, abbreviated, straitjacketed events—recalcitrant events and *recalcitrant lives*—whose very retelling by historians is made possible by calling into question the terms on which the 'Big Story' (as the popular idiom of modern times would call it) or the Master Narrative (as we understand it) is told and assented to both in the profession and within the nation. Alternative histories are not local histories; they are not alternatives to history; alternative histories are histories written from within the profession; ideally, they are also accessible to those outside the profession, that is, they ought to become, one day, the Big Story.

It serves little purpose to lay down the conditions for the possibility of such histories in advance of the actual writing. With Ghazi Miyan, this book has tried to make narrative and historical sense of the hagiographic, sectarian, demotic and performative literature about the 'Prince of Martyrs' that have been refused entry into Clio's estate on the grounds of evidential inadmissibility. Beyond the question of evidence, the story of the Ghazi groom—and the continued persistence of his multi-religious cult over almost a millennium—carry important implications, I suggest, for the imagination of India as a community with a far from homogenous population and citizenry.

It is now widely accepted that the political community of Indian nationals contains differences that would be unhealthy for the nation state to brush aside: regional, linguistic, caste, gender, and community affirmations are here to stay. The question is: if one can find traces of these differences and conflicts in our history, how may we relate these to the present life of the community of Indian nationals? This is a radical and serious issue which Indian historiography must address itself if it is to reach out from the family of like-minded historians to the persons-in-communities who are struggling against the homogenising currents that are constantly and dangerously seeking merely to define the 'New Indian National'.

Appendix 1

The Ballad of Basauri Dafali, Recorded Near Rudauli, May 1994

I

एक तो जग में रुत्बा आया सैयद सालार का
सैयद सालार का, गाजन ऐसे पीर का
"   "   "   "   "

पल में सारी ईंट लागी, गारा लागा दूध का
रौजे भीतर गाजन लेटे, वो दिन के इतवार का
सैयद सालार बाबा का, घर त रहा सऽतरीख
एक तो जग में … … …

बाड़ा उनका सबज बना है, मकनापुर हमीरऽ
सैयद सालार बाबा, जोहरा बीबी ब्याह्ने आए
सैयद सालार बाबा, जोहरा बीबी ब्याह्ने आए
चारों मुलुक में डंका बाजे, सैय्यद सालार का
सुरत-बम्बई-कुबेत-सितारा-ओ-बंगाल का
चारों मुलुक में साखा फूटे, सैय्यद सालार का
सैयद सालार का, गाजन ऐसे पीर का

II

जोहरा बीबी ब्याह्ने आए, अब तो रुदौली का...जोहरा बीबी ......
खास रुदौली ब्याह्ने आए, दिनऽ, एतवार का,
बोलन लागी उनकी अम्मा, मय्या मामूलाऽऽ... बोलन लागी उनकी...
सैयद सालार बाबा, सादी नाहिं करऽऽ,
बुढ़वा तुम्हरे बाबा अब तो, काऽ तुमका कहिएँ
अपने-अपने हाथ से, अपनी सादी करिहैं
बाबा बुढ़वा अब तो बहुत, तुमरे खफा होइहैं

बहुत से मकसूद ग़ाज़ी, खफा अम्मा से होते
हुवहैं से ऐनी हम तौ, रुदौली से करऽ
जात केरी सैय्यद, वा लड़की आहे हउए
जोहरा बीबी अब तो, जोहरा बीबी कैसे लगिहेंऽ
आँखी की नबीना अब तो, जोहरा बीबी सौहैं
दोनों आँखी की अब त, नाबीना जोहरा बीबी
सैय्यद सालार, काऽ हमरे सूझी

III

बुढ़वा अब तौ घरवा केनी, जल्दी तऽ घर का
आए केनी घर के अब तऽ, बुढ़वा बाबा पहुँचे
बोलन लागी मय्या अब तो, मामुल अब तो काही
जोहरा बीबी केरा साथ, ब्याह-ओ अब-तो राची
कहें, आप हाथ से, सादी कैसे करिहौ
कलजुग अबहीं बहुत दूर, बेटा कैसे होइहौ

लिखा अब तो बाबा ओ तौ, टाऽरे नाहिं टरे
कैसे कातौं ओहवां पार, खबर अब तो पायो
जात की नाबिनिया जोहरा, सोहौं होइहैं

IV

तोलिन केरे घर माँ जोहरा, बीबी गईं हैं पाऽली
होवैं सेनी ब्याह लेके, अब करिहों
तेलवा के घर का सैय्यद, पीर अब तो कैसे

V

उन्हिंन के सोस [अफ़सोस], बुढ़वा बाबा मारे गए
उनका अब तो, परदा अब तो, आहैं
एतनी अब त बाते बुढ़वा, बाबा बहुत बोले
बेटा हमरे सादी कइहैं, बाप-माँ के छोड़ के

ओही अफ़सोस-माँ बुढ़वा बाबा खतम अब तो होइ गये

तेरा बरद [बरस] सादी, अब त चौदहाँ लागा
जोहरा बीबी अब तौ, कौन सन की राहीं
जोहरा अब तौ, कौन सन माँ पैदा भईं
सैय्यद कैरी लड़की बहुत, पढ़-लिखें हुईहैं
उन्हिंन केरी सादी अब तो, ऐसन कैसे होईहैं
बुढ़वा बाबा अब तौ उनके, हाथ [हार्ट]-फेल होइहैं

VI—VII

सैय्यद सालार मसूद गाजी, अब तौ रूदौली का पहुँचे
एक दिन रस्ता में लागा, दुई दिन माँ पहुँचे
रस्ता में इहाँ आँधी-पानी, उनके खूब लागी
ऐसे जोर से आँधी आई, सैय्यद सालार चटाए गए
जाएके रूदौली में अब तो, जाऽ के पहुँचे

जोहरा बीबी इन्दारा पे, तेलवा द्वारे बैठीं
कहे लागे [सैय्यद सालार] हमके, थोरा पानी दो पिलाई
अब तो जोहरा बीबी, खाफा होए लागी
अब तौ अब-त अंधरी-धुंधरी, कैसे का पियाई
सैय्यद सालार मकसूद गाजी, का खबरे नाहिं राही
हम का देखाओ अब तऽ, ताना दिए लागी

जोहरा अब तो बीबी कौन, घर उनके आवे
हमको एनका अब त देत, तुम पता-ओ बताई
जोहरा अब तो बहुत, खाफा होके बोलीं

हम तो अंधरी-धुंधरी, फिर काहे उनसे लागी
हमके हमरी आँखी अब तौ होई [दिआई?]

अल्ला से अरदास सैय्यद, सालार ने कीनी
उनकी अब मुराद सैय्यद, सालार की इजाहिर होई
अल्ला से अरदास सैय्यद सालार तब कीनी
इका ता परवर-दिगार, आँखी जल्दी दीहौ
हमरे तौ मारे प्यासन, जान हमरा जाई

पन्दरह साल की उमर से सैय्यद सालार फकीरी जाहिर होई

VIII—IX

अल्ला ने सुनवाई बहुत, जल्दी अब तो कीन्हा
उनकी तो मुराद जासा, अब तोऽ पाई
बोलन लागी जासवा बांझिन, एक तो बोली
कैसे का तुमरी आँखि, बहिनी कहाँ तू पायौ
बाबा अब तौ हमरे, अब तऽ, ई कहाँ से नियाए
एक तो [ठो] जन भइया देख दुअरे हमरे बैठे
कहा तुम जल्दी-जल्दी, घर को अपने काहे
लोटा लइबे पानी इनका, जल्दी हम पिलैबे
शक्कर नाहिं, मिठाई नाहिं, राब घोलके लइबे

सैय्यद सालार मसूद ग़ाज़ी, खूब खायके अब पियएँ
खाना उनका नाहिं अब त, पेट में सरबत गईऽ
सैय्यद सालार मसूद ग़ाज़ी, काहे लागे
हमका अब तौ छुट्टी दीहो, अपने [घर] ता हम जाई

जोहरा बीबी अब तो, कहे उनसे लागी
घाम अब तौ धूप बहुत, जोर न हुई आके
जल्दी-से आराम थोरा, लेओ फरमाई
जल्दी-से आराम थोरा...

X

उनकी अम्मा, जोहरा बीबी की, अब तो आईं
कहे लागीं अच्छी आँखी, कैसे का होई आई
कहिन अब तो, मैया अब तो, कहे जल्दी लागी
हमका तनका (तनिका) तौ, पानी देओ पिलाई

हम तौ कहा हमके आँखी, नाहिं कौसूँ करऽ,
अल्ला से अरदास रोवे, रोवे काहै लागे
इतौ है नाबीना इनका, आँखी जल्दी दीहऽ,
अल्ला हमरी आँखी अब त, जल्दी से मँगवाई
इन्हिन केरे साथ मइयाँ, सादी अब त करबै
एतनी अब तौ बात सैय्यद, सालार जौन जब सुनै
उठके जल्दी भागै लागे, जोहरा बीबी धकरे-पकरे

सादी का इन्कार तोअरा, एक्को नाहिं चालै
अपना देवो पता अब, हमरा तुम ले जावो
हमरे अब तौ सादी अब-त, साथ तुम्हरे होइबे
जोहरा बीबी का हमका, देओ पहले बताई...
इन्हिन केरी [साथ] री अम्मा, हम त उन्हिन चलबै

XI

सच्चा जोहरा बीबी सैय्यद, सालार से बताई
अपना पता उनका दीन्हा, दिहा अपना पता बताओ
सैय्यद सालार वजू तो बनावैं,
पूछे लागे, जोहरा बीबी, महजीद कहूँ त बताओ
नमाज पढ़ो घर में, अब तो कहूँ नाहिं जाओ
जोहरा अब तो बीबी लाके, पानी उनके दीना
वजू तो सैय्यद सालार, ग़ाज़ी तो बनाएँ
अच्छा-अच्छा तखत, झार-पोछ (जोहरा बीबी) बिछावें
सैय्यद सालार गाजी, नमाज अब पढ़ेंऽ...

जोहर की नमाज सैय्यद सालार, पढ़े अब त लागेऽ,
जल्दी-जल्दी जोहरा बीबी, वजू त बनाएँ
उन्हिंन के पीछे जोहरा बीबी, नमाज पढ़े लागी
सैय्यद सालार-मसूद-ग़ाज़ी को, खबर नाहिं राही
कौनो आलम सलाम के, अलावा नहीं देखी

XII—XIII

अपना अब त पता सैय्यद, सालार से लीहैं
खोल के नमाज दोनों, जनें गुजरें
जोहरा बीबी जल्दी से, कुरान अब तो ले आवें
खोल के कुरान, सैय्यद सालार के आगे धरें
कौन सी तुमरी पैदाइश, जल्दी अब-त बताई
सैय्यद सालार मसूद कहें, पैदाइश जेठ में हमरी
हमरी ओही पैदाइश, अब त सादी अच्छी लिखी
जोहरा बीबी कऽहे, उनके नाहिं खबर

कुरान शरीफ खोज, गरीबनवाज (मुइन-उद्दीन चिश्ती) आए
पैगम्बर सब जितने रहे, बिटुर के आए

ख़्वाजा ग़रीब नवाज़ कहन लागे यह क्या कह रहे हो
—इसकी सादी नहीं लिखी है.

सादी इसके ब्याह में, इसके पचखा लागी
तेल होई, मेल होई, ब्याह में पचखा लागी
इनको-जोहरा बीबी कऽ, खबर नाहिं होती
जोहरा बीबी अब तो, काहे अब तो लागी
अब त हम तो बाबा से, वादा करे लागी

जबरदस्ती सादी किसी की नहीं लिखी

XIV

सुनो हमरे हजरत, पैगम्बर हमरे सुनौ
अल्ला-ताला हमका त, नाबीना दोनों आँखी

सैय्यद सालार मसूद ग़ाज़ी, इनका नाम तौ डंका में बाजी
इनके अब त कारन से, हम त आँखी पाही
दुनिया में इहाँ कोहू, आदमी के हम नाहिं देखी

उन्हिन हमरे साथ जो, कुछ सलूक कीन्हा
अब तो पैगम्बर सुनौ, हमरी तौ बातें
कोई पैगम्बर खफा भये, कोई पैगम्बर खुसी भये, कहा: सादी नहिं लिखी है

XV

मैय्या मामूला को, खबर जब गईऽ
पूछत-पूछत पूछत-पूछत, दूर से आई
मैया मामूलाऽ, बाभन को बुलावाई
उहो बाभन बैठे आँगन में
सोवाचो(बाँचो) न, मेरे पीर की लगनियाँ
बाभन साइत बिछाई लागा-इनका सादी ना होइहै
तेल होइहै, मेल होइहै, ब्याह माँ पचखा लागी
मैया मामूल रोए-रोए काहे लागी
अच्छी-अच्छी साइत वाचो

--तुमरी रमायन खुदा की कसम

तब बाभन गुस्सा होके कहा – जौन दिन सैय्यद सालार के सादी होईहै
वोही दिनिया, सैय्यद सालार मसूद ग़ाज़ी न होइहैं (रहिहैं)
या जौन दिन सादी जोहरा बीबी की होइहैं
ओही दिन जोहरा बीबी न होईहैं

--बाभन साइत बताकर चला गया

सैय्यद सालार मसूद ग़ाज़ी रुदौली शरीफ से
तैयारी करत हैं अब त कहाँ जात हैं?

इधर जाएँ-उधर जाएँ, सैय्यद सालार रस्ता न पावें
पूछत-पूछत अपने घर का, सिधारे अब लागें
"   "   "   "   "   "   "

XVI

जाके सतरिख माँ, दुसरे रोज पहुँच-लागे
बुढ़वा-बाबा का सब, बस्ती [के] काहे लागेऽ
तुम्हारे अफ़सोस में तुम्हरे वालिद मर गए,
कहा, "फकीरों को काम यही है, मरना तो सब का है
कुछ इंतज़ाम खुदा के लिए करो"

सब गाँव के लोग उनको, फातिहा-दुरूद का लिए भेजा
उनकी पक्की तुरबत बँधाएके, अब ता बिदा कर दिया
—उनका उलूस बनवाया

सैय्यद सालार मसूद ग़ाज़ी के ऊपर फ़क़ीरी का सवाल आया

XVII

उन्नीस साल में बुढ़वा बाबा से, अब सलाम करके चल दिए
कहाँ पर गए- बहराइच के जंगल का
देओ (देव) रहा - सात कोस का जंगल था, बहराइच गाँव नहीं था
सारा आदमी- हिंदु मुसलमान देओ खाय लेता, एक हठीले और बरेहना दोनों जने बचे
ए क्या काम किया - एक बहुत बड़ा दरख़्त रहा, ऊपर सवार हुए
ऊपर चढ़ कर सिंहासन पर बहुत दूर गए
सैय्यद सालार मसूद ग़ाज़ी जब सिधारा, कहा कहाँ जाते हौ- अब तौ राज-दरबार
तुम्हारे गम में चल गए
कहा कि अब त फ़क़ीरी का लिहाज अब कुछ करें
तो कैसे पैदा करेगें फ़क़ीर, के देव सब खाय लेता है
कहा बहराइच तो दूर है, कै रोज का रास्ता है
अब गढ़ गजनी के चले जाओ -- अपने ननिहाल का

कहा काहे भाई, कहा लिल्ली मामा का तुम्हारे गढ़-गजनी माँ ...
लिल्ली का सुन के, बहुत खुश हुए -- जाके गढ़-गजनी अब पहुँचे

XVIII

कहा लागे अपने अब त, मामा से सूनऽ
मामा हमका लिल्ली देओ --सिकार हम तो खेलबै

कहा [मामा/महमूद गज़नवी ने] लो कौन बेटा लिल्ली माँगे कैसे तुम आयो
गयारा साल की उमर माँ, तो लिल्ली वो बाँधी
लिल्ली कहाँ मामा अब त, कोठरी कहाँ बाँधेउ
सात तेरे ताबक अली, मुरतज़ा गए बाँधे
अली अ मुरतज़ा अब तौ, परदा दुनियाँ में कर गए
लिल्ली उन्हिन बाँधकर, बेटा चले गएऽ
हसन और अब हुसैन तऽ, दूनों है ई अब तो
लड़ाई अब जंग माँ, ओही अब तो...

बेटा उन्हिन लिल्ली, बाँध के चले अब गए
किसी केरे मान की, बाग बेटा नाहिं

सैय्यद सालार मसूद ग़ाज़ी जज़्बा में आए --

XIX

मामा हमका अब तो, दिया अब बताई
मारे गुस्सा के [महमूद गज़नवी] सैय्यद सालार को, कुंजी अब त दीहैं
एक कोठरी खोलें, अब त दुई खोलै लागे
धीरे-धीरे सात कोठरी, तल्ला जायके पहुँचे;
सात नीचे, सात ऊपर, चौदह ताबक गए
चौदह अब त ताबक केरे, जमीन असमान बाँधे
पकर के चुरऽकी [बाल], लिल्ली निकारें
चढ़ के अब ता जाबै अब तौ, बहराइच का, शिकार खेलबै

XX

थोड़ी दूर में ईहाँ है, बहराइच गौवाँ
मनहि एक्को नाहिं रह गवा हुआं, हम तौ जाबे
तनिक त लगाम बाबा हमका, रहतिन में देते
पक्का बेटा सवा मन की, ये लगाम बाबा टाँग गए
जैवन उससे उतरिहै बेटा, जाओ गवन (उसको) बुलावो
हम तो बेटा ईका सारी जिंदगी, लग्गा से खाना, इसके अब तौ देते
लग्गा से (ही) पानी लिल्ली, कहियाँ (को) देते
आहा! तुम तो बेटा इसकी, चुरकी पकड़ खाड़े

लगाम सैय्यद सालार मसूद ग़ाज़ी, बिस्मिल्ला करके उतारै
एक हाथ से पकर केनी, अपने मामा को दिखाते
तुम तो कहो मामा, सवा मन के लगमिया
ऐसा कहके तीन बार उनके, उठा के तऽ दिखावें

मामा उनके देखकर, हैरत खावें जल्दी
औनैस साल के सैय्यद सालार मसूद, कैसा-का दिखाएँ
एतनी अब त ताकत एही, अली मुरतजा सेरे (खुदा)
अली मुरतजा अब तो, उन्हिन से उतारें
उन्हिन त लगमिया ईके, अबही त चढ़ाए
उनसे अब चार जामा, अब तो उनसे माँगे लागे
बारह-बारह साल बेटा, लगाम कार देते
कपड़ा रहा बेटा अब त, पानी में लगाव भीगते

अली मुरतजा सेरे-खुदा, अब त खत्म हो गए
बेटा उनके साथ मैयौं, कपड़ा-चादर मँगाये
अली मुरतजा सेरे-खुदा -- ऐसन चढ़े रहे बेटा – आसमान निय बात करेऽ
लिल्ली बेटा ई बेटा, जल्दी बाँध आवा

लाएन मामा, ई की चाल, तब हम देखबै
ये ही पेर चढ़कर, हम देव का मरबै
अली मुरतजा बेटा इका, त उन्हिन तऽ चऽढ़
दुनिया में हियां गश्त, बेटा उन्हिन तऽ लगाएँ
अली मुरतजा सेर-ए-खुदा, हम का अबऽ तौ देखें
हमई लग्गा से, खाना-पानी देते
इतना लिल्ली केरी ताकत, कौन्हूँ घोड़ी के नाहिं
अली मुरतजा सेर-ए-खुदा, परदा बेटा कर गए
तुमरे मान के बात नाहिं, ईपर कैसे चढ़िहे।

XXI

बिस्मिल्ला कर के अब तो, सैय्यद सालार तौंपे चढ़ैंऽ
मारा एक एड़ा सर से, निस जा के अब ता पहुँचैंऽ

गाँवा में [बहराइच के जंगल] में कौनो नाहिं, कैसे का बतावें
इनकी तऽ नज़र, जंगल के लग्गे गई
देव त हा-हा करे, लगा सब का
हठीले और बरहना पीपल चढ़े बैठे,
महिया डरन के, इहाँ उतरन नाहिं पावें
जाय अब त सैयद सालार, मसूद ग़ाज़ी पहुँचे
कहे लागे धिक्कार तुमरी, फकीरी पे नालत भेजे
हठीले बाबा बोले बरहना बाबा बोले, अब त तुमरी करामत इ महिमा दिखाओ

हमरे पास करामात नाहिं, तुम त जल्दी दिखाओ
हमरे तऽ मुरीद तुम तऽ, जल्दी अब तो होवो
" " " " " "

हमका तऽ थोरा सा, पानी त पिलाओ
आठ रोज हमका अब बीत गए, पानी-दाना नाहिं पाए
देख तो मनहि सारा, गाँव-का खान करे
सारा मनहि देव तऽ खाए अब तऽ गवा
सात केरे जंगल अब तौ, सात कोस केरा लागे
देव आए अब तऽ, हा हा करे हाहाकारे
सैय्यद सालार मसूद ग़ाज़ी, अब तऽ उतरें
पहिला अब तऽ कदम अब तऽ, रसूल अब बनाएँ
लिल्ली केरी टाप देखा, आज बनही अबहीं
......परे (पढ़े) दाल पर फातिहा होवे
कदम रसूल अब तो सैय्यद सालार ने बनवाए

XXII

देव अब तऽ हा हा हा हा कर के अब तऽ आवै
सैय्यद सालार मसूद ग़ाज़ी, का नाहिं पावै
बहुत बारी अब तऽ, देव देखो खौरावै
इनको वो ता देखौ, नाहिं अब त पावें एक्को
हठीले बाबा बोले, अगर हुकूम दिओ तऽ हम मारी
इसे तुम पार नाहिं, एक्का जन पइहो
सैय्यद सालार मसूद गाजी, बरेहना से बोले:

सोरह सौ बरेहना अब तऽ, जल्दी पैदा करौ
बरेहना अब बाबा अब तऽ, खिसियाए अब तो लागे

हमरे तऽ मुरीद अब त जल्दी से अब होओ
बाबा बरेहना और हठीले अब तऽ, (मुरीद) होते
सैय्यद सालार मसूद ग़ाज़ी की, करामात परवर दिखावौ
परवर अब दिगार से, [मसूद ग़ाज़ी] चिरौरी करें
सोरह सौ बरेहना अब तऽ, एक तौ पैदा होवें
कैसा कहा बरेहाना अब तऽ, दूनों जने बोले
खोल के लंगोट केरी पट्टी देओ झरियाई
सोरह सौ बरेहना अब त, पैदा जल्दी भए
दोनों बरछी-भाला बाँधे, कायद अब तऽ करें
मारत-मारत कायद एक तो, अब तऽ देव का करें
जान से दीहो काहे, नाहिं अब तऽ मारे
कैद कर के सैय्यद सालार के कदम पर पटकैं

– हुआ खिस्सा खत्म छोड़ा अब तऽ अजगैबी तारा, आज
सेनी अब त टूटे अजगैबी अब तऽ तारा आज सेनी अब तऽ टूटे

तेल होवे मेल होवै, ब्याह में पचखा लागी

सैय्यद सालार के ऊपर अब तऽ, तारा बारह बजे टूटे
सैय्यद सालार मसूद ग़ाज़ी का, शहीद दर्जा मिले
शहीद केरा दर्जा, सैय्यद सालार ने पाई

XXIII

अंधरे [आँख] और काया, कोढ़िया अब तौ पावैं
साथ-ओ बाँझनिया अब-तौ, बालक ओही पावैं
काहे लागे... कोरान शरीफ में देखा
इतना-इतना डंका, दुनिया में बाजे लागै
जितना किला दुनिया में रहा
जितना झंडा रहा, सैय्यद सालार ने तोड़ा
डंका सैय्यद सालार का, हरदम रहाऽ बजताऽ

लगतै जेठ का गाजन सैय्यद, सालार की सादी होवे
डोली पलंग-पीढ़ी-सजावट, जात है तेली के घर से
उसके घर में सारे घर में, आग लग जाती
अजगैबी अब तो आग देखो, उसके घरऽ

– सारा घर जलने लगा पीढ़ी पलंग जब निकल जाता है रुदौली से अच्छा-अच्छा सब घर बना है, कुछ नुकसान जला-भुना नहीं

एक तो जग में रुत्बा आया, सैय्यद सालार का
सैय्यद सालार का, गाजन ऐसे पीर का
पल में सारी ईंट लागी, गारा लागा दूध का
रौजे भीतर गाजन लेटे, वो दिन के इतवार का
सैयद सालार बाबा का, घर त रहा सतरीख
एक तो जग में... ... ...

The Ballad of Basauri Dafali, Recorded Near Rudauli, May 1994 (English translation)

I

The glory of Syed Salar, or Gajan-Pir, has spread to the four corners of the world. The bricks for his shrine were laid in an instant; with milk for lime and mortar they were cemented. It was on a Sunday that Pir Gajan (or simply Gajan), lay down in his grave [was martyred]. His home is in Satrikh [on the outskirts of the town of Bara Banki]. Syed Salar Baba came to wed Johra (Zohra) Bibi; in the four corners of the world [here *muluk* or countries], the gong of his fame reverberated; all over the land—in Surat-Bombay, Kuwait [!], Satara and Bengal, the branches [of the cult] of our Gajan-Pir have sprouted.

II

On a Sunday, it was that he came to town Rudauli to wed Johra Bibi. Mamula—Bibi Mamula, his mother—cautioned Syed Salar against taking the matter of matrimony in his own hand, warning the son that *Burhwa Baba,* his old man, would be most annoyed at such impertinence. Hearing this [rebuke], Maqsud Gaji [Masud Ghazi] got angry at his mother. 'Though lacking sight, Johra Bibi—(the one I have chosen for my bride)—is a regular Syedani [that is, born of high Syed lineage], he retorted.

III

When Burhwa (Baba) returned home, Mamula, his wife, told him about Masud Ghazi's affairs of the heart, and his decision to choose his bride. Mother Mamula repeated her point of view before her husband, exhorting Masud: 'Beta, Kaljug is still far away [when such things may come to pass], how can you take your own decision in such matters?' Masud remained adamant about wedding blind Johra.

IV

[Now Masud introduces a new element], for though of elite Syed lineage, Johra has been brought up in the household of a low-caste Teli oil presser of Rudauli.

V

Unable to take the shock of his son ignoring the wishes of his parents and persisting with choosing a blind Syedani-Telin of Rudauli for a wife, his Old Man died of *haath-fail* —heart failure!

VI–VII

Syed Salar Masud Ghazi reached Rudauli after encountering innumerable hurdles on the way. Seeing Johra Bibi sitting by a well near the Teli's house, he asked her to draw some water for him. She got angry and retorted with the taunt that if he wished to have a patently blind person quench his thirst, he had better get her eyesight restored first! Syed Salar, who had acquired saintly powers at the tender age of fifteen, now began to beseech Allah on her behalf. 'O Almighty!' he prayed, 'fast infuse her eyes with light, for here I am dying of thirst [and only this woman can draw water from the well for me].'

VIII–IX

Allah heeded [Syed Salar's prayer] instantly; [and infertile Jaswa, who in another story had been rid of her curse due to the intercession of Syed Salar with the Almighty, asked Johra]: 'Tell me sister, how did you get your eyes back—*kaise ka tumri ankhi bahini kahān tu payo*?' 'It was due to this gentleman come to my door for a drink of water', replied Johra. 'Now I am rushing home; I'll get a *lota* for drawing water from the well, and offer him not plain water, but a drink sweetened with treacle.' Having had his fill of the sherbet, the Ghazi sought leave of Johra. But Johra Bibi; she would not let go of him so easily: 'It's scorching hot out there [on the road], why not rest awhile, yes, rest a little here at our place', she pleaded.

X

At this point Johra's mother came rushing from the house to the well side, and enquired about the sequence of events: '[This gentleman] asked for a drink of water, and when I replied that I was blind as a bat, he started imploring Allah: "she is a *nabeena*—one without sight, O Almighty Allah! grant her eyesight fast." And in this way he "got me my sight back real quick." Amma! I have made up my mind, it is this gent and none else that I shall wed!' Taken completely by surprise, Syed Salar got up and tried to run away, but Johra, she wouldn't let him off the hook so fast: 'No way you are going to get out of this marriage, no you aren't': *sādi ka inkār toara ekko nāhin chali*, she asserted [much to the surprise of Masud, and possibly of her mother as well]. Going a step further, she exchanged addresses with him—*apna pata devo ab, hamra tum le jāvo*.

XI

Forced, in effect, to part with his 'correct address', Syed Salar performed the ritual ablutions preparatory to offering the noon prayers. (Johra was still, in a sense, tailing him.) When Salar asked for the way to the nearest mosque, Johra insisted that he go nowhere, but offer *namaj* at her house. She brought him water for the ablutions (*waju*), and readied a wooden takhat, a diwan, spreading a clean bedcover over it to serve as a prayer mat. As Salar began his noon prayer, Johra hurriedly abluted herself, and stood behind him (as laity do behind an Imam) to offer *namaj*. Engrossed in prayers, Salar Gaji had no inkling of Johra following his every [ritual] move behind his back.

XII–XIII

Having shared addresses and prayed in unison, Johra rushes out and procures a copy of the Quran; opening it at random she pushes the Book in Masud's face: 'Tell me the month of your birth, and I shall mine', she gushes.* 'The month of Jeth,' replies Masud; 'so is mine', Johra chimes in excitedly. 'It is written', she says excitedly, 'our marriage is fated to take place.'

---

* *Istikhāra*: Finding meaning or significance by opening randomly a verse of Koran and interpreting it in terms of the current issue or problem.

At this, Gharib Nawaj (Muin-ud-din Chishti) showed up; besides, all the prophets also made their appearance. Khwaja Gharib Nawaj put a dampener: 'What is this you are saying? His marriage is blotted out of Fate. The preparatory rituals will go on a'right; the groom will be anointed (with unguents), but his marriage, the marriage itself will be stymied—*pachkha* (adverse celestial configurations) will come in the way.' Johra Bibi—she was unaware, and paid no heed: 'I have decided, it is a promise, that I am to wed this gentleman', she retorted ruefully. Saints and prophets intoned: no marital resolve can get the better of what is fated; it is written that this marriage shall not take place. *No one can get married by forcing the hand of Fate.*

XIV

Listen to me you prophets and great personages! It is because of Syed Salar Masud Gaji's intercession that Allah-tala has infused light in my two opaque eyes; the gong of this Gaji's fame is soon to reverberate all round. I have eyes in the world only for him—it is but him, and no one else I going to set my eyes on. Some of the prophets were pleased at what Johra had to say; others responded sternly: *This marriage is blotted out of Fate.*

XV

Hearing all this, Maiya Mamula, Salar Masud's mother, reached Rudauli [from Satrikh]. Straightaway, she called for a Brahman priest, and asked him to work out an auspicious date for her darling son's marriage. Spreading his almanac, the priest intoned: 'The preparatory rituals will proceed alright; the groom will be anointed (with unguents), but his marriage, his marriage will be stymied—*byāh mein pachkha lāgi*—adverse celestial configurations will come in the way'. In a tearful voice mother Mamula pleaded, 'By your Ramayan-Khuda [!], have another look into your almanac; take out an auspicious date (*acchi-acchi saet bācho*) and say auspicious things. At this the priest got angry and warned: 'The day of Syed Salar's wedding would be the end of Salar—the day when Syed Salar Mashud Gaji would be no more; or the day Johra Babi is to wed, that day Johra Bibi would cease to be.'

Reading into his almanac the Brahman departed. Now Syed Salar prepares to leave Rudauli sharif. And where does he go? He goes this way and that way, but is unable to find a destination. Asking for directions, he reaches his home.

XVI

He reached Satrikh the next day. There, people told him that his father had died of grief. (The Gaji responded): 'This is the way of the pious—the faqirs. Everyone is to die one day; what is required is to serve Khuda.' The village people buried the old man with the proper rituals, and built a pukka tomb over his grave.

And now Syed Salar Masud Gaji started thinking of the question of Fakiri—of leading a detached and pious life in this world.

XVII

At nineteen years of age [Syed Salar] bid goodbye to his father's grave and left Satrikh [for good]. And where did he go? He went to the big Bahraich jungle. In that jungle lived a Deo, an ogre, and Hindu or Musalman, he devoured them equally. There were just Hathile and [Baba] Birahna who had survived by climbing up a large tree. Salar Masud was told to go to Garh Gajni—his maternal grandfather's home [Ghazni/Ghazi-abode]. He asked why, and was told about (the wondrous) Lilli, which was tethered at that place. Hearing of Lilli, Salar Masud was delighted and straightaway made his way to Garh-Gajni.

XVIII

In Garh Gajni, he told *mama* (his mother's brother Mahmud Ghazni), '*mama*', he said, 'give me Lilli mare so that I may go on shikar.' The uncle was surprised at the young lad asking for Lilli, which he said belonged to Ali Murtaza (the Prophet's son in law) which *he* had tethered seven floors deep. And now that Ali Murtaza had left the world after tethering her deep down, there was no one left who could rein in that vicious mare.

XIX

On Masud insisting, his uncle in a fit of anger gave the keys to the dungeons wherein Lilli was kept to Syed Salar. Masud managed to reach the lowest dungeon and [fearlessly] holding her by the mane, brought Lilli out. 'Now riding this mare, I'll go hunting in the Bahraich jungle', he told his uncle.

XX

He repeated that not far (from Garh Gajan) was Bahraich—it was not a village then, just a jungle—and astride Lilli he would go hunting there. All he wanted were the reins of the horse. [Syed Salar had brought out and controlled an unbridled Lilli.] Uncle [Mahmud] said that it was a very heavy (*sawa man*) rein [and that a lad like Masud would be unable to lift it]. But the nineteen-year-old had done what only Ali Murtaza, the lion hearted, had managed before. Said uncle [Mahmud Gajni], 'I haven't approached this vicious mare all these years—and have been content with giving her water by a long tube, at a safe distance from her. It was the legendary Ali who could ride Lilli, and beta, you a sapling lad, have managed to tame her so. And Ali Murtaza is no more, beta it is not in your power to actually ride Lilli.'

XXI

Invoking the name of Allah, Masud jumped on to Lilli's back. Spurring her on, he reached Bahraich in no time. But that place was empty. There was no one to be seen in the village of Bahraich. Making a thunderous noise—*ha ha ha* (*kār*)—the ogre appeared. Hathile and [Baba Birahna] who had sought refuge high up on a tree, now sought the protection of Salar Masud, who shamed them for lacking in 'fakiri'—virtue and prowess. They admitted the diminution of their virtue in face of the Ogre of Bahraich, and requested Syed Salar to show his miraculous powers [so as to be able to subdue the Deo]. Syed Salar asked them to become his devotees. Dismounting from his high horse, Lilli, the Salar first built a Qadam Rasul (lit., the footprint of the Prophet at that spot), and performing *fatiha*, prepared to wrestle with the Ogre of Bahraich.

XXII

The Ogre kept coming at Masud, but armed with superior powers, the young lad kept stepping adroitly aside . This made the ogre increasingly tired and frustrated. Now Hathile Baba asked for permission to kill the Deo but was told by Salar Masud to step aside. He turned instead to Birahna (lit., 'the naked) to produce 1,600 Birahna-alikes immediately. Embarrassed at his inability to perform such a miracle, Birahna looked sheepishly sideways, upon which Salar asked him to become his *murīd* (devotee). Both Hathile and Baba Birahna immediately became Masud's devotees. Now, Salar Masud began praying to the Almightly, 'Please Allah, let 1600 Birahnas be born.' He asked Baba Birahna to loosen his *langot* (an ascetic's jockstrap) and unfurl it in the air (egged on, so to speak, by the Gaji's prayers), the coming into contact of a congealed reproductive seed with fresh air enabled the siring of 1,600 Birahnas. Laced with lances and spears, this army [of Birahna-naked warriors] crushed the Bahraich ogre into submission in no time. Now vanquished, the deo who would devour the locals irrespective of their religion—*Hindu Musalman deo sab khai let raha*—was thrown at the feet of Syed Salar.

Here ends the qissa—[this tale of the Basaurhi Dafali about Ghazi Miyan]. And then an unseen star/meteorite rained down the sky and broke the chest [of Syed Salar], [that is, Salar Masud was slain by an unseen hand]. At 12 noon, an *ajgaibi-tara* star broke over Syed Salar; and in this way, Syed Salar Masud Ghazi attained the high rank of a martyr.

For, as had been foredoomed, the [Ghazi-groom] will be anointed, all the rituals would be performed, but the marriage will be stymied—*Tel hove mel hovai, byāh mein pachkha lāgi.*

XXIII

The blind regained sight, lepers were cured of their affliction and infertile-*banjhaniya*s of their *bānjhness.* Syed Salar conquered all the forts there were; defeated all his enemies; the gong of his success reverberated in the four corners of the world. With the beginning of the month of *Jeth* (May), a palanquin, nuptial cot and the trousseau (of Johra Bibi) leaves the house of the Rudauli Teli; the oil presser's house catches fire—the entire house is engulfed in flames—but as the *palang-peerhi* departs from the town of Rudauli, the house is restored to its original condition, with no damage whatsoever.

The glory of Syed Salar, or Gajan-Pir, has spread to the four corners of the world. His shrine was built in an instant, with milk for lime and mortal. It was on a Sunday that Pir Gajan [or simply Gajan], lay down in his grave (was martyred). His home is in Satrikh. The glory of Syed Salar …

Appendix 2

The Ballad of Set Mahet, Recorded, c. 1900 by W. Hoey[1]

I

1.

Crowds were moving through the city,
Wedding guests in garments gay:
Bibi Mámúl[2] sent for *mehndi*:
And 'twas brought upon a tray
Gájan's[3] hands she coloured with it,
On his neck a garland bound,
While to all the guests assembled
Betel leaf was handed round.

2.

And she sprinkled *atar* on the
Saiyads of the Prophet's race,
And she summoned Khwája Nádir, [?]
Set him in the middle place.
How the squibs and rockets crackled,
Scent of aloe-wood arose,
How the blue stars burst and faded
Nathmal Lall[4] the story knows.

3.

Saiyad Rána[5] came with *mehndi*
And the garden[6] went before.
How bright it bloomed!—An elephant
On his back a haudah bore.

Came the maiden in a litter,
Borne along in bridal state;
Saiyad Ránа's train pressed onward
And the *mehndi* reached the gate.

4.

Bibi Mámúl's love waxed stronger
When she heard they thronged the way,
And her maidens all uprising
Broke into this nuptial lay
'Spread ye now the sandal *chauki*,
'On it now the bridegroom seat:
'Dye ye well his hands with *mehndi*:
'Give him gilded *pán* to eat.'

5.

Mámúl scattered gold and silver,
And she seated Gájan bold:
On his wrist he wore a bracelet,
Pearls inlaid in purest gold.
In his hand he held a dagger
While she spread the *mehndi*'s hue:
Then with rice she decked the pitcher,
Finishing maternal due.

II

The Gwallas danced to mark the day
In forest wild with mirth;
The townsfolk came their joy to share,
And Indra stooped to earth.
A Sunday for those rites was fixed,
Which never were to be,
A Day for war, not nuptials, marked
By Allah's firm decree.

III

1.

On guild the Raja Rudal Mal[7]
Was bent and now he rose

And swore a lie. No king hath fear
Bo bond in oath who knows.
'Pir bála's[8] marriage feast to-day
'They keep with banquet high:
'So I shall seize on Gaura Got
'And on my gods rely.'

2.

Then uprose Rája Suhil Dal;
'My brother king,' quoth he,
'To arms we'll call our armies all
'And I shall go with thee,
'The Gwallas kill and Sálar's kine
'Our booty be to-day.'
A wanton king was Suhil Dal
And would not brook delay.

IV

1.

The Gwalla clan at Gaura Got,
They were seven hundred strong:
Nand Mahar[9] was their sturdy chief:
His retinue was long.
To him the Raja Suhil Dal
For tribute sent request;
Of curds and milk on Mahar Nand
He laid a strong behest.

2.

When thus the Raja Suhil Dal
Demanded milk and curds,
Nand Mahar heard but heeded not
The raja's haughty words:
'Gájan my master is,' said he,
'Whom fealty I owe:
'And to his wedding feast to-day
'My milk and curds shall go.'

3.

The raja heard but gave no thought
To what Nand Mahar said:
He drew his army out in line
And Bág Mal went ahead.
He went and fell on Gaura Got[10]
Where dwelt the bold Ahir,
And thus that wanton raja seized
The cattle of the *Pir*.

4.

Nand Mahar rose in mighty wrath,
His retinue was long:
He called the Gwalla clan to rise;
They were seven hundred strong:
'Hear me my Gwáls,' said he, 'be brave
'And to your salt be true.
Be up and bear in mind to-day
'The Mián's claims on you.'

5.

The Gwallas rushed to battle all
With axes and with bows:
Where'er they saw the stoutest foe
They dealt their boldest blows.
The sturdy Gwallas fought like men
While Mahar cheered the fray,
And he for one remembered well
The Mián's claims that day.

6.

Among them all was Harbans Lall,
The bravest of their band:
A double sword was in his belt,
A rocket in his hand.
Like thunderbolt he forward leaped
Into the thickest fight:
He drew his sword and brandished it
Around him left and right.

7.

Then trembled warriors of the field
And back they stood appalled:
Matchless he was and fought alone;
On Gájan's name he called.
The wounded fell upon the ground
And corpses headless rolled:
He slaughtered chiefs and warriors,
And bravest cheeks grew cold.

8.

Then quailed the raja Suhil Dal;
He left the cows and fled:
But many of that Gwalla clan
That erst were few, were dead.
Then Rája Bahar Mal reviled
His brother Suhar:[11] 'Shame!
'To turn thy back on Nand and bring
'A stain upon our name'!

V.

1.

The Gwallas to Nand Mahar cried:
'Come, now the wine cup drain.'
'This is no time for wine,' said he,
But 'gainst them strove in vain.
By clamour led, seven hundred cups
Their chief before them laid:
They drank full deep and sank in sleep
In the cool forest shade.

2.

And now the raja Suhil Dal
A priestly pandit sought:
And horses five and garments five
And weapons five were brought,
'Pandit,' the Rája said, 'those gifts

'To Mahar Nand present:'
The Brahman hied to Gaura Got
Upon this message bent.

3.

He went among the Gwallas all
And straight the gifts he showed:
'Ho! Mahar Nand!' a Gwalla said,
'What do these presents bode?'
'They are,' Nand answered, 'merely gifts
'From Suhil Dal to me,
'These horses five, and garments five
'And weapons five I see.'

4.

'But are these gifts,' the Gwalla asked,
'For thee or for the clan?'
To all his tribe Nand Mahar spoke:
'Go, let him mount who can.'
And killed those noble nags,
Those weapons five they broke in twain,
And rent the robes in rags.

5.

The pandit saw this woeful spite
And out Nand Mahar spake:
Go Maharáj! To Suhil Dal,
'And back this message take:
"'The Kunwar Kandhaiya is my son,
"'Thy child Singhásan fair:
"'The *tilak* send full soon or I
"'Nor thee nor thine, will spare.'"

6.

'All will I tell,' the priest replied:
His face he homeward set:
No haste made he; he halted at
Each staging post he met.
Arrived—the raja asked him how
At Gaura Got he fared:

He bent his head and omens sought
And auspices compared.

7.

The Raja Bág Mal bade him speak:
'Say is the omen fair:'
The pandit spread his tables out
The tokens to declare.
'Hear, Suhil dal,' he quick replied,
The auspices are bright:
'The Gwallas all are lying drunk.
'Rise, Suhil Dal, and fight.'

8.

A ruthless king was he and called
His forces to the fray:
He Raja Bág Mal sent ahead,
And there was no delay.
He summoned all his men to arms
And rajas great of note:
He placed his guns in front and led
His hosts to Gaura Got.

9.

He fell a thunderbolt upon
The herds in drunken drowse:
A futile fight they fought and fell:
He swept off all the cows.
Their bodies on the field exposed
A feast for vultures lie:
Like garnered sheaves their corpses fall
And floods of blood run high.

10.

The king thus slew the sleeping Gwáls,
And captive Mahar made,
And with him on his elephant
His captive ride he bade:
'Thus with the Gwalla Chief he rode
And there was no delay.

But Mahar Nand uprose and said:
'Hear, Raja, what I say:'

11.

'Whoe'er shall see me ride with thee,
'Without a shade of doubt
'Will say this day that I am king
'And thou art my *mahaut*.'
The Rája roused, a dagger plunged
Into the chieftain's breast:
Then onward with the cows alone
Towards his fort he pressed.

VI.

1.

'Jáso, bring curds,' Mámúla said,
'For lucky is my star':
Nand Mahar's wife she was, replied
'Long live our lord Sálár'!
The women of her clan she called:
Each head a milk pail bore,
And round her form from waist to head
One sheet each milkmaid wore.

2.

When Jáso drew near Gaura Got
And kites and vultures saw
And felt the stillness in the air,
Her soul was filled with awe.
Corpse upon corpse she saw the dead;
With grief she cried aloud:
The robe she wore in twain she tore
And made a mourner's shroud.

3.

She searched in vain among the slain;
Her Nand not here she found,
But on she strayed and saw him laid
Alone upon the ground:

'Oh Mahar Nand, my sun and moon!'
She cried, 'O husband mine!
'Who thus hath killed our Gwallas all
'And driven away our kine?'

4.

She gently raised Nand Mahar's head
And laid it on her knee,
While of his Jáso's tenderness
Thus heedless answered he:
'O unclean! what art thou? vulture,
'Tiger, jackal, art thou?
'Wilt not wait my parting spirit
'But gnawest at me now.'

5.

'Tiger, jackal none,' said Jáso,
'Vulture or kite is nigh:
'She for whom thy flowers were looted,[12]
'Thy boyhood's wife am I:
'Swámi, I am come to tend thee'—
'O Wife,' he answered low,
'Be thou my wife of early life,
'Prithee for water go.'

6.

'My lord, I will,' quoth she, 'but say
'Who killed and why our band"
'Did our cows eat the rája's crops
'Or trespass on his land?'
'Our cows,' said he, 'nor ate his crop
'Nor trespassed on his land:
'This ruthless raid and massacre
'He worked with want on hand.'

7.

A tank she sought and raised her hands:
'*Pir khwájah*! hear me pray:
'If in my cloth the water stay
'My husband's debt I'll pay.'

While thus she prayed the water stayed
Within her apron pent:
She had the Sálár Gházi's *pir*
Addressed and back she went.

8.

The draught she brought to Mahar's lips
And sped his parting breath:
Then to her maids: 'Your vestments steep
'In this red flood of death:
'Your pails seven hundred fill with blood
And backward with me turn'
The [sic] while she speaks her heart and cheeks
With hot resentment burn.

9.

And to the Mián Jáso came,
Her crimson plaint she spread:
'To thee I look: our cows are gone,
'A hundred thousand head.'
The words she said like arrows sped
And kindled Gájan's pride:
He washed the *mehndi* from his hands,
His bracelets flung aside.

10.

His sword he grasped and kissed the blade
And straight his mother sought:
'O hear me, mother mine,' he said,
'Great wrong the king hath wrought,
'He hath our kine as plunder seized
'And all our Gwallas killed:
'Jáso hath come to me: the air
'With cries for blood is filled.'

11.

'O hearken, Saifu'd-din;[13] the tale
'To me hath Jáso told;
'Who kills my Gwáls and steals my kine,
'A traitor king I hold.'
'O son!' ('tis now his mother speaks)

'Thy wedding feast is laid:
'Gájan, thou treasure of my heart
'What new resolve is made?'

12.

'There reigns but one desire supreme
'Within thy mother's heart,
'That see she may thy wedding day
'And in it bear a part:
'I would thy nuptials celebrate
'And welcome home thy bride:
'Might I but gratify this wish,
'I have no wish beside.'

13.

'Nay, mother mine, but bid me go,'
Bold Gájan quick replied,
'And I shall fight the traitor king;
'The Prophet's on our side:
'Say *Bakshá-dudh*[14] and I shall go
'The Moslem faith to spread,
'Bring back the kine, and with my sword
'Cut off the rája's head.'

14.

'Or I shall fight and victor be
'And come to wed this maid
'Or I shall fall and on my grave
'My wedding wreath be laid.
'For what should all my kinsmen say
'If I disgraced our name:
'Nay with this king I swords will cross,
'And turn his pride to shame.'

15.

Then Chishti[15] rose to interpose,
But Gájan's way was won:
His mother said: 'God go with thee;
'*Dudh-bakshá*, go my son.'
So now for Ajab[16] Gájan sent

And asked for ink and pen:
He cleared accounts up to the day
And paid up all his men.

16.

He bid them gird them for the fight:
His armoury they sought,
And arms of every kind they took
And rockets out they brought.
His mother heard the order given
And ran with naked feet,
And clasped her arms around his neck
His filial love to entreat:

17.

'O son, on this thy wedding day
'Haste not to leave my side:
'A maid with locks as dark as night
'I bring thee for thy bride:
'The noble Saiyads all are here,
'Thy wedding guests are they,
'And maidens singing bridal songs,
'They sing for thee to day.'

18.

'Nay, mother, nay' he said, 'there waits
'A martyr's death for me:
'A mausoleum and a mosque
'My monument shall be.
'I shall be laid in Hind to rest
'But still my fame shall grow,
'And all the four worlds hither come
Their tribute to bestow.'

19.

'Saddle and mail on Lilla[17] bind
'My charger mount will I:
'My double quiver strap in front:
'Two wardrums on her tie.'
He said and went his blood to prove,

True crescentader he,
With force so great that earth did quake
His moving hosts to see.

20.

All this the rája Suhil hears
And he is sore afraid:
The Mián's army ready is
And no delay is made.
On flags and banners waving went
And crossed the Ghágra's tide:
The Mián to the Ka'bah prayed
For blessings on his side.

21.

All green the garment were he wore
From Kábul or Qandhár:
One lakh and thousands thirty-six
Of Saiyads went to war.
Their tents went first, their cannons next,
And elephants in rear:
Full many days they marched; at last
They drew to Hind Mulk near.

22.

The Gabar[18] king the tidings hears
How Gájan's tents are near,
How flags and banners court the breeze
And lines of shops appear:
A sight is his Urdu bázár:[19]
The people come and go,
And sweets are piled and bakers squat
And at their ovens blow.

23.

Vendors of grain and spices here
And money changers sit,
And on the sutler's hostel hearth[20]
The cheery fire is lit:
Greengrocers vegetables bring

Upon the ground to spread:
The goldsmiths deftly work with gold
And pearls for earrings thread.

24.

And *guriyas* from river beds
Have gourds and melons brought,
And *dhímars*[21] offer fish for sale
In running rivers caught:
And who's kotwál to hear complaints?
'Tis Nirmal Parihár.
Thus well arranged and busy is
Gájan's Urdu bázár.

VII

1.

When this the Gabar king had heard,
His queen Nauráni said:
'O Sire! against thy fort his hosts
'Hath Mián Gájan led.
'The army of the 'Dín' has come
'To lay thy fortress low:
'O king, they will thy soldiers kill
'And streams of blood will flow.'

2.

'Mad art thou, woman,' said the king,
And mighty wroth grew he,
'For him good grace is second place:
'Why name the Turk[22] to me?
'For I can boast an equal host,
'Be still and wait the strife.'
'Twas thus the king with anger rude
Strove to put down his wife.

3.

Again Nauráni spoke: 'O Sire!
'To fight this Saiyad dread

'Who takes the field, a stoutest shield
'Must hold above his head:
'Through bone he cleaveth clean, and what
'Avails thy sword of thread?
'A foe we face who shows no grace
'And dyes the earth in red.'

4.

But Bahar Mal had been forewarned
And hurried to prepare
The ancient fort of Teliyagarh[23]
And put it in repair.
The king now staked his spear, and viewed
The fort with heart elate:
He bade them tie his elephant
Beside his palace gate.

5.

And next he summoned his mahaut
And usages explained:
The driver went at once to where
The elephant was chained;
Saluted first the royal beast,
Rubbed ochre on his head
Then a red housing bound with fringe
Upon his back he spread.

6.

To Bhairon then and Hanuman
And Narsingh he appealed,[24]
And then of stout rhinoceros hide
He took a studded shield
With burnished boss, which fast across
His giant head he tied.
Then roared that elephant and shook
The walls on every side.

7.

Now, Lalla with due caution speak:
Such elephant 'twould need

With driver bloated and obese,
Twelve villages to feed.
A sword he gave that elephant
Within his trunk to hold:
At which he grew intoxicate
With warlike fury bold.

8.

When sleep o'ercame the elephant—
Now hear the tale I tell—
Sháh Mardán bore him in a dream
Down to the gate of hell.
While here he stood, a scorching blast
Of flame upon him blew,
And upward to the golden gate
Of Paradise he flew.

9.

Sarwar Rasul[25] came to the gate:
'My son, in heaven,' said he,
'Till thou with Gájan cast thy lot,
Thy portion cannot be.'
The dream was o'er that broke his rest,
The elephant awoke:
Nor longer tarried Night, for now
The dawn of morning broke.

10.

The Raja Suhil Dal aroused
For news despatched a scout,
And Raja Rudal Mal advised
Him lead his army out.
The Raja rode his elephant,
His army on he led:
The war-drums beat to war in front
And firm was every tread.

11.

The Hindus clashed with Moslems, while
Their king on Somnáth calls:

The Moslems opened with grenades,
Hindus with musket balls.
And thus that battle fierce began
While loud the war-drums beat:
Those hosts were numberless and earth
Vibrated 'neath their feet.

12.

The high born Rajput fought, nor once
Their faces turned away:
Tora in turban, clad in red,
Conspicuous were they.
'God keep my name,' the raja cried:
The Rajputs heard him call;
The fight he led, his foes he slew,
The foremost he of all.

13.

Loud Gájan's war-drums beat; he placed
In front each bravest man;
The 'fátiha' recited he
And Ajab led the van
Hari Singh Náth the standard high
Amid the fight displayed:
He drew his sword, it flashed like fire,
Nine maunds his armour weighed.

14.

It was the doughty Hari Singh
Who struck with surest stroke:
He mowed the forces of the king
And Káfirs' noses broke.[26]
How Raja Suhil Dal was grieved
This carnage sore to see:
His hands he raised to heaven
And wept—'oh! woe is me!'

15.

The Pír[27] fought on; great tuskers fell;
No fear was on his brow:

He hailed the haudah-mounted king:
'Cowstealer! whither now?'
Barahna raised his spear and charged
Like raging tempest blast;
Hindu and Moslem made him way;
The monarch breathed his last.

16.

To Ajab Mián Gájan called:
'Set spurs to thy brown mare;
'On Bahar Mal with sword advance
'And hold him in the rear.'
Mián himself his Lilla spurred,
To Allah he appealed,
His sword he drew and Bahar Mal
Rolled dead upon the field.

17.

Mián hailed Nirmal Parihár;
Then from his quiver full
He took a shaft, and drew his bow,
And picked off Sahar Mal.
By God's decree thus Gájan killed
Those kings who wisdom lacked:
He took possession of their fort,
Their palace razed and sacked.

18.

'Now by God's grace the day is thine,'
To Gájan Chishti said,
'And Somnáth[28] it behoveth us
Beneath our feet to tread.'
He said and straight upon that fort
The Moslem flag was shown:
He tore that house of idols down
And smashed the gods of stone.

19.

Whate'er my fame as poet, 'tis
Through Lalla Ustád[29] won:

The story true he told, I tell,
And now my tale is done.
The Saiyad Mián Gájan now
For Saiyad Míran[30] called,
And in the middle of the fort
As governor installed.

20.

The Moslem force to Gaura Got
Marched from the field of strife:
God gave the word and Gájan brought
The Gwallas back to life.
Like sunlit waves the spear-hands gleamed
And drums were loud in mirth:
Ajab Hatíla's spear had rest
Like sleeping snake in earth.

Appendix 3

A Poetical Description of the Ghazi Miyan Fair at Bahraich, c. 1800 by Cazim Ali Jawan

(Transcription and translation from Urdu by Mahmood Farooqui)

As I have been instructed by the Saheb
Write about the seasons and all the months
Describe the good events and customs
So that one may come to know all about them

The festivals of Hindus and Musalman
Write them down once and for all
Among the latter there are some people
Whose ways and mores I shall now tell you

In this month (of *Jeth*: May) they have this custom
Of erecting pennons with much fanfare
They call it the spear of their Pir
These pennons that they hold afloat
But the *ajlāf* (low born) mostly cling to this belief
That they regard this as their Pir

Some say Masud, some Ghazi, some Salar
And they chant his name repeatedly and *bār-bār*
Some address him as Bale Miyan
And remain forever in his tutelage

And know ye, one and all
That in town Bahraich his shrine falls

Every year the great Asaf-ud-daulah (the Awadh Nawab Bahadur)
The precious mother of pearl of the world of *Wazarat*
He used to visit the shrine just about every year
Always promptly he was there to witness the Fair
What I have told you thus far
Is just the prologue to that *mela*-fair

That on the day of the *urs* a great concourse assembles
And planting those flags by the bank of the river
They hold the pennons aloft each day thither
Ecstatic in their devotion and their faith are they

Round these they go a hundred times
How shall I descry their joyous ways?
One holds aloft a pennon, fixing it (with a belt) to his waist
Presenting a joyous spectacle in demotic splendour

And everybody is held spellbound
Spectators' stare at him, mouths agape
Others conjoin their hands with respect
Some jump around with joy
Prostrating themselves, yet others weep
I saw such scenes enacted there in wondrous sweep

And thousands of lamps of *ghee*
Are lit and placed under these pennons for all to see
(*Lahbar*s they call these in Gorakhpur, Azamgarh and Varanasi)
Thousands in dire need gather here
The afflicted supplicate for boons and welfare

Some bring flowers, sweets others proffer
Praying for fulfilment of their needs and desires
And playing the jhanjh and their Rabana
The Dafalis intone their songs-n-*gana*:

Whoever listens to the *sohlas* of the Gaji-groom
Would have his desires fulfilled in a jiffy or very soon.

And for miles those crimson and green pennons
Every year they get erected so
And beneath them highly decorated pots (*namgeere*)
Thousands of them are placed thither colourful and odorous

Fairy-like creatures flit about at several places,
I still cannot forget the sight of those lovely faces

What else shall I say to describe that joyful tamasha
With what words shall I descry that scene, and in which meter
Two roads converge and a bazaar springs to life
There everybody gets what they're looking for in a trice

And in those light ox-carts and *rath*-like chariots
One sees such captivating moon-faced beauties
That the heart only wishes and desires
Such stunning creatures' presence forever before one's eyes

From morning such a spectacle is mounted
That is visible to us through the night
And when the morn appears in its glory
They are all there to celebrate (their Pir's) glory
And those who wish to pay homage to the shrine
Go thither as their faith-n-devotion enjoins

Others who have a yen for a spectacle and a play
Go there to satisfy their fancy, inclination and taste
Or they go back to their homes
And return at night or in the morn

On the first Sunday in the month of Jeth
Is the day of his *Urs*, my friend, I say
And it has now become established

A wonderful show unfolds there—a cherished practice
The *menu peuple* with money in hand,
Prepare for his marriage this time again and again
And behold, the servitors of the dargah
Take out the saint's *lungi* and the *chauki*-stool every morn
And giving it a ceremonial bath
Collect the holy water as (life sustaining) *āb-i-hayāt*
Doling it out as benediction of a sort
Collect 'silver and gold' (in fact cowrie and pice)
As just return by way of the blessed gift's price

Although I have as yet not been there
But I have heard about it year after year
All the provision and arrangements and things
As befitting for Emperors and Kings
From the morning it starts in earnest
Assembled there one finds people of all bent and etiquette

Some get bestowed gifts and boons from there
Others receive a horse or a sword or a dagger
They say it is forever flowing
That river of bounty, grace and gifts that is the saint's doing

Thousands of blind, lame, lepers and handicapped
Lie around the drain all day long
And oft under trees or in front of the pavilion
Hundreds tie themselves around to these places (and around the pennons)

As I have descried and put down here
Such a spectacle unfolds there every year

And a scorching hot wind blows in that month
Reaching all the way up to the skies, the very heavens
And what we call a dust storm, or in the local tongue āndhi
They call a *toofān* in Bengali

And the devotees who go for his *urs*
They all come back and say unto us:
That such a miracle (the Ghazi) has wrought
That the ogre Makna Dev himself has showed up
(at the Ghazi Fair) to sweep-and-dust.

Map A.1 Ghazi Miyan fair sites in the United Provinces of Agra and Oudh

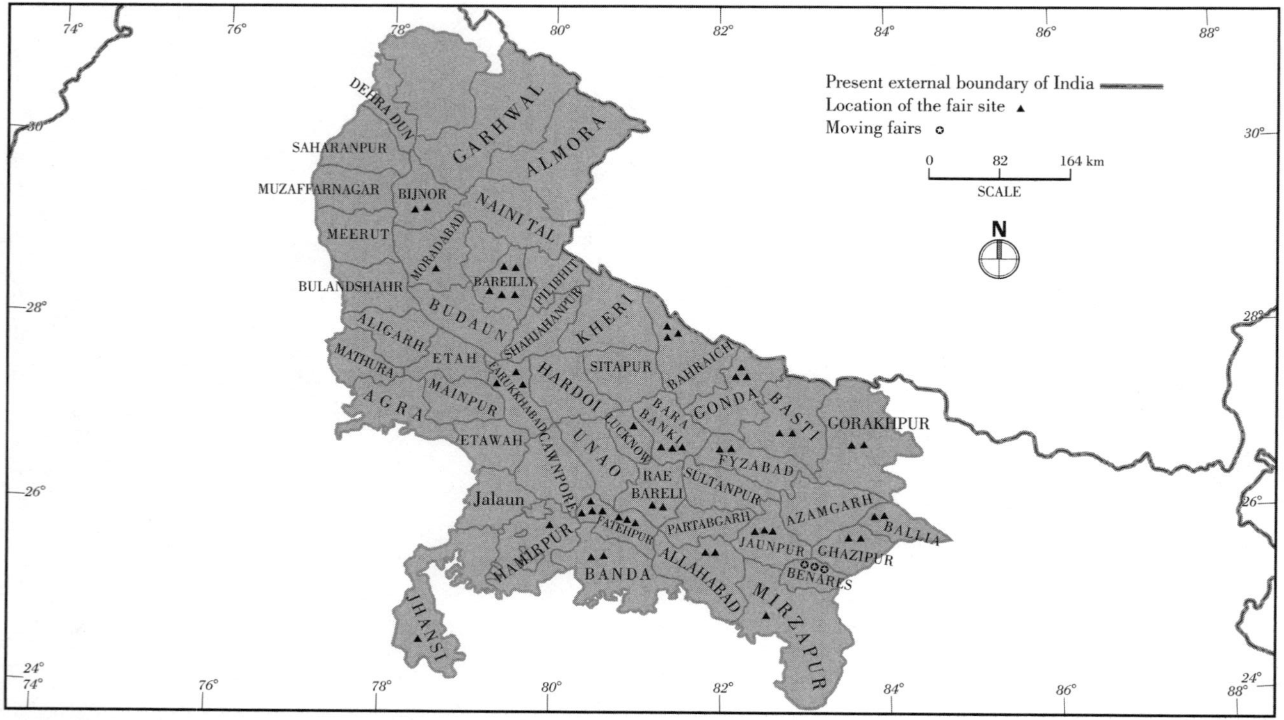

Source: Compiled from *UP District Gazetteers (Supplementary Notes and Statistics, 1913–36)*; Ramprasad Tiwari, *Ritiratnakar*; Abdul Bismillah, *Jhini Jhini Bini Chadariya*; Sanjay Sharma, written communication about Allahabad fairs

Frequency of local Ghazi Miyan fairs in various districts of the United Provinces of Agra and Oudh compiled from District Gazetteers, 1913–36

District	Tahsil	Pargana	Place of Fair	Name of Fair	Time
Lucknow	Bijnor	Bijnor	Bijnor	Sohbat	Jeth 17
Rae Bareli	Maharajganj	Bacharawan	Thulendi	Sohbat	1st Jeth Sudi
	Maharajganj	Simrauta	Atreha	Sohbat	1st Sunday Jeth
Faizabad	Akbarpur	Akbarpur	Ashrafpur Barwa	Syed Salar	1st week in Jeth
	Tanda	Tanda	Asupur	Syed Salar	Jeth Badi 1st
Gonda	Utraula	Mahadeva	Asokpur	Rauza	1st Sunday Jeth
	Tarbalganj	Digsir	Asokpur	Bale Pir	1st Sunday Jeth
Bahraich	Bahraich	Bahraich	Singha Parasi	Syed Salar Fair	1st and 2nd Sunday Jeth
	Bahraich	Bahraich	Shahpur Jot Yusuf	Rajab Hathila	1st Sunday Jeth
	Bahraich	Bahraich	Dikauli	Pir Nasrullah	1st Sunday Jeth
Barabanki	Nawabganj	Satrikh	Satrikh	Hazrat Sahu Salar	Jeth Puranmasi
	Ramsanehighat	Rudauli	Rudauli	Zohra Bibi	1st Sunday Jeth
	Ramsanehighat	Rudauli	Rudauli	Makhdum Shah Abdul Haqq	Jamadussani 12-15th
Gorakhpur	Bansgaon	Dhuriapur	Barhaj	Ghazi Rauza	1st Sunday Jeth
	Gorakhpur	Haveli	Bairampur	Sayid Salar	Jeth Mela Atwa

Basti	Khalilabad	Rasulpur	Usra Shahid	Ghazi Miyan	1st Sunday Jeth
	Khalilabad	Rasulpur	Dudhara	Ghazi Miyan	1st Sunday Jeth
Jaunpur	Sahibganj	Ungli	Kheta Sarai	Sohbat Ghazi Miyan	Baisakh Sudi 11th
	Sahibganj	Razi	Sarokhanpur	Sohbat Ghazi Miyan	Jeth Badi 6th
	Machhlishahr	Ghiswa	Machhlishahr	Sohbat Ghazi Miyan	Jeth Badi 11th
Jhansi	Moth	Jhansi	Pichor	Zahir Pir Ka Mela	Bhadon Badi 9th
Ballia	Ballia	Ballia	Sagar Pali	Ghazi Miyan	Rabi-us-Sani 1st
Bareilly	Baheri	Richa	Richa	Bale Miyan	1st Sunday Jeth
	Baheri	Chaumahla	Banjoria	Bale Miyan	1st Sunday Jeth
	Baheri	Kali	Shergarh	Bale Miyan	Jeth Badi 1st
	Faridpur	Faridpur	Khata	Urs of Syed Salar Masood	Ist Sunday Jeth
	Nawabganj	Nawabganj	Khata	Bale Miyan	1st Sunday Jeth
Bijnor	Bijnor	Bijnor	Bijnor	Neza Bale Salar	Last Wednesday Chait
	Bijnor	Daranapar	Mandwar	Neza Bale Salar	2nd Thursday Chait
Moradabad	Amroha	Pooranpur	Pooranpur	Neza Bale Salar	1st March
Farukhabad	Farukhabad	Pahara	Fatehgarh	Ghazi Miyan	Jeth Sudi 1st
	Tiwra	Saurikh	Saurikh	Ghazi Miyan	1st Sunday Chait
	Chhibrama	Saurikh	Saurikh	Ghazi Miyan	Ist Sunday Jeth

Fatehpur	Haswa	Haswa	Tesi	Ghazi Miyan	1st Sunday Jeth
	Haswa	Haswa	Semari	Ghazi Miyan	1st Sunday Jeth
	Kora	Kora	Kamasi	Ghazi Miyan	1st Sunday after Baisakh Sudi 15th
Banda	Banda	Banda	Gusyari	Ghazi Miyan	Baisakh
Ghazipur	Ghazipur	Ghazipur	Ghazipur	Ghazi Miyan	1st Sunday Jeth
	Ghazipur	Saidpur	Pahlwanpur	Ghazi Miyan	Baisakh Sudi 6th
Hamirpur	Maudaba	Khanna Circle	Gusyari	Ghazi Miyan	Every Sunday of Jeth

ENDNOTES PREFACE

1. Pierre Briant, *Darius in the Shadow of Alexander* (Cambridge, Mass.: Harvard University Press, 2015); Nathan Wachtel, *The Vision of the Vanquished: The Spanish Conquest of Peru through Indian Eyes, 1530–1570* (Hassocks: Harvester Press, 1977).
2. Carlo Ginzburg, *The Cheese and the Worms: The Cosmos of a Sixteenth Century Miller* (London: Routledge and Kegan Paul, 1981), p. 155.

ENDNOTES INTRODUCTION

1. Manan Prasad Dwivedi Gajpuri, *Musalmani Rajya ka Itihas: Pahila Bhag*, ed. Shyam Sundar Das (Varanasi: Kashi Nagari Pracharini Sabha, samvat 1976/1920 CE), pp. 1–2.
2. On Manan Prasad Dwivedi Gajpuri, who also wrote satirical pieces under the nom de plume 'Mucchandar Nath', see Shri Durga Prasad Singh, *Bhojpuri ke Kavi aur Kavya* (Patna: Bihar Rashtrabhasha Parishad, 1959), pp. 227–28, and Premchand's obituary notice in his *Vividh Prasang*, vol. 3, (Allahabad: Hans Prakashan, 1962), pp. 403–04. For his satirical writings on 'Gandhi Baba', see Shahid Amin, 'Gandhi as Mahatma: Gorakhpur District, Eastern U.P., 1921-22', in Ranajit Guha (ed.), *Subaltern Studies*, vol. 3 (Delhi: Oxford University Press, 1984), pp. 49–50.
3. Partha Chatterjee, *The Nation and its Fragments: Colonial and Postcolonial Histories* (Princeton: Princeton University Press, 1993), p. 102.
4. Ibid., p. 99.
5. Cited in Sudhir Chandra, *The Oppressive Present: Literature and Social Consciousness in Colonial India* (New Delhi: Oxford University Press, 1992), p. 123.
6. Camal Kafadar, *Between Two Worlds: The Construction of the Ottoman State* (Berkeley: University of California Press, 1995), p. 20.

7. Edward Sachau (ed.), *Alberuni's India* (New Delhi: Low Price Publications, 1993, reprint. First published 1910), p. 22. It has been suggested that this 'scattering' refers probably to 'an exodus of Brahman literati from the Punjab' rather than Hindus from all of Hindustan, an unlikely demographic eventuality in the short run. See Andre Wink, *Al Hind: The Making of the Indo-Islamic World—The Slave Kings and the Islamic Conquest, 11th-13th Centuries,* vol. 2 (Leiden: Brill, 1997), pp. 103–04.
8. Tarinicharan Chattopadhyay, 'Bharatversher Itihas', cited in Chatterjee, *The Nation and its Fragments*, pp. 103–04. In a similar vein, see 'Foreword', in R. C. Majumdar (ed.), *The History of India and Culture of the Indian People: The Struggle for Empire,* vol. 5 (Bombay: Bhartiya Vidya Bhavan, 1957), pp. 7–29; Ram Gopal Misra, *Indian Resistance to Early Muslim Invaders upto 1206* (Meerut: Anu Books, 1983).
9. Peter Hardy, 'Mahmud of Ghazna and the Historian', *Journal of the Punjab University Historical Studies* 14, December 1962; C. E. Bosworth, 'Mahmud of Ghazna in Contemporary Eyes and in Later Persian Literature', *Iran* 4, 1966, pp. 85–92; Richard H. Davis, *Lives of Indian Images* (Princeton: Princeton University Press, 1997), ch. 3.
10. K. A. Nizami (ed.), *Politics and Society during the Early Medieval Period: Collected Works of Professor Mohammad Habib*, vol. 1 (New Delhi: People's Publishing House, 1974), pp. 3–122.
11. Nizami, *Politics and Society*. For scholarly consensus around this view see Wink, *Al Hind*, pp. 124–25; Peter Jackson, *The Delhi Sultanate: A Political and Military History* (Cambridge: Cambridge University Press, 1999), p. 6; Richard Eaton, 'Temple Desecration and Indo-Muslim States', in David Gilmartin and Bruce B. Lawrence (eds), *Beyond Turk and Hindu: Rethinking Religious Identities in Islamicate South Asia* (Gainsville: University of Florida Press, 2000), p. 251.
12. Nizami, *Politics and Society*, pp. 21–23, 116.
13. Ibid., pp. 22–23.
14. Ibid., pp. 113–14.
15. Simon Digby, 'The Sufi Shaikh as a Source of Authority in Medieval India', *Purushartha* 9, 1986, pp. 57–77; Simon Digby, *Encounters with Jogis in Indian Sufi Hagiography* (London, mimeo, 1970).
16. See the detailed consideration of the build up of the image of Khwaja Muinuddin Chishti 'as pioneering Islamizer' of the subcontinent (c. 1200) from the second half of the fourteenth century in Muzaffar Alam, *The Languages of Political Islam, c. 1200–1800* (New Delhi: Permanent Black, 2004), pp. 154–57, 164.
17. Alam, *Languages of Political Islam*, pp. 156–57; cf. Chaudhury Syed Ali Mohammad Zaidi, *Bara Banki: Jugrafiya, Tarikh wa digar aham waqiat wa rawaiyat waghaira* (Lucknow: Nami Press, 1984); Ali Mohammad Zaidi, *Apni Yaden, Rudauli ki Baten* (Rudauli: Azmi publishers, 1977); Interview with Maulvi Khalid saheb, village Kinhaura, Bara Banki, December 1994;

Ballad of the Capture of Palihar by Hathile, aka Ajab Salar, sung by Zainullah Dafali, Chittaura (Bahraich), May 1996.

18. Tony Stewart, 'Alternate Structures of Authority: Satya Pir on the Frontiers of Bengal', in David Gilmartin and Bruce B. Lawrence (eds), *Beyond Turk and Hindu: Rethinking Religious Identities in Islamicate South Asia* (Gainsville: University of Florida Press, 2000); Aditya Behl, 'The Magic Doe: Desire and Narrative in a Hindavi Sufi Romance, circa, 1503', in Richard M. Eaton (ed.), *India's Islamic Tradtions, 711–1750* (Delhi: Oxford University Press, 2003); Aditya Behl and Simon Weightman (trans.), *Madhumalati: An Indian Sufi Romance,* Oxford World Classics Series (Oxford: Oxford University Press, 2000).

19. Alam, *Languages of Political Islam*, p. 97.

20. Garcin de Tassy, *Memoirs sur des Particularites des la Religion Musulmane dans l'Inde d'apres les Ouvrages Hindoustani* (Paris: Libraire de la Societe Asiatique, 1869, second edition), translated by M. Waseem, as *Muslim Festivals in India* (New Delhi: Oxford University Press, 1995). See also M. Mujeeb, *Indian Muslims* (London: Allen Lane, 1963), ch. 1.

21. For a recent overview, see Sanjay Subrahmanyam, 'Before the Leviathan: Sectarian Violence and State in Pre-Colonial India', in Kaushik Basu and Sanjay Subrahmanyam (eds), *Unravelling the Nation: Sectarian Conflict and India's Secular Identity* (New Delhi: Penguin India, 1996), pp. 44–80; see also Susan Bayly, *Saints, Goddesses and Kings: Muslims and Christians in South Indian Society, 1700-1900* (Cambridge: Cambridge University Press, 1999), ch. 5.

22. Richard Eaton, *The Sufis of Bijapur 1300–1700: The Social Role of Sufis in Medieval India* (Princeton: Princeton University Press, 1978), p. 33.

23. H. M. Elliot, *The History of India, As Told by Its Own Historians: The Muhammadan Period,* ed. John Dowson (Delhi: Low Price Publications, 2001, reprint. First published 1869), p. 160 (Hereafter abbreviated as *MM* E for the section dealing with the translation of 'Mirat-i-Masudi'); Allami Abul-Fazal, *The Ain-i-Akbari*, trans. H.S. Jarett, vol. 2 (New Delhi: Low Price Publications, 1989, reprint. First published 1894), p. 187.

24. Iqtidar Husain Siddiqui, 'A Note on the Dargah of Salar Mas'ud in Bahriach, in the Light of the Standard Historical Sources', in Christian W. Troll (ed.), *Muslim Shrines in India: Their Character, History and Significance* (New Delhi: Oxford University Press, 1989), pp. 44–47, esp. p. 45 from which the reference about Amir Khusro is taken.

25. Elliot, *History of India*, vol. 3, p. 363.

26. S. H. Askari (ed.), *Sirat-i-Ferozshahi, Nuskha Khudabaksh* (Patna: Khudabaksh Library, 1999), pp. 27–28.

27. Simon Digby, 'Dreams and Reminiscences of Dattu Sarwani: A Sixteenth-Century Indo-Afghan Soldier' (in two parts), *Indian Economic and Social History Review* 2(1&2), 1965, p. 59.

28. Digby, 'Dreams and Reminiscences', pp. 189–90.

29. Shaikh Raziqullah Mushtaqi, *Waqiat-i-Mushtaqi* (Rampur: Raza Library, 2002), p. 19; Shireen Moosvi (ed. and trans.), *Episodes in the Life of Akbar: Contemporary Records and Reminiscences* (New Delhi: National Book Trust, 1994), pp. 21–22.
30. See 'Saiyid Salar Trust', in 'List of Endowments and Miscellaneous Trusts in the Province of Oudh for 1878', Oudh Gen. File 1769/1878-79, Uttar Pradesh State Archives (UPSA). *Harek sāl Asaf-ud-daula Bahadur wazārat ke sadaf be bahadur, tamashe* [*Urs*] *ke liye jata tha us ja, muqarrar tha ki woh dekhe tha mela*: Cazim Ali Jawan, *Barah Masa: A Poetical Description of the Year in Hindoostan* (Calcutta: Hindoostanee Press, 1812), p. 29.
31. Mohammad Umar (trans.), *Sanskriti ke Saat Adhyay: Qateel dwara krt, 'Haft Tamasha' ka Hindi anuvad* (Aligarh: Kitab Ghar, 1990), pp. 84-85; Jawan, *Barah Masa*, section on the month of Jeth.
32. *MM* E, p. 160; Abul-Fazal, *Ain-i-Akbari*, p. 187.

ENDNOTES PART ONE

2 The Hagiography

1. C. A. Rieu, *Persian Literature: A Bio-Bibliographic Survey* (London: Luzac and Co, 1927), pp. 1105–07.
2. Alam, *Languages of Political Islam,* p. 165.
3. Ibid., pp. 92, 94, 165.
4. Abdur Rahman Chishti, *Mirat-i-Masudi,* text, MS. Or. 1837, British Library, p. 10 (hereafter *MM* F). Partial English translation in H. M. Elliot, 'Nobel, G: *Mirat-i-Masudi*', in *History of India,* vol. 2, pp. 513–49. I have at places modified Elliot's translation in the light of two recent translations of the complete text done in Urdu and English in India: Jagdeo Singh, *Mirat-i-Masudi*: *Izzat mab Abdur Rahman Chishti ki Ma'ruf tasneef* (Lucknow: Books India International, 1997, Urdu translation), p. 33; H. A. Qureshi (trans.), *Sufis Classics-II*: *Mirat-i-Masudi of Abdur Rahman Danethwi* (Lucknow: New Royal Book Company, 2009), pp. 28–29.
5. Inayat Husain, *Tarikh Salar Masud Ghazi Masud Ghazi, be-ihtemam... Mohammad Abdullah Siddiqui, Lakhnavi, tajir Kutub-wa chikan, Chowk* (Lucknow: Matba-i-Mujtabai, 1916), p. 9 (hereafter *MM* IH).
6. Roderic Vasie, 'Persian Interpretations of the Bhagvadgita in the Mughal Period with Special Reference to the Sufi version of Abd al-Rahman Chishti' (PhD diss., School of Oriental and African Studies, London University, 1988), p. 49 and note 6, citing Simon Digby, 'Abdul al-Quddus Gangohi (1456–1537): The Personality and Attitudes of a Medieval Indian Sufi', in *Medieval India: A Miscellany*, vol. 3 (Bombay: Asia Publishing House, 1975).
7. *Mirat-ul-Asrar*, cited in Vasie, 'Persian Interpretations', p. 49. Evoking the same religious experience, Abdur Rahman recounted in the middle of the *Mirat-i-Masudi*: 'This slave once, in the beginning of [his spiritual] life, looked upon the Sultan [us Shuhda] in a vision. From that hour his heart grew cold to the business of the world and for three or four years he lost thoughts of self in the pain of separation from him'. *MM* E, p. 536.
8. *MM* E, pp. 513–14; Paul Ricoeur, 'The Hermeneutics of Testimony', in *Essays in Biblical Interpretation* (Philadelphia: Fortune Press, 1980). See also

David Cook, *Martyrdom in Islam* (Cambridge: Cambridge University Press, 2007), pp. 16–17.

9. Vasie, 'Persian Interpretations', pp. 49–50. See the comprehensive work, Hazrat Shaikh Abdur Rahman Chishti, *Mirat-ul-Asrar,* c.1635–1654, trans. Wahid Baksh Syal (Lahore, 1993), Urdu translation.

10. *MM* E, p. 514.

11. *MM* F, p. 97aff.

12. *MM* E, pp. 547–48.

13. Saiyid Athar Abbas Rizvi, *A History of Sufism in India*, vol. 1 (Delhi: Munshiram Manoharlal, 1997), p. 313.

14. *MM* E, p. 548.

15. Ibid. p. 104.

16. Muhammad Nazim in his monograph on Mahmud Ghazni characterises it as 'a history mixed with a liberal supply of pious fiction', and leaves it at that. Mohammad Habib in an earlier (1927) study skips any mention of the hagiography altogether. See Muhammad Nazim, *The Life and Times of Sultan Mahmud of Ghazna* (Cambridge: Cambridge University Press, 1931), p. 14. See also Nizami, *Politics and Society*, vol. 2, pp. 36–104, 389–92. For a recent extended discussion of the *Mirat* and also the frontier region of Bahraich, see Sunil Kumar, *The Emergence of the Delhi Sultanate, 1192-1286* (Ranikhet: Permanent Black, 2007), pp. 347–50.

17. The mid-nineteenth-century editor of the printed English translation maintained that Abdur Rahman's references from the standard historical sources like the *Rauzat-us-Safa* 'are fair, though somewhat abridged, and stripped of redundant ornament'. Prefatory note, *MM* E, p. 514. Simon Digby, on the basis of a close reading of the same Persian manuscript, was of the view that 'a number of citations by Abdur Rahman Chishti … are wholly mendacious, and that the author has taken existing place names such as Kabul and Kalinjar and compounded them into his own "coinages" as Kabuliz and Kalihar/Kahilar'. Written communication, Simon Digby, 12 April 2004. For a historicist reading of the *Mirat* and the attempt to collate all the extant copies in India, see Maulvi Muhammad Abbas Saheb Sherwani, Collector, *Hayat-i-Masudi, yani Sawan-e-Umri, Hazrat Sipah Salar Masud Ghazi Shaheed* (Aligarh: Aligarh Muslim University, 1935). See now the extended Introduction, along with a full translation from the collated master text of Sherwani, in Qureshi, *Mirat-i-Masudi*, esp. pp. 1–20.

18. *MM* E, p. 515.

19. Ibid., p. 516.

20. *MM* F, pp. 16–16a, *MM* E, pp. 517–18.

21. *ba qudrat haq … hamān shab … Salar Masud az pusht-i-pidar dar rahm-i-mādar dar āmad. MM* F, p. 17. 'Through the power of the Almighty God, that

very night ... Salar Masud left the loins of his father and entered the womb of hs mother'. *MM* E, p. 318.
22. *MM* E, pp. 518–19.
23. Ibid., p. 520.
24. *MM* C, pp. 3, 5; *MM* F, p. 25a. Chapman's translation modified.
25. *MM* C, p. 5a.
26. Ibid., p. 6a.
27. Ibid., p. 6.
28. *MM* E, p. 520.
29. 'Kalihar' appears to be a non-existent place, unknown in the sources of the eleventh century. Variant texts specify Kabuliz in its stead, both places missing from the physical geography of north India. The same seems to hold true for the place Rawal (see the story in the chapter about the Raja of Rawal who tries to poison Masud).
30. The text of Abdur Rahman has *khusr-pura*: a 'wife's brother', *MM* F, p. 28. The north Indian affinal term is *sāla*, a common expletive.
31. *MM* E, p. 519.
32. *MM* F, p. 28a.
33. *MM* E, p. 523.
34. Ibid.
35. Ibid., p. 524.
36. Ibid., p. 116.
37. *MM* C, p. 8a. I have modified Chapman's translation of this passage, including the verse (attributable to Hafiz) in terms of *MM* F, p. 32, and Joginder Singh's Urdu translation (see *MM* JS, pp. 50–51).
38. *MM* C, p. 15.
39. *MM* E, p. 525.
40. See *inter alia*, the fictionalised accounts in Kanhaiya Lal Munshi, *Jai Somnath, c. 1940* (Nai Dilli: Rajkamal Paperbacks, 1977); Acharya Chatursena Shastri, *Somnath, c. 1954* (Dilli: Hind Pakit Buks, 2002).
41. For a discussion of the sack of Somnath, see Nazim, *Sultan Mahmud of Ghazna; Habib, Collected Work*, vol. 2; Davis, *Lives of Indian Images*, ch. 3; Romila Thapar, *Somanatha—The Many Voices of a History* (New Delhi: Penguin India, 2005).
42. The quotation is from Nazim, *Sultan Mahmud of Ghazna*, p. 121. For details, see Mahdi Hasan (ed.), *Futuhus-Salatin, or Shahnamah-i-Hind of Isami*, vol. 1 (Bombay: Asia Publishing House, 1967, English translation), pp. 83–86.
43. Nazim, *Sultan Mahmud of Ghazna*, p. 135.
44. *MM* E, p. 119.
45. Davis, *Lives of Indian Images*; Thapar, *Somanatha.*
46. Nazim, *Sultan Mahmud of Ghazna*, p. 136.

47. *MM* C, p.130.
48. *MM* E, pp. 528–29.
49. *MM* C, p. 13a.
50. Ibid. The Persian text ascribes the verse to a *buzurg*, a 'wise man'; Chapman in his translation reads it to refer to the great Iranian poet Hafiz Shirazi.
51. *MM* E, p. 532.
52. Satrikh, the abode of seven sages or *rishi*s: saptarishi>satrich>satrikh. Compare Kosambi: 'The seven sages (*saptarishis*) are not only an Indian group, but highly reminiscent of the seven Mesopotamian antediluvian sages, whose images are actually found buried in groups of seven'. See D. D. Kosambi, 'Development of the Gotra System', in *Combined Methods in Indology and Other Writings* (New Delhi: Oxford University Press, 2002), p. 131.
53. Asaf-ud-daulah, the Nawab of Awadh and Mir Taqi Mir, the Delhi poet, during his residence in Lucknow, went hunting annually to Bahraich in the early nineteenth century. Written communication, C. M. Naim, 22 November 2009.
54. *MM* F, p. 57; *MM* E, p. 534.
55. *MM* F, pp. 56a–58; *MM* E, pp. 534–35.
56. *MM* F, p. 58; *MM* E, p. 535.
57. Mohammad Habib and Khaliq Ahmad Nizami (eds), *A Comprehensive History of India: The Delhi Sultanate*, vol. 5, pt. 1 (New Delhi: People's Publishing House, 1992), pp. 171–78.
58. I wish to thank the late Simon Digby for his reading of the history of the phrase *bāla dast* and *firo dast* as these occur in the *Mirat-i-Masudi*.
59. *MM* E, p. 535.
60. Irfan Habib, *An Atlas of the Mughal Empire: Political and Economic Maps with Detailed Notes, Bibliography and Index* (Delhi: Oxford University Press, 1986), map 8B.
61. Kumar, *Emergence of the Delhi Sultanate*, p. 350.
62. *MM* F, pp. 66–67.
63. Based on the perusal of the same manuscript copy as used by R.W. Chapman for his partial translation of the *Mirat-i-Masudi*, reproduced in Elliot, *History of India as Told by its Own Historians*, vol. I, Appendix, the late Simon Digby had pointed out that Chapman had misread *Bāla rich/rikh* as the somewhat meaningless *Bāla rukh* (written communication, 12 April 2004).
64. *MM* F, pp. 66–67. On *Bāl* = sun, see George Weston Briggs, *Gorakhnath and the Kanphata Yogis* (Delhi: Motilal Banarsidass, 1975, reprint. First published 1938), p. 101; Abul-Fazal, *Ain-i-Akbari*, p. 319: 'In the middle of the Sindh sagar near Shamsabad is the cell of Balnāth Jogi which is called

Tilah Balnath'. In a footnote, Col. Jerret, the translator of the *Ain*, makes the connection to sun worship explicit: 'The full name is Gorakhnāth ka Tila, the more ancient Balnāth ka Tila, both derived from the temple on the summit dedicated to the sun as Balnath, but now devoted to the worship of Gorakhnath, a form of Shiva'.

65. *MM* E, p. 538.

66. *MM* C, p. 23a.

67. *MM* E, p. 539.

68. *MM* F, pp. 72–72a, 76a.

69. A *nala* of the Rapti river, locally called Phenkala or Kathela nadi, according to the local informants. Interview with Haji saheb at the Bahraich Dargah, 17 May 1996. Most probably, it is the 'Kauriala' river, the common name for the big river Saru or Saryu in its upper reaches of Bahraich country. See Irfan Habib, *Atlas of the Mughal Empire*, map 8B, and notes, p. 30, under 'Rivers', column 3.

70. *MM* E, p. 543; *MM* F p. 77. Translation modified. In the ballads about Salar Masud or Ghazi Miyan, 'the cattle of the army' become 'cows and cowherds belonging to Ghazi Miyan'—an interesting case of the forging of an affective relationship between the Ghazi and his herdsmen.

71. For such 'bhomias', as they are called in Rajasthan, see Rustom Bharucha, *Rajasthan: An Oral History: Conversations with Komal Kothari* (New Delhi: Penguin India, 2003), pp. 105–08. For Gangetic north India, see the last battle of the hero against cow rustlers in both *Lorikayan* and *Chandayan*, the latter an Awadhi epic, c. 1370s, dealing with a virile cowherd hero Lorik and his paramour Chanda.

72. Mahua (*Bassia latifolia*), *gulchampa* in Abdur Rahman's text, is a slow-growing 'large deciduous tree, indigenous in the forests of the Central Provinces ... it extend[s] from Kangra, Kumaon, and Oudh through the Central Provinces and Chutia [Chota] Nagpur to the Western Ghats, and distributed in the south-east to Ava ... Each of its products is of considerable commercial, medicinal and alimentary value: it yields a white milky gum from incisions and cracks in the bark, the bark is often used as an adjunct in dyeing where dark colours or black are desired; along with its leaves it is sometimes employed as a tan; it yields a greenish oil, which besides being used for lighting is also used as an inexpensive substitute for ghee ... The fruit is sometimes eaten, but the principle edible structure is the succulently-developed flowers (i.e., corollas); these are eaten raw or cooked, or in the form of sweetmeats. Liquor, resembling Irish whiskey, is fermented from the flowers in NWP and Oudh in the eastern and southern districts'. See George Watt, *A Dictionary of Economic Product,* vol. 1, pp. 405ff, from which this description is taken. The three products of the mahua tree—leaves, corolla and nut—also figure in the origin myth of grain parchers, distillers and oil-

pressers: a primeval father allots the leaves for firing the oven to the grain parcher; the distiller is entitled to ferment the corolla; and the oil presser to extract oil from the mahua nut. See William Crooke, *The Tribes and Castes of North-Western Provinces and Oudh*, vol. 4 (Allahabad: Superintendent Government Press, 1896), s.v. 'Teli'.

73. Pradip Krishen, *Trees of Delhi: A Field Guide* (Delhi: Dorling Kindersley, 2006), pp. 140–41; Wheeler M. Thackston (ed. and trans.), *The Baburnama: Memoir of Babur, Prince and Emperor* (New York: Oxford University Press, 1996), p. 342; see also *Crooke, Tribes and Castes,* s.v. 'Teli'.

74. W. C. Bennett, 'Introduction', in *Gazetteer of the Province of Oudh*, vol. 1 (Delhi: Low Price Publications, 1993, reprint. First published 1877–78), pp. v–vi, emphasis added.

75. *MM* E, p. 541.

76. The polar opposite of mahua in terms of its relation to cultivation was the mango tree—the rightful lord of the arborial kingdom of Awadh. 'Never found wild', noted the Gazetteer, 'there is no village and hardly any respectable family which is without its plantation, and even members of the lower castes will think no effort thrown away to acquire a small patch of land on which to plant a few trees'. *Oudh Gazetteer*, p. vi.

77. *MM* E, p. 542, emphasis added.

78. Ibid., pp. 543–44.

79. Ibid., p. 544.

80. Ibid., p. 546.

81. There is a cult of *khing-sawār*, the grey or piebald rider at Ajmer which antedates the establishment of the cult of Muinuddin Chishti at that place in the thirteenth century: S. H. Askari, *Islam and Muslims in Medieval Bihar* (Patna: Khuda Baksh Library, 1989), p. 22. See also Qureshi, *Mirat-i-Masudi*, p. 131.

82. *MM* E, pp. 546–47.

83. *MM* F, p. 8a; *MM* Q, p. 26. Towards the end of his work, Abdur Rahman tries to draw a convoluted parallel between the stages by which both light and life were infused into the body of Adam, from the upper portion to the middle and lower parts, and the spread of Islam from Arabia (Mecca) into north India. *MM* F, pp. 95–96a. 'Abdur Rahman is here in trouble from the fact that they are both in the 'second clime' *(iqleem)*, as fixed by astronomical observation'. Simon Digby, written communication, 12 April 2004.

84. *MM* C, p. 239.

85. An earlier version in use during the thirteenth–fourteenth centuries was *chauntra*: Nizamuddin Auliya's tomb in Delhi is built on *chauntra-i-yārān.*

86. *MM* C, p. 31, emphasis added.

87. Two rajas of the hills convey their acceptance of Masud's suzerainty in these parts before the final battle with Sohal Deo and a confederacy of

twenty-two other rajas. *MM* Q, p. 112. By contrast, conversion of kings, clan chiefs, courtiers and clansmen are widespread motifs in the Ghazi stories in Bengal, and in the conversion myths of the various islands of the Indonesian archipelago and Inner Asia. For Bengal, see Abdur Rahim, *Gaji Kalu-o Champabati Kanyari Puthi*, c. 1870 (Dhaka: Hamidiya Library 1961); Edward Yazijian, 'The Story of Ghazi in Bengal' (Typescript, Chicago, May 2000); Russell Jones, 'Ten Conversion Myths from Indonesia' in Nehemia Levtzion (ed.), *Conversion to Islam* (New York: Holmes and Meir, 1979), pp. 129–58; Devin DeWeese, *Islamization and Native Religion in the Golden Horde* (Pennsylvania: Pennsylvania State University Press, 1994).

88. I have used the fuller translation by Digby of the highly embroidered seventeenth-century exposition of the legend of Ajmer and Muinuddin Chishti as presented in Ilahdiya Chishti's *Siyar al-Aqtab*. Digby, 'The Sufi Shaikh as a Source of Authority', p. 73.

89. The *Mirat-i-Masudi* provides an abbreviated account of the successful contest waged by the Khwaja to win Ajmer as a sacred site for Islam (see *MM* E, p. 548). For a fuller discussion, see Simon Digby, 'Encounters with Jogis', pp. 14–15.

90. *MM* F, p. 94a.

3 An Urdu Mirror of Masud

1. Moin Ahmad Ali, '*Mirat-i-Masudi* (Notes on Different Manuscripts)', *Mushir-i-Awqaf* 3(1), 1976, in H. A. Qureshi, *Sufis Classics-I*, pp. 32–38; Qureshi, *Mirat-i-Masudi;* Sherwani, *Hayat-i-Masudi,* pp. 29–30. Though two early nineteenth-century compendia touch upon popular beliefs about Salar Masud and brief descriptions of his shrine, there appears to have been little discussion of the *Mirat-i-Masudi* text among the literati or the elites of Awadh. See Meer Sher Ulee Ufsos, *Araish-i-Mulhfil, Being a History, in the Hindoostanee Language of the Hindoo Princes from Joodishtur to Pithoura: Compiled from Khoolasut-ool-Hind and other Authorities—By Meer Sher Ulee Ufsos, Head Monshee in the Hindoostanee Department of the College* (Calcutta: Hindoostanee Press, 1808), p. 98; Mirza Qatil, 'Haft Tamasha, c. 1811–12', in *Sanskriti ke Saat Adhyay: Qatil dwara krt 'Hafta Tamasha' ka Hindi Anuvaad,* trans. Mohammad Umar (Aligarh: Kitab Ghar, 1990), pp. 83ff. This last text has a section on Salar Masud Ghazi Bahraichi [sic!], pp. 194–197, but this is an appendix added by its twentieth-century translator, and so of very little use as description of conditions and narratives of the eighteenth century, the time period when the original Farsi text of 'Haft Tamasha' was written.

2. Sujan Rai Bhandari. *Khulasatu-t-Tawarikh,* ed. Zafar Hasan (Delhi: J. & Sons Press, 1918), p. 43.

3. *MM* E, pp. 514–15.
4. Developments in the late nineteenth-century Hindi literary and social sphere are discussed extensively in Vasudha Dalmia, *The Nationalization of Hindu Traditions: Bharatendu Harishchandra and Nineteenth-Century Banaras* (Delhi: Oxford University Press, 1997). For a nuanced understanding of the relationship between memories of north India's medieval Muslim past and historical and mnemonic consciousness as found in Hindi literary texts of the period, see Sudhir Chandra, 'Communal Consciousness in Late 19th Century Hindi Literature', in Mushirul Hasan (ed.), *Communal and Pan-Islamic Trends in Colonial India* (Delhi: Manohar, 1981); Chandra, *Oppressive Present.* See also Francesca Orsini, *The Hindi Public Sphere, 1920-1940: Language and Literature in the Age of Nationalism* (New Delhi: Oxford University Press, 2002), esp. ch. 3, 'The Uses of History'; Shahid Amin, ' Representing the Musalman: Then and Now, Now and Then', in Shail Mayaram, M. S. S. Pandian and Ajay Skaria (eds), *Muslims, Dalits and the Fabrication of History: Subaltern Studies,* vol. 12 (New Delhi: Permanent Black, 2005) and Part IV of this book.
5. *MM* IH.
6. *MM* F, pp. 16–16a.
7. *MM* E, p. 517, emphasis added.
8. *MM* IH, p. 24.
9. *Koi gãnje ka dam laga-kar, ankhen charha kar tarang mein aya, munh bana kar zabān par laya: aji hum ko bhi kal se zukām hai, hamāra yahān kya kām hai ... āo baitho daya karo, dam tambāku lo, gānje ki chillum lo, Dada ko jangal phir āne do, humko bhi lete chalo.*

Koi Barahman baccha beresha bola: hamāra pothi bichār-kar sāet batāna kām hai, Panditon mein nām hai, Raja-Babu āo-bhagat se bulāte hāin ... Chandni ke hawāle hokar bhang ka istemāl karte thei, fasād ki surat se darte thei; khūn to khūn peshāb dekh kar ghash khāte thei, nashtar ke nām se mar jāte the. Ab hatiya [hatya] pare gi, dharm jāye ga, zeest [?] *pe bhi harf aega ... Hum aise rozgār se kināra karenge, bheek māng kar khāna gawāra karenge, halwa-poori, kachauri na pā sakenge, bhaunri laga lenge ... kutte ki maut to na marenge. MM* IH, p. 25.
10. *Chūn matlab mahaz shahādat būd*: 'What was sought was nought but martyrdom', and so, after a purificatory bath, wearing a regal 'shahāna dress', with a dagger and sword tucked in his waist band, Masud happily rode out on his very special *asp-i-māda-i-khing* (grey mare). *MM* F, pp. 83–83a.
11. *MM* IH, p. 75.
12. Compare, for example, *Tarikh-i-Masudi: Tarikh Syed Salar Masud Ghazi, Hasab Farmaish Ghani Ahmad Tajir-i-Kutub, Chowk, Lucknow* (Lucknow: Nami Press, n.d., c. 1950), which is a reprint in large parts of Inayat Husain's version of the *Mirat.*

4 The Author as Hero

1. I am relying here on Captain Wolseley Haig, 'The Legendary Account of Shah Abdur-r-Rahman-i-Ghazi, the Warrior Saint of Berar', *Journal of the Asiatic Society of Bengal*, (hereafter *JASB*) 71 (3.1), 1901, pp. 10–16. Unless indicated, all quotations in this chapter are from his article, which is abbreviated as 'Legendary Account'.
2. A ballad from Patan, western India, recounts the story of a Muslim faqir, punished for his proselytisation, similarly appealing to the Ghazni Sultan for succour. James Tod, *Travels in Western India* (London: W. H. Allen, 1839), pp. 344–51; Major J. W. Watson, 'The Fall of Patan: Ballad of the Fall of Patan', *Indian Antiquary* 8, June 1879, pp. 153–61.
3. The Elichpur history, 'Tarikh-i-Ahmadi', cited in Haig, 'Legendary Account', p. 11. I have modified Haig's spelling 'Ilicpur' to Elichpur.
4. See Ch. 15, 'The Bahraich Shrine'.
5. Emphasis added. She advises him, 'saying that the example of Fatimah, who had given the head of her son Husain as an offering for the freedom of all Muslims, prompted her to advise him thus'. Haig, 'Legendary Account', p. 12.
6. Haig, 'Legendary Account', p. 12.
7. Ibid., pp. 13–14.
8. The only differences between the two genealogies are a different father and a gap of one generation, so that Syed Ataullah, the grandfather of Ghazi Miyan, here figures as the great grandfather of the Elichpur Ghazi. See, 'shijra' Salar Masud Ghazi in Mansur Ali Khadim, *Karamat-i- Ghazi* (Bahraich, n.d.), pp. 4–5; Haig, 'Legendary Account', p. 14.
9. Subuktigin died in August 997 CE, and Sultan Mahmud was preoccupied in Central Asia till the early 1000s, the time of the Abdur Rahman's battles in Elichpur. For the historical record, see Nazim, *Sultan Mahmud of Ghazna*, Ch. 5–6.
10. Haig, 'Legendary Account', p. 14.
11. Satyendra, *Jaharpir: Guru Gugga* (Agra: Agra University Press, 1956).
12. See R. Greeven, *The Heroes Five (Panchon Pir): An Attempt to Collect Some of the Songs of the Pachpiriya Ballad-Mongers in the Benares Division* (Allahabad: Pioneer Press, 1898), p. 107.
13. Mangal Khan, *Gulzar-i-Masudi, aur Kitab Lajawab Jamei—Halaat Syed Salar Musud Ghazi Alia Rahmatullah, Az tasneef Janab Mangal Khan Sahib Nighat Banarasi, Shagird Janab Maulana Zakir Ali Sahib Marhoon Banarasi* (Bahraich: Ikleel Press, 1914), pp. 70–71.
14. A. C. Lyall (ed.), *Gazetteer for the Haidarabad and Assigned Districts, Commonly Called Berar* (Bombay: Education Society Press, 1870), p. 144.
15. Haig, 'Legendary Account', p. 15; Notice on Elichpur, in Lyall, *Gazetteer*, p. 144, footnote.

16. Haig, 'Legendary Account', p. 16, emphasis added.

17. Rahim, *Champabati Kanyati Puthi*; Asim Roy, *The Syncretic Tradition in Bengal* (Princeton: Princeton University Press, 1983), pp. 213–18, 236–41; James Wise. 'The Muhammadans of Eastern Bengal', *Journal of Asiatic Society of Bengal* 63, 1894, pp. 41–45. Sarat Chandra Mitra, 'On a Musalmān Legend about the Sylvan Saint Bona-Bibi and the Tiger Deity Dakshina Rayā', *University of Calcutta: Journal of the Department of Letters* 10, 1923, pp. 154–72.

18. Soon after sighting the sun tank at Bahraich, Masud had a dream: 'He thought he saw [his father] ... encamped with a large army on the banks of the Ganges whither he had just joined him'. Inside the private pavilion Salar Sahu presided 'over a festive assembly'. With a garland of roses in her hand, Masud's mother now beckoned: 'Hasten hither my child Masud, we have prepared this feast for thee. Salar Masud approached and she crowned him with a garland [tiara] of roses'. The Dervishes 'with one accord declared that he who had seen such a vision would certainly be a martyr for the faith'. *MM* C, p. 23a. See Chapter 2 of this volume.

ENDNOTES PART TWO

5 Tales and the Text

1. Mahdi Hasan (ed. and trans.), *The Rehla of Ibn Battuta (India, Maldive Islands and Ceylon)*, Gaekwad's Oriental Series no. 122 (Baroda: Oriental Institute, 1953), pp. 109–10.
2. *MM* JS, pp. 89–90; *MM* E, p. 103.
3. *MM* Q, p. 10.
4. Ibid. citing the chroniclers Gardizi and Bahqaqi. See also the extracts from the *Majma-i-Wasaya*, in Elliot and Dowson, *The History of India as Told by its Own Historians*, vol. 2, appendix, pp. 504–05 ('Mahmud and Ahmad Hasaan Maimandi'), where the wazir is cast in the role of a veritable eleventh-century Sherlock Holmes!

6 Reproductive Anxiety

1. *Jise pūt Mahboob diya na, sun Mamul! / usey kaun kare ahiwāti*: Saint Zinda Madar of Makanpur to Mamula in a ballad recorded in the late nineteenth century. Greenven, *Heroes Five*, p. 6, line 50; s.v. '*Ahiwāti*'/*Ahibāti*' in Shahid Amin (ed.), A *Concise Encyclopaedia of North Indian Peasant Life* (New Delhi: Manohar Books, 2005), p. 178, para 633 for the slightly different meaning of 'a woman whose husband is alive'.
2. The expression is *bitiyahi mori kokh*. See Ram Naresh Tripathi, *Gramya Geet: Sohar, Annprashan, Mundan, Janeu, Nahcchu aur Vivah ke Geet* (Prayag: Hindi Mandir, 1951), sohar songs nos 1–52, especially no. 17, pp. 110–11; Bernard S. Cohn, 'The Camars of Senapur: A Study of the Changing Status of a Depressed Caste' (PhD diss., Cornell University, 1954), p. 210.
3. Tripathi, *Gramya Geet*, sohar no. 61, pp. 185–86. Even the plain-looking flouncing wife, whose *thunkan* for gold jewellery is turned down by a careless husband, knows the one sure way to make up: she prays devoutly to the sun god. Formulaically, as the ninth month yields the desired boon, the husband forgetting her ugliness rushes home with a three-stringed necklace. He shakes his tired, dark-skinned wife: 'Rani, My Queen', he says cuddling up to her: 'Spit

the hurt out, here is the jewellery I had denied you'. Now it is the turn of the beaming Madonna to retaliate —'black as a koel-bird, ugly as a skunk' is what he had called her. 'Don't you clamber on to my bed', she taunts him, 'My dark skin might rub off on you'! 'Raja, now that I have my own priceless gem, I need no tri-stringed *tilari-hār*'; 'It is because of your dharma that the Lord has given me a son', she says self-effacingly. See Tripathi, *Gramya Geet*, no. 68, pp. 194–96.

4. Tripathi, *Gramya Geet*, sohar, no. 5, couplet 1, p. 87. See also Udai Narain Tiwari, *The Origin and Development of Bhojpuri*, Asiatic Society Monograph Series, vol. 10 (Calcutta: Asiatic Society 1960), pp. 212–13, where the term 'Brijbasini', as used in this song, is rendered as 'a wanton woman'.

5. *Dharti! Tumhin saran ab dehu bānjhin nām chhutei ho;*
Jahwān se tum āeu lauti uhān jāo, tumhin ham na rākhab;
Bānjhin! Tonh-ka jo hum rākhi lei, hamhaun hob usar ho.

6. 'Gaura Got'—*go-ghat*/*gau-ghāt*, it seems, refers to a watering place for cattle. In a stylised history of Ahir or cowherds, collected in the submontane *tarai* region, it was the custom here that the Ahir chiefs would have the cows under their charge drink only at the tanks constructed by them. See 'Ahwal Qaum Gobari, yani Ahir', H. M. Elliot Papers, OR 1733, OIOC, British Library (BL). Even where circular masonry tanks, with steps leading down to the water level were constructed, one side with a slope was usually left open (*go-ghāt*) to allow cattle access to the water body. See the notice on the Surajkund in Delhi, in Sir Syed Ahmad Khan, *Asar-us-Sanadid* (Delhi: Urdu Akademi, 2000, reprint. First published 1847, 1854), p. 157.

7. *Tere ghar tiriya be-ausān;*
Hum na laibe bānjhiniya ke dān;
Aré uska tay diya deuta pūji nahin pāe. Ballad of Jaswa, sung by Bashir Dafali at the Bahraich Fair, mid-May 1996.

8. The thought that the husband may equally share in the inadequacy to produce a child—a 'modern' idea—is rarely encountered in adages and folklore. There is however one pithy 'women's song' from Farrukhabad in UP, recorded in the late nineteenth century, that splits the blame equally between husband and wife: *ya to kachu kokh mein kaj meri hai, ya tum mein kachu kaj hai balma; teri jawāni mein rahi bānjh ré balma*: 'Either in my womb is a twist not right, Or you my darling, are not quite fit; I am barren, spouse, your youth despite' (trans. modified); s.v. *kokh* in S. W. Fallon, *A New Hindustani Dictionary with Illustrations from Hindustani Literature and Folklore* (Banaras: E. J. Lazarus, 1879). The best historical discussion of barrenness in north India is to be found in Anshu Malhotra, *Gender, Caste and Religious Identities: Restructuring Class in Colonial India* (Delhi: Oxford University Press, 2004)

9. 'Jaswa' sung by Shubrati Dafali, Bahraich, December 1995 (hereafter Shubrati, 'Jaswa').

10. *Banjh ka guzāra ek lahza-bhar nahin*: Shubrati, 'Jaswa'.
11. Shubrati, 'Jaswa'.
12. Ibid.
13. *Aré Lal! Nauven mein upjen dunon jahān; / Mere Jasa Lāl! Jasa ke upje Kanhaiya Lāl.*
14. For 'gobal/gobali/gopal', see *MM* F, pp. 99–99a; Akbar Ali ibn Mohammad Baksh, *Khulasah Tarikh-i-Masudi* (Lucknow: n.p., 1876), p. 12; *MM* IH, p. 87 for Ahir and *bānjh*, and for the later reference to the husband's vow of bringing in sweets as offerings every week once his wife conceived; for the use of the composite 'gaddi-gwala', see the Hindi text Babu Chote Lal, *Syed Salar Leela jisko Babu Chote Lal wald Babu cheda Lal, senior grade sub-assistant sarjan, Kasganj Zila Eta niwasi, Incharge shafakhana, Tajganj Agra-ne, yatriyon-ke faidey-ke liye banaya, Matbae Mufid aam Agar mein Qadar Ali Khan Sufi ke ehtaman-se chapi* (1913), p. 11.
15. *MM* IH, p. 87; *MM* F, p. 100.

7 Zohra Bibi

1. Alam, *Languages of Political Islam*, pp. 92, 94.
2. *MM* F, pp. 100–01a.
3. Ibid., p. 100.
4. *MM* IH, p. 87.
5. Amir Khusro, the legendary Indo-Persian poet had stayed in Awadh some time during 1287–90, and had written about the *ud* (aloe-wood)-like scent spreading throughout Hindustan, that is, eastern UP and Awadh, from the grave of Sipahsalar. Siddiqi, 'A Note on the *Dargah* of Salar Mas'ud', p. 45.
6. *MM* F, pp. 100aff; Akbar Ali ibn Mohammad Baksh, *Khulsah Tarikh Masudi*, 1288 A.H., p. 13; *Aina-i-Masudi: al maruf bah Tarikh Syed Salar Masud Ghazi RA, hasab farmaish Haji Ahmad Saheb tajir kutub, Chowk, Lukhnau* (Kanpur: Razzaq Press, 1357/1358 AH, reprint. First published n.d., pp. 106–07.
7. *MM* F, pp. 102–03; *MM* IH, p. 89.
8. *MM* F, p. 103.
9. Based on field notes and *Dargah* pamphlets.
10. *MM* IH, pp. 89, 103; cf. *Aina-i-Masudi*, p. 108. See also Syed Mohammad Zaidi, *Apni Yaden*, pp. 242–44. I am grateful to janab S. M. Zaidi sahib *marhoom* for a discussion on the place of Rudauli in the cult of Ghazi Miyan.
11. *MM* F, p. 104.
12. Moosvi, *Episodes in the Life of Akbar*, pp. 21–22. The phrase *sarod guyān wa raqs kuna* (singing and dancing) does not appear in Emperor Akbar's account, but is used repeatedly in the *Mirat* to characterise the annual movement of pilgrims to the Bahraich shrine. See *MM* F, pp. 105a–106a.
13. See the discussion of this episode in the narrative section of the *Mirat*.

14. *MM* F, p. 103b.
15. *MM* F, p. 104a; compare *MM* JS, p. 107; *MM* Q, p. 144. Here, Abdur Rahman combines his own approval of the ways of the Bahraich pilgrims with the opinion of the great fourteenth-century Bihar Sufi Yahya Maneri on the Ulema's lack of understanding of the popular festivities around the shrines of the saints. See also Askari, *Medieval Bihar*, p. 16.
16. 'Kick and box those who term such rites (in honour of Ghazi Miyan and Zohra Bibi) un-Islamic, for such critics are ignoramus—nay ill-bred wretches pure and simple. And as for the finger-wagging Maulvis, these are nothing but religious imposters, reprobates and villains.' Mangal Khan, *Gulzar-i-Masudi*, p. 122.
17. Mohammad Umar interview, Rudauli, May 1994; Mangal Khan, *Gulzar-i-Masudi*, p. 122.
18. See Ram Gharib Chaube, 'Pachra Song—Chuhar Mal the Dusadh Hero Marrying a Brahman Girl', *North Indian Notes and Queries* (hereafter *NINQ*), 5(4), July 1894a, para 154.
19. Ballad sung at Karaundi village, near Rudauli by a Kingaria-Dafali from Basaurhi, 16 May 1994 (hereafter Basaurhi ballad recorded near Rudauli).
20. William Crooke, *A Rural and Agricultural Glossary for the N.W. Provinces and Oudh* (Calcutta: Government Press, 1888), s.v. *pachkha*: 'A conjunction of five unlucky stars: (*panchak*) a period of five days in the year from the twenty-second lunar asterism Sharavana to the twenty-seventh Revati, [that is, covering the zodiac signs Makara or Capricorn and Mina or Pisces] during which it is unlucky to do any work: persons who die during this time are thrown into a river, not burnt.'
21. Basaurhi ballad recorded near Rudauli.
22. An index of the assertion of lower-caste attachment to the warrior saint, the Teli upbringing of Zohra is not without interest, for two branches of Muslim Telis have taken the appellation 'Bahlim' (a moniker of Ghazi Miyan) and 'Turkiya' (from Turk).

8 **Birth–Marriage–Martyrdom**

1. *Jāge bans Mamul ke, jab hue Gājan aise pūt; kāt kufr Islam kiya, bhāge deo dānu dūt*. Greeven, *Heroes Five*, p. 120, lines 1–2.
2. Basaurhi ballad recorded near Rudauli. I am most grateful to Professor Khan Masud Ahmad, Vice Chancellor, Muinuddin Chishti University, Lucknow for arranging for Sanjay Kak's and my stay in Karaundi and persuading the *Kingaria* balladeer of an adjacent village to come over and perform his version of the Ballad of Ghazi Miyan, which interestingly combines several episodes in the saga of the Ghazi, recorded separately in the late nineteenth-century ethnographic collections of Greeven and Crooke.

3. Calling a woman 'barren' was one of the worst kind of abuse that could be heaped on her, and so '… women were under tremendous pressure to reproduce, preferably sons…'. Malhotra, *Gender, Caste and Religious Identities*, p. 171.
4. Greeven, *Heroes Five*, pp. 120–21, lines 14–18. Compare, 'Loosened unbraided hair is a gesture of humility and submission that the supplicant employs while soliciting divine help'. See Ghalib Lakhnavi and Abdullah Bilgrami, *The Adventures of Amir Hamza*, trans. Musharraf Ali Farooqi (New York: Modern Library, 2007), Translator's note no. 1, p. 944.
5. Greeven, *Heroes Five*, p. 7, line 69.
6. The usual expression for stressing one's connection with a particular place as home is to assert: *is āngan mein mere purkhon ki nāl gari hui hai*, that is, 'the navel strings of my ancestors are buried in the courtyard of this very house'.
7. Compare, 'Now, Nona Chamain, the midwife, was a sorceress, and she overpersuaded Mamula, saying "Is not a navel string unclean? How then shall thou appear with it before the Saint?"', *NINQ* 3(1), April 1893, para 25. In another version: *yeh sun Nona Chamarin āi, nār cheen, paisa bahut pāi / dua det apne ghar jāve, bihise bāram-bāra*. Greeven, *Heroes Five*, p. 8, line 74.
8. Greeven, *Heroes Five*, p. 8, line 84.
9. William Waterfield (trans.), *The Lay of Alha: A Saga of Rajput Chivalry by Minstrels of Northern India*, ed. G. A. Grierson (Oxford: Oxford University Press, 1923), p. 196.
10. G. A. Grierson (ed. and trans.), 'The Song of Alha's Marriage: A Bhojpuri Epic', *Indian Antiquary*, August 1885, pp. 219–20, and p. 227, lines 530–51 of the Bhojpuri text.
11. Mahdi Hasan, *The Rehla of Ibn Battuta*, p. 79. See also Syed Athar Abbas Rizvi (trans.), *Tughlaq Kaleen Bharat*, vol. 1 (Aligarh: Department of History, Aligarh Muslim University, 1956), pp. 201–02, which specifically mentions the forcible dismounting of the bride's party by the groom's in the battle with bamboo-staffs.
12. R. C. Temple, 'The Marriage of Ghazi Salar' as recorded by the author from the private kaithi MS kept by the singer for his own information, in *The Legends of Punjab*, vol. 1 (Patiala: Department of Languages, Punjab, 1998, second reprint. First published c. 1844); W. Hoey, 'Set Mahet', *JASB*, 1, extra no., 1892 (hereafter Set Mahet ballad).
13. In the Ambala ballad, the Ghazi's *mandwa* is made of sandalwood.
14. Temple 'The Marriage of Ghazi Salar', pp. 98–99, lines 30–49; G. A. Grierson, *Bihar Peasant Life*, pp. 377–79, paras 1372–76; Anon., 'Customs and Ceremonies of the Natives of Eastern N.W.P.', c. 1900, Grierson MS E-223, South Asia Section, British Library; Field Notes, May 1994. See also Barbara Stoler Miller and Mildred Archer (eds), *Songs for the Bride: Wedding*

Rites of Rural India (New York: Columbia University Press, 1985), pp. 25ff; Sankata Prasad and W. G. Archer (eds), *Bhojpuri Gramya Geet* (Patna: Patna Law Press, 1943).

15. Grierson, *Bihar Peasant Life*, p. 378, para 1376.

16. s.v: '*Mānjha*' in 'Azamgarh Glossary', reprinted in Amin, *Encyclopedia of North Indian Peasant Life*.

17. Ahmad Behbahani, *India in the Early 19th Century: An Iranian's Travel Account*, trans. A. F. Haider (Patna: Khuda Baksh Oriental Public Library, 1996), pp. 60–61.

18. A feature (usually scoffed at as 'un-Islamic'), still retained at the Bahraich shrine to signify the number of days remaining to the saint's May-marriage after the initial 'fixing' of the date at a smaller gathering in mid-January. Interview at the *Dargah*, May 1996.

19. Sayyid Ahmad Dehlavi, *Rusum-i-Dehli* (Delhi: Urdu Akademi, 2006, reprint. First published 1905), p. 120. I have here transposed the lines of this marriage song, prevalent among the Muslims in early-twentieth-century Delhi to the 'time' of Ghazi Miyan's marriage.

20. *Jaswa ka ahwāl sun hue jalāl tayyār; bāndha tegh-talwār, churi katāri bhāla, sab hathiyār lāge; itni bāt suni mayya Mamal Bala ke pās chal āi; Tum mat jāo ran ko la[l]re, tumhen bare bhāg se pāe[i]*. Greeven, *Heroes Five*, p. 124, lines 77–82, 84.

21. Set Mahet ballad, p. 30.

22. Greeven, *Heroes Five*, pp. 124–25, lines 89–90.

23. *Ro-ro Māmul sir dhunne, tan mein lāgi āg / Ghazi mera ran ko chala, phūta hamara bhāg....* Greeven, *Heroes Five*, p. 125, line 110.

24. *Main kātun sees Sohal ka, aur jad main byāh rachāun; Jaisa phirūn, jab karūn byāh, nahin sehra kabr charhāun*. Amballa ballad, Temple's translation modified.

25. Set Mahet ballad, p. 30.

26. The usual rite at this stage is the symbolic touching of the mother's breast as a recognition of the fact that the milk of the mother, which has nurtured the son, is priceless. Compare, Ambika Prasad Suman, *Krishak-sambandhi Braj Bhasha Shabdavali*, vol. 2 (Ilahabad: Hindustani Akedemi, 1961), p. 498, para 1349. I am grateful to Bhagwati Prasad for discussion on this issue.

27. *Lilli Peeth charhe Bahlim ruksat Amma se mānga: Tum dūdh baksh do, Amma, mera leo khol kangan ka dhāga*. Greeven, *Heroes Five*, p. 125, line 106.

28. Khalilabad Dafali, recorded near Chittaura, Bahraich Fair, May 1996.

29. Ibid.

30. Set Mahet ballad, p. 36, sec. 17–18.

31. Temple, *Legends of Punjab*, p. 106, lines 269–70. Translation modified.

32. *Main khenchu tegh*, he challenges Sohal, *ghārat kar dālun, deen Nabi ka barehga*. Greeven, *Heroes Five*, p. 126, line 111.

33. *Jāge bans Mamal ke, jab hue Gājan aise pūt; Kāt kufr Islam kiya, bhāge deo dānu sab dūt.* Greeven, *Heroes Five*, p. 120, lines 1–2.
34. Khalilabad Dafalis, interview, *Dargah*, mid-May 1996.
35. Greeven, *Heroes Five,* p. 127, line 139; Bashir Dafali, interview, Bahraich, May 1996.

9 Ghazi Miyan and Cowherds

1. Set Mahet ballad, p. 22.
2. Ibid., p. 25. The Jaswa ballad ends with Nand, the cowherd chief of Gaura Got, being blessed with the birth of the young Ahir boy Krishna.
3. Set Mahet ballad, p. 26.
4. Ibid., pp. 26–27; the quote is from p. 27.
5. Set Mahet ballad, pp. 9ff, 28–29.
6. Ibid., p. 36.
7. *Kāhe mosei lagan lagāe re sanwalia;*
Lagan lagāe hāi bedardi, kubja-ke ghar jāe re, sanwalia;
Us bepir ahir tain , kaul-karār bhulāe-re sanwalia;
Sāwan beeta kajri āi, tain na suratiya dekhāe-re sanwalia;
Jhutain prem dekhāe 'Premghan', bhal hamke tarsāe-re sanwalia.
'Grihastinon-ki lai: sthānik stri-bhāsha', in Prabhakareshvar Prasad Upadhyay (ed.), *Golokvasi Chaudhuri Pt. Badri Narayan Upadhyay 'Premghan', Premghan Sarvasya, pratham bhag* (Prayag: Hindi Sahitya Sammelan, 1884, second edition), p. 518.
8. Zainullah Dafali, interview, Chittaura Tal, near Bahraich, mid-May 1996. Various hyperbolic numbers of cows under Ghazi Miyan are mentioned by other Dafalis as well.
9. Mohamad Mushir Khan, interview, Gulheria, December 1995.
10. Roy, *Syncretic Tradition*, pp. 223–24; James Wise, 'The Muhammadans of Eastern Bengal', p. 43.
11. *Indian Notes and Queries* (hereafter *INQ*), February 1887, no. 351.
12. Shyam Manohar Pandey, *The Hindi Oral Epic Lorikayan*: *The Tale of Lorik and Chanda* (Allahabad: Sahitya Bhavan, 1987), pp. 3–10, 110–48, verses 240–60.
13. Pandey, *Hindi Oral Epic Lorikayan*, pp. 3756–4000, verses 301–2708. The story about the raja tying a tag around the neck of the new-born girl is mentioned in a recent study based on an oral version current in Ghazipur District. See Nityanand Tiwari, *Madhyakalin Romanchak Akhyan: Lorikayan ke Maukhik aur Likhit Pathyarup par Adharit* (Dilli: National Publishing House, 1977).
14. Maulvi Khaled, interview, village Kinhaura, 15 December 2014.

15. छीर जो माँगत चीर गहे, अजी लेहु जे केतिक छीर अचैहौ, चाखन के मसि माखन माँगत, लेहु जे माखन केतकि खैहौ; जानत हौं जिय की "रसखान, सो काहे को मों संग रार बढ़ैहौ, गौरस के मिस जो रस चाहत सो रस कान्हा नैकू न पैहौ. Text from Simon Digby manuscript collection of medieval Braj-bhasha poetry, reproduced in Rupert Snell, *The Classical Tradition: A Braj Bhasha Reader* (London: SOAS, 1991). See also Figure 9.1. I am grateful to Professor Harish Trivedi of the Department of English, University of Delhi for the translation.
16. Verrier Elwin, *Folksongs of Chhattisgarh* (Madras: Oxford University Press, 1946), pp. 287–92; Putlibai D. H. Wadia, 'The Ballad of Gujari', *Indian Antiquary*, August 1889; 'Eladi Ahirin: Ahiron ka Pauranic Kavya', *Lokvarta* (Tikamgarh) 1, 1944, pp. 186–91.
17. The Gwalin who daydreams of saving money, dressing up and catwalking her way to a major fair is the object of a morality tale in a language primer. As she imagines herself, all decked up, hips swaying, arms slicing languorously through the air, she allows herself a pronounced lurch. With that the pot-full of curd crashes down from her head, and with it, crashes the dream of the Gwalin of being the cynosure of every eye at the next big fair. See Radha Lal, *Hindi Kitab, Dusra Numbur* (Calcutta, 1873), Fable XI, cited in Amin, *Encyclopedia of North Indian Peasant Life*, p. 360. I am grateful to Aishwarj Kumar for procuring a copy of this Hindi reader for me.
18. Pandey, *Lorikayan*, pp. 344–47, 486–87.
19. Elwin, *Folksongs of Chhattisgarh*, pp. 287–90; Divya Varma; 'Mr Devendra Satyarthi in Bundelkhand', *Rural India* 7, 1943, pp. 43ff, cited in Elwin, *Folksongs of Chhattisgarh*, p. 287; Wadia, 'The Ballad of the Gujari', pp. 242–44. See also the song about the Ahirin Eladi, in 'Eladi Ahirin', pp. 186–91.
20. Elwin, *Folksongs of Chhattisgarh*, p. 290.
21. Maulvi Khaled, interview, Kinaura village, Bara Banki district, 28 December 1995.
22. Simon Digby, 'Before Timur Came: Provincialization of the Delhi Sultanate through the Fourteenth Century', *Journal of the Economic and Social History of the Orient* 47(3), 2004, p. 304. See also Kumar, *Emergence of the Delhi Sultanate*, pp. 334–36.
23. Digby, 'Before Timur Came', p. 303, citing Amir Hasan Dihlavi, *Fawad-ul Fawad*, 1966, pp. 227–28; ballads of Ghazi Miyan.
24. The quotation in this paragraph is from Simon Digby, 'Dreams and Reminiscences', pp. 194–63.
25. Marshal Hodgson, *The Venture of Islam: Conscience and History in a World Civilization—The Expansion of Islam in the Middle Periods*, vol. 2 (Chicago: University of Chicago Press, 1977), p. 156.
26. Pandey, *Lorikayan*, pp. 5–31 of text, pp. 452–65 of translation.
27. Ibid., pp. 12–15, lines 386–450, pp. 976–78.

27. Ibid., pp. 12–15, lines 386–450, pp. 976–78.
28. Ibid., pp. 471–72, 475; *MM* Q, p. 126.
29. Cook, *Martyrdom in Islam*, p. 42; Mansur Ali Khadim, *Gaed Dargah Hazrat Syed Salar Masud Ghazi RA* (Bahraich, 1985), p. 5.
30. Bharucha, *Rajasthan*, p. 95.
31. The Rajasthan story is complicated by the fact that Jhindrav, the local strongman, is the husband of Pabuji's sister, an alliance struck to avoid a family feud consequent upon the slaying of his father by the hero. The affinal bond had remained tenuous ever since.
32. Bharucha, *Rajasthan*, p. 96.
33. J. D. Smith, *The Epic of Pabuji* (Cambridge: Cambridge University Press, 1991), p. 422, lines 2952–62.
34. Ibid., p. 285, line 325.
35. In an early 1379 version of this epic by the Awadh-based Sufi Mulla Daud, the text ends abruptly with the cows being taken away in Lorik's absence, but by the aggrieved husband of Lorik's paramour and not by any tribal group colluding with Turks. See Parmeshwari Lal Gupta, *Maulana Daud Dalmai Krit Chandayan* (Bumbai: Hindi Granth Ratnakar, 1964), *panwara* 452, p. 335.
36. Diane M. Coccari, 'The Bir Babas of Banaras: An Analysis of a Folk Deity in North Indian Hinduism' (PhD diss., University of Wisconsin, 1986), pp. 224, 228.
37. W. G. Archer, *The Vertical Man: A Study in Primitive Indian Sculpture* (London: George & Unwin, 1947).
38. Ibid., pp. 106–07. This need to propitiate the unnamed Muslim arises, suggests Archer, 'from the heavily Muhammadan tone of the area with its Moghul traditions, its memories of Muhammadan power and continued presence of Muhammadans in the villages ... Its total impact involves an effort of adjustment by the Ahirs … a need to assert Ahir superiority, a need to declare Ahir friendship and a need to appease Muhammadan violence'. Archer, *Vertical Man*, p. 107.
39. Smith, *Pabuji*, p. 449 and fn. 301; Bharucha, *Rajasthan*, pp. 103–04.
40. Bharucha, *Rajasthan*, p. 104.
41. Ibid., p. 108.

10 Grey Mare, Lilli

1. *Leela ghora leeli zeen tāpe baitha Mohammada Veer.* Chaudhuri Baldev Singh, *Ahir-jati ke liye Char Nuskhe* (Ilahabad, 1923), p. 39.
2. In several eastern UP folksongs, it is 'Lille ghora' which the brother rides home, after the sister, getting over an earlier altercation, invites him belatedly to her wedding:

āge- āge chaura changerwa piyari gahāgah;
Lille ghore bhaiya aswār to dāndiya bhāvuj mori.

'In front (servants are carrying on their heads) a bamboo-basket full of the gift of rice and a dhoti, dyed deep-yellow; following this retinue of gift-bearers, astride a *nile* (blue) horse is my brother, and in the palanquin my sister-in-law. See Ram Naresh Tripathi, *Gramya Geet*, pp. 322–23. Compare, *Lili-si ghoriya, pātar aswāra; chaley hain kaun Lala bahin lene hāra*. Azhar Ali Faruqi, 'Dafaliyon aur Mujawiron ke Geet: Sohile', *Hindustani* 27(1), 1966, p. 128.

3. *Leele-neele ghorwa chhail aswārwa kurkhete hanai nisān/ khirki ughār-ke amma jo dekhai dhiya dasauri hoin; Leel-leel ghorwa kanwar aswāra re, kurkhete uth gaili ghūr/ chandra jharokhan thārhi māta nihāireli, dhiya dasāwar hoe re*. See Tripathi, *Gramya-Geet*, pp. 278, 362. For another reference to the rider coming for the girl astride a 'Leela ghorwa', see song no. 89, in Prasad and Archer, *Bhojpuri Gramya Geet*.

4. Anon, 'Village Hymns in Itawa District, no. 16: 5', *Indian Antiquary* 19, 1910, p. 281: *Bharmat phirain aswāri nadi pai; Leela ghora, zeen sonehra / Kalu Khan bhayo aswār / Kahān Lela garad bhare? Kahan bhari sāmal sēj? Ganga pār Leela gard bhare; wahīn katthin chali talwār / Nadi pae bharmat phiren Kalu Khan aswār*.

5. *MM* IH, p. 74; *MM* C, p. 29; *MM* E, p. 140.

6. John Renard, *Islam and the Heroic Image: Themes in Literature and the Visual Arts* (Columbia: University of South Carolina Press, 1993), p. 208.

7. Mangal Khan, *Gulzar-i-Masudi*, p. 97.

8. Compare, Grierson, *Bihar Peasant Life*, p. 243; R. Greeven, 'Benares—The Worship of Panchon Pir', *NINQ* 3(2), May 1892, p. 22, para 85; s.v. 'leer' in Fallon, *New Hindustani Dictionary*.

9. Zainullah Dafali, interview, Chittaura, May 1996.

10. Greeven, 'Benares', pp. 21–22; Greeven, *Heroes Five*, pp. 86–87.

11. Anon., 'A Song about Forest Godlings: The Cow and the Lion', *Indian Antiquary* 39, October 1910, pp. 276–77.

12. *Khula karam bakhat mora jāga / bhala ki bahina jo tu āi*, says Mahmud welcoming his sister, but after the denial of Lilli, she curses him roundly: *Marey bhāi sher jawān / Aur bhāwaj howe rānr; Yisne ādar bahin nahin rakha*. See Greeven, 'Benares', para 85, fns 1, 4.

13. Ibid., para 149, p. 37.

14. *NINQ* 2(4), June 1892, para 153.

15. Ibid.

16. Ibid.

17. *Kitna deota ban men bhāg gae, kitne Ganga mein dūbe mar,*
Debi Durga leke murga sinni dona bhar-bhar:
'Ham par rahm karo Miyan Gaji, tere ghorwan ke dāna, deben [*debai*] *dar dar'*

lāge dard mard Gaji ke, diha chor nāk nishāni kāt-kar. Greeven, *Heroes Five*, p. 106, lines 116–29.

18. See Finbarr B. Flood, *Objects of Translation: Material Culture and Medieval 'Hindu-Muslim' Encounter* (Princeton: Princeton University Press, 2009), pp. 166–72.

19. David Hardiman, *Feeding the Baniya: Peasants and Usurers in Western India* (New Delhi: Oxford University Press, 1996), pp. 228–30, 233–35; C. M. Naim, written communication, 22 November 2009.

20. Shubrati, 'Jaswa'; Haji saheb, interview, Dargah Bahraich, 17 May 1996.

21. Vishwanath Tripathi, *Nangatalai ka Gaon*: *Smriti-Akhyan* (Nai Dilli: Rajkamal Prakashan, 2004), p. 15.

22. *MM* F, pp. 10, 104a.

11 Cooking for a Turkic Brother

1. Hari S. Upadhyaya, 'The Joint Family Structure and Familial Relationship Patterns in the [sic] Bhojpuri Folksongs' (PhD diss., Folklore Institute, Indiana University, 1967), pp. 77, 143–44.

2. In Punjabi folk songs, the brother arrives astride a *neela* (*leela* in Bhojpuri) horse. Devendra Satyarthi, *Dheere Baho Ganga*! (Nai Dilli: Praveen Prakashan, 1993), pp. 85–86.

3. Ram Naresh Tripathi, 'Chakki ke Geet', no. 1 in *Hamara Gramya Sahitya* (Prayag: Hindi Mandir, 1940), pp. 113–14.

4. Ibid.

5. Ibid., pp. 114–117. For a stylised description of the hardships suffered by a married woman in her husband's home, as recounted to her brother who has come to visit her, see George A. Grierson, 'Some Bhojpuri Folk-songs', *JASB*, 1886, song no. 64, pp. 240–42. For a contemporary recording of a similar version from eastern UP, see 'Brother Don't Tell', in Smita Tewari Jassal, *Unearthing Gender: Folksongs of North India* (Durham: Duke University Press, 2012), pp. 45–46.

6. *Kedri ban mein khele hain shikar, hain Salar, hain piyāse ban mein. Kadli/kedri-ban* is a stock locality in both mystic and martial popular accounts. The kadli grove is the same stretch of forest where Rama and Sita 'had shared many intimacies during their long exile'. Behl, 'The Magic Doe' p. 196; Digby, 'Encounters with Jogis', p. 32; R. C. Temple, *The Legends of Punjab*, vol. 1 (Patiala: Department of Languages, Punjab, 1998, second reprint. First published c. 1884), p. 520. Bhava-bhuti, *Rama's Last Act*, trans. Sheldon Pollock (New York: Clay Sanskrit Series, 2007), pp. 196–97.

7. *Kuanan-mein khele hain shikār, hain Salar,*
Hain piyāse ban mein,
Miyan batohi rovela,

Miyan kuaen mein roven hain panihār
Hain piyāse ban mein. Amina Sati ballad, Bahraich Dargah, May 1996.

8. *Akru nagar dulma des / Na kihu āwe ne kahae sandes:* Greeven, *Heroes Five*, p. 56. Translation modified.

9. *Jāke panhuche Panchon Pir Amina ke duār / Bahin bahin kar ke liha pukār;*
Bheetar se nikali hai Amina Māi / ānke kaure gai thahrāe.
Amin Panchon Pir ke cheenhat bāe / Tum sab koi hamre naihar se āe.
Kaho naihar ki bāten arthāe / tab ham tūke pāni deun piyāi
'Tuhari naihar Amin khem-kushal bāe kul paliwār.
Hum to Amin baithat bāten rāt-dina tuhre duāre'. Greeven, *Heroes Five*, p. 57, lines 32–36.

10. Vishwanath Tripathi, *Nangatalai ka Gaon: Smriti-akhyan*, p. 25.

11. *Aarsh se utral Amina sonawa kai thāri.* Greeven, *Heroes Five*, p. 57, lines 50–54.

12. *Rasoi ke peeche hoi tuhār buri bhāg.*
Hamke Ramchand jon likhe hun[*hauwwen*?] *banbās;*
Kekare bhāg se bhogab ranwās .... Greeven, *Heroes Five*, p. 58, lines 60–62.

13. Greeven, 'Benares', p. 110; Greeven, *Heroes Five*, p. 58, line 74, translation modified.

14. *NINQ* 2(7), October 1892, no. 413.

15. *Kaisan sās tuhre deswa ki chalya bāi;*
taune tharya Nurchand jewen jeonār
taune tharya Turukan diya jhutār. Greeven, *Heroes Five*, p. 59, lines 92–94.

16. *NINQ* 2(7), October 1892, no. 413.

17. This final chapter of the Ramayana is now available in an excellent translation of Bhavabhuti's Sanskrit play *Uttar Ramcharitmanas* in Bhavabhuti, *Rama's Last Act.*

18. Greeven, *Heroes Five*, p. 61, lines 146–47.

19. Ibid., lines 165–66.

20. *NINQ* 2(7), October 1892, no. 413.

21. Greeven, *Heroes Five*, p. 61, lines 177–78.

22. *NINQ* 2(3), January 1893, no. 606, emphasis added.

23. Crooke, *Tribes and Castes*, vol. 3, p. 390.

24. Ballad of Amina Sati by Banaras Dafali, Bahraich Fair, May 1996.

25. Bashir Dafali, interview, Bahraich Fair, 17 May 1996; Field notes, Dikauli, 18 May 1996.

26. Ballad of Amina Sati by Bashir Dafali, Bahraich Fair, May 1996.

27. *Chirke bakhri mein dhoi-dhoi charanwa Amina / Bakhri hui gulzār, āi Angan mein bahār, bana le āie jevnār gulzār / Panchon Pir ke sevat hain bhojanwa Amina ... laibe gāhre din mein khabariya Amina.* Ballad of Amina Sati by Bashir Dafali, Bahraich Fair, May 1996.

28. 'The Lay of Saint Amina', in Greeven, *Heroes Five*, p. 55.

29. I am grateful to Professor Bijoy Boruah of Indian Institute of Technology Delhi for a discussion on this theme and the subsequent written exchange after the presentation of an earlier version of this chapter at the Indian Institute of Advanced Studies, Shimla, and to Director Peter Ronald deSouza for facilitating this exchange.
30. Greeven, *Heroes Five,* p. 56.

12 **Idols**

1. See Chapter 2 of the current volume.
2. Greeven, 'Benares', *NINQ* 2(4), July 1892, no. 217, p. 55. Compare, Faruqi, 'Dafaliyon aur Mujawiron ke Geet', pp. 128–29.
3. Greeven, *Heroes Five*, p. 105, lines 88–90.
4. Ibid., pp. 105–06, lines 110–15. By the fourteenth to sixteenth centuries, this Hindawi term and the shape of the *badhna*, perhaps adopted from the earlier Buddhist sacred water vessel (*vardhanika*), was commonly associated with the Muslims of the Gangetic plains, from Awadh to Bengal. See Askari, *Medieval Bihar*, p. 79; Crooke, *A Rural Glossary*, s.v. 'badhna'; James Wise, 'The Muhammadans of Eastern Bengal', p. 30.
5. *Bhagua chor Bhagwan purāne Mahadeo bhāge, bol Har! Har*!
Kitna deota ban mein bhāg gae, kitne Ganga mein dūbe mar.
Debi Durga leke murga sinni dona bhar-bhar:
'*Ham par rahm karo Miyan Gaji, tere ghorwan ke dāna deben* [*debai*] *dar-dar*'; *lāge dard mard Gaji ke, diha chor nāk nishāni kāt-kar*. Greeven, *Heroes Five*, p. 106, lines 116–29.
6. Greeven, *Heroes Five*, pp. 100–01.
7. *NINQ* 2(5), August 1892, no. 302.
8. Greeven, *Heroes Five*, p. 107.
9. Ibid., p. 107, lines 137–47.
10. Compare the Hindi writer Bhartendu Harishchandra: *Tuv yāvanan tu dharm nari dhan tinhon leenhon.*
11. Greeven, *Heroes Five*, p. 99. In his *Lives of Indian Images*, Richard Davis notes specifically with regard to peninsular India: Under pressure of iconoclasm, concealment and flight became important means [by temple priests] for the preservation of portable idols. Images might find refuge underground, or they might abandon their wealthy and vulnerable temple for more out-of-the way sanctuaries. The assumption, or at least the hope, behind these evacuations was that, when the danger had passed, the image would return to their accustomed homes. In fact the text *Vimānārcanākalpa* outlined the procedures priests were to follow when ritually burying images in the wake of iconoclastic assaults on south Indian temples from the conquering armies of the expanding Sultanate of Delhi in the early thirteenth

century. 'As soon as the danger has passed', the same text suggested, 'the priest should disinter the image, clean it with tamarind, perform a rather lengthy reconsecration, return it to the temple, and finally thereafter transfer the divine presence back into the resurrected icon'. Davis, *Lives of Indian Images*, pp. 127–28.

12. Cf. Mary Searle-Chatterjee, 'The Muslim Hero as Defender of Hindus: Mythical Reversals and Ethnicity among Benares Muslims', *Social Analysis* 28, 1990, pp. 70–81, esp. pp. 75–77.

13. *Jab pārti-ke sāth gāyit hai, mastāna-logan ke sāmne gāyit hai, tab note-jhar-jhara ke girat lāge hai.* Bashir Dafali, interview, May 1996.

14. Greeven, *Heroes Five.*

15. Compare: *Dagmag macha shahar mein ghera hai ek dam se,*
Jitne thei bhoot-deuta kāta hai nāk jar-se,
to Sobhnath-deuta jāwe zameen-mein dhans-ke; ...
Jab kartal se nikli talwār waār karti,
Bhagi hain devi-Durga jo roz khassi khātīn;
Sanka pari jigar mein kuen-beech kūd parteen,
abki dafa bachi to tāb-e-umar samajhteen...

Extract from the Ballad of Banaras, sung by Bashir Dafali at the Bahraich Fair, May 1996.

16. Greeven, 'Benares', para 78. I suggest that Greeven's *pūhi* may be read more appropriately as *peerhi*: a small stool, sitting atop which the groom is ritually cleansed with unguents.

17. Abdul Bismillah, *Jhini Jhini Bini Chadariya* (Nai Dilli: Rajkamal Paperbacks, 1987), p. 62.

18. Ibid.

19. *Sone-chāndi ka kalash hai, palang-peerhi—200-250 ādmi girat, bhahrāhat, gāri-motor par nishān lekar āte hain.* Interview with the Banaras party, Bahraich Fair, 19 May 1996.

ENDNOTES PART THREE

13 Altars

1. William Crooke, 'Panchpiriya', in J. Hastings (ed.), *Encyclopaedia of Religion and Ethics* [*ERE*], vol. 9 (Edinburgh: T. T. Clark, 1908–27), p. 601; Muhammad Enamul Haq, 'Panch Pir', *Journal of the Asiatic Society of Pakistan* 20(2), 1970, pp.110–27.

2. *Report, North-Western Province and Oudh, Census of India, 1891*, 9, pt. 4 (Allahabad: North-Western Province and Oudh Press, 1891), para 192 (hereafter *Census, NWP FO*).

3. Greeven, 'Benares'; *NINQ* 4 July 1835, no. 86; also cited in William Crooke, *An Introduction to the Popular Religion and Folklore of Northern India,* vol. 2 (hereafter *PRFL*) (Allahabad: North-Western Provinces and Oudh Government Press, 1893), p. 205; Ram Gharib Chaube, 'Ceremonies and Festivals', *NINQ* 5(1), 1895, para 1. Parihar or Palihar, the demon captured from Lanka, for example, was for some in the tribal belt of Mirzapur the most important Panchpiriya.

4. Dharkars, see Crooke, *Tribe and Castes*, vol. 2, p. 285; Biar, p. 137; Kahar, vol. 3, p. 98; Kumhars, p. 338–39, Luniya, p. 390.

5. The Kingiriyas sang the ballads of Ghazi Miyan on their two-stringed lute, worshipped Kali Bhawani in 'their house kitchen in the [monsoon] month of Sawan with an offering' of fried 'puri' and 'halwa'; Churihars, see Crooke, *Tribes and Castes*, vol. 3, p. 232; Saiqalgars, vol. 4, p. 258; Ghosi, vol. 2, p. 420; Dafali, p. 243; Kingariya, vol. 3, pp. 280–82. 'Puris' are rendered more correctly as deep-fried bread.

6. Grierson, *Bihar Peasant Life*, s.v. 'Panchopir', para 1456, p. 40, emphasis added.

7. E. A. H. Blunt, *The Caste System of Northern India, with Special Reference to the United Provinces of Agra and Oudh* (London: Oxford University Press, Humphrey Milford, 1931), p. 292. Blunt was the Census Commisioner of the Province in 1911.

8. Mir Afsos Ali, *Jild Awwal Kitab Araish-i-Mahfil, Hasil Mazmoon Khulasa Al Hind Araish-i-Mehfil* (Kalkatta: Hindoostani Press,1808), p. 98.

9. For the caste composition of pilgrims, see, 'Report on the Arrangement of the Syud Salar Fair [1873]', by Syad Ali Ukber, Extra Assistant Commissioner, para 27, Ans. to Question nos 5 & 12 of Civil Surgeon. Office Files of the Faizabad Commissioner, Bundle no. 173, Sr. no. 13: Syad Salar Fair, 1873, UP State Regional Archives, Allahabad. I am grateful to Sanjay Sharma for providing me with a copy of the relevant portions of this file.
10. 'Report on the Arrangement of the Syud Salar Fair', para 5.
11. Ibid.
12. See Shahid Amin, *Event, Metaphor, Memory: Chauri Chaura, 1922–1992* (Berkeley: University of California Press, 1995), ch. 33–34.
13. 'Maur': headdress worn by groom, made of talipot leaves. 'Mauri': the bride's headdress, made of date leaves. Grierson, *Bihar Peasant Life*, para 1326. 'Mureth': 'a head dress', 'a piece of ordinary cloth, even a gamcha, worn round the head'. Crooke, *Tribes and Castes*, vol. 4, p. 374 (Teli); Grierson, *Bihar Peasant Life*, para 724; *Tribes and Castes*, vol. 2, p. 224; Thathera, vol. 4, p. 408.
14. *PRFL*, vol 1. p. 138; Crooke, *Tribes and Castes*, vol. 4, p. 363.
15. Crooke, *Tribes and Castes*, vol. 4, p. 338 (Kumhar).
16. *PRFL*, vol. 1, p. 139; Ramsanehi Pal, *Hardaul Bhajnawali* (*urf*) *Hardaul-ka Bhat* (Kanpur: Shri Janta Book Stall, n.d.).
17. A Methodist missionary's account, c. 1880 of the postponement that year of Ghazi Miyan's marriage due to a storm, speaks of 'a grand black sand storm, darting out flashes of fire and sending forth rolling peals of thunder over the *mela* [fair] and the city'. Knowles, *Gospel in Gonda: Being a Narrative of Events in Connection with the Preachings of the Gospel in the Trans-Ghaghra Country* (Lucknow: Methodist Publishing House, 1889), p. 168. An early nineteenth-century poetic description of the festivals of north India refers to the popular belief that the storm is caused every year at the Bahraich Fair by the ogre Makana trying to sweep the fairground clean. Jawan, *Barah Masa*, p. 31. On 16 May 1996, it was a brewing dust storm that was taken as a climatic sign requiring the postponement of Ghazi Miyan's marriage.
18. W. Sleeman, *Rambles and Recollections of an Indian Official*, vol. 1 (London: J. Hatchard and Son, 1844), pp. 131–32; also cited in Crooke, *Popular Religion and Folklore*, vol. 1, pp. 121–22; Chandrabhan 'Visharad', 'Banda prant ke gram devta', *Lokvarta* (Tikamgarh) 1, 1944, pp. 173–74.
19. *PRFL*, p. 120.
20. Crooke, 'Panchpiriya', p. 601.
21. Coccari, 'The Bir Babas of Banaras', p. 132.
22. *Census, NWP&O, 1891*, Report, para 192, pp. 216–17.
23. Ibid., emphasis added. For the attack on the Ghazi Miyan cult, see Part IV of this volume.
24. 'Police Report on the Barwars of Gonda', n.d., cited in *Oudh Gazetteer*, vol. 1, pp. 507–09. The long quotation is from p. 509. Interestingly, this 'lugra

bread' of a late nineteenth-century 'criminal tribe' on the margins of rural society, is the same *lagdahwa roti* (pulse of gram mixed with rice and wheat) which is an essential component of the offerings to the saint in central Awadh even today. Bashir Dafali, interview, 16 May 1996.

25. For the domestic worship of the Ghazi in Mewati villages in the neighbourhood of Delhi in the 1870s, see Monier Williams, 'Notes on Indian Folklore, etc.', *Indian Antiquary*, August 1879, pp. 209–10.

26. Jack M Planalp, 'Religious Life and Values in a North Indian Village', PhD diss., Cornell University, 1954, pp. 770–71.

27. Ibid.

28. Ibid., pp. 771–74.

14 *Dafalis* and Servitors

1. The phrase '36 jatis' is a notional one, meant to cover the entire hierarchy of castes. Regarding the wide range of Hindu castes coming to the Bahraich Fair, see *Mukhtasar Sawaneh Umri Hazrat Syed Salar Masud Ghazi Rahmatullaliya* (Gorakhpur: Anjuman Hifazat-i-Islam, 1925), p. 8.

2. Bashir Dafali, interview, Bahraich Fair, May 1996.

3. Ibid.

4. *Kandūri* meant both 'tablecloth' and 'feast'. Askari, *Medieval Bihar*, p. 75, s.v. 'kandūri': *Encyclopaedia of Islam* (Leiden: E.L. Brill, 1991, second edition); Sayyid Ahmad Dehlavi (ed.), *Farhang-i-Asafiya* (Dilli: Tarraqi-i-Urdu Board, 1974).

5. Zainulla Dafali in the course of a long interview at Chittaura, 15 June 1996: 'Hathile Baba is Hanumanji; Barhana Baba is a Brahman, Bare Pir (Bare Purukh) is Ram Lakshman Singh of Ajodhya ... Nirmal Palihar is an Ahir ... Syed Salar Masud is the sole Turkiya'.

6. Bashir Dafali, interview, 16 May 1996.

7. Compare: *gharaz razale ... anwāe-aqsām ke sāng lāte hain aur apne gumān mein usi sabab se murāden pāte hain*. Ufsos, *Araish-i-Mahfil*, p. 98.

8. See the painting of Khwaja Muinuddin Chishti and devotees at Ajmer, c. 1660–70 from the Victoria and Albert Museum, London, reproduced in Bonnie C. Wade, *Imaging Sound: An Ethnomusicological Study of Music, Art, and Culture in Mughal India* (Chicago: University of Chicago Press, 1998), fig. 114 and pp. 143–47.

9. M. Martin (ed.), *The History, Antiquities, Topography, Statistics of Eastern India: Behar (Patna City) and Shahabad* (London: W. H. Allen & Co., 1838), vol. 1(Behar and Patna), p. 145, and vol. 2 (Bhagalpur), pp. 112–13.

10. J. R. Reid, 'Azamgarh Glossary', 1881, reprinted in Amin, *Encyclopedia of North Indian Peasant Life*, Appendix, p. 503.

11. *Dafali ke sang khēti kiya, ga-baja ke wahi liya*, in Surya Narain Trivedi, *Gawar Masla, or Village Wits* (Samastipur, 1923), proverb 231.

12. Crooke, *Tribes and Castes*, vol. 2, p. 243.
13. *NINQ* 2(8), November 1892, no. 487: Kingaria.
14. Blunt, *The Caste System of Northern India*, p. 205.
15. Planalp, 'Religious Life', pp. 101–02.
16. Syed Ali Mohammad Zaidi, *Apni Yaden, Rudauli ki Baten* (Rudauli: Azmi Publishers, 1977), p. 83.
17. Bashir Dafali, interview, Bahraich Fair, May 1996,.
18. Crooke, *Tribes and Castes*, vol. 2, p. 243 (Dafali).
19. Grierson, *Bihar Peasant Life*, p. 405; *PRFL*, vol. 1, pp. 142–44, 146,169–70; Bashir Dafali, interview. For a discussion on such transferences of disease in rural India, see Ranajit Guha, *Elementary Aspects of Peasant Insurgency in Colonial India* (Delhi: Oxford University Press, 1983), pp. 242–44.
20. Ibn Battuta, *Ajaib al Asfar*, vol. 2, trans. Maulvi Mohammaf Husain (Islamabad: National Institute of Historical and Cultural Reseach, 1983, reprint), p. 190, cited in Siddiqui, 'Note on the Dargah of Salar Masud', p. 46; Saiyid Ahmad Khan (ed.), *Tarikh-i-Ferozshahi of Ziaa-al Din Barani, under the superintendence of W. Naussau Lees and Mawalvi Kabir Al-Din* (Calcutta: Bibliothica India, Asiatic Society of Bengal, 1862), p. 491. See also the Hindi translation in Syed Athar Abbas Rizvi, *Tughlaq Kaleen Bharat*, vol. 1, p. 57.
21. On *madad-i-māsh* holders in the province of Awadh, see Muzaffar Alam, *The Crisis of Empire in North India: Awadh and Punjab, 1707–48* (Delhi: Oxford University Press, 1986), pp. 110ff.
22. Urdu translation of Parwana, dated 25 Jamadil awwal 1180, A.H. by Shah Shujauddaula Bahadur, Awadh, kept at the Dargah, in Mansur Ali Khadim, *Mukhtasar Sawaneh Hazrat Syed Salar Masud Ghazi, R.A.* (Bahraich, n.d.), pp. 32–33.
23. In the English translation of the petition by one of the Bahraich *khadims* (1887), we read: 'The ancestors of the Petitioner and the executors of the Trust were always loyal to the Government since the amalgamation of Oudh.' See Petition dated 26 August 1887 of Doulat Ali (English Translation), para 3, Oudh Rev. File 227B/1888, UPSA. I am grateful to Professor C. M. Naim for pointing out that this passage is not to be found in the original Urdu petition in *shikasta* hand. For the proclamation shutting up a mosque in mauza Masudgaon in Chayal (Chail pargana), Allahabad District, see Public Notification, dated 18 June 1857, H/724a, Kaye Papers, BL, p. 159.

15 The Bahraich Shrine

1. R. H. Montgomery, DC, Bahraich to Commr, Fyzabad, 1 July 1878: 'Report on the *Dargah* Sayyad Salar Fair for 1878', para 9, BR Oudh, Bahraich File 257/1874-83, UPSA.
2. 'Report on the Dargah Sayyad Salar Fair for 1878', para 9, Bd. Rev. Oudh, Bahraich File 257/1874-83, UPSA.

3. *Jeevan Parichay, Hazrat Syed Salar Masud Ghazi RA, Bahraich*[i] (Bahraich: Ikleel Press, n.d.), p. 23 (hereafter *Dargah Pamphlet*).
4. Askari, *Medieval Bihar,* p. 96. The word variously deciphered as *chithraha/chethara/chathraha* has been read alternatively as rags or umbrella. Going by the nineteenth-century usage, these terms seem to refer to some sort of large flags. Cazim Ali Jawan in his 1812 description of the Bahraich Fair uses the terms *neza, jhanda* (flag), *chariyān* and *chatriyān* interchangeably.
5. Ufsos, *Araish-i-Mahfil,* p. 97.
6. On Qalandars and Madaris and their connection with Ghazi Miyan, see Askari, *Medieval Bihar,* p. 96. It was the failure of an Afghan soldier to honour his pledge to pay his respects to Salar Masud at the Bahraich shrine, consequent on regaining his health, that had led the warrior saint despatch a Madari Dervesh to admonish this subaltern serving in the Afghan army in the early sixteenth century. See Simon Digby, 'Dreams and Reminiscences', p. 189. On the demilitarisation of the peasantry in the Great Revolt of 1857, see Rudrangshu Mukherjee, *Awadh in Revolt: A Study of Popular Resistance* (New Delhi: Oxford University Press, 1984).
7. For a characterisation of 'sohala', see Abul-Fazal, *Ain-i-Akbari,* vol. 3, pp. 271–72. For evidence of ghee-fed propitiary earthen lamps, see Mirza Cazim Ali Jawan, *Barah Masa,* p. 30; Field notes, Chittaura Tal, Bahraich, May 1996.
8. Williams, 'Notes on Indian Folklore, etc.', p. 209. This description of many such standards in the Meo country near Delhi refers to the local *mujawirs* celebrating the marriage of Ghazi Miyan in their own locality. The Mughal Emperor had personally encountered pilgrims en route to Bahraich outside his capital city of Fatehpur, abutting the Meo countryside. Compare: '... pilgrims visit ... [Bahraich] from distant parts, forming themselves in bands and bearing gilded banners'. Abul-Fazal, *Ain-i-Akbari,* vol. 2, p.182.
9. N. L., Rockey, 'Progress of Islam in Oudh', *Muslim World* 3(3), 1913, p. 253.
10. J. R. Reid, 'Azamgarh Glossary' (1881), s.v. 'Bale Miyan', reprinted in Amin, *Encyclopaedia of North Indian Peasant Life,* p. 583.
11. In eastern UP, this 'lahbar' was ritually shaved on an auspicious date, to the refrain: *lahbar suhāi lilār, murao Rama lahbar ho*—'the forelocks on the newborn look fetching, shave the lahbar, O Rama!' Chaube, 'Customs and Ceremonies', translation modified.
12. The official notice announcing the date and other details of the Fair in April–May 1996 enumerates ten such cases, mostly of vitiligo patients being cured at the dargah (*bars se nijāt*), along with the case of a son being born to a couple after eighteen years. For a denunciation of 'false lists' of cured people circulated at the fair, see the anti-Ghazi Miyan tract, Nand Kishore Jaiswal, *Ghazi Miyan: Arthat Masud Ghazi ka Saccha Jeevan Charitra* (Prayag, 1916).
13. See, for instance, the case of the martyr of Elichpur in Chapter 4 of this volume. A 'Chandan shaheed', mentioned in Banaras-based accounts, got

decapitated in that holy city, but rode heedless all the way to Sahasra where he lies buried. Mangal Khan, *Gulzar-i-Masudi*, p. 71. For the headless Malik Ambar, see Notice on Bijlaur town, near Lucknow, *Oudh Gazetteer* 1, p. 308.

14. H. M. Elliot, *Supplement to the Glossary of Indian Terms* (Roorkee: Thomason College Press, 1860), s.v. 'Ghazee Meean', p. 384.

15. Compare, *Gānwn mein mazedār ādmi bhi rahte hain—Beni Maharaj kahte hain: 'Jeth mās mein Bale Miyan binu sheesh jata phatkārte hain.' Dwādash-varsheeya sapūt bol utha, 'eh Babua, jette bare Bale Miyan tetti bari pūnch.'* Manan Prasad Dwivedi Gajpuri, *Ramlal: Grameen Jeevan ka ek Samajik Upannyas* (Allahabad: Indian Press, 1913), p. 20.

16. Rockey, 'Progress of Islam', p. 253.

17. Knowles, *Gospel in Gonda*, pp. 162–63. This article was first published in the May 1884 issue of the *Indian Witness* (Allahabad).

18. Rockey, 'Progress of Islam', p. 253.

19. Knowles, *Gospel in Gonda*, p. 162.

20. E. G. Clark and H. Scott Boys, *Bahraich Settlement Report* (Lucknow: North-Western Province and Oudh Government Press, 1873), p. 76. The Gorakhpuri 'kaccha paisa', minted in Butwal in the Nepal tarai was in any case getting steadily devalued against the standard coin since the 1840s.

21. In a novel that portrays with great acuity the mores and mentalité of nineteenth-century Delhi, a somewhat fearsome holy female recluse living besides the old Eidgah accepts only cowries from both elite and subaltern women come seeking her benediction to help them tide over their existential problems. And so Wazir Khanum, the tragic but wilful heroine of the novel, sends her maid servant to the bazaar in Chandni Chowk to buy two rupees worth of cowries from the moneychanger; in all, 10,000 cowries, somewhat dearer of late, which are carried by her *khadima* in two small sacks to the makeshift 'hospice' of the devout 'Baiji saheb'. Shamsur Rahman Faruqui, *Kai Chand Thei Sare Aasman* (Nai Dilli: Yatra Books/Penguin Books, 2010), pp. 669–75, translated by Naresh 'Nadeem' as *The Mirror of Beauty* (New Delhi: Penguin Books, 2013).

22. John S. Deyell, 'Cowries and Coins: The Dual Monetary System of the Bengal Sultanate, *Indian Economic and Social History Review* 47(1), 2010, pp. 73–75.

23. Mahdi Hasan (ed.), *The Rehla of Ibn Battuta*, p. 201, cited in Deyell, 'Cowries and Coins'.

24. Rough calculations based on Rockey's 'Progress of Islam' estimate that £100 sterling worth of small coins were thrown at the dome on the crucial days of the month-long fair.

25. This would have been a Teli or oil presser-trader. See, 'List of Claims made in Captain Nobles' Ishtehar inviting Claims, April 1873', claim no. 118 of Nunkoo Tailee, BR Oudh, Bahraich File 257/1874-83, UPSA.

26. Mirza Khudadad Beg Dehalvi, *Tarannum Khudadad der Zikr-i-Masud* (Lucknow: Matba Ijaz-i-Muhammadi, 1891), cited in Moin Ahmad Alvi, 'Saiyyid Salar Masud Ghazi ka Tarikhi Aastana: Ek Purani Kitab ki Roshni Mein', *Qaumi Awaz* (Zamima), 31 December 1972, translated with notes by Qureshi, *Sufis Classics-I,* p. 53.

27. 'जो होता जेठ का पहला एतवार, उन्हों के उर्स का दिन है ऐ यार; मगर मामूल ये ही हो गया है, अजब आलम है, तरीका माजरा है; कि उनके ब्याह की तैय्यारी हर साल, करे है छोटी उम्मत होके खुशहाल; सुनो है लुत्फ है खुद्दाम-ए-दरगाह, लगा कर लुंगी और चौकी सहर गाह; करे है जमा आब-ए-गुस्ल बाहर; यह अज़ आब-ए-हयात उसको समझकर, तबर्रूक़ की तरह करते है तक़सीम, एवज़ में उसके ज़र लेते है और सीम; नहीं मैं वाँ गया हूँ गरचे, गाहे, पर ये सुन्ता रहा हूँ साल-ओ-माहे; तमास असबाब वाँ कारखाना, मोहय्या रोज़-ओ-शब है खुस्त्रवाना'.

Jawan, *Barah Masa*, p. 31. See also, de Tassy, *Muslim Festivals in India,* esp. pp. 84–85 which provides a summary of this important text.

28. 'Mortgage debt of 6 anna of *nāli-i-āb ziyārat* [*tāhārat*?], i.e., drainage of the Holy "pilgrimage" [pure/purifying/holy] water', states a tabular 'List of Claims made in Captain Noble's [Offg. Dist. Commr.] Ishtehar Inviting Claims in April 1873', claim no. 56, Dargah File, UPSA.

29. Irwin's Report on the Offerings at the Shrine, 1875, Oudh Rev. File 227B/1888, UPSA.

30. *Istehāq khairāt ... i- ām jāta raha ... Haq tauliyat aur khadimāt ka jāta raha; asar mulāzamat ka paida hua, jisko koi qayām aur istehkām nahin hai ... Kabhi intezām iska kisi ahad mein ya kisi waqt mein sarkari ya Badshahi nahi hua'.* I am grateful to C. M. Naim for providing a reading from the *shikasta* script of this document. Urdu Petition of Daulat Ali to Lt. Governor, NWP and Oudh, 26 August 1887, paras 1, 7, Oudh Rev File 227B of 1888, UPSA.

31. The Religious Endowments Act XX of 1863, in *Government of Bengal: Legislative Department: Bengal Code in Five Volumes* (Alipore, 1939, fifth edition), vol. 1, pp. 378-86, sec. 22, extracted in Mohammad Motiur Rahman Khan, 'The Institution of Waqf in Mughal India: A Study of the Land grants to the *Dargah* of Ajmer up to [the] 1860s' (MPhil diss., Department of History, University of Delhi, 2009). See also, Judicial Commissioner, Oudh's ruling in a case filed by Daulat Ali and Inayatullah, *khadims* of Bahraich dargah against the Govt. of Oudh [1899?], cited in Commissioner, Fyzabad Division to Chief Secretary, North-Western Province and Oudh, 7 October 1899, GAD April 1901, A Progs. no. 27, para 3.

32. 'It is evidently cosmopolitan, and the mass of people rather than any sect have to be considered. There is no reason why it should be maintained for the private advantage of a particular family, or the descendants of the original attendants.'

33. The entry under Saiyid Salar Trust in an official list reads: 'Donor: King of Delhi in Hijri 979 (1564 A.D.), Khoja [sic] Ain-ud-din, Nazim [Oudh] in 1207 Hijri (1792 A.D.); Purpose: Maintenance of dargah of Saiyid Salar;

Details: "Revenue-free lands, rents from shops, stalls, and fair offerings, yielding in all about Rs. 6000 per annum, and Rs. 15,000 deposited in Government Savings Bank"'. See 'List of Benevolent Endowments and Miscellaneous Trusts in the Province of Oudh for 1878', Oudh Gen. File 1769/1878–79, UPSA. The legislation that could be invoked against the shrine was Act XXIII of 1871.

34. DC, Bahraich to Commissioner, Fyzabad, 31 August 1878, BR Oudh, Bahraich File 257/1874–83, UPSA.

35. Compare, *Koi razala us buzurg ko gājna Dulha [kahta hai] aur koi rajali [razali] chināl. Wajah uski yeh hai ki jo randi uske gumbad mein jāti hai, badhāl ho kar āti hai, par woh murdār yeh samajhti hai ki saheb-i-qabr ne mujhe chūs liya. Lānat uski samajh par, aur lānat uski būjh par.* Ufsos, *Araish-i-Mahfil*, p. 98.

36. H. M. Elliot, citing Ufsos, *Araish-i-Mahfil*, suggests that it is because of the nuptial presents made by pilgrims that Ghazi Miyan 'is partly called Gajna Doolha, and Salar Chhinula'. Elliot, *Supplement to Glossary*, s.v. 'Ghazee Meean', pp. 384–85.

37. Mahdi Hasan, *The Rehla of Ibn Battuta*, pp. 110–11.

38. DC, Bahraich to Commissioner, Fyzabad, 31 August 1878, BR Oudh: Bahraich File 257/1874–83, UPSA.

39. For an evocative description of the thermantidote in sultry Calcutta in the 1830s, see Amitav Ghosh, *The Sea of Poppies* (New Delhi: Penguin Books, 2008), p. 253.

40. Compare, 'They [the pilgrims] have even begun to place upon it offerings of pice, cowries and flowers; and in two or three years these will doubtless form a recognised source of income to the *khadims* and be mortgaged, fought over and sued for with as much earnestness as if the origins of the tribute were lost in the mist of antiquity.' DC, Bahraich to Commissioner, Fyzabad, 31 August 1878. Compare Henry Crossley Irwin, *The Garden of India, or Chapters on Oudh History and Affairs*, vol. 1 (London: W. H. Allen, 1880), p. 64.

41. Daulat began by making a pointed gesture to the syncretic nature of the shrine: 'a religious trust of both Muslims and Hindus'. He then went on to categorise the shrine 'as a kind of place of worship of the Muslim community'. The two propositions were only seemingly contradictory: apart from the mammoth summer fair, the *Urs* of the saint on 12–14 Rajab and the annual *meelād* on the day of the Prophet's birthday were two specifically Islamic moments in the shrine's ritual calendar. See the Urdu petition by Daulat, Oudh Rev File 227B of 1888, UPSA.

42. Judgement of the Judicial Commissioner, cited in J. Hooper, Commissioner, Fyzabad to Chief Secretary, North-West Province and Oudh, 7 October 1899, GAD April 1901, A Progs, no. 27. UPSA.

43. See Qureshi, *Sufis Classics*-I, pp. 70–72 for details about problems with management, beginning with the official takeover in 1876 to the 1960s.

16 Sites and Cenotaphs

1. The *Mirat-ul-Asrar*, a compendium of the biographies of prominent Sufis from the seventh to the seventeenth centuries CE, devotes a longish section on Salar Masud and his military campaigns in northern India.
2. Hazrat Shaikh Abdur Rahman Chishti, *Mirat-ul Asrar*, p. 450.
3. Hazrat Shaikh Abdur Rahman Chishti, *Mirat-ul Asrar*, p. 448; Khalilabad Dafalis, interview, Bahraich, mid-May 1996.
4 The term 'tasarruf' like *jalāl* has a residual fearsome, ominous sense to it.
5 *Jo tasarrufāt mein mumtāz hain aur bare jawān mard hain*; *yeh faqir kātib-i-hurūf wahān hazir hokar baharmand ho chuka hai*. Hazrat Shaikh Abdur Rahman Chishti, *Mirat-ul Asrar*, p. 449.
6. *MM* Q, pp. 116–17.
7. See the account of the province of Awadh in Sujan Rai Bhandari, *Khulasatu-t-Twarikh*, ed. Zafar Hasan (Delhi: J and Sons Press, 1918) p. 43 and Introduction by Zafar Hasan, esp., p. v. I am grateful to Rajeev Kinra for providing me a copy of the text and translation of the passages relating to Bahraich and Salar Masud.
8. Notice on Bijlaur Town (Lucknow), *Oudh Gazetteer* 1, p. 308.
9. Notice on 'Bawan', tahsil Hardoi, *Oudh Gazetteer* 1, p. 221, emphasis added. See also, p. 275 and Notice on 'Mallawan', *Oudh Gazetteer* 2, p. 441.
10. *Oudh Gazetteer* 1, pp. 576–77, 584–85, 41–42; 'Sayyad Salar Masud', *NINQ* 2(9), December 1892, no. 534; E. T. Atkinson (ed.), *Statistical, Descriptive and Historical Account of North-Western Provinces of India* (Allahabad: North-Western Provinces Government Press, 1874–86), vol. 2, part I, p. 77; vol. 5, p. 90; vol. 14, pp. 80, 84, 162–63 (hereafter *NWP Gazetteer*).
11. A. F. Millett, *Report on the Settlement of the Land Revenue of District Sultanpur* (Allahabad: North-Western Province and Oudh Government Press, 1873), p. 107.
12. Patrick Carnegy, *Notes on the Races, Tribes and Castes inhabiting the Province of Oudh* (Lucknow: Oudh Government Press, 1868), p. 68.
13. See Irwin, *Garden of India*, p. 75.
14. C. A. Elliot, *The Chronicles of Oonao: A District in Oudh* (Allahabad: Mission Press, 1862), pp. 84–85, note 2. 'Connected with the Muhammadan invasion of India, there is no one of whom more wild legends are recorded than Sipah Salar Masud, the prince of martyrs', noted the section on 'History', c. 1875, of the Meerut Division, *NWP Gazetteer* 2(1), 1875, p. 77
15. Notice on Deoband, *NWP Gazetteer* 3(1), pp. 264–65. Regarding the name Deogaon in Azamgarh, there was a legend 'that when Syed Muhammad

Baghdadi took possession of it, after driving out a demon, he so far had mercy upon the latter that the name of the place was allowed to bear testimony to the demon's prior occupation of it'. See *NWP Gazetteer* 1(13), p. 155. For an early medieval textual example of the switch over between 'dev' and 'deo', see Habib, 'The Campaigns of Alauddin Khalji, being the English Translation of [Amir Khusrau] The Khazainul Futuh', in Nizami, *Politics and Society*, vol. 2 , pp. 187, 198, note 27.

16. *Oudh Gazetteer* 1, pp. 318–19.

17. Ibid., pp. 18–19.

18. *MM* Q, p. 70. I have modified this passage in the light of *MM* JS, p. 55 and *MM* E, p. 525, which give the name as 'Kalu', It was with reference to this incident that Abdur Rahman Chishti could suggest in his *Mirat-ul Asrar* that 'Shaikh Abū Muhammad Chishtī blessed and fought, even if only spiritually, with the army of Mahmūd of Ghazni, the first, according to the author, to bring the power of Islam to India.' See Muzaffar Alam, 'The Debate Within: A Sufi Appraisal of Religious Law, Tasawwuf and Politics in Mughal India', unpublished typescript, 2011.

19. Notice on Charda, *Baharich DG.*, p. 116, 165. Compare: '... it is more than probable that the dynasty of the treacherous Kosla king Virudhaka ended with Suhil Deo, who fell in conflict with Salar Masud's force: and the tomb at Mahet on the site of the king's palace is that of the Kotwal left behind by the invading Moslems', Set Mahet ballad, p. 12.

20. H. R. Nevill, *Gonda DG* (Allahabad: Superintendent Government Press, 1909), pp. 169–70.

21. Alois Anton Führer, *The Monumental Antiquities and Inscriptions in the North-Western Provinces and Oudh* (Allahabad: Superintendent, Government Press, North-Western Provinces, 1891), p. 304.

22. Ibid.

23. Ibid., pp. 304–05.

24. Abdur Rahman Chishti, *Mirat-ul Asrar*, pp. 450–51; Vasie, 'Persian Interpretations', p. 48; *MM* Q, p. 2.

25 Maulvi Khalid saheb, interview, Kinaura village, Bara Banki, 28 December 1995; Interviews in Belkhara village on the banks of the Ghaghra, 27 December 1995.

ENDNOTES PART FOUR

17 Investing the Ghazi

1. Mushtaqi, *Waqiat-i-Mushtaqi*, p. 19.
2. *MM* Q, p. 145.
3. *MM* IH, p. 91; A further elaboration of the reply of Salar Masud in a twentieth-century *masnavi* reads as follows: *Kaha ek nāi tumse na wān rukh saka, yahān āti hai ek khalk-i-khuda; yeh sab mujh akele-se kyun ruk saken, jhuka den zamīn-ko jidhar yeh jhuken; isi se to aie mard-i-āli tabār, yeh māmūl pāya hai apna qarār; ke hota hai jab-tak yeh fisk-o-fijūr, raha karta hun qabr-se dūr-dūr; khalayāk jo karti hai yān azdahām, hefāzat mein rahta hūn unke madām; yeh ja leti hai khalk jab sar basar, to phir qabr mein apne rakhta hūn sar.* Mangal Khan, *Gulzar-i-Masudi*, p. 117.
4. See the sectarian tract by Syed Ahmad Shaheed (trans.), 'Sirat-i-Mustaqim', *JASB* 11, 1832, pp. 489–90.
5. Jawan, *Barah Masa*; Umar,'Haft Tamasha', pp. 84–85; Jaffur Shurreef, *Qanoon-e-Islam: Or the Customs of the Mussulmans of India, Comprising a Full and Exact Account of their Various Rites and Ceremonies from the Moment of Birth to the Hour of Death*, ed. and trans. G. E. Herklots (New Delhi: Asian Educational Services, 1991, reprint. First published 1863).
6. Avril A. Powell, 'History Textbooks and the Transmission of the Pre-Colonial Pasts in North-Western India in the 1860s and 1870s', in Daud Ali (ed.), *Invoking the Past: The Uses of History in South Asia* (New Delhi: Oxford University Press, 1999), p. 117 et seq.
7. Ram Lal, *Banitabuddhiprakashini,* [by] *Awwal Muddaris Zilla School, Hamirapur* (Ilahabad: Government Chapakhana, 1871), p. 69.
8. Pandit Ramprasad Tiwari, *Ritiratnakar* (Allahabad: Government Chapkhana, 1872).
9. Ibid., p. 30.
10. Ibid., p. 31.
11. Ibid, p. 35.
12. Ibid., pp. 29–36, esp. p. 36.

18 Demotic Warfare

1. Inayat Husain, *Tarikh Salar Masud Ghazi, be-Ihtemam ... Mohammad Abdullah Siddiqui, Lakhnavi, Tajir Kutub-wa Chikan, Chowk,* third edition (Lucknow: Matba-i-Mujtabai, 1916).
2. On the braiding of reason and religion in Arya Samaj popular tracts, see Gyan Prakash, *Another Reason: Science and the Imagination of Modern India* (Princeton: Princeton University Press, 1999), esp. pp 76–77, 106–09. For an elaboration of this argument, see Amin, 'Representing the Musalman'.
3. Braj Mohan Jha, *Bahraich ke Saiyid Salar Masud ka Jeevan Charitra* (Etawah, 1916); Jaiswal, *Ghazi Miyan;* Devkali Prasad, *Balark Teerth Rahasya* (Bahraich, 1923).
4. Jha, *Bahraich ke Salar Masud*, p. 1.
5. Prasad, *Balark Teerth Rahasya*, pp. 1–2.
6. Jaiswal, *Ghazi Miyan*, pp. 1–19.
7. Ibid., pp. 8–9.
8. Jaiswal, *Ghazi Miyan*, p. 44; Jha, *Bahraich ke Salar Masud*, p. 4.
9. Jha, *Bahraich ke Salar Masud*, p. 19. Compare Set Mahet ballad, p. 12.
10. Jha, *Bahraich ke Salar Masud*, p. 19. For a similar Ahir kingly role, see 'Haal Qaum Gobari yani Ahir', H.M. Elliot MSS. OR. 1733. BL.
11. See Chapter 2 in this volume.
12. Jha, *Bahraich ke Salar Masud*, pp. 24–25.
13. Jaiswal, *Ghazi Miyan*, p. 57; Jha, *Bahraich ke Salar Masud*, p. 57.
14. Jha, *Bahraich ke Salar Masud*, p. 57.
15. Ibid., p. 41. Such dialogues are found in the *Mirat-i-Masudi* as well, buttressed by Abdur Rahman's claim that he was basing the work on an old contemporary chronicle of the Life of Masud.
16. Jha, Bahraich ke Salar *Masud*, p. 14.
17. *MM* Q, pp. 25–26.
18. Jaiswal, *Ghazi Miyan*, p. 42.
19. Ibid., p. 43.
20. Jha, *Bahraich ke Salar Masud*; Jaiswal, *Ghazi Miyan*; Prasad, *Balark Teerth Rahasya*; Premanand Banprasthi, *Ghazi Kaun Hai* (Awadh, 1927); Premanand Banprasthi, *Musalmani Gorakhdhandha*, published by Secretary, Arya Samaj, Sultanpur (Allahabad: Leader Press, 1927).
21. The best discussion of Sufis, landed colonisation and literary output in the vernaculars in the fourteenth century is by Digby, 'Before Timur Came'.
22. C. A. Elliot, *Chronicles of Oonao:* pp. 84–85, note 2.
23. Jha, *Bahraich ke Masud Salar*, p. 54.
24. Jaiswal, *Ghazi Miyan*, pp. 16, 49, 53, 57; Jha, *Bahraich ke Masud Salar*, p. 51.
25. For a detailed discussion of the 'Saintly Dead', see *PRFL*, vol. 1, pp. 174–229.

26. Such practices persist in parts of the province to the present day. I know of one such person blessed by the shrine of Masud at Sikandara, near Allahabad (the one which was the object of popular version and elite Hindu derision in the text *Ritiratnakar*), who is called Ghazi Lal at home. I am grateful to Dr Sanjay Sharma of Ambedkar University, Delhi for a discussion on the theme of personal names such as 'Ghazi Lal' and 'Dargahi' in UP today.
27. Jaiswal, *Ghazi Miyan*, pp. 6–8; Banprasthi, *Musalmani Gorakhdhandha*, pp. 16–17.
28. For a recent discussion, see Charu Gupta, *Sexuality, Obscenity, Community: Women, Muslims, and the Hindu Public in Colonial India* (New Delhi: Permanent Black, 2002), pp. 281–98.
29. See Chaudhuri Baldev Singh, *Ahir-jati*, pp. 40–42, 50ff.; Chaudhuri Baldev Singh, *Ahir Jati mein 31 Rog* (Aligarh: Abhir Mahasabha, 1924); Baijnath Prasad Yadav, *Ahir Jati ki Niyamavali* (Banaras City, 1948), pp. 30–31; Munshi Munni Lal Rathore, *Teliyon ki Vanshavali aur Shakha-Vyakhya: Teli Jati Ka Sampurna Itihas* (Farrukhabad: Pradyuman Krishna Gulhare ke prabandh se Karmyogi press, 1924), p. 24.
30. Manu is quoted as saying: *vandhyāshtame dhivettu dashmetu mrt praja; ekādasho stri janani saddyās priyavādini*. Chaudhuri Baldev Singh, *Ahirjati*, p. 29; see also pp. 36–37. For Manu see, 'Manusmriti' 9.81 in Wendy Doniger O'Flaherty and Brian K. Smith (trans.), *The Laws of Manu* (Harmondsworth: Penguin Books, 1991); the operative part reads: 'a barren wife may be superseded in the eighth year'. I am grateful to Naina Dayal for the citation from Manu.
31. Chaudhuri Baldev Singh, *Ahir Jati*, p. 40.
32. Ibid., pp. 29, 36–37, 41.
33. To blow a benediction over the head of an infant, in this reasoning, was to spit on his face: *Jo munh-se maara phoonk, to kas-na nikra thook*. Coming from a Muslim, this was doubly polluting, wrote another pamphleteer. Jaiswal, *Ghazi Miyan*, p. 15.
34. Yadav, *Ahir Jati ki Niyamavali*, pp. 30–31. See also Charu Gupta, *Sexuality, Obscenity, Community*, pp. 273–81 for a fuller discussion of this economic and social boycott.
35. G. R. Thursby, *Hindu-Muslim Relations in British India: A Study of Controversy, Conflict and Communal Movements in Hindu Northern India, 1923–28* (Leiden: E. J. Brill, 1975). Charu Gupta brings much new Hindi material into focus from Uttar Pradesh in *Sexuality, Obscenity, Community*, Chapter 6. The key Muslim text that was especially targeted in the anti-Ghazi Miyan tracts of the 1920s was Khwaja Hasan Nizami, *Dai-y-Islam: Yeh Risala Har Musalman ko Dai-i-Islam Banane aur Hefazat wa Ishat-i-Islam ke liye Khwaja Hasan Nizami Dehalvi ne Likha aur Chauthi Baar Chapwa-kar Shaya*

Hua (Delhi, 1927, third edition) (I am grateful to Farhat Hasan for procuring a copy of this text for me.)
36. See for instance, Swami Vicharanand Saraswati, 'Hindu Samaj aur Ghazi Miyan', Swadesh, 26 April 1928, Swami Vicharanand Saraswati, 'Bale Miyan ki Puja Anuchit Hai: Bale Miyan ka Mela aur Ghazi Miyan ki Puja ka Gupt Rahasya', *Swadesh*, 26 April 1928.
37. UP Police Abstracts of Intelligence (PAI), 22 May and 29 May 1926, 5 June and 19 June 1927. For one such *patiya* reproduced in a propaganda tract, see Banprasthi, *Musalamani Gorakhdhandha*, pp. 6–7. See also Charu Gupta, *Sexuality, Obscenity, Community*, pp. 281–98, esp. pp. 290–91 for a detailed discussion of the boycott campaign.
38. UP PAI, 22 May, 29 May 1926, 5 June and 19 June 1927. I am grateful to Ram Narayan Rawat for accessing this archive on my behalf.

19 Downplaying the Iconoclast?

1. Abdur Majid Raza Khan Sherwani, *Saiyed Salar Masud Ghazi ka Mukhtasar Jeevan Charitra* (Bahraich: Ikleel Press, 1926) (hereafter Dargah Hindi pamphlet, 1926). This is a translation of an Urdu pamphlet released a year earlier, with the one major difference that the Urdu version has a detailed announcement about the Sufi ceremony of the *urs* of the saint on 12–14 Rajab of the Islamic calendar. See *Hayat-i-Masudi, Yani Hazrat Saiyed Salar Masud Ghazi ... Bahraich ke Mukhtasar Halaat ka Majmua* (Bahraich: Ikleel Press, 1925).
2. Dargah Hindi pamphlet, 1926, p. 16.
3. Ibid., pp. 22–23. The pamphlet summarises in Urdu the following passage by Sir H. M. Elliot: '[The] incidents [described by Abdur Rahman Chishti] seem to be borrowed rather than invented, and, as he used a contemporary work which is not known to us, it may be that some of his novel statements may be true, or may serve to explain, or elucidate other writers, though no reliance can be placed on them when unsupported.' *MM* E, p. 515.
4. Dargah Hindi pamphlet, 1926, p. 22.
5. See Mohammad Khalil Ansari, *Tazkira Ghazi Bale Miyan* (Delhi: Printing Works, 1927). This pamphlet on Salar Masud was a pendant to the more general Muslim response to the Hindu organisations' effort to reconvert some quasi-Muslim castes back into the fold of Hinduism, the 'shuddhi' movement, epitomised in the tract. Nizami, *Dai-i-Islam*.
6. Ansari, *Tazkira Ghazi Bale Miyan*, pp. 12–13.
7. The tract is a rich storehouse of information on popular worship of the Ghazi in the provinces of Bihar (Maner) and deltaic Bengal where Khalil Ansari had functioned in various administrative capacities. Ansari, *Iazkira Ghazi Bale Miyan*, pp. 6–8, 12–15.

8. Ibid., p. 2 et. seq.
9. UP Police Reports of Intelligence, 1922.
10. See Planalp, 'Religious Life', pp. 769–74; B. S. Cohn, 'The Changing Status of a Depressed Caste', in *An Anthropologist Among Historians and Other Essays* (Delhi: Oxford University Press, 1987) pp. 263–64. In Senapur, as in neighbouring Madhopur, the village studied by Cohn, the domestic worship of Ghazi Miyan went, as elsewhere, under the name of 'Panchon Pir'.
11. At the Bahraich Fair, the Arya Samaj Staff had provisions for purification by the regulation fire sacrifice for those returning from the dargah. A small portable *havan* had been installed in the tent for the purpose; a pamphlet titled *Ghazi Miyan ki Puja aur Hindu* along the lines of the 1920s tracts was also on sale. Field notes, May 1996. See also Badri Narayan Tiwari, 'Memories, Saffronising Statues and Constructing Communal Politics', *Economic and Political Weekly* 41(45), 2006, pp. 4695–701.

ENDNOTES PART FIVE

20 Everyday Memories

1. Wachtel, *Vision of the Vanquished.*
2. Richard Swedberg, *The Max Weber Dictionary: Key Words and Central Concepts* (Stanford: Stanford University Press, 2005), p. 29.
3. For a detailed consideration of the cult of Ghazi Miyan in Nepal and north India generally, see Marc Gaborieau, 'Légende et Culte du Saint Musalman Ghazi Miyan au Nepal Occidental et en Inde du Nord', *Objets et Monde* 15(3), 1975, pp. 289–312; and specially Marc Gaborieau, 'Les Saintes, les Eaux et les récoltes en Inde', in Mohammad Ali Amir Moezzi (ed.), *Cultes et Cultures de l'Afrique et Java* (Paris: Autrement, 1996), pp. 239–54. For north India, see Tahir Mahmood, 'The Dargah of Sayyid Salar Masud Ghazi in Bahraich: Legend, Tradition and Reality', in Christian W. Troll (ed.), *Muslim Shrines in India: Their Character, History and Significance* (New Delhi: Oxford University Press, 1989); Kerrin G. V. Schwerin, 'Saint Worship in Indian Islam: The Legend of Martyr Salar Masud Ghazi', in Imtiaz Ahmad (ed.), *Religion and Politics Among Muslims in India* (Delhi: Manohar, 1981); Kerrin G. V. Schwerin, 'The Cow-saving Muslim Saint: Elite and Folk Representation of a Tomb Cult in Oudh', in Mushirul Hasan and Asim Roy (eds), *Living Together Separately: Cultural India in History and Politics* (New Delhi: Oxford University Press, 2005).
4. V. A. Smith, 'Benares', in J. Hastings (ed.), *Encyclopaedia of Religion and Ethics* (Edinburgh: T. T. Clark, 1980), p. 466.
5. There is reason to suppose that these, especially the one about Zohra Bibi, the blind girl, were such 'utterings of the locals' as the learned Sufi of Rudauli tried to rein in his hagiography of the saint.
6. For the carnivalesque elements of the mourning, see Shurreef, *Qanoon-e-Islam*, Chapter 15, pp. 98–151, esp. pp. 126–41. For Muharram in Trinidad, see Madhavi Kale, *Fragments of Empire: Capital, Slavery and the Indian Indentured Labour Migration in the British Caribbean* (Philadelphia: University of Pennsylvania Press, 1989), esp. p. 153; Prabhu P. Mohapatra, 'The Hosay Massacre of 1884: Class and Community among Indian Immigrant Labourers in Trinidad', in Arvind N. Das and Marcel van der Linden (eds),

Work and Social Change in Asia: Essays in Honour of Jan Breman (New Delhi: Manohar, 2003), pp. 186–230.

7. Ram Gharib Chaube, 'The Time when the Mango First Begins to Ripen', *NINQ* 4(8), July 1894, no. 319, para 319; for a twentieth-century literary allusion to Bale Miyan's marriage and the first ripening of mangoes in rural Awadh, see Qurratulain Hyder, *Chandini Begum,* trans. Wahajuddin Alavi (Nai Dilli: Bhartiya Gyanpeeth Prakashan, 1997), p. 201.

8. *Shakkar-i-Misri na dāram kaz Arab gūyam jawāb / Turk-i-Hindustāniyam dar Hindawi gūyam jawāb*, cited in Alam, *Languages of Political Islam*, p. 148.

9. On 'Banaudha', see *Oudh Gazetteer*, vol. 1, Introduction, p. xxxiv; compare Banprasthi, *Musalmani Gorakhdhanda*, p. 11.

10. Askari, *Medieval Bihar,* p. 16; Subrahmanyam, 'Before the Leviathan, pp. 68–69.

11. '.... Salar Masud ... buried [at] ... Bahraich ... was connected by blood with Mahmud Ghaznavi, and sold his life bravely in battle and left an imperishable name'. See Abul-Fazal, *Ain-i-Akbari,* vol. 2, p. 187.

12. Moosvi, *Episodes in the Life of Akbar*, p. 21.

13. Marc Bloch, *The Royal Touch: Sacred Monarchy and Scrofula in England and France*, trans. J. E. Anderson (London: Routledge and Kegan Paul, 1973), p. 48.

14. Ibid., pp. 233–34.

15. Ibid., p. 243.

16. See Alam, *Languages of Political Islam*, p. 165.

17. Carlo Ginzburg, *The Cheese and the Worms: The Cosmos of a Sixteenth-Century Miller* (London: Routledge and Kegan Paul, 1980), esp. pp. 154–55.

18. Bloch, *Royal Touch*, p. 232.

19. R. G. Collingwood, 'Limits of Historical Knowledge', *Journal of Philosophical Studies* 3(10), 1928, p. 221.

20. Eric Hobsbawm, *On History* (New York: New Press, 1997), pp. 5–6.

21. Sanjay Subrahmanyam, 'Violence, Grievance, and Memory in Early Modern South Asia', in *Explorations in Connected History: From the Tagus to the Ganges* (New Delhi: Oxford University Press, 2005), p. 89.

22 'Introduction', in Partha Chatterjee and Anjan Ghosh (eds), *History and the Present* (New Delhi: Permanent Black, 2002), pp. 18–19.

23. Ibn Khallikan, *Biographical Dictionary,* vol. 3, trans. Bn MacGuckin de Slane (Paris: General Translation Fund of Great Britain and Ireland, 1868), pp. 333–34.

24. Cf: *dar qasba Bahraich az mazār mātbar Sipah Salar hamān Hindustan bu-e-ūd giraft ast.* Amir Khusrau, *Ijaz-i-Khusravi,* Risala I (Lucknow: Neval Kishore Press, 1867), p. 155; Mahdi Hasan, *The Rehla of Ibn Battuta*, pp. 109–10.

25. Phyllis Granoff, 'Tales of Broken Limbs and Bleeding Wounds: Responses to Muslim Iconoclasm in Medieval India', *East and West* 41(3–4), 1991, pp. 189–203.
26. I am grateful to my student Ravikant who during his long research into the 'language of Hindi Cinema' dug out this gem from the film *Majhli Didi*, (1967), starring Meena Kumari, the tragedy queen of Indian cinema of the 1960s.
27. *Thora karen Ghazi Miyan, bahut karen Dafali*. Fallon, *New Hindustani Dictionary*, s.v. Ghazi Miyan.
28. Shiv Narain, *Awadh-deshiya Bhugol* (Lakhnau: Neval Kishore, 1870), p. 37; Babu Shivprasad, *Bhugol Hastmalak, or The Earth As (a Drop) of Clear Water in Hand*, vol. 1(Kalkatta: Sanskrit Press, 1859), pt. 1, p. 186.
29. Testimony Recorded by Braj Kishore Prasad at Bettiah on 23 April 1917, Rajendra Prasad Papers, Champaran Documents, vol. 2, National Archives of India, New Delhi.

21 **Epilogue**

1. Post Master General, United Provinces of Agra and Oudh (compiled), *Village Directory of the United Provinces of Agra and Oudh*, vols 1–12 (Allahabad: Government Press, 1902).
2. Rahi Masoom Raza, *Adha Gaon* (Nai Dilli: Rajkamal Prakashan, 1984), translated by Gillian Wright as *The Feuding Families of Village Gangauli* (Delhi: Viking, 1994)
3. Ismat Chughtai, *Dil ki Duniya* (Nai Dilli: Rajkamal Prakashan, 2009, Hindi edition. Urdu edition first published 1862).
4. Alok Rai and Mushtaq Ali (eds), *Samaksh: Premchand ki Bees Urdu-Hindi Kahaniyon ka Samanantar Paath* (Ilahabad: Hans Prakashan, 2002), pp. 26–37, esp. pp. 28–29.
5. Grierson, *Bihar Peasant Life*, s.v. 'Panchopir', para 1456, p.
6. Suniti Kumar Chatterjee, 'Daraf Khan Ghazi', *Sanskrit I*, 1368 B.S.
7. Thapar, *Somanatha*.

Bibliography

RECORDS

Census of India, 1891. Allahabad: North-Western Province and Oudh Press, 1891.

Files in the Board of Revenue, Oudh, General Administration, Revenue and Police Departments of NWP and Oudh (subsequently UP), 1860–1925, UP State Archives, Lucknow.

Files of the Faizabad Commissioner, 1873, UP State Regional Archives, Allahabad.

Police Abstracts of Intelligence, 1925–7, UP, Lucknow.

EUROPEAN LANGUAGES

Abul-Fazal, Allami, *The Ain-i-Akbari*, translated by H. S. Jarett, vol. 2. New Delhi: Low Price Publications, 1989, reprint. First published 1894.

Alam, Muzaffar, *The Crisis of Empire in North India: Awadh and Punjab, 1707–48*. Delhi: Oxford University Press, 1986.

——, *The Languages of Political Islam, c. 1200–1800*. New Delhi: Permanent Black, 2004.

——, 'The Debate Within: A Sufi Appraisal of Religious Law, Tasawwuf and Politics in Mughal India'. Unpublished, typescript, 2011.

Alvai, Moinuddin,'*Mirat-i-Masudi aur Uska Musannif*, *Mushir-i-Awqaf* 3(1), 1976, translated in H. A. Qureshi, *Sufi Classics II: Mirat-i-Masudi of Abdur Rahman Danethwi* (translations). Lucknow: New Royal Book Company, 2009.

Alvi, Moin Ahmad, '*Mirat-i-Masudi* (Notes on Different Manuscripts)', *Mushir-i-Awqaf* 3(1), 1976,. in H. A. Qureshi, *Sufi Classics I*. Lucknow: New Royal Book Company, 2009.

Amin, Shahid, 'Gandhi as Mahatma: Gorakhpur District, Eastern U.P., 1921–22' in Ranajit Guha (ed.), *Subaltern Studies*, vol. 3. Delhi: Oxford University Press, 1984.

——, *Event, Metaphor, Memory: Chauri Chaura, 1922–1992*. Berkeley: California University Press, 1995.

Amin, Shahid, 'Representing the Musalman: Then and Now, Now and Then', in Shail Mayaram, M. S. S. Pandian and Ajay Skaria (eds), *Muslims, Dalits and the Fabrication of History: Subaltern Studies*, vol. 12. New Delhi: Permanent Black and Ravi Dayal Publishers, 2005.

——— (ed.), *A Concise Encyclopaedia of North Indian Peasant Life*. New Delhi: Manohar Books, 2005.

Anon., 'Customs and Ceremonies of the Natives of Eastern N.W.P.', c. 1900, Grierson MS E-223, South Asian Section, British Library.

Anon., 'Village Hymns in Itawa District', no. 16: 5, *Indian Antiquary* 19, 1910.

Anon., 'A Song about Forest Godlings: The Cow and the Lion', *Indian Antiquary* 39, October 1910.

Archer, W. G., *The Vertical Man: A Study in Primitive Indian Sculpture*. London: George and Unwin, 1947.

Askari, S. H., 'The Malfuzat and Maktutat of a Sufi Saint of North India of a Fourteenth Century Saint of Bihar', *Journal of the Bihar Research Society* 34(3–4), 1948.

———, *Islam and Muslims in Medieval Bihar*. Patna: Khuda Baksh Library, 1989.

Atkinson, E. T. (ed.), *Statistical, Descriptive, Historical Account of the North-Western Province of India*, vols 1–9 (Allahabad: North-Western Province Government Press, 1874–86).

Battuta, Ibn, *Ajaib al Asfar*, vol. 2, translated by Maulvi Mohammad Husain. Islamabad: National Institute of Historical and Cultural Research, 1983.

Bayly, Susan, *Saints, Goddesses and Kings: Muslims and Christians in South Indian Society, 1700–1900*. Cambridge: Cambridge University Press, 1999.

Behbahani, Ahmed, *India in the Early 19th Century: An Iranian's Travel Account*, translated by A. F. Haider. Patna: Khuda Baksh Oriental Library, 1996.

Behl, Aditya, 'The Magic Doe: Desire and Narrative in a Hindavi Sufi Romance, circa 1503', in Richard Eaton (ed.), *India's Islamic Traditions: 711–1750*. New Delhi, Oxford University Press, 2003.

Behl, Aditya and Simon Weightman (trans.), *Madhumalati: an Indian Sufi Romance*, Oxford World Classics Series. Oxford: Oxford University Press, 2000.

Bennett, William C. (ed.), *Gazetteer of the Province of Oudh*, vols 1–3. Lucknow: Government Press, Oudh, 1877–78.

Bharucha, Rustom, *Rajasthan: An Oral History: Conversations with Komal Kothari*. New Delhi: Penguin India, 2003.

Bhavabhuti, *Rama's Last Act*, translated by Sheldon Pollock. New York: Clay Sanskrit Series, 2007.

Bloch, Marc, *The Royal Touch: Sacred Monarchy and Scrofula in England and France*, translated by J. E. Anderson. London: Routledge and Kegan Paul, 1973.

Blunt, E. A. H., *The Caste System of Northern India, with Special Reference to the United Provinces of Agra and Oudh*. London: Oxford University Press and Humphrey Milford, 1931.

Briant, Pierre, *Darius in the Shadow of Alexander*. Cambridge: Harvard University Press, 2015.

Bosworth, C. E., 'Mahmud of Ghazni in Contemporary Eyes and in Later Persian Literature', *Iran* 4, 1966.

Briggs, George Weston, The *Chamars*. London: Oxford University Press, 1920.

———, *Gorakhnath and the Kanphata Yogis*. Delhi: Motilal Banarsidass, 1975, reprint. First published 1938.

Carnegy, Patrick, *Notes on the Races, Tribes and Castes Inhabiting the Province of Oudh*. Lucknow: Oudh Government Press, 1868.

Chandra, Sudhir, 'Communal Consciousness in Late 19th Century Hindi Literature', in Mushirul Hasan (ed.), *Communal and Pan Islamic Trends in Colonial India*. Delhi: Manohar, 1981.

———, *The Oppressive Present: Literature and Social Consciousness in Colonial India*. New Delhi: Oxford University Press, 1992.

Chapman, R. W., 'Mirat-i-Masudi', English translation. Addl. MS. 30776, BL.

Chatterjee, Partha, *The Nation and its Fragments: Colonial and Postcolonial Histories*. Princeton: Princeton University Press, 1993.

Chatterjee, Partha and Anjan Ghosh (eds), *History and the Present*. New Delhi: Permanent Black, 2002.

Chaube, Ram Gharib, 'Pachra Song—Chuhar Mal the Dusadh Hero Marrying a Brahman Girl', *North Indian Notes and Queries*, 4(4), July 1894, no. 152.

———, 'The Time when the Mango First Begins to Ripen', *North Indian Notes and Queries* 4(8), November 1894b, no. 319.

———, 'Ceremonies and Festivals', *North Indian Notes and Queries*, 5(1), April 1895, no.1.

———, 'Ethnographic Notes on Eastern U.P.' Grierson Papers, MS Eur. E-223, BL.

Clark, E. G., and H. Scott Boys, *Bahraich Settlement Report*. Lucknow: North-Western Province and Oudh Government Press, 1873.

Cleghorn, Maude L., 'Observations on the Bat-Flowers of the Mohwa (*Bassia latifolia*)', *Journal of the Asiatic Society of Bengal* 18(ns), 1922.

Coccari, Diane M., 'The Bir Babas of Banaras: An Analysis of a Folk Deity in North Indian Hinduism'. PhD diss., University of Wisconsin, 1986.

Cohn, Bernard S., 'The Camars of Senapur: A Study of the Changing Status of a Depressed Caste'. PhD diss., Cornell University, 1954.

———, 'The Changing Status of a Depressed Caste', in *An Anthropologist Among Historians and Other Essays*. Delhi: Oxford University Press, 1987.

Collingwood, R. G., 'Limits of Historical Knowledge', *Journal of Philosophical Studies* 3(10), 1928.

Cook, David, *Martyrdom in Islam*. Cambridge: Cambridge University Press, 2007.

Crooke, William, *A Rural and Agricultural Glossary for the N.W. Provinces and Oudh*. Calcutta: Government Press, 1888.

———, *An Introduction to the Popular Religion and Folklore of Northern India*. Allahabad: North-Western Provinces and Oudh Government Press, 1893.

———, 'The Battle of Banaras—A Local Ballad sung by Dafalis in Eastern Districts of the North-Western Provinces', *North Indian Notes and Queries* 2(12), March 1893.

———, *The Tribes and Castes of North-Western Provinces and Oudh*, 4 vols. Allahabad: Superintendent Government Press, 1896.

———, 'Panchpiriya', in J. Hastings (ed.), *Encyclopaedia of Religion and Ethics*, vol. 9. Edinburgh: T. T. Clark, 1908–27.

Dalmia, Vasudha, *The Nationalization of Hindu Traditions: Bharatendu Harishchandra and Nineteenth-Century Banaras*. Delhi: Oxford University Press, 1997.

Davis, Natalie Zemon, *The Return of Martin Guerre*. Cambridge, MA: Harvard University Press, 1983.

Davis, Richard H., *Lives of Indian Images*. Princeton, NJ: Princeton University Press, 1997.

de Tassy, Garcin, *Mémoirs sur des Particularites des la Religion Muslamane dans l'Inde d'apres les Ouvrages Hindoustani*. Paris: Libraire de la Societé Asiatique, 1869. Translated and edited by M. Waseem as *Muslim Festivals in India and Other Essays*. (New Delhi: Oxford University Press, 1995).

DeWeese, Devin, *Islamization and Native Religion in the Golden Horde*. Pennsylvania: Pennsylvania State University Press, 1994.

Deyell, John S., 'Cowries and Coins: The Dual Monetary System of the Bengal Sultanate', *Indian Economic and Social History Review* 47(1), 2010.

Digby, Simon, 'Dreams and Reminiscences of Dattu Sarvani: A Sixteenth-Century Indo-Afghan Soldier' (in two parts), *Indian Economic Social History Review* 2(1&2), 1965.

———, 'Encounters with Jogis in Indian Sufi Hagiography', London, mimeo, 1970.

———, 'The Sufi Shaikh as a Source of Authority in Medieval India', *Purushartha* 9, 1986.

———, 'The North Indian Kissa Tradition and the Nepali Madhumalti', typescript, 1996.

———, 'Before Timur Came: Provincialization of the Delhi Sultanate through the Fourteenth Century', *Journal of the Economic and Social History of the Orient* 47(3), 2004.

———, 'Abd-al-Quddus Gangohi (1456–1537): The Personality and Attitudes of an Indian Sufi', in *Medieval India: A Miscellany*, vol. 3. Bombay: Asia Publishing House, 1975.

———, 'Some Afghan Tall Tales'. Unpublished manuscript, c. 2008.

Eaton, Richard, *The Sufis of Bijapur, 1300–1700: The Social Role of Sufis in Medieval India*. Princeton: Princeton University Press, 1978.

———, 'Temple Desecration and Indo-Muslim States', in David Gilmartin and Bruce B. Lawrence (eds), *Beyond Turk and Hindu: Rethinking Religious Identities in Islamicate South Asia*. Gainsville: University of Florida Press, 2000.

Elliot, C. A., *The Chronicles of Oonao: A District in Oudh*. Allahabad: Mission Press, 1862.

Elliot, H. M., *Supplement to the Glossary of Indian Terms*. Roorkee: Thomason College Press, 1860.

———, *The History of India as Told by Its Own Historians*, ed. John Dowson, vols 1–8. New Delhi: Low Price Publications, 2001, reprint. First published 1869.

Elwin, Verrier, *Folk Songs of Chhattisgarh*. Madras: Oxford University Press, 1946.

Encyclopaedia of Islam. Leiden: E. J. Brill, 1991, second edition.

Fallon, S. W., *A New Hindustani Dictionary: With Illustrations from Hindustani Literature and Folklore*. Banaras: E. J. Lazarus, 1879.

Farooqi, N. R., 'The Legend of Saiyyid Salar Masud Ghazi', *Islamic Culture* 75(3), 2001.

Faruqi, Shamsur Rahman, *The Mirror of Beauty*. New Delhi: Penguin Books, 2013.

Flood, Finbarr B., *Objects of Translation: Material Culture and Medieval 'Hindu-Muslim' Encounter*. Princeton: Princeton University Press, 2009.

Führer, Alois Anton, *The Monumental Antiquities and Inscriptions in the North-Western Provinces and Oudh*. Allahabad: Superintendent, Government Press, North Western Provinces, 1891.

Gaborieau, Marc, 'Légende et Culte du Saint Musalman Ghazi Miyan au Nepal Occidental et en Inde du Nord', *Objets et Monde* 15(3), 1975.

———, 'Les Saintes, les Eaux et les récoltes en Inde', in Mohammad Ali Amir Moezzi (ed.), *Cultes et Cultures de l'Afrique et Java*. Paris: Autrement, 1996.

Ghosh, Amitav, *The Sea of Poppies*. New Delhi: Penguin Books, 2009.

Ginzburg, Carlo, *The Cheese and the Worms: The Cosmos of a Sixteenth-Century Miller*. London: Routledge and Kegan Paul, 1980, 1981.

Government of Bengal: Legislative Department: *Bengal Code in Five Volumes*. Alipore, 1939, fifth edition.

Granoff, Phyllis, 'Tales of Broken Limbs and Bleeding Wounds: Responses to Muslim Iconoclasm in Medieval India', *East and West* 41(3–4), 1991.

Greeven, R., 'Benares—The Worship of Panchon Pir', *North Indian Notes and Queries* 2(2), May 1892.

Greeven, R., *The Heroes Five (Panchon Pir): An Attempt to Collect Some of the Songs of the Pachpiriya Ballad-Mongers in the Benares Division*. Allahabad: Pioneer Press, 1898.

Grierson, G. A. (ed. and trans.), 'The Song of Alha's Marriage: A Bhojpuri Epic', *Indian Antiquary*, August 1885.

Grierson, G. A., *Bihar Peasant Life: A Descriptive Catalogue of the Surroundings of the People of that Province*. Calcutta: Government Press, 1885.

———, 'Some Bhojpuri Folk-songs', *Journal of Royal Asiatic Society'* (NS), 1886.

Gruzinski, Serge, 'Mutilated Memories: Reconstruction of the Past and the Mechanisms of Memory among 17th Century Otomis', *History and Anthropology* 2, 1986.

Guha, Ranajit, *Elementary Aspects of Peasant Insurgency in Colonial India*. Delhi: Oxford University Press, 1983.

Gupta, Charu, *Sexuality, Obscenity, Community: Women, Muslims, and the Hindu Public in Colonial India*. Delhi: Permanent Black, 2002.

Habib, Irfan, *An Atlas of the Mughal Empire: Political and Economic Maps with Detailed Notes, Bibliography and Index*. New Delhi: Oxford University Press, 1986.

Habib, Mohammad, *Politics and Society during the Early Medieval Period: Collected Works of Professor Mohammad Habib*, edited by K. A. Nizami. New Delhi: People's Publishing House, 1974.

Habib, Mohammad and Nizami Khaliq Ahmad (eds), *A Comprehensive History of India, The Delhi Sultanate*, vol. 5, pt. 1. New Delhi: People's Publishing House, 1992.

Haig, Captain Wolseley, 'The Legendary Account of Shah Abdur-Rahman-i-Ghazi, the Warrior Saint of Berar', *Journal of the Asiatic Society of Bengal* 71(3.1), 1901.

Hamilton, Charles, 'A Description of the Mahwah Tree', *Asiatic Researches* 1, 1798.

Haq, Muhammad Enamul, 'Panch Pir', *Journal of the Asiatic Society of Pakistan* 20(2), 1970.

Hardiman, David, *Feeding the Baniya: Peasants and Usurers in Western India*. New Delhi: Oxford University Press, 1996.

Hardy, Peter, 'Mahmud of Ghazna and the Historian', *Journal of the Punjab University Historical Studies* 14, December 1962.

Hasan, Mahdi (ed. and trans.), *The Rehla of Ibn Battuta (India, Maldive Islands and Ceylon)*, Gaekwad's Oriental Series no. 122. Baroda: Oriental Institute, 1953.

——— (ed.), *Fatuhus-Salatin, or Shahnamah-i-Hind of Isami*, English translation, vol. 1. Bombay: Asia Publishing House, 1967.

Hasan, Mushirul, *Nationalism and Communal Poltics in India, 1885–1930*. New Delhi: Manohar, 1991.

Hastings, J. (ed.), *Encyclopaedia of Religion and Ethics*, vols 2 and 9. Edinburgh: T. T. Clark, 1908–27.

Hertig-Skalicka, Jitka, 'Fifty Bhojpuri Songs from Ballia District: Text, Translation, Commentary, Skeletal-Grammar and Index'. PhD diss., University of Basel, 1974.

Hobsbawm, Eric, *On History*. New York: New Press, 1997.

Hodgson, Marshall G. S., *The Venture of Islam: Conscience and History in a World Civilisation—The Expansion of Islam in the Middle Periods*, vol. 2. Chicago: University of Chicago Press, 1977.

Hoey, W., 'Set Mahet', *Journal of the Asiatic Society of Bengal* 1, extra no., 1892.

Hyder, Qurratulain, *River of Fire*. Delhi: Kali for Women, 1998.

Ibn Khallikan, *Biographical Dictionary*, translated from Arabic by Bn MacGuckin de Slane. Paris: General Translation Fund of Great Britain and Ireland, 1868.

Irwin, Henry Crossley, *The Garden of India*, or *Chapters on Oudh History and Affairs*, vol. 1. London: W. H. Allen, 1880.

Jackson, Peter, *The Delhi Sultanate: A Political and Military History*. Cambridge: Cambridge University Press, 1999.

Jassal, Smita Tewari, *Unearthing Gender: Folksongs of North India*. Durham: Duke University Press, 2012.

Jones, Russell, 'Ten Conversion Myths from Indonesia', in Nehemia Levtzion (ed.), *Conversion to Islam*. New York: Holmes and Meir, 1979.

Kafadar, Camal, *Between Two Worlds: The Construction of the Ottoman State*. Berkeley: University of California Press, 1995.

Kale, Madhavi, *Fragments of Empire: Capital, Slavery and the Indian Indentured Labour Migration in the British Caribbean*. Philadelphia: University of Pennsylvania Press, 1989.

Keene's Handbook for Visitors: Allahabad, Cawnpore and Lucknow. Calcutta: Thacker, Spink and Co., 1896.

Keir, Archibald, 'On the Method of Distilling as Practiced by the Natives of Chatra in Ramgur, and in other Provinces, Perhaps, with a Little Variation', *Asiatic Researches* 1, 1793.

Khan, Mohammad Motiur Rahman, 'The Institution of Waqf in Mughal India: A Study of the Land Grants to the Dargah of Ajmer upto [the] 1860s'. MPhil diss., Department of History, University of Delhi, 2009.

Knowles, S., *The Gospel in Gonda: Being a Narrative of Events in Connection with the Preachings of the Gospel in the Trans-Ghaghra Country*. Lucknow: Methodist Publishing House, 1889.

Kosambi, D. D., *Combined Methods in Indology and Other Writings*. New Delhi: Oxford University Press, 2002.

Krishen, Pradip, *Trees of Delhi: A Field Guide*. New Delhi: Dorling Kindersley, 2006.

Kumar, Sunil, *The Emergence of the Delhi Sultanate, 1192–1286*. Ranikhet: Permanent Black, 2007.

Lakhnavi, Ghalib and Abdullah Bilgrami, *The Adventures of Amir Hamza*, translated by Musharraf Ali Farooqi. New York: Modern Library, 2007.

Lyall, A. C. (ed.), *Gazetteer for the Haidarabad Assigned Districts Commonly Called Berar*. Bombay: Education Society Press, 1870.

Mahmood, Tahir, 'The Dargah of Sayyid Salar Masud Ghazi in Bahraich: Legend, Tradition and Reality', in Christian W. Troll (ed.), *Muslim Shrines in India: Their Character, History and Significance*. New Delhi: Oxford University Press, 1989.

Majumdar, R. C. (ed.), *The History of India and Culture of the Indian People: The Struggle for Empire*: Bombay: Bhartiya Vidya Bhavan, 1957.

Malhotra, Anshu, *Gender, Caste and Religious Identities: Restructuring Class in Colonial India*. Delhi: Oxford University Press, 2004.

Martin, M. (ed.), *The History, Antiquities, Topography, Statistics of Eastern India: Behar (Patna City) and Shahabad*. London: W. H. Allen & Co., 1838.

Miller, Barbara Stoler and Mildred Archer (eds), *Songs for the Bride: Wedding Rites of Rural India*. New York: Columbia University Press, 1985.

Millett, A. F., *Report on the Settlement of the Land Revenue of District Sultanpur*. Allahabad: North-Western Province and Oudh Government Press, 1873.

Mirza, Mohammad Wahid, *The Life and Works of Amir Khusro*. Lahore: Panjab University, 1975.

Misra, Ram Gopal, *Indian Resistance to Early Muslim Invaders upto 1206*. Meerut: Anu Books, 1983.

Mitra, Sarat Chandra, 'On a Musalmān Legend about the Sylvan Saint Bona-Bibi and the Tiger Deity Dakshina Rāya', *University of Calcutta: Journal of the Department of Letters* 10, 1923, pp. 154–72.

Mohapatra, Prabhu, 'The Hossay Massacre of 1884: Class and Community among Indian Immigrant Labourers in Trinidad', in Arvind N. Das and Marcel van der Linden (eds), *Work and Social Change in Asia: Essays in Honour of Jan Breman*. New Delhi: Manohar, 2003.

Moosvi, Shireen (ed. and trans.), *Episodes in the Life of Akbar: Contemporary Records and Reminiscences*. New Delhi: National Book Trust, 1994.

Mujeeb, M., *Indian Muslims*. London: Allen Lane, 1963.

Mukherjee, Rudrangshu, *Awadh in Revolt: A Study of Popular Resistance*. New Delhi: Oxford University Press, 1984.

Nazim, Muhammad, *The Life and Times of Sultan Mahmud of Ghazna*. Cambridge: Cambridge University Press, 1931.

Nizami, K. A. (ed.), *Politics and Society during the Early Medieval Period: Collected Works of Professor Mohammad Habib*. New Delhi: People's Publishing House, 1974.

Nevill, H. R., *Gonda District Gazetteer*. Allahabad: Superintendent Government Press, 1909.

Pandey, Shyam Manohar, *The Hindi Oral Epic Lorikayan: The Tale of Lorik and Chanda*. Allahabad: Sahitya Bhavan, 1987.

Planalp, Jack M., 'Religious Life and Values in a North Indian Village'. PhD diss., Cornell University, 1954.

Post Master General, United Provinces of Agra and Oudh (compiled), *Village Directory of the United Provinces of Agra and Oudh* vols 1–12. Allahabad: Government Press, 1902.

Powell, Avril A., 'History Textbooks and the Transmission of the Pre-Colonial Pasts in North-Western India in the 1860s and 1870s', in Daud Ali (ed.), *Invoking the Past: The Uses of History in South Asia*. New Delhi: Oxford University Press, 1999.

Prakash, Gyan, *Another Reason: Science and the Imagination of Modern India*. Princeton: Princeton University Press, 1999.

Qureshi, H. A. (trans.), *Sufis Classics-I*. Lucknow: New Royal Book Company, 2007.

——, (trans.), *Sufis Classics-II: Mirat-i-Masudi of Abdur Rahman Danethwi*. Lucknow: New Royal Book Company, 2009.

Raza, Rahi Masoom, *Adha Gaon*. Nai Dilli: Rajkamal Prakashan, 1984, Translated by Gillian Wright as *The Feuding Families of Village Gangauli* (Delhi: Viking, 1994).

Renard, John, *Islam and the Heroic Image: Themes in Literature and the Visual Arts*. Columbia: University of South Carolina Press, 1993.

Ricoeur, Paul, 'The Hermeneutics of Testimony', in *Essays in Biblical Interpretation*. Philadelphia: Fortune Press, 1980.

Rieu, C. A., *Persian Literature: A Bio-Bibliographic Survey*. London: Luzac and Co, 1927.

Rizvi, Saiyid Athar Abbas, *A History of Sufism in India*, vol. 1. Delhi: Munshiram Manoharlal, 1997.

Rockey, N. L., 'Progress of Islam in Oudh', *Muslim World* 3(3), 1913.

Roy, Asim, *The Syncretic Tradition in Bengal*. Princeton: Princeton University Press, 1983.

Sachau, Edward (ed.), *Alberuni's India*. New Delhi: Low Price Publications, 1993, reprint. First published 1910.

Schwerin, Kerrin G. V., 'Saint Worship in Indian Islam: The Legend of the Martyr Salar Masud Ghazi', in Imtiaz Ahmad (ed.), *Religion and Politics Among Muslims in India* Delhi: Manohar, 1981.

——, 'The Cow-saving Muslim Saint: Elite and Folk Representation of a Tomb Cult in Oudh', in Mushirul Hasan and Asim Roy (eds), *Living Together Separately: Cultural India in History and Politics*. New Delhi: Oxford University Press, 2005.

Searle-Chatterjee, Mary, 'The Muslim Hero as Defender of Hindus: Mythical Reversals and Ethnicity among Benares Muslims', *Social Analysis* 28, 1990.

Shurreef, Jaffur, *Qanoon-e-Islam: Or the Customs of the Mussulmans of India, Comprising a Full and Exact Account of their Various Rites and Ceremonies from the Moment of Birth to the Hour of Death*, edited and translated by G. E. Herklots. New Delhi: Asian Educational Services, 1991, reprint. First published 1863.

Siddiqui, Iqtidar Husain, 'A Note on the Dargah of Salar Mas'ud in Bahraich in the Light of the Standard Historical Sources', in Christian W. Troll (ed.), *Muslim Shrines in India: Their Character, History and Significance*. New Delhi: Oxford University Press, 1989.

Sikand, Yoginder, 'Arya Shuddhi and Muslim Tabligh: Muslim Reactions to Arya Samaj Proselytisation (1923-30)'. Typescript.

Sleeman, W., *Rambles and Recollections of an Indian Official*. London: J. Hatchard and Son, 1844.

Smith, V. A., 'Benares', in J. Hastings (ed.), *Encyclopaedia of Religion and Ethics*, vol. 2. Edinburgh, T. T. Clark, 1980.

Smith, J. D., *The Epic of Pabuji*. Cambridge: Cambridge University Press, 1991.

Snell, Rupert L., *The Classical Tradition: A Braj Bhasha Reader*. London: SOAS, 1991.

Subrahmanyam, Sanjay, 'Before the Leviathan: Sectarian Violence and State in Pre-Colonial India', in Kaushik Basu and Sanjay Subrahmanyam (eds), *Unravelling the Nation: Sectarian Conflict and India's Secular Identity*. New Delhi: Penguin India, 1996.

——, 'Violence, Grievance, and Memory in Early Modern South Asia', in *Explorations in Connected History: From the Tagus to the Ganges*. New Delhi: Oxford University Press, 2005.

Swedberg, Richard, *The Max Weber Dictionary: Key Words and Central Concepts*. Stanford: Stanford University Press, 2005.

Temple, R. C., 'The Marriage of Ghazi Salar', in *The Legends of Punjab*, vol. 1. Patiala: Department of Languages, Punjab, 1998, second reprint. First published c. 1884.

——, *The Legends of Punjab*, vol. 1. Patiala: Department of Languages, Punjab, 1998, second reprint. First published c. 1884.

Thackston, Wheeler M. (ed. and trans.), *Baburnama: The Memoirs of Babur, Prince and Emperor*. New York: Oxford University Press, 1996.

Thapar, Romila, *Somanatha—The Many Voices of a History*. New Delhi: Penguin, 2005.

Thursby, G. R., *Hindu-Muslim Relations in British India: A Study of Controversy, Conflict and Communal Movements in Northern India, 1923-28*. Leiden: E. J. Brill, 1975.

Tiwari, Badri Narayan, 'Memories, Saffronising Statues and Constructing Communal Politics', *Economic and Political Weekly* 41(45), 2006: 4695–701.

Tiwari, Udai Narain, *The Origin and Development of Bhojpuri*. Asiatic Society Monograph Series, vol. 10. Calcutta: Asiatic Society, 1960.

Tod, James, *Travels in Western India*. London: W. H. Allen, 1839.

Todorov, Tzvetan, *The Conquest of America: The Question of the Other*. New York: Harper Collins Perennial Edition, 1992.

Upadhyaya, Hari S., 'The Joint Family Structure and Familial Relationship Patterns in the [sic] Bhojpuri Folksongs'. PhD diss., Folklore Institute, Indiana University, 1967.

Varma, Divya, 'Mr Devendra Satyarthi in Bundelkhand', *Rural India* 7, 1943.

Vasie, Roderic, 'Persian Interpretations of the Bhagvadgita in the Mughal Period with Special Reference to the Sufi Version of Abd al-Rahman Chishti'. PhD diss., School of Oriental and African Studies, London University, 1988.

Wachtel, Nathan, *The Vision of the Vanquished: The Spanish Conquest of Peru through Indian Eyes, 1530-1570*. Hassocks, Sussex: Harvester Press, 1977.

Wade, Bonnie C., *Imaging Sound: An Ethnomusicological Study of Music, Art, and Culture in Mughal India*. Chicago: Chicago University Press, 1998.

Wadia, Putlibai D. H., 'The Ballad of the Gujari', *Indian Antiquary*, August 1889.

Waterfield, William, 'The Nine Lakh Chain', *Calcutta Review*, 1875.

———, (trans.), *The Lay of Alha: A Saga of Rajput Chivalry by Minstrels of Northern India*, edited by G. A. Grierson. Oxford: Oxford University Press, 1923.

Watson, Major J. W., 'The Fall of Patan: Ballad of the Fall of Patan', *Indian Antiquary* 8, June 1879.

Watt, George, *A Dictionary of Economic Products*, vol. 1. New Delhi: Periodical Exports, 1972, reprint. First published 1893.

Williams, Monier, 'Notes on Indian Folklore, etc.', *Indian Antiquary*, August 1879.

Wink, Andre, *Al Hind: The Making of the Indo-Islamic World—The Slave Kings and the Islamic Conquest vol. 2, 11th-13th Centuries*. Leiden: E. J. Brill, 1997.

Wise, James, 'The Muhammadans of Eastern Bengal', *Journal of Asiatic Society of Bengal* 63, 1894.

Yazijian, Edward, 'The Story of Ghazi in Bengal'. Typescript, Chicago, May 2000.

PERSIAN AND INDIAN LANGUAGES

Aina-i-Masudi: *al Maruf bah Tarikh Syed Salar Masud Ghazi RA, hasab farmaish Haji Ahmad Saheb tajir kutub, Chowk, Lukhnau*. Kanpur: Razzaq Press, 1357 AH, reprint. First published n.d.

Ali, Chaudhuri Mohammad, *Kashkol Mohammad Ali Shah Faqir*. Lucknow: Nami Press, 1951.

Ali, Mir Afsos, *Jild Awwal Kitab Araish-i-Mahfil, Hasil Mazmoon Khulasa Al Hind Araish-i-Mehfil*. Kalkata: Hindoostanee Press, 1808.

Alvi, Moin Ahmad, 'Saiyyid Salar Masud Ghazi ka Tarikhi Aastana: Ek Purani Kitab ki Roshni Mein', *Qaumi Awaz* (Zamima), 31 December 1972.

Translated with notes by H. A. Qureshi, *Sufis Classics I*. Lucknow: New Royal Book Company, 2007.

Ansari, Mohammad Khalil, *Tazkira Ghazi Bale Miyan*. Delhi: Printing Works, 1927.

Askari, S. H. (ed.), *Sirat-i-Ferozshahi, Nuskha Khudabaksh*. Patna: Khudabaksh Oriental Library, 1999.

Baksh, Akbar Ali ibn Mohammad, *Khulasah Tarikh-i-Masudi*. Lucknow: n.p., 1876.

Banprasthi, Premanand, *Ghazi Kaun Hai*. Awadh, 1927.

——, *Musalmani Gorakhdhandha*, published by Secretary, Arya Samaj, Sultanpur. Allahabad: Leader Press, 1927.

Battuta, Ibn, *Ajaib al Asfar*, vol. 2, translated by Maulvi Muhammad Husain. Islamabad: National Institute for Historical and Cultural Research, 1983, reprint.

Bhandari, Sujan Rai, *Khulasatu-t-Tawarikh*, ed. Zafar Hasan. Delhi: J. & Sons, 1918.

Bismillah, Abdul, *Jhini Jhinin Bini Chadariya*. Nai Dilli: Rajkamal Paperbacks, 1987.

Chatterjee, Suniti Kumar, 'Daraf Khan Ghazi, *Sanskriti I*, 1368 B.S.

Chauhan, Vibha Singh, *Ganga Jamuna Beech*. Dilli: Alekh Prakashan, 2007.

Chishti, Abdur Rahman, *Mirat-i-Masudi*. MS. Or. 1837, British Library.

Chishti, Hazrat Shaikh Abdur Rahman, *Mirat-ul-Asrar*. Translated into Urdu by Capt. Wahid Baksh Syal. Lahore, 1993.

Chote Lal, Babu, *Syed Salar Leela, jisko Babu Chote lal, wald Babu Cheda Lal, senior grade sub-assistant sarjan, Kasganj zila Eta niwasi, incharge shafakhana, Tajganj Agra-ne, yatriyon-ke faidey-ke liye banaya, matbae Mufid aam Agra mein Qadar Ali Khan Sufi ke ehtamam-se chapi*. 1913.

Chughtai, Ismat, *Dil ki Duniya*. Dilli: Rajkamal Prakashan, 2009, Hindi edition. Urdu edition first published 1962.

Dehlavi, Sayyid Ahmad (ed.), *Farhang-i-Asafiya*. Dilli: Tarraqi-i-Urdu Board, 1974.

Dehlavi, Syed Ahmad, *Rusum–i-Dehli*. Delhi: Urdu Akademi, 2006.

'Eladi Ahirin: Ahiron ka Pauranic Kavya', *Lokvarta* Tikamgarh 1, 1944.

Farooqi, Azhar Ali, 'Dafaliyon aur Mujawairon ke Geet: Sohile', *Hindustani* 27(1), 1966.

Faruqi, Shamsur Rahman, *Kai Chaand Thei Sar-i-Asmaan*. Nai Dilli: Yatra/ Penguin Books, 2010.

Gajpuri, Manan Prasad Dwivedi, *Ramlal: Grameen Jeevan ka ek Samajik Upannyas*. Ilahabad: Indian Press, 1913.

——, *Musalmani Rajya ka Itihas, Pahila Bhag*, ed. Shyam Sundar Das. Varanasi: Kashi Nagri Pracharini Sabha, samvat 1976/1920.

Ghazi Miyan: *Jeevan Parichay*. Bahraich dargah, n.d.

Gupta, Parmeshwari Lal (ed.), *Maulana Daud Dalmai krit Chandayan: Mool Path, Pathantar, tippini aevam khojpurna samagri*. Bumbai: Hindi Granth Ratnakar, 1964.

Hayat-i-Masudi, Yani Hazrat Saiyed Salar Masud Ghazi ... Bahraich ke Mukhtasar Halaat ka Majmua. Bahraich: Ikleel Press, 1925.

Husain, Inayat, *Tarikh Salar Masud Ghazi Masud Ghazi, be- ihtemam... Mohammad Abdullah Siddiqui, Lakhnavi, tajir kutub-wa chikan, chowk*. Lucknow: Matba-i-Mujtabai, 1916.

Hyder, Qurratulain, *Chandini Begum*, translated by Wahajuddin Alavi. Nai Dilli: Bhartiya Gyanpeeth Prakashan, 1997.

Jaiswal, Nand Kishore, *Ghazi Miyan: Arthat Masud Ghazi ka Saccha Jeevan Charitra*. Prayag, 1916.

Jawan, Cazim Ali, *Barah Masa: A Poetical Description of the Year in Hindoostan*. Calcutta: Hindoostanee Press, 1812.

Jeevan Parichay, Hazrat Syed Salar Masud Ghazi RA, Bahraich [i]. Bahraich: Ikleel Press, n.d.

Jha, Braj Mohan, *Bahraich ke Saiyid Salar Masud ka Jeevan Charitra*. Etawah, 1916.

Khadim, Mansur Ali, *Jeevan Parichay, Hazrat Saiyid Salar Masud Ghazi rahmatullah alehi*. Bahraich, n.d.

———, *Karamaat Ghazi*. Bahraich, n.d.

———, *Mukhtasar Sawaneh Hazrat Syed Salar Masud Ghazi, R.A*. Bahraich, n.d.

———, *Gaed Dargah Hazrat Syed Salar Masud Ghazi RA*. Bahraich, 1985.

Khan, Mangal, *Gulzar-i-Masudi, aur Kitab Lajawab Jamei—Halaat Syed Salar Masud Ghazi Alia Rahmatullah, az Tasneef Janab Mangal Khan Sahib Nighat Banarasi, Shagird Janab Maulana Zakir Ali Sahib Marhoom Banarasi*. Bahraich: Ikleel Press, 1914.

Khan, Saiyid Ahmad (ed.), *Tarikh-i-Ferozshahi of Ziaa-al Din Barani, under the superintendence of W. Naussau Lees and Mawalvi Kabir Al-Din*. Calcutta: Bibliothica India, Asiatic Society of Bengal, 1862.

Khan, Sir Syed Ahmad, *Asar-us-Sanadid*. Delhi: Urdu Akademi, 2000, reprint. First published 1847, 1854.

Khusrau, Amir, *Ijaz-i-Khusravi*, Risala 1, 2. Lucknow: Neval Kishore Press, 1867.

Lal, Radha, *Hindi Kitab, Dusra Numbur*. Calcutta, 1873.

Lal, Ram, *Banitabuddhiprakashini*, [by] *awwal muddaris zilla school, Hamirapur*. Ilahabad: Government Chapakhana, 1871.

Mukhtasar Sawaneh-Umri Hazrat Syed Salar Masud Ghazi Rahmatullaliya. Gorakhpur: Anjuman Hifazat-i-Islam, 1925.

Munshi, Kanhaiya Lal, *Jai Somnath, c. 1940*. Nai Dilli: Rajkamal Paperbacks, 1977.

Mushtaqi, Shaikh Raziqullah, *Waqiat-i-Mushtaqi*. Rampur: Raza Library, 2002.

Narain, Shiv, *Awadh-deshiya Bhugol*, Lakhnau: Neval Kishore, 1870.

Nizami, Khwaja Hasan, *Dai-i-Islam: Yeh Risala Har Musalman ko Dai-i-Islam Banana aur Hefazat wa Ishat-i-Islam ke liye Khwaja Hasan Nizami Dehalvi ne Chauthi Baar Likha aur Chapwa-kar Shaya Hua*. Delhi, 1927, third edition.

Pal, Ramsanehi, *Hardual Bhajnawali (urf) Hardaul-ka Bhat*. Kanpur: Shri Janata Book Stall, n.d.

Pandey, Shyam Manohar (ed.), *Lok Mahakavya Chanaini: Lorik aur Chanda ki Lok-gatha*. Allahabad: Sahitya Bhavan, 1982.

Prasad, Devkali, *Balark Teerth Rahasya*. Bahraich, 1923.

Prasad, Sankata and W. G. Archer (eds), *Bhojpuri Gramya Geet*. Patna: Patna Law Press, 1943.

Premchand, *Vividh Prasang*, vol. 3. Allahabad: Hans Prakashan, 1962.

——, 'Jeevan Saar', in *Premchand ki Shreshth Kahaniyan*. Dilli: Vishv Books, 2008.

Qatil, Mirza, 'Haft Tamasha, c. 1811–12', in *Sanskriti ke Saath Adhyay: Qatil dwara krt 'Haft Tamsha' ka Hindi Anuvaad*, translated by Mohammad Umar. Aligarh: Kitab Ghar, 1990.

Rahim, Abdur, *Gaji Kalu o Champabati Kanyari Puthi, c. 1870*. Dhaka: Hamidiya Library, 1961.

Rai, Alok and Mushtaq Ali (eds), *Samaksh: Premchand ki Bees Urdu-Hindi Kahaaniyon ka Samanantar Paath*. Ilahabad: Hans Prakashan, 2002.

Rathore, Munshi Munni Lal, *Teliyon ki Vanshavali aur Shakha-Vyakhya: Teli Jati ka Sampurna Itihas*. Farrukhabad: Pradyuman Krishna Gulhare ke prabandh se Karmyogi Press, 1924.

Rizvi, Syed Athar Abbas (trans.), *Tughlaq Kaleen Bharat*, vol. 1. Aligarh: Department of History, Aligarh Muslim University, 1956.

Saraswati, Swami Vicharanand, 'Hindu Samaj aur Ghazi Miyan', *Swadesh*, 26 April 1928.

——, 'Bale Miyan ki Puja Anuchit Hai: Bale Miyan ka Mela aur Ghazi Miyan ki Puja ka Gupt Rahasya', *Swadesh*, 26 April 1928.

Satyarthi, Devendra, *Dheere Baho Ganga!* Nai Dilli: Praveen Prakashan, 1993.

Satyendra, *Jaharpir: Guru Gugga*. Agra: Agra University Press, 1956.

Suman, Ambika Prasad, *Krishak-sambandhi Braj Bhasha Shabdavali*, vol. 2. Allahabad: Hindustani Akedemi, 1961.

Shaheed, Syed Ahmad (trans.), 'Sirat-i-Mustaqim', *Journal of the Asiatic Society of Bengal* 11, 1832: 489–90.

Shastri, Acharya Chatursena, *Somnath, c. 1954*. Dilli: Hind Pakit Books, 2002.

Sherwani, Abdur Majid Raza Khan, *Saiyed Salar Masud Ghazi ka Mukhtasar Jeevan Charitra*. Bahraich: Ikleel Press,1926.

Sherwani, Maulvi Muhammad Abbas Saheb, Collector, *Hayat-i-Masudi, yani Sawan-e-Umri, Hazrat Sipah Salar Masud Ghazi Shaheed*. Aligarh: Aligarh Muslim University, 1935.

Shivprasad, Babu, *Bhugol Hastmalak, or The Earth As (a Drop) of Clear Water in Hand*, 2 vols. Kalkatta: Sanskrit Press, 1859.

Singh, Chaudhuri Baldev, *Ahir-jati ke liye Char Nuskhe*. Ilahabad, 1923.

———, *Ahir Jati mein 31 Rog*. Aligarh: Abhir Mahasabha, 1924.

Singh, Durga Prasad, *Bhojpuri ke Kavi aur Kavya*. Patna: Bihar Rashtra Bhasha Parishad, 1959.

Singh, Jagdeo, *Mirat-Masudi: Izzat mab Abdur Rahman Chishti ki ma'ruf tasneef*. Lucknow: Books India International, 1997, Urdu translation.

Tarikh-i-Masudi: Tarikh Syed Salar Masud Ghazi, Hasab Farmaish Ghani Ahmad Tajir-i-kutub, Chowk, Lucknow. Lucknow: Nami Press, n.d., c. 1950.

Temple, R. C., 'Git Shadi Sayyid Salar Saheb Ka', in *Legends of Punjab*, vol. 1. Patiala: Department of Languages, Punjab, 2000, second reprint. First published c. 1880s.

Tiwari, Pandit Ramprasad, *Ritiratnakar*. Ilahabad: Government Chapkhana, 1872.

Tiwari, Nityanand, *Madhyakalin Romanchak Akhyan: Lorikayan ke Maukhik aur Likhit Pathya rup par Adharit*. Dilli: National Publishing House, 1970.

Tripathi, Ram Naresh, *Hamara Gramya Sahitya*. Prayag: Hindi Mandir, 1940.

———, *Gramya Geet: Sohar, Annprashan, Mundan, Janeu, Nahcchu aur Vivah ke Geet*. Prayag: Hindi Mandir, 1951.

Tripathi, Vishwanath, *Nangatalai ka Gaon: Smriti-Akhyan*. Nai Dilli: Rajkamal Prakashan, 2004.

Trivedi, Surya Narain, *Gawar Masla, or Village Wits*. Samastipur, 1923.

Ufsos, Meer Sher Ulee, *Araish-i-Mahfil, Being a History, in the Hindoostanee Language of the Hindu Princes from Joodishtur to Pithoura: Compiled from Khoolasut-ool-Hind and other Authorities By Meer Sher Ulee Ufsos, Head Monshee in the Hindoostanee Department of the College*. Calcutta: Hindoostanee Press, 1808.

Umar, Mohammad (trans.), *Sanskriti ke Saat Adhyay: Qatil dwara krt 'Hafta Tamasha' ka Hindi Anuvaad*. Aligarh: Kitab Ghar, 1990.

Upadhyay, Krishnadev, *Bhojpuri Lok-sanskriti*. Prayag: Hindi Sahitya Sammelan, 1991.

Upadhyay, Prabhakareshvar Prasad (ed.), *Golokvasi Chaudhuri Pt. Badri Narayan Upadhyay 'Premghan', Premghan Sarvasya, pratham bhag*. Prayag: Hindi Sahitya Sammelan, 1884, second edition.

Vaid, Ram Kumar Upadhyay, *Vaid ki Lachari*. Jaunpur, 1942.

'Visharad', Chandrabhan, 'Banda prant ke gram devta', *Lokvarta* (Tikamgarh) 1, 1944.

Yadav, Baijnath Prasad, *Ahir Jati ki Niyamavali*. Banaras City, samvat 1948.

Zaidi, Ali Muhammad (Maluf), *Apni Yaden, Rudauli ki Baten*. Rudauli: Azmi Publishers, 1988.

Zaidi, Chaudhuri Syed Ali Mohammad, *Bara Banki: Jugrafiya, Tarikh wa Digar Aham Waqiyat wa Rawaiyat Waghaira*. Rudauli: Irshad Manzil, 1984.

Acknowledgements

As with the life of its protagonist, this work too has been in the making for a considerable period of time. There is a long list of people and institutions that have made the research, writing and publication of this book possible. The idea of this project was first mooted as a proposal, on the suggestion of Sudhir Kakar, for a year's stay at the Wisenschaftskolleg zu Berlin. I am grateful to Wolf Lepenies and Joachim Nettlebeck of Wiko (for keeping faith with me), and the wonderful set of co-Fellows, historians Jürgen Kocka and Luisa Passerini; the anthropologist Jack Goody; co-editor of Einstein Papers, Robert Schulmann and the theoretical biologist Eörs Szathmáry, for conviviality and intellectual companionship at 19, Wallotstrasse over two decades ago.

I wish to thank the librarians and archivists at Wissenshaftskolleg, specially Frau Bottomley and her colleagues; the India Office and Library, London and Shabana Mahmud, Richard Bingle, Graham Shaw and Leena Mitford in particular; Jim Nye of the Regenstein Library, University of Chicago and James Simon of the Centre for Research Libraries, Chicago; Ames Library, University of Minnesota; the Columbia University library system; the Uttar Pradesh State Archives, Lucknow; St. Stephen's College Library; my own Department of History Library at Delhi University; and the library of the Centre for Studies in Developing Societies, Delhi.

I am also beholden to Sanjay Kak and Aishwarj Kumar for accompanying me on my field trips to Bara Banki and Bahraich during the hot month of *Jeth* (May) in 1994 and 1996, and to Alok Sinha and Atul Bagai, UP civil servants, for facilitating my travel and stay in Lucknow and northern Awadh. A special word of thanks to the genial Mr Kaul for proving a home on my extended trips to Bahraich. Janab Khursheed Anwar Rizvi, Officer on Special Duty at the *rauza* of Ghazi Miyan, enabled access to the shrine during the festive period and also introduced me to the records and the *khuddam* of the shrine. This study would not have been possible without the help and camaraderie of the Dafalis of Bahraich, Gonda, Fyzabad, Sultanpur, Khalilbad, Rudauli and Basaurhi. I wish to thank in particular Bashir Dafali of Tharia Kalan, Shubrati of Salar Tola, Zainullah of Gonda and the unassuming Kingaria of Basaurhi for allowing me to record their ballads and for the patient explication of the finer points of their compositions.

My several trips to Rudauli sharif and the Bhatiana tract abutting it were materially aided by my old friend Professor Khan Masud Ahmad of Jamia Millia Islamia, now Vice Chancellor of the Muinuddin Chishti Urdu University, Lucknow. It is a pleasure to recollect our travels on the Ghazi Miyan trail through Sohbatia Bagh, Neura, Gulheria, Karaundi, Kinhaura, Ram Sanehi Ghat and Belkhara in the winter of 1995. It was through Professor Masud that I got to meet Chaudhury Syed Ali Mohammad Zaidi, the venerable *rais* and local historian, who not only agreed to discuss aspects of the Ghazi cult, but also gifted me two priceless histories of Rudauli and Bara Banki that he had authored. In Gorakhpur, Habib Ahmad sahib advocate, once again acted as key informant, helping me variously, as he has done on my other academic ventures. Mahesh Rangarajan, Ram Narayan Rawat, Devyani Gupta, Ashutosh Kumar, Saumya Gupta, Arun Kumar and Sanjay Sharma have helped in ferreting out difficult to access material from repositories in London, Lucknow and Allahabad. Heather Joshi, Dinesh Bhugra and David Page have continued to be gracious hosts in London, enabling short stints of research at the British Library.

I am grateful to the Universities of Chicago, Columbia University and the Centre for Early Modern History, Minnesota for electing me to Visiting Professorships in 2000 and 2007. This enabled me to bounce off the formative ideas of this book with a group of extraordinary graduate students. I wish to put on record my appreciation of the contributions of Manan Ahmed, Rajeev Kinra, Venkat Dhulipala, Abhishek Kaicker and Anand Taneja to the making of this book. Drs. Ahmed and Kaicker have, in addition, functioned as my gateways to difficult-to-access (from here in India) online materials, which, despite the openness of the web, are very often restricted to US-based users. Shuddabrata Sengupta, sojourner of *sarais* and watering holes has over the years been a dissentient interlocutor.

Earlier chapters were written during my stint at Chicago and Columbia and during a month-long sojourn in the elevating surroundings of the Indian Institute of Advanced Studies, Shimla. The Centre for Studies in Developing Societies (CSDS), Delhi accorded me the honour of electing me to the Rajni Kothari chair during the academic year 2012–13 which materially helped in the writing of this book. I wish to thank the Director, Rajeev Bhargava and the fellows of CSDS, specially Aditya Nigam, Awadhendra Sharan, Ashis Nandy, Shail Mayaram, Rakesh Pandey, Ravi Vasudevan and Ravi Sundaram for their comradeship and the long after-hour sessions at that intellectual oasis at 29, Rajpur Road, a stone's throw from my own University of Delhi. My long-time doctoral student Ravi Kant, also a member of CSDS, knows all too well the innumerable ways in which he has been of help in the writing and preparation of this manuscript. Ambarish Satwik, artistic wielder of both the laser knife and the quill has helped me with my composition, and much else besides. Mahmood Farooqui, historian, *dastango*-storyteller and fellow *poorabia* has helped rid the earlier drafts of a good deal of blubber, and also transcribed and translated a late eighteenth-century poetical description of the Ghazi Miyan Fair. Shobhit Mahajan of Delhi University has over the last decade shared with me over our bi-weekly meetings each and every idea that has been discarded, or indeed gone into the making of this book.

Parts of this manuscript were first presented at seminars at New School University and New York University, Amherst College, the University of Cape Town, the South Asian Institute at Harvard and Heidelberg, Sydney Institute of Technology, University of California Berkeley, the Department of Sociology, Delhi University, the Advanced Institute at Shimla and as the Rajni Kothari Lecture at CSDS, Delhi. And then there is a long list of fellow academics and friends who have commented on different portions of the manuscript. Sheldon Pollock, Gyan Prakash, Veena Das, Romila Thapar, Bhavani Raman, Mukul Kesavan, Muzaffar Alam and Naina Dayal have gamely plodded through several drafts of this book, and offered much useful advice. Prachi Deshpande, Sugata Bose, Homi Bhabha, Gayatri Chakravorty Spivak, Talal Asad, Arjun Appadurai, Ajay Skaria, Akeel Bilgrami, Mahmood Mamdani, Roma Chatterjee, Nicholas Dirks, David Lelyveld, Veena Talwar Oldenburg, Qadri Ismail, Gloria Raheja,

Janaki Bakhle, Pradeep Jeganathan, Manu Goswami, David Ludden, Allison Busch, Rahul Govind, the late Carol Breckenridge, Heather Godhall, Bijoy Baruah and Peter Ronald DeSouza, have helped clarify several ideas and arguments during seminars and talks. C. M. Naim, emeritus Professor at University of Chicago, has been specially helpful, guiding me through Persian and Urdu materials, and being my own personal Google for all things concerning the Warrior Saint. Professor Muzaffar Alam, a true Alim among medievalists, has been my constant companion in this intellectual journey now for over two decades. I offer my heartfelt *shukriya* for all that he has done to bring this project to fruition. Aparna Balachandran and Farhat Hasan have helped in different ways in the birth of this book. Chairperson Upinder Singh has gone out of her way to allow access to the History Department's meagre resources, so as to enable a 'retiring' colleague to see his book through the press. I wish to thank Ms Ankita for cheerful secretarial assistance. Anubhuti Maurya, Mughal historian and friend, has provided intellectual support and sound advice while keeping a 'neighbourly oversight' during the long gestation period of this manuscript.

Natalie Zemon Davis has engaged with this project from its inception, appreciating the texture of the warrior-saint story beyond its Turkic and Indo-Gangetic specificities, and offering suggestions to make it intelligible beyond area-specific boundaries. This book, among other things, is a token of my appreciation of her friendship and scholarly camaraderie across continents and centuries. Ranajit Guha, my guru in matters historical, has once again asked the most challenging questions. Partha Chatterjee and Dipesh Chakrabarty, comrades-in-arms of four decades, have contributed immensely to the shaping of this manuscript as well.

The late Simon Digby, scholar extraordinaire—a Cambridge-trained Sufi, if there ever was—has influenced this telling of the Ghazi Miyan story the most. Signs of my immense debt to Simon Baba, as he came to be called in our household, would be found scattered through the notes to this volume; a former acknowledgement is inscribed on the dedication page of this book. Richard Harris, friend, Urduphile and literary executor of Simon Digby's estate rummaged through the trove of Digby's papers at Jersey and dug out the one manuscript of seventeenth-century Brajbhasha poetry that had a direct bearing on the Ghazi saga. His photograph of the relevant page, held in place by a decorative dagger belonging to the Simon Digby collection, is reproduced in this book (see Figure 9.1), and has also been incorporated into the cover design of the South Asia edition, produced by Siddharth Chatterjee and Anitha Balachandran with loving care and affection. Lastly, I wish to thank Professor Irfan Habib for having agreed to, and then spent a considerable amount of time identifying the sites connected with the cult of Salar Masud. The two excellent maps produced by him and cartographer Faiz Habib have been redrawn slightly by the cartography department of the publishers, in terms of their in-house conventions.

Unlike everything else I have published, this, alas, is one book that Ravi Dayal, historian, friend and father figure to Oxford University Press, India did not live to see in print; leafing through its endnotes, he would no doubt have chuckled at the 'scaffolding of scholarship', strung together with the native bamboo and *munja* rope that are intended to support it.

Mohammad Amin not only nurtured me as a historian, as he had done numerous others at St. Stephen's College, Delhi, he also provided key ethnographic depth to the story of the Ghazi. It will be my lasting regret that 'the albatross', as he lovingly called this long-delayed manuscript, has at long last taken flight when he is no longer with us to share in the familial joy. My wife Bano has watched and waited, not always patiently, with the waxing and waning of this manuscript. I hope I'll be able to convince her one day that my obsession with the saint of Bahraich is finally over, and that the noble spirit of the Ghazi has taken leave of our home and hearth. My son Adil, now training to be a cosmologist, would surely recognize the strains of the Basaurhi Dafali's ballad—printed here as an appendix—as one of the earliest songs he tried singing as a five-year-old. More than me, it is he who has willed this book into being. *Tum ahl-o-ayāl ho to jahān hai.*

Finally, I wish to thank my publishers, Vidya Rao and Mimi Choudhury of Orient BlackSwan and Priya Nelson of University of Chicago Press, and the two anonymous referees for making the book possible. A very special thank you to my editor Sucharita Ray who really gave shape to the manuscript (*nok-palak durust*, as one says in Urdu) and has helped make what I intended to say clearer.

I am grateful to Permanent Black Press, Delhi, the editors of *Annales* and Hatje Cantz Verlag for permission to include material that was published in variant forms in Partha Chatterjee and Anjan Ghosh (eds), *History and the Present*; *Annales*: *Histoire, Sciences Sociales*, 60 (2), Mars–Avril, 2005; and in Okwui Enwezor (ed.), *Experiments with Truth: Transitional Justice and the Processes of Truth and Reconciliation*: Documenta 11_Platform 2.

29 June 2015

Shahid Amin
Cavalry Lines
Delhi University

Index